Principles and Practice of Sustainable Business Models

Principles and Practice of Sustainable Business Models

Editor: Jamie Mason

New York

Published by NY Research Press
118-35 Queens Blvd., Suite 400,
Forest Hills, NY 11375, USA
www.nyresearchpress.com

Principles and Practice of Sustainable Business Models
Edited by Jamie Mason

International Standard Book Number: 978-1-64725-459-9 (Hardback)

Cataloging-in-Publication Data

Principles and practice of sustainable business models / edited by Jamie Mason.
    p. cm.
Includes bibliographical references and index.
ISBN 978-1-64725-459-9
1. Business enterprises--Environmental aspects. 2. Industrial management--Environmental aspects.
3. Sustainable development. 4. Business planning. I. Mason, Jamie.
HD30.255 .P75 2023
658.408--dc23

Contents

Permissions

List of Contributors

Index

Preface

Sustainable business models are the business models that can be implemented by businesses in conducting business activities in a manner that they do not have any negative influence on the environment. Sustainability in business is translated into the triple bottom line, which requires the businesses to manage the financial, environmental and social implications of their actions. A sustainable business model is a company's strategy for earning a profit, while taking into consideration the effects of its decisions and operations on the environment and people. It outlines the products or services that the company offers, the people who will use them, the expenses involved as well as the supply and distribution network. The notion of environmental and social values is combined in sustainable business models along with the conventional business dimension. This book elucidates the concepts and innovative models around prospective developments with respect to sustainable business models. It aims to serve as a resource guide for students and experts alike and contribute to the growth of study on this topic.

This book has been a concerted effort by a group of academicians, researchers and scientists, who have contributed their research works for the realization of the book. This book has materialized in the wake of emerging advancements and innovations in this field. Therefore, the need of the hour was to compile all the required researches and disseminate the knowledge to a broad spectrum of people comprising of students, researchers and specialists of the field.

An eye disease can refer to any of the diseases or disorders that affect the human eye. Eye problems are treated within the field of ophthalmology. Age-related eye diseases are the leading cause of blindness and low vision. A few major eye diseases are macular degeneration, cataract, diabetic retinopathy and glaucoma. Amblyopia and strabismus are other common eye disorders. Most eye diseases have no early symptoms. The patient might not notice any pain or changes in the vision until the disease has become quite advanced. The book aims to shed light on some of the unexplored aspects of eye diseases. It includes contributions of experts and researchers which will provide clinical perspectives on these diseases.

At the end of the preface, I would like to thank the authors for their brilliant chapters and the publisher for guiding us all-through the making of the book till its final stage. Also, I would like to thank my family for providing the support and encouragement throughout my academic career and research projects.

Editor

Sustainable Business Models in Hybrids: A Conceptual Framework for Community Pharmacies' Business Owners

Caterina Cavicchi *[ID] and Emidia Vagnoni

Department of Economics and Management, University of Ferrara, 44121 Ferrara, Italy; vgnmde@unife.it
* Correspondence: cvccrn@unife.it

Abstract: Community pharmacies have recently been asked to contribute to sustainable healthcare systems through active participation in an integrated model of care and by playing a major educational role for environmental conservation. Therefore, dramatic changes in their institutional context have led to increasing competition in the drugs retail sector and a shift toward a service-oriented business. These factors urge rethinking of the business model of these hybrid organizations, which combine a profit-oriented, social, and more recently addressed, environmental identity. This paper aims at discussing a sustainable business model (SBM) that could allow community pharmacies to contribute to public health through pharmacists' current role and development of that role. The effects of the COVID-19 pandemic suggest that human health should be at the center of the sustainable development agenda; the pandemic raises questions about the traditional role of community pharmacies, such as extending patient-oriented services. The SBM for community pharmacies represents an opportunity to enhance their role among the healthcare workforce, especially in a time of global pandemics. In addition, the SBM can support community pharmacies to integrate sustainability in day-to-day pharmacy practice, although it should be customized based on the contextual characteristics of the business and on differences between countries, such as health policies and regulations.

Keywords: sustainable business model; community pharmacies; pharmacy practice; public health; COVID-19

1. Introduction

The community pharmacies are subject to heterogeneous value logics that reflect their hybridity; indeed, they stand at the interface between the profit and not-for-profit sectors. On the one hand, community pharmacies are entrepreneurial organizations that are subject to profit maximization, but on the other hand, they dispense medication and provide counselling and other care-related services that contribute to societal welfare. Community pharmacies operate in a regulated market shaped by a country's healthcare institutions [1]; therefore, their hybridity is characterized by: (1) environmental determinism, as they are operating under the reimbursement schemes of a government's health and pharmaceutical policies; and (2) strategic choices, which are based on customers' needs [2]. As community pharmacies can enhance people's well-being, they also tend to incorporate social duties within their mission; they have recently been asked to strengthen this role in order to address the challenges posed by UN Sustainable Development Goals (SDGs) [3–5]. These heterogeneous value logics, which combine both commercial and sustainability elements, affect their business model, which comprises strategic and organizational value choices adopted in response to the institutional context [6].

Scholars have only recently started to focus on strategic orientation and organizational structures that can enhance sustainability in the context of community pharmacies. As health-related organizations, community pharmacies are part of the healthcare system and are expected to "optimize social, environmental, and economic outcomes" [7]. Indeed, the integration of the three performance dimensions of sustainability, also known as the triple bottom line [8], represented one of the pioneering lenses used to interpret the sustainable management of community pharmacies [9,10] and their sustainable business model (SBM). An SBM focuses on Elkington's (1997) concept of the triple bottom line [11,12] and "aligns interests of all stakeholder groups, and explicitly considers the environment and society as key stakeholders" [11] (p. 44). This integration between profit orientation and social and ecological goals for organizations is recommended, because the different purposes can mutually reinforce each other to create competitive advantage [13] and generate shared value [14]. To this end, profit is an outcome but also a lever to implement social and environmental sustainability [15].

In the literature, we find attempts at theoretical grounding around SBMs and business model innovation for sustainability both empirically and conceptually [11,15–19]. However, despite the growing interest of scholars in SBM research, studies on SBM innovation (and the design and implementation of SBMs) continue to be limited [20] due to a lack of consensus and consistency on business model concepts [17]. Consequently, knowledge on business model innovation for sustainability is dispersed [14]; researchers [18] urged to develop SBM research as an integrative field [21]. Moreover, to date, no studies have discussed SBM for pharmacies, which represent hybrid organizations. To this end, scholars suggested the testing of patterns characterizing SBMs and their combinations in different contexts, based on empirical evidence [18].

Although not empirically, this paper aims to address this gap by, first, discussing the ideal features of an SBM both in terms of its strategic and organizational dimensions within these hybrids in the light of the environmental turbulence affecting their activities. Indeed, the extent to which hybrids' business models differ from the business model of traditional businesses is under-investigated [22].

Second, from a theoretical point of view, the paper contributes to SBM innovation [20] by providing a conceptual framework for community pharmacies. It contends that an SBM for community pharmacies can be drawn considering the combination of outside–in and inside–out approaches [12] to business model innovation for sustainability. Thus, an SBM for community pharmacies is designed considering the relevant literature in the field and internal elements of these organizations acting as propellers to the adoption of sustainability practices. The paper allows clarification of the strategic and organizational structures that pharmacies need in order to develop an SBM and respond to institutional plurality.

Third, adopting both managerial and organizational perspectives, the paper discusses the potential of learning–action networks for the development of an SBM for community pharmacies [23]. Indeed, in managerial studies on sustainable business modelling, a systemic approach is recommended [15,19], and the mutual relation with stakeholders of the organization's value network is the lever to develop innovative and sustainable solutions beneficial to the business, society, and the ecosystem [24]. In organizational studies, this mechanism involves hybridization [25,26] of the value network that is investigated in the paper.

The SBM could allow community pharmacies to contribute to public health through extending patient-oriented services, especially in the time of COVID-19 emergency. Then, this paper aims at discussing SBM for community pharmacies as an opportunity to enhance their role among the healthcare workforce, especially in a time of global pandemics. In addition, the SBM can support community pharmacies to integrate sustainability in day-to-day pharmacy practice: the framework, which is discussed in the paper should be customized based on the contextual characteristics of the business and on differences between countries, such as health policies and regulations that may affect pharmacy practice.

The paper is organized as follows: Section 2 discusses the institutional context of community pharmacies; Section 3 introduces the theoretical background on sustainable business modelling. Sections 4 and 5 discuss, respectively, the ideal strategic and organizational structures of an SBM for community pharmacies. Section 6 discusses the evolution of SBM for community pharmacies in the light of COVID-19 emergency. In Section 7, some theoretical contributions, practical implications, and further research are proposed.

2. Community Pharmacies' Institutional Context

During the past 20 years, the community pharmacies of many countries have experienced dramatic changes due to deregulation and liberalization policies, so that the distribution of drugs, which was considered their core activity, lost importance in favor of patient-centered services and the selling of healthcare-related products, which were not based on drugs [27]. For instance, in European countries, the main criticalities community pharmacies currently face are the following [27,28]:

- Increase in competition on prices of over-the-counter (OTC) drugs;
- Regulations facilitating pharmacy chains and introducing new competitors such as grocery retailers in the OTC drugs market;
- Increase in competitiveness on complementary medicine;
- A shift from the dispensary role of community pharmacists (left to hospital pharmacies) to the management of professional services, introduced by countries' health policies and related cost-saving measures;
- The advent of information technology that reshaped competitiveness (e-pharmacy; electronic prescribing matched with marketing tools to tailor offerings based on customers' preferences and reduce the amount of time dedicated to dispensing activities);
- Diversification of big retailers and supermarkets into non-conventional fields.

These criticalities have pushed pharmacy business owners to focus on: improving their business models through new competitive strategies [29], increasing their professional reputation, and achieving operational efficiency to sustain competitiveness [30].

More recently, community pharmacies were also asked to strengthen their contribution to sustainable healthcare policies, which were set by the SDGs. For instance, SDG 3 stated, "ensure healthy lives and promote well-being for all at all ages" and highlighted targets such as achieving universal coverage through access to essential safe and effective medications and vaccines and the reduction of mortality rates and chronic diseases. The SDG targets place major responsibilities on the health workforce and require the professional development of the health workforce including pharmacists [3]. Given these challenges, international health institutions and associations have started to set out a sustainable development agenda for community pharmacies [4]. For example, the International Federation of Pharmacists (2017) underlined the importance of pharmacists' counseling activities for sustainability given that "as medicines experts, the pharmaceutical workforce plays a key role in improving health outcomes through responsible use of medicines and optimizing effective choice and use." Furthermore, the Pharmaceutical Group of the European Union [31] recommended a list of actions that they expected European countries to implement in order to enable community pharmacies to contribute to high-quality, inclusive, and sustainable healthcare systems. This list of actions included:

- The expansion of community pharmacies' services as an integral part of primary care;
- Improved access to innovative medicines by increasing their supply via community pharmacies;
- Incentivization of the uptake of generic drugs through community pharmacies;
- Involvement of community pharmacies in national health policies to improve vaccination coverage and risk minimization plans for other medicinal therapies.

These developments are expected to broaden the traditional expertise of community pharmacies on the dispensing of drugs and counseling to ensure the achievement of SDGs.

The environmental turbulence affecting community pharmacies' activities requires business model innovation aimed at supporting these organizations in their response to calls for more sustainable healthcare systems while maintaining competitiveness. Indeed, sustainable business modelling can help these organizations to respond to the heterogeneous value logics that characterize the institutional context [6].

3. Sustainable Business Modelling: Theoretical Background

Business model innovation helps to align a business model with environmental complexity, where the business model includes the definition of the purpose and goals of a firm and the organizational design affecting its effectiveness, efficiency, and agility [32]. A business model incorporates the ways in which a firm creates and delivers value to customers and how it is able to convert this value into profit [33,34]; so, a business model's functions consist of value creation, delivery, and capture [35]. However, the tools of traditional profit-normative business models are unable to address the complexity of sustainability issues [36].

Sustainability requires organizations to rethink how they do business [37]; therefore, orientating business model innovation toward sustainability represents a key capability for them. In the literature pertaining to SBMs, a company's value capture consists of capturing "economic value while maintaining or regenerating natural, social, and economic capital beyond its organizational boundaries" [23] (p. 6), so that a holistic view that considers both benefits and costs for stakeholders, such as society and the environment, is generated [24]. Sustainability encourages organizations to move from a firm-centric to a network-centric operational logic, as they have to deal with a plurality of actors [37]. SBMs therefore represent "business models that incorporate pro-active multi-stakeholder management, the creation of monetary and non-monetary value for a broad range of stakeholder, and hold a long-term perspective" [20] (p. 404). Organizations that adopt an SBM "increase their ability to create multiple forms of value beyond financial gains" [18] (p. 147), so that financial viability as well as SDGs can be met [18].

The literature provides studies that aim at delineating the meaning, the ideal features and the process of construction of SBMs. For instance, Stubbs and Cocklin (2008) adopted an ecological modernization perspective in order to discuss internal, cultural, and structural capabilities that are needed to adopt an SBM and achieve both firm-level and system-level sustainability [15]. Other scholars proposed value mapping as a tool that an organization can use to assess its current value proposition for its value network and identify opportunities for business model redesign and realignment of different stakeholders' interests [24,38]. Abdelkafi and Täuscher (2016) used a systemic thinking approach to explain that SBMs are built on reinforcing a feedback loop among value creation for customers, value captured by the firm, and the value to the natural environment [16]. Roome and Louche (2016) focused on the organizational transformation leading to the development of an SBM [19]. Bocken et al. (2014) proposed archetypes as mechanisms to build SBMs [11]. Evans et al. (2017) introduced a unified theoretical perspective to generate business model innovations that can lead to better economic, social, and environmental performance of organizations [17]. Lüdeke-Freund et al. (2018) [18] identified patterns of SBMs to be applied "to solve specific problems at the nexus of business and sustainability" (p. 159) while providing social, economic, or ecological value or the integrations between them.

In order to sum up the main features of SBM research, Lüdeke-Freund and Dembek (2017) argued that empirical and theoretical studies on SBMs show: "(i) an explicit sustainability orientation, integrating ecological, social and economic concerns, (ii) an extended notion of value creation, questioning traditional definitions of value and success, (iii) an extended notion of value capture in term of those for whom value is created, (iv) an explicit emphasis on the need to consider stakeholders and not just customers, and (v) an extended perspective on the wider system in which SBM is embedded" [21] (p. 1670).

When discussing SBM innovation, the literature introduces two main approaches [12]: the outside–in approach through which a firm adapts its business model to well-known archetypes in order to embed sustainability in the business' activities and processes; and the inside–out approach, which addresses the potential elements within an organization that can support its change toward sustainability. With reference to the first, Bocken et al. (2014) cited by Joyce and Paquin (2016) [11,12] proposed the following as archetypes for SBMs: (a) maximize material productivity and energy efficiency (do more with less resources—lean, eco-efficiency); (b) create value from waste; (c) substitute with renewables and natural processes; (d) deliver functionality rather than ownership; (e) adopt a stewardship role; (f) encourage sufficiency, such as reducing overconsumption (market for second-hand goods, eliminating superfluous or overly complex functionality from products as they increase the consumption of natural resources); (g) re-purpose the business for society and the environment in which a partial solution is represented by hybrid entities that pursue profit but a part of it is reinvested in their second non-profit business; and (h) develop scale-up solutions, such as radical change to consumption patterns through collaboration with different partners and open innovation. Scholars [18] extended the discussion on ideal features of SBMs trying to fill the gap in knowledge dispersion. The authors [18] identified patterns that can represent businesses' response to sustainability problems and classified them on the basis of the social, economic, and environmental value each business model solution brings.

With regards to the inside–out approach, this is based on the analysis of the internal elements of a firm that can act as facilitators to implement sustainable business practices; it is based on the use of planning tools, such as the Triple Layered Business Model Canvas developed by Joyce and Paquin (2016) starting from acknowledging the limits of Osterwalder and Pigneur's (2010) traditional Business Model Canvas [12,39]. This latter tool however does not take into account the social and ecological context and its links with the business when addressing sustainability [36].

In this paper, the two approaches to SBM innovation derived from the literature, the outside–in and the inside–out approaches, are combined and adapted to the specific operational features and professional expertise of community pharmacies to create an ideal SBM for community pharmacies (Figure 1).

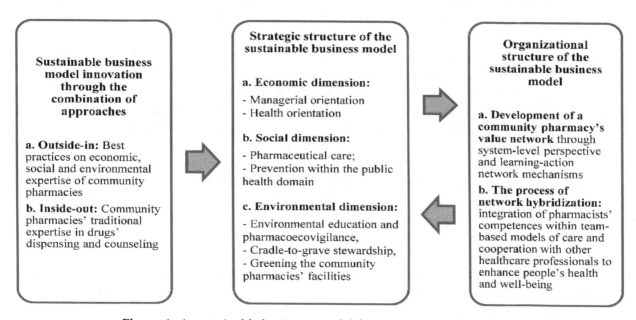

Figure 1. A sustainable business model for community pharmacies.

In the box on the left, SBM innovation through the combination of the outside–in and inside–out approaches is applied to the context of community pharmacies. On the one hand, the outside–in approach is related to best practices related to community pharmacies that have developed economic, social, and environmental expertise to respond to the challenges of the institutional environment. On the other hand, inside–out is related to competences that are already available in community pharmacy practice, which are generally related to drugs' dispensing and counseling. Sustainable business innovation drives the construction of the strategic structure of the SBM, consisting of economic, social, and environmental practices; these practices can be adopted by community pharmacies in order to create value for both the business and the value network; indeed, community pharmacies are hybrid organizations that have to satisfy a multitude of stakeholders' interests. An arrow pointing from sustainable business innovation to the strategic component of the SBM represents this relation. In turn, the strategic component of the SBM drives the organizational design, which is functional to the achievement of long-term goals (the two arrows between the strategic component box and the organizational structure box represent this mutual relation). The variables in the model are discussed in the next section.

4. SBM and Community Pharmacies: Strategic Structure

In next subsections, the strategic structure of an SBM for community pharmacies is proposed, focusing on economic, social, and environmental practices that can be adopted to allow sustainable value creation for both the pharmacy and its value network.

4.1. Economic Dimension

The economic dimension of the strategic structure of the business model for community pharmacies is explained in relation to managerial orientation and health orientation.

4.1.1. Managerial Orientation

Community pharmacies operate within a regulated environment where the health provider or insurer for retailing often defines remuneration and dispensing functions. New payment mechanisms are slowly emerging in the arena of patient-centered services as reforms extend the role of pharmacists as primary care health professionals [40]. Decreasing margins caused by increasing competitiveness [29] led to community pharmacies being perceived as entrepreneurial organizations that rely on profit generation and cost control to gain financial viability. Factors of deregulation and the emergence of new market players in the segment of drug distribution progressively required community pharmacies to develop a managerial attitude based on creativity and innovation [28] and to differentiate their offering [29]. With reference to managerial orientation, Al-Arifi (2013) described the tasks that the pharmacist, owner, and manager of a small community pharmacy should perform to enable their firm to reach optimal productivity levels. The tasks include: the selection and motivation of human resources; layout management; strategizing and marketing; management of the warehouse and inventory; and the correct use and management of information systems, such as accounting tools (collection and provision of data to the pharmacy staff), for management control of activities carried out coherently with changing regulations and markets [41]. Many studies have underlined the need for small pharmacies to use marketing mix levers adapting to the socio-demographic characteristics of the consumers to tailor offerings toward their preferences [28,42]. In addition, competences and relational skills were found to be a source of consumers' trust [27,30] and can help community pharmacies to develop brand personality to compete with the new market's players [30]. Key managerial competences for pharmacists are to comprehend the strategic and operational levels of activities: the strategic level of activities includes risk taking, capacity to innovate, competitor analysis, and budgeting/financial planning; the operational level of activities includes the ability to negotiate with suppliers, cooperation with other health professionals, and staff coordination tasks [43].

4.1.2. Health Orientation

Community pharmacies generally represent a first reference point for people for the dispensing of drugs and counseling activities. More recently, community pharmacies were asked to extend their role beyond the dispensing of medications and counseling to contribute to societal healthcare [44,45]. A recent study [46] underlined that community pharmacies could become financially sustainable centers for health and personal care if they shifted from a product-oriented business model to a service-oriented business model characterized by: (a) connecting people with healthcare professionals and (b) focusing on the quality and quantity of patients' outcomes achieved. This implies the abandonment of traditional management approaches and the sole commercial orientation of community pharmacies in order to "(1) be focused on optimizing care, (2) use patient care business models, and (3) be conducive to patients 'receiving care' rather than purchasing products" [46] (p. 3). At the same time, the expansion of superior quality professional pharmacy services could represent a source of competitive advantage [44,47].

4.2. Social Dimension

The social dimension of the business model for community pharmacies has been deployed in two main areas: pharmaceutical care (PC) and disease prevention within the public health domain.

4.2.1. PC

The role of the pharmacist "is patient-centered care with all the cognitive functions of counseling, providing drug information and monitoring drug therapy, as well as technical aspects of pharmaceutical services, including medicines supply management" [48] (p. 4). According to this statement, pharmacists have a huge responsibility in developing a generative safety culture oriented to patients where risk management is routinized to prevent errors and mitigate their impacts (Ashcroft et al., 2005). In addition to their roles of drugs' dispenser and counselors, pharmacists can play a crucial role within the healthcare system in contexts such as PC, disease prevention, and public health delivery. PC has been defined as "the responsible dispensing of drug therapy in order to achieve defined outcomes that improve the quality of life of the patient" [49] (p. 539). Coherent with this approach, the pharmacists' role is to promote safe and effective use of medicines and identify potential and existing drug-related problems for patients through three main activities: (a) assessment of appropriateness, effectiveness, and safeness; (b) set care plans in accordance with patients and other healthcare professionals (drug therapy but also preventive activities such as the promotion of healthy lifestyles); and (c) the monitoring of compliance with/effectiveness of drug therapy, such as identification of adverse effects, abuse, and misuse of drugs, but also the assessment of patients' progress during the therapy [50]. This approach to PC requires an involvement of the pharmacist in the design, implementation, and monitoring of therapeutic plans in collaboration with other health professionals [49,51].

Ensing et al. (2019) found evidence of positive cooperation between community pharmacists and healthcare organizations in addressing patients' drug-related problems after hospital discharge [52]. PC by community pharmacies has resulted in: (a) improving patients' clinical outcomes (through promoting an improvement in patients' adherence to therapy, avoiding drug interactions, and monitoring in order to avoid or minimize adverse drug reactions, etc.); (b) reducing medical costs including physician and laboratory visits, hospitalization, and so on for the healthcare system; (c) improving the productivity of patients through decreased days of sickness; and (d) improving customers' satisfaction and loyalty with reference to pharmacists' role [53–57]. Witnessing the need for greater involvement of community pharmacists in patients' care, Franco-Trigo et al. (2017) conducted a stakeholder analysis [58]. They underlined the potential benefits pharmacists could provide in cardiovascular diseases prevention and management including: patients' education on the use of medicines, monitoring of adherence to drugs' therapy, elaboration of the patients' medication profile (or a check if it is provided by a general practitioner), empowerment of patients in the management of their diseases, promotion of healthy habits, provision of services in rural areas, and patients' referral to healthcare professionals when it is advisable. Despite the above mentioned benefits of community pharmacists playing a major role in the delivery of PC services, some barriers persist; among them the public's and doctors' misperception of the role and competences of community pharmacists, the lack of collaboration between healthcare professionals that impacts their knowledge of patients' clinical paths and their needs, the lack of an adequate remuneration system for those pharmacy services delivered under an agreement with the national healthcare system, and so on [58].

It is important to remember that PC has different features depending on the context in which it is implemented [59]; so, the modality through which it is practiced and the benefits from its adoption can change depending on the health system under examination. In fact, PC has had multiple connotations in different countries over time: in the Netherlands, it is based on a consolidated cooperation culture between general practitioners and pharmacists to discuss patients' pharmacotherapy; in Sweden, PC is linked to the introduction of monitoring infrastructures such as the national register of patients' dispensed drugs to set PC initiatives that are voted on to identify and solve drug-related problems; in the UK, PC comprises a major counseling and prescribing role of pharmacists; in Germany, PC is related to cognitive pharmaceutical services and some programs such as diabetes counseling are certified; while in Italy, PC is typically part of a hospital's pharmacy practice [59], and only recently have national health institutions discussed actions to extend it to community pharmacies. Therefore, translating PC into sustainable practices will depend very much on the regulatory environment in which the community pharmacy under scrutiny operates.

4.2.2. Disease Prevention within the Public Health Domain

From a perspective of societal well-being, pharmacies can also contribute to public health because they can provide support to a national healthcare systems' campaign on disease prevention and healthy lifestyles, providing patients with the right information on how to improve and maintain their health [60]. Opportunities to support patients to make healthy living choices, in domains such as diet and nutrition, physical activity, and a reduction in alcohol consumption and tobacco smoking, and to support people with long-term conditions have been identified [61] and represent ways in which community pharmacies can contribute to public health [62]. Examples of best practices related to pharmacies that have become healthy living and information centers were already present when Anderson (2000) reviewed health promotion in community pharmacies in the UK [63]; the author proposed an improvement in the abilities of the workforce of community pharmacies through ad hoc training to integrate health promotion with PC and provision by paymasters of an adequate refund for community pharmacies' services. Currently, the situation does not seem to have changed and the criticalities that tend to persist concern the scarce representation of pharmacists by their association within healthcare policies, a lack of strong relationships with other healthcare professionals, a lack of collaboration between pharmacists in order to establish a common strategy for the provision of PC services, a lack of involvement of patients in the design of services, and so on [64]. A stakeholder analysis conducted in Nazar and Nazar's study (2018) revealed a major need for community pharmacies to collaborate with healthcare professionals at various levels in order to become the patients' port of call for services and advice [64].

Constraints due to social context can hinder the development of a new SBM [65]. Community pharmacies could be socially sustainable if such limitations were addressed not only reconsidering pharmacists' value in health policies, but also giving them professional and managerial tools to get actively involved in the provision of pharmaceutical and public healthcare services. To this end, effective promotional campaigns on the skills and competences of pharmacists are needed to increase the perception of all relevant stakeholders (patients and healthcare professionals) of the ability of community pharmacies to provide such services; patient-centered education should be included in pharmacy curricula to prepare pharmacists in the management of their relationship with customers; in addition, a change in contractual arrangements and a higher participation in the definition of healthcare policies are needed to increase pharmacists' involvement in the delivery of such services [66].

4.3. Environmental Dimension

The environmental dimension of the strategic structure of the business model is discussed considering the major role business owners of community pharmacies can play in environmental education and pharmacovigilance, cradle-to-grave stewardship, and the greening of community pharmacies' facilities.

4.3.1. Environmental Education and Ecopharmacovigilance

Greening the pharmacy requires embedding sustainability in its organizational system and processes through ways of changing people's behavior [67]. In particular, "green pharmacy practice in a community setting, is measured by the ability of both independent and corporate pharmacy organizations to reduce pharmaceutical waste, educate consumers on the proper disposal of medicines, and provide solutions for reducing pharmaceutical contamination" [10] (p. 363). In order to prevent the environmental impact of dispensed medicines, pharmacists can act as environmental educators [68]. In particular, they can increase the awareness of consumers of the environmental consequences of their choice to consume pharmaceuticals and personal care products and advise them about greener alternatives [68–70]. In fact, the active pharmaceutical ingredients (APIs) of unused, unwanted, and expired drugs can enter ground and water systems once disposed of and cause damage to the ecosystem; indeed, pharmaceuticals and personal care products are disposed of via industrial and household sewage and waste [69,71]. To scholars [71,72], the increase of APIs in the environment is exacerbated by: (a) promotions by manufacturers, such as the release of free samples to healthcare professionals, and advertising that creates prescription expectations in patients; (b) over and extra-label prescribing, therapy switches, and prescriptions to treat side effects exacerbating polypharmacy; (c) dispensing, which includes availability of free and low-cost drugs and the presence of automated dispensing machines; (d) ineffective administration of healthcare, for instance unused drugs left over in hospitals and unknown duration of therapy; (e) consumer involvement and behavior, such as purchase of excessive quantity of OTC products, stockpiling drugs for future use, and filling prescriptions with no intention to use them; and (f) non-adherence and non-compliance due to both real and perceived ineffectiveness of therapy, under-dosing of drugs, aversion to use drugs, and fear of adverse reaction. Although the effects of these substances on humans are poorly known, APIs could represent incalculable risks for the whole ecosystem in the long term and the seriousness of the risks should be taken into account [73].

Discouraging patients' misuse of drugs can also positively reduce waste with cost savings to the healthcare system and to customers' own expenditure. In this field, more integrated information systems between healthcare professionals (such as the so-called electronic medical record if shared by general practitioners and pharmacists) could enable a major monitoring of patients' consumption of medicines by pharmacists and help prevent their abuse and misuse [71,73]. Healthcare professionals can then contribute to ecopharmacovigilance through prescribing and dispensing practices that are both able to orient patients to the correct use of drugs and decrease the environmental impact of these drugs [71]. Indeed, ecopharmacovigilance "can be defined as the science and activities concerning detection, assessment, understanding and prevention of adverse effects or other problems related to the presence of pharmaceuticals in the environment, which affect both human and the other animal species" [74] (p. 963). Pharmacies can also help in reducing the environmental footprint of medicines by decreasing their inventories and counseling patients about a reasonable quantity of medication to be purchased [72].

4.3.2. Cradle-to-Grave Stewardship

Community pharmacies can act to green the supply chain [75] in several ways: they can choose contract distributors, which use storage, transport methods, and packaging with a low environmental impact and that have environmental certifications; they can exert pressure on the pharmaceutical industry through buying behavior in order to encourage the design and production of greener drugs; and they can provide facilities for wasted drugs take-back programs [68,70,75]. The more information (and time to absorb it) is made available to pharmacists about environmental problems, and the more conscious they become, the more they will enact green purchasing practices [76]. Greening the supply chain means to consider medicines' lifecycle, from production to correct disposal and degradation processes, and to provide good alternatives to reduce drugs' environmental footprint [77]. To implement a cradle-to-grave product stewardship starting from the pharmaceutical industry, which is responsible for design, development, and manufacturing, can provide, in the long term, environmental and cost-effective benefits [69].

4.3.3. Greening Community Pharmacies' Facilities

With reference to greening community pharmacies' facilities, the literature discusses possible business practices such as: energy saving in heating, air conditioning, water, and energy use; a choice of electronics that is labeled as energy efficient and can be part of a take-back program at the end of life; renovations based on sustainable materials; investigation of sources of indoor pollution in order to reduce emissions; collaboration with municipalities in disposal programs and supporting customers in separate disposal of waste programs [10,68,70]. The literature shows that customers prefer community pharmacies that engage in drugs take-back programs [78]; so, pharmacies participating in these projects can contribute to reducing the environmental impact of the pharmaceutical supply chain while increasing their customer base [79]. As scholars have underlined, pharmacists are aware of the link between the use of drugs and the persistence of active ingredients in the environment when medicines are disposed of; they recognize the importance of prevention strategies, although they see their contributions limited to supporting drugs disposal or to consultancy. Therefore, educational programs are recommended in order to help pharmacists to develop and sustain their capabilities in the field of sustainable pharmacy [73].

5. SBM and Community Pharmacies: Organizational Structure

The next subsections shed light on the design of the organizational structure of an SBM for a community pharmacy: the development of the community pharmacy's value network and the process of network hybridization that can help achieve the strategic goals of the firm.

5.1. The Development of a Community Pharmacy's Value Network

Community pharmacies are hybrid organizations characterized by both utilitarian and normative identities: their utilitarian identity refers to profit maximization through competitiveness, while their normative identity concerns the provision of care activities; therefore, business owners are engaged in balancing the tensions between the two in order to meet both financial goals and improve stakeholders' health. The peculiarities of hybrids stem from these two different institutional logics [6] leading to ambiguity in performance management and measurement, and to a major need to be accountable to diverse stakeholders [22,80]. During the past decade, the pharmacies' context has progressively redefined the traits and characteristics of pharmacies and, currently, calls for a greater contribution from pharmacies to the sustainability of the health system. For instance, in 2006, the Wiedenmayer et al. (2006) in collaboration with the International Pharmaceutical Federation, released the document "Developing pharmacy practice. A focus on patient care" in which they addressed the change in pharmacy practice over the past 40 years [48]. In the document, pharmacists were depicted as playing a number of different roles within society including the roles of caregiver, decision-maker, communicator, manager, life-long learner, educator, leader, and researcher. Indeed, pharmacy practice delves into a plurality of tasks including: the ability to manage resources, the use of information technology to provide quality services; the intermediation between drugs' prescribers and patients; an educational role for patients; the capability to use evidence-based pharmacy practice to advise the healthcare system about the effective and rational use of drugs; and the ability to take the lead within multidisciplinary healthcare teams for patients' well-being [48].

Awareness of the role that pharmacists can play within this modern frame of health and sustainable development policies is revealed in the literature that recommended a major role for pharmacists in multidisciplinary healthcare teams in order to contribute to societal healthcare needs and SDGs [50,81]. Pharmacists could contribute to SDGs if their role was extended to disease prevention, to wellness services, and to environmental factors (Woodard et al., 2018); in support of this, there would also be a greater preference of patients and pharmacists for healthcare delivery through community-based pharmacies [46]. From an organizational point of view, the literature proposed that community pharmacies should become part of networks in which their skills are shared with those of other health professionals for the provision of personalized treatments. In organizational studies, this process has been called hybridization extending beyond organizational forms [25], and it occurs in "hybrid process, practices and expertises that create and enable lateral rather than vertical transfers of information and knowledge, and that in so doing produce new forms of expertise" [26] (p. 961). In more recent studies on sustainable business modelling that combine both strategy definition and organizational design, knowledge sharing of this kind is considered to bring considerable benefits if developed at the system level, with the involvement of different social actors and therefore outside organizational barriers [15,19]. Scholars tend to use network theory to describe the ways in which the system approach that an organization develops through mutual relations with stakeholders can contribute to economic, social, and environmental value for both; in this way, value networks represent the locus in which to promote sustainable solutions balancing manifold interests and responsibilities [17,24,38]. These studies are based on the idea that value networks create social and economic good by ways of exchange of tangible and intangible value [82]. The literature has underlined that the transition toward sustainable development requires the adoption of both a firm-level and a system-level perspective on value creation, so that an SBM is constructed to provide value for the organization and the socio-economic-technical environment to which it belongs [19]; this is possible when the engagement of social actors is promoted and learning–action networks are developed in order to "create, capture and distribute value in novel ways" [19] (p. 4). In this paper, it is contended that when the managerial and organizational perspectives are combined, value networks become a lever to innovative sustainable solutions developed by community pharmacies' hybridization and the business model.

5.2. The Process of Network Hybridization

Hybridization for community pharmacies is expected to be characterized by the emergence of new expertise that could, from one side, benefit patients and communities as the major recipients of care and well-being services, and, from the other, guarantee healthcare system sustainability while increasing the competitive advantage of these organizations. Some studies highlighted that the network ties pharmacists create and maintain with their stakeholders, such as health providers and patients, can support them in successfully taking part in team-based care models [83,84]. For instance, Turner et al. (2018) reported that collaboration with a public health agency on the management of high-risk patients has increased the ability of pharmacists to deal with such users and support care managers with patients that had a high rate of emergency room visits [83]. Sharing information with healthcare providers on patients' adherence to drugs use and on drugs regimes, assisting them in annual wellness visits and collaborating to furnish new services within community pharmacies have increased healthcare providers' knowledge of the clinical competences of pharmacists [83]. Ties with patients and cooperation with drugs' delivery drivers were also useful to identify patients' unexpressed problems and preferences for service, and to tailor staff's competences toward these complex needs [83]. Kozminski et al. (2011) reported that healthcare professionals acknowledged the benefits of the integration of pharmacists in a medical homes project, such as medication therapy management, medication reconciliation post-hospital discharge, patient chart review and patient phone follow-up [84]. In some cases, this knowledge is already internally available and can be put at the service of new sustainable practices recalling the inside–out approach to business model innovation for sustainable development [12]. In other cases, pharmacists' competences need to be strengthened through adequate interdisciplinary education to facilitate the process of integration with other healthcare practices [40]. These networks can be considered real learning–action networks affecting the creation of community pharmacies' SBMs [23], where the sharing of information on patients and cooperation developed to provide personalized care, lead to the creation of value not only for those who will benefit from the service, but also for those who have generated it. Indeed, entering innovative working environments can enable community pharmacies to respond effectively to the changes in the institutional environment through satisfying patients' unmet needs. This is coherent with the mutual reinforcing cycle that is created between profit generation and social and ecological goals' achievement [13].

6. Community Pharmacies' SBM in Time of COVID-19

Hakovirta and Denuwara (2020) argued that the emergence of public health issues with COVID-19 "has reprioritized the sustainable development goals" within the United Nations agenda as "health is no longer only a demographic or an individual-level issue, but rather a global pandemic"; so, human health should be included as a fourth pillar of the sustainable development framework [85] (p. 3). Following this orientation, the community pharmacy SBM is put to the test to face COVID-19 emergency. As the literature pointed out, countries' response to COVID-19 pandemic "will unleash the full potential of community pharmacists and thus appears more likely to accelerate the paradigm shift from dispensing and indirect clinical focus to more direct clinical and patient centered healthcare relationship with patients/customers as well as other healthcare professionals" [86] (p. 1). In fact, social distancing and self-isolation measures will require pharmacy services to adopt new methods of service delivery [87]. New roles have thus been envisaged for community pharmacists that will sometimes be accompanied by a change in regulations to respond to COVID-19 emergency: for instance, in some countries pharmacists have been authorized to continue dispensing for patients with long-term conditions to improve patients' adherence, to compound drugs because of the shortage of medicines used in the treatment of patients with COVID-19, to extend prescriptions or pass prescriptions to other pharmacists, and deliver prescriptions to patients' homes for patients requiring controlled drugs [86,87]. In addition, their support in prevention campaigns and the provision of personal protective equipment was also recognized. As argued, during the pandemic, community pharmacists remained "at the frontline of public health by serving as direct point of access for their patients" [88] (p. 1); for instance, they provided triage services reducing the burden on healthcare facilities and helped patients by providing direct support.

A prospective major role for pharmacists is telepharmacy and home delivery services to decrease direct contact with patients and to compensate for counselling. Scholars outlined that the telepharmacy criticalities that emerged during COVID-19 pandemic could be overcome if supported by adequate government and professional bodies' interventions in terms of resources and pharmacists' education initiatives [89]; indeed, emphasis must be placed on vulnerable patients with limited digital skills and health literacy, as they need special support in the use of such services [89].

The role of community pharmacists in the management of COVID-19 pandemic is and will be, however, country specific because pharmacy legislation across the world is not homogeneous. For instance, in some countries community pharmacists do not have the right to prescribe drugs; in a pandemic situation, their role could be extended to maintaining the continuity of repeat prescriptions for older patients and people with long-term conditions [87].

The response of different countries in implementing SBM to support human health pillar will vary depending on their specific contexts. In developing countries, the SBM approach was based on the bottom of the pyramid approach; the aim of this approach was to overcome issues related to poverty and the lack of resources so that SBM had a positive impact on the local community [90]. Evidence on SBM implementation in different countries and contexts was provided in Dentchev et al.'s (2018) literature review [91]. They found papers dealing with manifold approaches to sustainable business modelling in 23 different countries. They emphasized the extent to which SBM may vary across cultural, industrial, and organizational contexts, and variation in the level of analysis, which could be individual, team, organizational, inter-organizational, and of multinational type [92]. They also emphasized the need for governmental support to foster the implementation of SBM and called for "research at the intersection of political preoccupations and the development and trajectories of SBMs across different institutional regimes to examine potential convergence, but also divergence of paths to sustainability in different countries and regions" [91] (p. 701). Culture and governmental support can affect the implementation of SBMs [92], which leads to variation in countries' approaches to SBM depending on the institutional context. Given the scarcity of empirical studies on such differences, further research is recommended to test the effect of countries' different institutional frameworks on SBM development, especially on the concerns of community pharmacies and their role in facing COVID-19 emergency.

7. Discussion and Conclusions

This conceptual paper discussed the strategic and organizational structures of an ideal SBM for community pharmacies in the light of the emergent institutional context [6]; it addressed the specificities of these hybrid organizations [22], whose competitive advantage depends on the satisfaction of multiple interests pertaining to their value network.

The paper also addressed the call of Geissdoerfer et al. (2018) for studies on business model innovation for sustainability [20]. Indeed, the paper combines best practices found from the literature and the internal knowledge assets that are already available within these organizations in order to discuss the ideal features of an SBM for community pharmacies; this new perspective comes from the combination of outside–in and inside–out approaches to SBM innovation [12]. The inside–out approach is related to competences that are already available within the community pharmacy, such as being a reference point for communities for dispensing drugs and counseling activities [48], while the outside–in approach is related to best practices found in the literature on pharmacists' competences that can be developed starting from positive experience in economic, social, and environmental areas. If these competences are combined, they form the basis for strategic planning around sustainability. From the organizational design side, a systemic approach [15,19] was adopted to explain the relevance of cooperation within pharmacists' value networks to make sustainable value creation, delivery and capture, effective. Indeed, the organizational structure supports the strategic structure of the SBM. To this end, pharmacists' capabilities become relevant if integration with other healthcare professionals is pursued in the name of personalized care paths for patients, through the mechanism of learning–action networks, whose role in the context of sustainable business modelling was conceptually addressed by Schaltegger et al. (2016) [23].

With respect to managerial implications, we contend that discussion of an SBM for community pharmacies could be useful to those business owners who strive to integrate sustainability into their pharmacy practice, showing that the co-existence of social, economic, and ecologic missions is possible and beneficial for both the business and its stakeholders: on the one hand, the business model that is proposed in this paper can support the development of economic, clinical, and environmental expertise for community pharmacies in order to contribute to people's health; on the other hand, its adoption can help enhance the perception of community pharmacies' professionalism and reputation, which represent sources of competitive advantage for community pharmacies.

In addition, the paper aims to raise awareness among those working in the field of health of the relevance of pharmacists in the achievement of the goals of sustainable healthcare systems, as the potential contribution of community pharmacists to SDGs is still under-evaluated in practice. The paper's recommendations are twofold. On one side, this research urges that health planning policies focus more on the concepts of value networks to ensure greater coverage of different disciplines within team-based models of care for the good of social and natural environments. Indeed, good governance based on the involvement of stakeholders, characterized by participation and involvement of stakeholders, has been discussed as a potential enabler of sustainable health [93]. On the other side, community pharmacists were at the forefront of the COVID-19 pandemic and represented the first point of contact with the healthcare system, providing patients with prompt support. This asks for health policies to contribute to a new valorization of the profession and a possible extension of the role of community pharmacists, especially in those countries in which their tasks are limited by regulations and support for the implementation of new pharmaceutical care services in response to the pandemic has been limited.

Suggestions for new research in this field are multiple. Further studies are needed to test the SBM for community pharmacies, discussed in the paper, through empirical research. In particular, longitudinal case study research may shed light on organizations that have started the journey toward SBM and monitor the efficacy and consequences of such choices [37]. These changes may not be radical in the short term due to the presence of contextual elements acting as constraints [65]. In the community pharmacies literature, we found examples of these criticalities, for instance: pharmacists' training is inadequate to the challenges of sustainable development, the limited interdisciplinary nature of the various paths of health education, and the lack of trust and collaboration between health professionals at various levels. For these reasons, evidence of best practices that have developed in some community pharmacies' contexts can enable understanding of the extent and the modality through which these criticalities can be overcome and a long-term oriented SBM can grow. As we discussed elsewhere in the paper, existing differences in community pharmacy practice among countries and contexts do exist, so that our conceptualization of an SBM for community pharmacies should be customized, based on contingent variables affecting its construction and development. Given the limited evidence on such differences, further research is recommended to test the effect of countries' different institutional frameworks on SBM development with reference to community pharmacies and their role in facing the COVID-19 emergency.

Author Contributions: Authors contribution are the following: conceptualization, E.V. and C.C.; methodology, C.C.; validation, E.V. and C.C.; formal analysis, C.C.; investigation, C.C.; writing—original draft preparation, C.C.; writing—review and editing, C.C. and E.V.; supervision, E.V. All authors have read and agreed to the published version of the manuscript.

References

1. Nunes, F.G.; Anderson, J.E.; Martins, L.M.; Wiig, S. The hybrid identity of micro enterprises: Contrasting the perspectives of community pharmacies' owners-managers and employees. *J. Small Bus. Enterp. Dev.* **2017**, *24*, 34–53. [CrossRef]
2. Joldersma, C.; Winter, V. Strategic management in hybrid organizations. *Public Manag. Rev.* **2002**, *4*, 83–99. [CrossRef]
3. Dugani, S.; Duke, T.; Kissoon, N. Transforming health through sustainable development. *Can. Med. Assoc. J.* **2016**, *188*, E213–E214. [CrossRef] [PubMed]
4. Rutter, V.; Chan, A.H.Y.; Tuck, C.; Bader, L.; Bates, I. Weaving the health and pharmaceutical care agenda through the themes of the commonwealth heads of government meeting (CHOGM), London 2018. *J. Pharm. Policy Pract.* **2018**, *11*, 1–4. [CrossRef]
5. Bader, L.; Duggan, C. FIP's Commitment to Action on the WHO Astana Declaration: Transforming pharmacy for better health for all. *Res. Soc. Adm. Pharm.* **2020**, *16*, 724–726. [CrossRef]
6. Laasch, O. Beyond the purely commercial business model: Organizational value logics and the heterogeneity of sustainability business models. *Long Range Plan.* **2018**, *51*, 158–183. [CrossRef]
7. Institute of Medicine. *Green Healthcare Institutions: Health, Environment, and Economics: Workshop Summary*; Frumkin, H., Coussens, C., Eds.; National Academies Press: Washington, DC, USA, 2007. [CrossRef]
8. Elkington, J. *Cannibals with Forks: The Triple Bottom Line of 21st Century Business*; Capstone: Oxford, UK, 1997.
9. Breen, L.; Garvey, O.; Mosan, G.; Matthias, O.; Sowter, J. Do we need to be Sustainable? An examination of purpose and intention behind Sustainability practice in Community Pharmacies in the National Health Service (UK). In Proceedings of the British Academy of Management Conference, Warwick, UK, 5–7 September 2017.
10. Webster, L.; Floyd, M. Green pharmacy practice. In *Pharmacy Practice Today for the Pharmacy Technician*; Webster, L., Ed.; Mosby: Maryland Heights, MO, USA, 2014; pp. 358–363.
11. Bocken, N.M.; Short, S.W.; Rana, P.; Evans, S. A literature and practice review to develop sustainable business model archetypes. *J. Clean. Prod.* **2014**, *65*, 42–56. [CrossRef]
12. Joyce, A.; Paquin, R.L. The triple layered business model canvas: A tool to design more sustainable business models. *J. Clean. Prod.* **2016**, *135*, 1474–1486. [CrossRef]

13. Osterwalder, A.; Pigneur, Y. Aligning profit and purpose through business model innovation. In *Responsible Management Practices for the 21st Century*; Palazzo, G., Wentland, M., Eds.; Pearson Education France: Paris, France, 2011; pp. 61–75.

14. Porter, M.E.; Kramer, M.R. The big idea: Creating shared value. *Harv. Bus. Rev.* **2011**, *89*, 2–17.

15. Stubbs, W.; Cocklin, C. Conceptualizing a "sustainability business model". *Organ. Environ.* **2008**, *21*, 103–127. [CrossRef]

16. Abdelkafi, N.; Täuscher, K. Business models for sustainability from a system dynamics perspective. *Organ. Environ.* **2016**, *29*, 74–96. [CrossRef]

17. Evans, S.; Vladimirova, D.; Holgado, M.; Van Fossen, K.; Yang, M.; Silva, E.A.; Barlow, C.Y. Business model innovation for sustainability: Towards a unified perspective for creation of sustainable business models. *Bus. Strategy Environ.* **2017**, *26*, 597–608. [CrossRef]

18. Lüdeke-Freund, F.; Carroux, S.; Joyce, A.; Massa, L.; Breuer, H. The sustainable business model pattern taxonomy—45 patterns to support sustainability-oriented business model innovation. *Sustain. Prod. Consum.* **2018**, *15*, 145–162. [CrossRef]

19. Roome, N.; Louche, C. Journeying toward business models for sustainability: A conceptual model found inside the black box of organisational transformation. *Organ. Environ.* **2016**, *29*, 11–35. [CrossRef]

20. Geissdoerfer, M.; Vladimirova, D.; Evans, S. Sustainable business model innovation: A review. *J. Clean. Prod.* **2018**, *198*, 401–416. [CrossRef]

21. Lüdeke-Freund, F.; Dembek, K. Sustainable business model research and practice: Emerging field or passing fancy? *J. Clean. Prod.* **2017**, *168*, 1668–1678. [CrossRef]

22. Spieth, P.; Schneider, S.; Clauß, T.; Eichenberg, D. Value drivers of social businesses: A business model perspective. *Long Range Plan.* **2018**, *53*, 427–444. [CrossRef]

23. Schaltegger, S.; Hansen, E.G.; Lüdeke-Freund, F. Business models for sustainability: Origins, present research, and future avenues. *Organ. Environ.* **2016**, *29*, 3–10. [CrossRef]

24. Bocken, N.; Short, S.; Rana, P.; Evans, S. A value mapping tool for sustainable business modelling. *Corp. Gov.* **2013**, *13*, 482–497. [CrossRef]

25. Kurunmäki, L. A hybrid profession—The acquisition of management accounting expertise by medical professionals. *Account. Organ. Soc.* **2004**, *29*, 327–347. [CrossRef]

26. Miller, P.; Kurunmäki, L.; O'Leary, T. Accounting, hybrids and the management of risk. *Account. Organ. Soc.* **2008**, *33*, 942–967. [CrossRef]

27. Castaldo, S.; Grosso, M.; Mallarini, E.; Rindone, M. The missing path to gain customers loyalty in pharmacy retail: The role of the store in developing satisfaction and trust. *Res. Soc. Adm. Pharm.* **2016**, *12*, 699–712. [CrossRef] [PubMed]

28. Schmidt, R.A.; Pioch, E.A. Community pharmacies under pressure: Issues of deregulation and competition. *Int. J. Retail Distrib. Manag.* **2004**, *32*, 354–357. [CrossRef]

29. Gavilan, D.; Avello, M.; Abril, C. Shopper marketing: A new challenge for Spanish community pharmacies. *Res. Soc. Adm. Pharm.* **2014**, *10*, e125–e136. [CrossRef] [PubMed]

30. Perepelkin, J.; Di Zhang, D. Brand personality and customer trust in community pharmacies. *Int. J. Pharm. Healthc. Mark.* **2011**, *5*, 175–193. [CrossRef]

31. International Federation of Pharmacists. Advancing the Global Pharmaceutical Workforce towards Achieving Universal Health Coverage and the UN Sustainable Development Goals, 2017. Available online: https://fip.org/files/fip/PharmacyEducation/2017/WHA_2017.pdf (accessed on 25 September 2020).

32. Fjeldstad, Ø.D.; Snow, C.C. Business models and organization design. *Long Range Plan.* **2018**, *51*, 32–39. [CrossRef]

33. Baden-Fuller, C.; Haefliger, S. Business models and technological innovation. *Long Range Plan.* **2013**, *46*, 419–426. [CrossRef]

34. Teece, D.J. Business models, business strategy and innovation. *Long Range Plan.* **2010**, *43*, 172–194. [CrossRef]

35. Chesbrough, H. Business model innovation: Opportunities and barriers. *Long Range Plan.* **2010**, *43*, 354–363. [CrossRef]

36. Upward, A.; Jones, P. An ontology for strongly sustainable business models: Defining an enterprise framework compatible with natural and social science. *Organ. Environ.* **2016**, *29*, 97–123. [CrossRef]

37. Pieroni, M.P.; McAloone, T.; Pigosso, D.A. Business model innovation for circular economy and sustainability: A review of approaches. *J. Clean. Prod.* **2019**, *215*, 198–216. [CrossRef]

38. Short, S.W.; Rana, P.; Bocken, N.M.P.; Evans, S. Embedding Sustainability in Business Modelling through Multi-stakeholder Value Innovation. In *Advances in Production Management Systems. Competitive Manufacturing for Innovative Products and Services*; Emmanouilidis, C., Taisch, M., Kiritsis, D., Eds.; Springer: Berlin, Germany, 2012; pp. 175–183.

39. Osterwalder, A.; Pigneur, Y. *Business Model Generation: A Handbook for Visionaries, Game Changers, and Challengers*; John Wiley & Sons, Inc.: Hoboken, NJ, USA, 2010.

40. Mossialos, E.; Courtin, E.; Naci, H.; Benrimoj, S.; Bouvy, M.; Farris, K.; Noyce, P.; Sketris, I. From "retailers" to health care providers: Transforming the role of community pharmacists in chronic disease management. *Health Policy* **2015**, *119*, 628–639. [CrossRef] [PubMed]

41. Al-Arifi, M.N. The managerial role of pharmacist at community pharmacy setting in Saudi Arabia. *Pharmacol. Pharm.* **2013**, *4*, 63. [CrossRef]

42. Pioch, E.A.; Schmidt, R.A. Community pharmacies as good neighbours? A comparative study of Germany and the UK. *Int. J. Retail Distrib. Manag.* **2004**, *32*, 532–544. [CrossRef]

43. Ottewill, R.; Jennings, P.L.; Magirr, P. Management competence development for professional service SMEs: The case of community pharmacy. *Educ. Train.* **2000**, *42*, 246–255. [CrossRef]

44. Moullin, J.C.; Sabater-Hernández, D.; Fernandez-Llimos, F.; Benrimoj, S.I. Defining professional pharmacy services in community pharmacy. *Res. Soc. Adm. Pharm.* **2013**, *9*, 989–995. [CrossRef]

45. Woodard, L.J.; Kahaleh, A.A.; Nash, J.D.; Truong, H.; Gogineni, H.; Barbosa-Leiker, C. Healthy People 2020: Assessment of pharmacists' priorities. *Public Health* **2018**, *155*, 69–80. [CrossRef]

46. Schommer, J.C.; Olson, A.W.; Isetts, B.J. Transforming community-based pharmacy practice through financially sustainable centers for health and personal care. *J. Am. Pharm. Assoc.* **2018**, *59*, 306–309. [CrossRef]

47. Singleton, J.A.; Nissen, L.M. Future-proofing the pharmacy profession in a hypercompetitive market. *Res. Soc. Adm. Pharm.* **2014**, *10*, 459–468. [CrossRef]

48. Wiedenmayer, K.; Summers, R.S.; Mackie, C.A.; Gous, A.G.S.; Everard, M.; Tromp, D. *Developing Pharmacy Practice. A Focus on Patient Care*; World Health Organization and International Pharmaceutical Federation: Hague, The Netherlands, 2006.

49. Hepler, C.D.; Strand, L.M. Opportunities and responsibilities in pharmaceutical care. *Am. J. Health Syst. Pharm.* **1990**, *47*, 533–543. [CrossRef]

50. Kehrer, J.P.; Eberhart, G.; Wing, M.; Horon, K. Pharmacy's role in a modern health continuum. *Can. Pharm. J.* **2013**, *146*, 321–324. [CrossRef] [PubMed]

51. Bernsten, C.; Björkman, I.; Caramona, M.; Crealey, G.; Frøkjær, B.; Grundberger, E.; Gustafsson, T.; Henman, M.; Herborg, H.; Hughes, C.; et al. Improving the well-being of elderly patients via community pharmacy-based provision of pharmaceutical care. *Drugs Aging* **2001**, *18*, 63–77. [CrossRef] [PubMed]

52. Ensing, H.T.; Koster, E.S.; Dubero, D.J.; van Dooren, A.A.; Bouvy, M.L. Collaboration between hospital and community pharmacists to address drug-related problems: The HomeCoMe-program. *Res. Soc. Adm. Pharm.* **2019**, *15*, 267–278. [CrossRef] [PubMed]

53. Cranor, C.W.; Bunting, B.A.; Christensen, D.B. The Asheville Project: Long-term clinical and economic outcomes of a community pharmacy diabetes care program. *J. Am. Pharm. Assoc.* **2003**, *43*, 173–184. [CrossRef] [PubMed]

54. Garrett, D.G.; Bluml, B.M. Patient self-management program for diabetes: First-year clinical, humanistic, and economic outcomes. *J. Am. Pharm. Assoc.* **2005**, *45*, 130–137. [CrossRef]

55. Munroe, W.P.; Kunz, K.; Dalmady-Israel, C.; Potter, L.; Schonfeld, W.H. Economic evaluation of pharmacist involvement in disease management in a community pharmacy setting. *Clin. Ther.* **1997**, *19*, 113–123. [CrossRef]

56. Park, J.J.; Kelly, P.; Carter, B.L.; Burgess, P.P. Comprehensive Pharmaceutical Care in the Chain Setting: Drug therapy monitoring and counseling by pharmacists contributed to improved blood pressure control in study patients. *J. Am. Pharm. Assoc.* **1996**, *36*, 443–451.

57. Wermeille, J.; Bennie, M.; Brown, I.; McKnight, J. Pharmaceutical care model for patients with type 2 diabetes: Integration of the community pharmacist into the diabetes team—A pilot study. *Pharm. World Sci.* **2004**, *26*, 18–25. [CrossRef]

58. Franco-Trigo, L.; Hossain, L.N.; Durks, D.; Fam, D.; Inglis, S.C.; Benrimoj, S.I.; Sabater-Hernández, D.

Stakeholder analysis for the development of a community pharmacy service aimed at preventing cardiovascular disease. *Res. Soc. Adm. Pharm.* **2017**, *13*, 539–552. [CrossRef]

59. van Mil, J.F.; Schulz, M. A review of pharmaceutical care in community pharmacy in Europe. *Harv. Health Policy Rev.* **2006**, *7*, 155–168.

60. Peña, C. Spanish pharmacy: Promoting sustainability through corporate social responsibility. *Int. Pharm. J.* **2011**, *27*, 1–52.

61. Vagnoni, E.; Biavati, G.R.; Felisatti, M.; Pomidori, L. Moderating healthcare costs through an assisted physical activity programme. *Int. J. Health Plann. Manag.* **2018**, *33*, 1146–1158. [CrossRef] [PubMed]

62. Root, D.; Varney, J. *Pharmacy: A Way Forward for Public Health Opportunities for Action through Pharmacy for Public Health*; Public Health England: London, UK, 2017; pp. 1–53.

63. Anderson, C. Health promotion in community pharmacy: The UK situation. *Patient Educ. Couns.* **2000**, *39*, 285–291. [CrossRef]

64. Nazar, H.; Nazar, Z. Community pharmacy minor ailment services in England: Pharmacy stakeholder perspectives on the factors affecting sustainability. *Res. Soc. Adm. Pharm.* **2018**, *15*, 292–302. [CrossRef]

65. Birkin, F.; Polesie, T.; Lewis, L. A new business model for sustainable development: An exploratory study using the theory of constraints in Nordic organizations. *Bus. Strategy Environ.* **2009**, *18*, 277–290. [CrossRef]

66. Saramunee, K.; Krska, J.; Mackridge, A.; Richards, J.; Suttajit, S.; Phillips-Howard, P. How to enhance public health service utilization in community pharmacy? General public and health providers' perspectives. *Res. Soc. Adm. Pharm.* **2014**, *10*, 272–284. [CrossRef]

67. Singleton, J. Greening pharmacy—Going green. *Aust. J. Pharm.* **2013**, *94*, 64–68.

68. Campbell, J. Creating an environmentally friendly pharmacy. *Pharm. Pract.* **2008**, *March/April*, 41–43.

69. Kreisberg, J. Greener Pharmacy. *Integr. Med.* **2007**, *6*, 50–52.

70. Wick, J.Y. Getting to Green: How's Pharmacy Doing? Available online: https://www.pharmacytimes. com/publications/issue/2013/November2013/Getting-to-Green-Hows-Pharmacy-Doing (accessed on 25 September 2020).

71. Daughton, C.G.; Ruhoy, I.S. Green pharmacy and pharmEcovigilance: Prescribing and the planet. *Expert Rev. Clin. Pharmacol.* **2011**, *4*, 211–232. [CrossRef]

72. Daughton, C.G. Cradle-to-cradle stewardship of drugs for minimizing their environmental disposition while promoting human health. I. Rationale for and avenues toward a green pharmacy. *Environ. Health Perspect.* **2003**, *111*, 757. [CrossRef] [PubMed]

73. Götz, K.; Deffner, J. Options for a more environmentally friendly handling of pharmaceuticals. In *Green and Sustainable Pharmacy*; Kümmerer, K., Hempel, M., Eds.; Springer: Berlin, Germany, 2010; pp. 149–163.

74. Velo, G.; Moretti, U. Ecopharmacovigilance for Better Health. *Drug Saf.* **2010**, *33*, 963–968. [CrossRef] [PubMed]

75. Xie, Y.; Breen, L. Greening community pharmaceutical supply chain in UK: A cross boundary approach. *Supply Chain Manag.* **2012**, *17*, 40–53. [CrossRef]

76. Schaper, M. Small firms and environmental management: Predictors of green purchasing in Western Australian pharmacies. *Int. Small Bus. J.* **2002**, *20*, 235–251. [CrossRef]

77. Kümmerer, K. Sustainable from the very beginning: Rational design of molecules by life cycle engineering as an important approach for green pharmacy and green chemistry. *Green Chem.* **2007**, *9*, 899–907. [CrossRef]

78. Kotchen, M.; Kallaos, J.; Wheeler, K.; Wong, C.; Zahller, M. Pharmaceuticals in wastewater: Behavior, preferences, and willingness to pay for a disposal program. *J. Environ. Manag.* **2009**, *90*, 1476–1482. [CrossRef]

79. Thach, A.V.; Brown, C.M.; Pope, N. Consumer perceptions about a community pharmacy-based medication take back program. *J. Environ. Manag.* **2013**, *127*, 23–27. [CrossRef]

80. Mair, J.; Mayer, J.; Lutz, E. Navigating institutional plurality: Organizational governance in hybrid organizations. *Organ. Stud.* **2015**, *36*, 713–739. [CrossRef]

81. Anderson, C.; Bates, I.; Beck, D.; Brock, T.P.; Futter, B.; Mercer, H.; Rouse, M.; Wuliji, T.; Yonemura, A. The WHO UNESCO FIP pharmacy education taskforce. *Hum. Resour. Health* **2009**, *7*, 45. [CrossRef]

82. Allee, V. Value-creating networks: Organizational issues and challenges. *Learn. Organ.* **2009**, *16*, 427–442. [CrossRef]

83. Turner, K.; Weinberger, M.; Renfro, C.; Ferreri, S.; Trygstad, T.; Trogdon, J.; Shea, C.M. The role of network

ties to support implementation of a community pharmacy enhanced services network. *Res. Soc. Adm. Pharm.* **2018**, *15*, 1118–1125. [CrossRef] [PubMed]

84. Kozminski, M.; Busby, R.; McGivney, M.S.; Klatt, P.M.; Hackett, S.R.; Merenstein, J.H. Pharmacist integration into the medical home: Qualitative analysis. *J. Am. Pharm. Assoc.* **2011**, *51*, 173–183. [CrossRef] [PubMed]

85. Hakovirta, M.; Denuwara, N. How COVID-19 Redefines the Concept of Sustainability. *Sustainability* **2020**, *12*, 3727. [CrossRef]

86. Nadeem, M.F.; Soumya, S.; Mustafa, M. Is the Paradigm of Community Pharmacy Practice Expected to Shift Due to COVID-19? Available online: https://www.ncbi.nlm.nih.gov/pmc/articles/PMC7255229/ (accessed on 25 September 2020).

87. Cadogan, C.A.; Hughes, C.M. On the frontline against COVID-19: Community pharmacists' contribution during a public health crisis. *Res. Soc. Adm. Pharm.* **2020**, in press. [CrossRef] [PubMed]

88. Bukhari, N.; Huma, R.; Bismah, N.; Zaheer-Ud-Din, B. Pharmacists at the frontline beating the COVID-19 pandemic. *J. Pharm. Policy Pract.* **2020**, *13*, 1–4. [CrossRef] [PubMed]

89. Koster, E.S.; Philbert, D.; Bouvy, M.L. Impact of the COVID-19 epidemic on the provision of pharmaceutical care in community pharmacies. *Res. Soc. Adm. Pharm.* **2020**, in press. [CrossRef]

90. Nosratabadi, S.; Mosavi, A.; Shamshirband, S.; Zavadskas, E.K.; Rakotonirainy, A.; Chau, K.W. Sustainable business models: A review. *Sustainability* **2019**, *11*, 1663. [CrossRef]

91. Dentchev, N.; Rauter, R.; Jóhannsdóttir, L.; Snihur, Y.; Rosano, M.; Baumgartner, R.; Nyberg, T.; Tang, X.; van Hoof, B.; Jonker, J. Embracing the variety of sustainable business models: A prolific field of research and a future research agenda. *J. Clean. Prod.* **2018**, *194*, 695–703. [CrossRef]

92. Birkin, F.; Cashman, A.; Koh, S.C.L.; Liu, Z. New sustainable business models in China. *Bus. Strategy Environ.* **2009**, *18*, 64–77. [CrossRef]

93. Sobczak, E.; Bartniczak, B.; Raszkowski, A. Aging Society and the Selected Aspects of Environmental Threats: Evidence from Poland. *Sustainability* **2020**, *12*, 4648. [CrossRef]

2

Industrial Symbiosis in Insect Production—A Sustainable Eco-Efficient and Circular Business Model

Chloé Phan Van PhI *, Maye Walraven, Marine Bézagu, Maxime Lefranc and Clément Ray

InnovaFeed, Route de Chaulnes, Lieudit Les Trente, 80190 Nesle, France;
maye.walraven@innovafeed.com (M.W.); marine.bezagu@innovafeed.co (M.B.);
maxime.lefranc@innovafeed.com (M.L.); clement.ray@innovafeed.com (C.R.)
* Correspondence: chloe.phan-van-phi@innovafeed.com

Abstract: Insect meal (IM) is a source of high-quality protein for aquafeed while insect oil (IO) is a source of fatty acids used in monogastric feed with identical or better performance than premium fishmeal (FM) or vegetable oils (VOs) respectively. Although insects' ability to feed on agricultural by-products and the entire valorization of insect products (IM, IO, frass) suggest insect production is sustainable, no studies have documented its environmental impact using industrial-scale production data. The present study is the first attributional life cycle assessment (A-LCA) based on data from an industrial-scale facility implementing an innovative symbiosis production model. This A-LCA was used to (i) assess the environmental performance of the symbiosis model vs. a no-symbiosis model and (ii) compare the environmental impacts of IM and IO production vs. their respective alternatives. The results revealed that the symbiosis model introduces a meaningful change in terms of environmental footprint by reducing CO_2 emissions by 80% and fossil resources depletion by 83% compared to the no-symbiosis model. The higher sustainability of the IM and IO produced using the symbiosis model was also demonstrated, as CO_2 emissions were reduced by at least 55% and 83% when compared to the best FM and VOs alternatives, respectively.

Keywords: industrial symbiosis; alternative protein; insect meal; insect oil; frass; sustainable production; environmental impact; circular economy; organic fertilizer

1. Introduction

Global food production has nearly tripled since 1960 to meet the demands of the growing population. Diet evolution has led to an increased need for animal protein: per capita fish food consumption grew from 9.0 kg in 1961 to 20.5 kg in 2018 [1] and per capita livestock consumption grew from 23.1 kg in 1961 to 43.2 kg in 2013 [2]. This increasing demand for animal protein also stimulated the demand for feed ingredients thereby intensifying the pressure on limited natural resources [3]. In this context, the Food and Agricultural Organization has pointed out the urgent need to use alternative feeds, as the requirement for traditional feed ingredients cannot be met even by the most optimistic forecasts [4]. In addition, the gap between the demand and supply of these ingredients is expected to widen in the upcoming decades. This provides a compelling reason to explore locally available feed ingredients.

Insects are part of the natural diet of multiple animals, and therefore several species have been investigated as potential sources of feed ingredients for fish, shrimp, poultry, and swine diets. Black soldier fly larvae (BSFL) have been identified as a source of high-quality protein and fatty acids necessary for animal development. Multiple studies performed with partial (50%) or total replacement of fishmeal (FM) by BSFL meal in aquafeed clearly demonstrated the validity of the latter in terms of nutritional demands [5–7]. Similarly, studies evaluating the replacement of VOs by BSFL oil in monogastric feed demonstrated similar growth performance for broiler chicks [8] and young turkeys [9], as well as similar meat quality, nutritional composition, and sensory profile of finisher broilers [10] and young turkeys [9]. In addition to showing at least equal performance to FM and VOs in aqua and monogastric feed, two reasons suggest that IM and IO could also be more sustainable than their respective alternatives. First, insects have the ability to transform low-value agricultural by-products into high-quality feed because insect production has extremely low water and land requirements [5,7,11]. Second, insects can be valorized entirely: IM as a source of high-quality protein for aquafeed, IO as a source of energy and lauric acid for monogastric feed, and frass (insect dejections) as an organic fertilizer thus closing the loop on nutrient cycling [11–13].

However, to meet the world's current and future demands for animal feed ingredients, insect rearing must be performed at industrial scale [14] and references therein. Likewise, to provide the most accurate environmental impact analysis, it is also at this scale that the sustainability of producing IM and IO has to be determined [12] and compared to that of their traditional alternatives [15]. Thus, it is vital to perform a life cycle assessment (LCA) of the entire production process to provide insights on which step(s) encompass environmental challenges, and thoroughly assess how sustainable the production of IM and IO is compared to that of traditional feed ingredients such as FM and VOs [12]. Few studies have performed such LCAs on the environmental impact of insect production [13] and references therein and all were based on partial or aggregated data derived from pilot-scale facilities. Following the change in European legislation (EU Regulation 2015/2283), which enabled the use of insect-based protein in aquaculture feed in 2017, the construction of several large-scale insect production facilities was announced. InnovaFeed, a French biotechnology company, has developed a unique and innovative symbiosis model in which the insect production unit is co-located with agro-industrials to recycle the by-products of these industries as feed for the insects and to benefit from energetic synergies during insect rearing. InnovaFeed's industrial-scale insect production facility was inaugurated in 2020.

The present study aimed to analyze the environmental impact of this innovative symbiosis model for BSFL production at industrial scale. Firstly, an attributional LCA (A-LCA) was conducted to evaluate the environmental impact of the symbiosis production model. Secondly, this impact was compared to that of a model without symbiosis (hereafter referred to as "no-symbiosis model") to evaluate the impact of the symbiosis. Finally, the environmental impacts of producing IM and IO using the symbiosis model were compared to that of producing their respective alternatives, i.e., FM and VOs, by contrasting the results from the current A-LCA with data available in the Agribalyse 1.3. database (https://app.agribalyse.fr) for these conventional feed ingredients.

2. Materials and Methods

2.1. Goal and Scope Definition of the A-LCA (ISO 14040)

To the best of our knowledge, the present A-LCA is the first using industrial-scale insect production data. Moreover, the environmental impact of producing IM, IO, and insect frass was based on data derived from InnovaFeed's industrial scale production facility in France that is co-located with two other industrial players: (i) a starch manufacturer that directly supplies local agricultural by-products to feed the larvae and (ii) a wood biomass turbine, installed in a renewable energy power plant, that powers the insect production facility. Using such data enabled assessing the potential environmental benefits of the symbiosis model vs. a no-symbiosis model but also the environmental impacts of the different production steps as well as that of each of the three products (IM, IO, and frass).

For the present A-LCA, the cradle-to-gate approach was used. It encompassed (i) feed preparation (raw materials' production and supply and BSFL feed preparation), (ii) BSFL growth and reproduction, (iii) IM and IO processing, and (iv) frass processing. These four steps are collectively referred to as "insect production" throughout the text.

To assess the environmental impact of the two different production models (symbiosis vs. no-symbiosis), 1 t IM + 0.35 t IO + 7 t frass was designated the Functional Unit (FU), as the three products were simultaneously produced at the 1:0.35:7 ratio at the insect production facility.

2.2. Inventory Analysis (ISO 14044)

2.2.1. Inventory Flows

The production of BSFL requires three types of inputs: (i) agricultural by-products (i.e., wheat bran and wheat slurry), (ii) food by-products both to feed BSFL; and (iii) energy to power the production facility. There are four output flows: three products (IM, IO and frass) and water.

In the case of the insect production facility examined here, agricultural by-products were supplied directly from the starch manufacturer located close to it via a pipeline connecting the two sites (Figure 1). As a result, agricultural by-products required no additional evaporation: wheat bran was provided with a dry matter (DM) content of 88% and wheat slurry with 15% DM; hence, no extra water was added to feed the BSFL. The co-location of the starch manufacturer and insect production facility also enabled the reception of slurry at 80 °C. The capture of this heat contributed to maintaining the appropriate temperature in the breeding zone thereby decreasing the overall energy needs of the insect production facility by 20%.

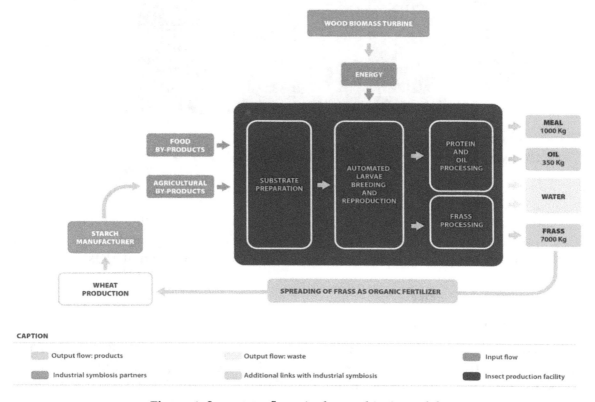

Figure 1. Inventory flows in the symbiosis model.

Similarly, the location of the insect production facility close to the wood biomass turbine of the renewable energy power plant enabled capturing the turbine's waste energy (i.e., energy that was previously dissipated in the atmosphere) in the form of water at 60 °C; the calorific capacity of this heated water was extracted at the insect production facility before the water was sent back to the turbine to be heated again. This waste energy corresponded to 53% of the production facility's energy need. The remaining 47% was sourced from the nearby energy power plant, consisting solely in renewable energy in the form of steam (8 bar, 29% of total consumption), and electricity (18% of total consumption).

2.2.2. Scenario Analysis

The environmental performance of the symbiosis model was compared to that of the no-symbiosis model (Figure 2) assuming the following scenario:

- Agricultural by-products were sourced dry (DM_{slurry} = 88%, DM_{bran} = 88%) from a starch manufacturer located 40 km away and transported by truck;
- Hence, additional water was required to mix the agricultural by-products and obtain a BSFL feed substrate with the same DM content as in the symbiosis model;
- Electricity was sourced from the French grid (standard renewable energy to fossil resources ratio);
- Heat was sourced from a gas furnace instead of using waste energy, steam, and warm slurry as in the symbiosis model.

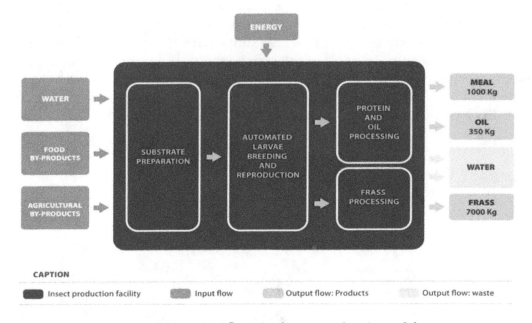

Figure 2. Inventory flows in the no-symbiosis model.

Feed and energy needs were assumed equal between models including larvae feed conversion ratio (FCR), substrate composition and total DM content, and total energy needs (in GWh/FU). Output flows including IM, IO, frass, and water were also assumed equal between models.

2.3. Impact Assessment (ISO 14044)

2.3.1. Methodology and Indicators

The assessment followed the standard A-LCA approach (ISO 14040, 2006; ISO 14044, 2006) using the SimaPro software (https://simapro.com). Three mid-point life cycle indicators were considered according to the IMPACT 2002+ methodology [16]: Climate change, fossil resources depletion, and land use. Economic allocation was applied to distribute the environmental impact across inputs (wheat bran and wheat slurry, as well as food by-products) and outputs (IM, IO, and frass).

2.3.2. Environmental Impact Calculation

For the no-symbiosis model, impact factors were sourced from Agribalyse 1.3, as implemented in SimaPro. In the symbiosis model, impact factors for wheat bran and wheat slurry inputs, as well as for the electricity input, were adapted to account for the specificities of the model:

- The impact of wheat slurry was adjusted to consider the cancelation of the drying step of the process as wheat slurry was supplied wet (15% DM) in the symbiosis model;

- The impact of electricity was adjusted to account for the use of at least 80% wood waste in the wood biomass turbine, as required by CREII certification;
- No impact was associated with the waste energy and heat captured from the wheat slurry nor with the transport of starch by-products in the symbiosis model as the latter are conveyed between partners through a direct pipeline;
- Finally, for wheat bran and wheat slurry, the replacement of nitrogen-phosphorous-potassium (NPK) mineral fertilizers by insect frass considered the NPK profile of the frass as well as the wheat NPK intake from mineral sources necessary for its growth. Based on the NPK required to produce the wheat by-products and on the NPK content of the produced frass, it was assumed that the latter could replace 100% of the NPK fertilizer required to produce the wheat by-products used as BSFL feed. This was the only consequential effect considered in this A-LCA.

2.4. Sensitivity Analysis

A sensitivity analysis was performed to assess if the environmental impact of BSFL production using the industrial symbiosis model could be further improved. This analysis tested the impact of improving larvae FCR. Given that insect feeding is the largest contributor to the environmental impact of insect rearing, improving larvae FCR might reduce the intake of the raw materials required for production. As so, BSFL feed intake was reduced by 2%, 5%, and 10% without changing the proportion of the feed components.

3. Results

3.1. Environmental Impacts of the Symbiosis Model

In the symbiosis model, the environmental impact of producing each FU (1 t IM + 0.35 t IO + 7 t frass) was estimated as 944 kg of CO_2 eq emitted, 17 GJ of fossil resources depleted, and 2179 m^2.yr of arable land occupied (Figure 3). Feeding BSFL was the main driver of the environmental impact of the symbiosis model across all three indicators studied (91% for climate change, 94% for fossil resources depletion, and 96% for land use). The environmental impact of the energy used for each of the different production steps, i.e., feed preparation, growth and reproduction, IM and IO processing, and frass processing, was further estimated. Growth and reproduction accounted for 47% of the overall environmental impact of energy used across all three indicators.

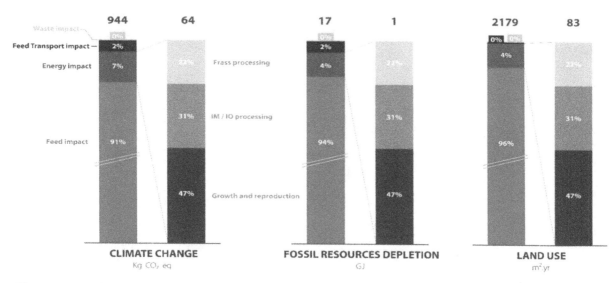

Figure 3. Breakdown of the environmental impact of each inventory flow (blue bars) and deep dive on the energy impact broken down across the different production steps (grey bars) of the symbiosis model.

3.2. Comparison of the Environmental Impacts of the Symbiosis and No-Symbiosis Models

The environmental impact of the symbiosis model was 80% and 83% lower than that of the no-symbiosis model considering climate change and fossil resources depletion, respectively, while the impact of land use was 3% higher. These differences are attributable to the four main differences between the two production models (Figure 4):

1. **The use of wet agricultural by-products**: In the symbiosis model, wheat slurry is received at 15% DM whereas in the no-symbiosis model it is dried up and received at 88% DM;

2. **The direct supply of by-products**: In the symbiosis model, wheat bran and wheat slurry are directly delivered from the starch manufacturer to the insect production facility through a pipeline whereas in the no-symbiosis model the same by-products are transported by truck over a 40 km distance;

3. **Energy mix optimization**: In the symbiosis model, the energy required to power the insect production facility is sourced from (i) the calorific capacity of the wheat slurry received at 80 °C, (ii) the calorific capacity of the water heated to 60 °C using the waste energy from the nearby wood biomass turbine, and (iii) the nearby wood biomass turbine itself; in the no-symbiosis model, the energy required to power the insect production facility is sourced from natural gas and electricity assuming the standard mix used in the French grid;

4. **The use of frass as fertilizer**: In the symbiosis model, the produced frass is assumed to be spread on agricultural lands thereby replacing 100% of the required mineral fertilizers to produce wheat bran and wheat slurry (the only consequential effect taken into account in this A-LCA); in the no-symbiosis model, no consequential effect related to the use of the produced frass was accounted for.

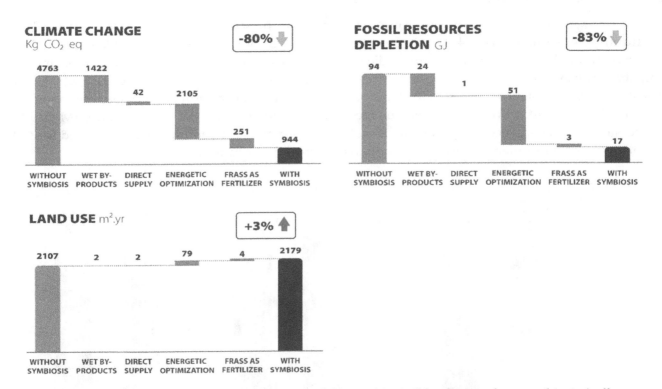

Figure 4. Comparative environmental impact of the symbiosis (blue bar) and no-symbiosis (yellow bar) models across the three indicators studied. The impact difference between models is broken down across each technological development implemented in the symbiosis model (grey bars).

Overall, the comparative analysis demonstrated that the use of wet by-products and optimization of the energy mix accounted for the larger proportion of the reduction in the environmental impact of the symbiosis model regarding climate change and fossil resources depletion [1422 kg CO_2 eq (30%) and 24 GJ (25%) reduction for the use of wet by-products; 2105 kg CO_2 eq (44%) and 51 GJ (54%) reduction for energy optimization; Figure 4].

In fact, the technology developed and implemented in the symbiosis model, which enabled capturing waste energy from the wood turbine and reducing energy requirement due to using wheat slurry at 80 °C, accounted for the majority of the reduction in climate change attributed to the energetic optimization (1533 kg CO_2 eq or 73%). The remaining of the reduction in CO_2 emissions attributed to energy optimization (572 kg CO_2 eq or 27%) stems from the use of renewable energy from the wood turbine as opposed to the French standard electricity and gas in the no-symbiosis model.

However, the use of wood biomass energy in the symbiosis model increased the impact on land use by 79 m^2.yr compared to the no-symbiosis model (Figure 4). This marginal increase of 3% is due to using wood resources to power the turbine, despite its CREII certification guarantee that at least 80% of the wood burnt is waste wood.

Finally, the replacement of mineral fertilizers by insect frass in the symbiosis model only marginally reduced the environmental impact of this model regarding climate change and fossil resources depletion (251 kg CO_2 eq or 5% and 3 GJ or 3%, respectively; Figure 4); yet, this step allowed closing the loop for the circularity of the model.

The split of the environmental impacts across the production steps also differed between models (Figure 5). Considering the climate change and fossil resources depletion indicators, the impacts of feed preparation and larvae growth and reproduction were more evenly distributed in the no-symbiosis model (55% and 33% for climate change and 46% and 37% for fossil resources depletion, respectively), while in the symbiosis model the impact of feed preparation step accounted for more than 90% (93% for climate change and 96% for fossil resources depletion).

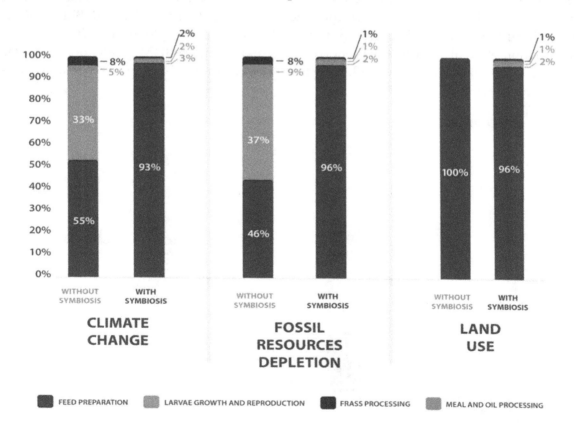

Figure 5. Breakdown of the environmental impact of each manufacturing step in the symbiosis and no-symbiosis models.

As for the environmental impact of each component of the FU (Table 1), i.e., IM, IO and frass, IM was attributed the largest impact share across all three indicators based on the economic allocation. This trend was maintained when the impact was calculated for each ton of product.

Table 1. Environmental impact of each fraction of the functional unit and of each ton of insect product.

	Climate Change	Fossil Resources Depletion	Land Use
	kg CO_2 eq	GJ	m^2.yr
Total of functional unit	944	17	2179
	Per fraction of the functional unit		
IM (1 t)	57%	86%	86%
IO (0.35 t)	8%	12%	12%
Frass (7 t)	35%	1%	1%
	Per ton of insect product		
IM (1 t)	536	9.39	1239
IO (1 t)	218	3.81	503
Frass (1 t)	47	0.02	2.59

3.3. Comparison of the Environmental Impacts of IM and IO with Their Alternatives

3.3.1. Comparison of IM and FM

For the comparison of IM and FM, 1 t of IM was considered nutritionally equivalent to 1.03 t of FM to account for the FCR reduction resulting from the replacement of FM with IM and for the difference in crude protein content (FM = 70%; IM = 65%). For this comparison, a fish basket representative of the most likely applications of IM in aquaculture was used (50% salmon + 10% trout + 40% shrimp). Two types of FM included in the Agribalyse 1.3 database were used for the comparison to consider the different FMs available in the market: FM from anchovies from Peru and FM from Blue Whiting from Norway. Using 1 t of IM instead of 1.03 t of FM resulted in 55–75% reduction of CO_2 emissions and 46–70% reduction of fossil resources depletion (Figure 6). As expected, IM production had a land use impact higher than that of FM, as the BSFL were fed on agricultural by-products whereas wild fish diet was not accounted for in the A-LCA.

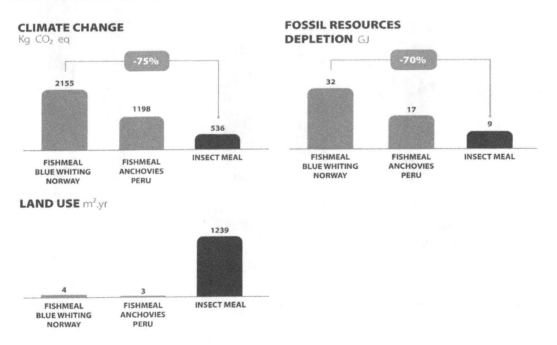

Figure 6. Environmental impact of producing insect meal and fishmeal as feed ingredients for a fish basket composed of 50% salmon, 10% trout, and 40% shrimp.

3.3.2. Comparison of IO and VOs

For the comparison of IO and VOs, particularly coprah and soy oils, 1 t of IO was considered nutritionally equivalent to 1 t of soy and coprah oils included in swine and poultry feed. To account for the traceability of the soy oil, two types (with and without deforestation) were retrieved from the Agribalyse 1.3 database and used for the comparison. Producing 1 t of IO compared to producing of 1 t of VOs showed an overall improvement of the environmental impact across all indicators: 83–95% reduction of CO_2 emissions, 77–91% reduction of fossil resources depletion, and 87–96% reduction in land use (Figure 7). These reductions were mostly driven by vertical insect farming, which uses limited space, and by the symbiosis of the three industries in which the waste of one is used as raw material for another.

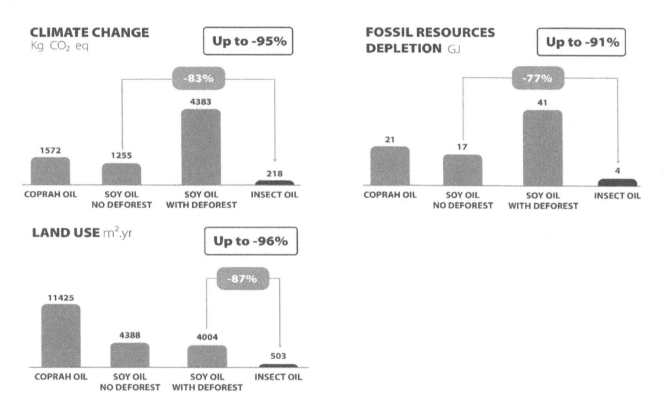

Figure 7. Environmental impact of producing insect oil, coprah oil, and soy oil, with and without deforestation, as feed ingredients for swine and poultry.

3.4. Sensitivity Analysis

Agricultural by-products required to feed the larvae were by far the inventory flow with the largest environmental impact across all three indicators. The sensitivity analysis performed to verify if the reduction of BSFL feed intake could improve the environmental impact of insect production revealed that a reduction of BSFL feed intake to 90% resulted in a proportional reduction (~10%) in the environmental impact across all indicators (Table 2).

Table 2. Environmental impact of feed reduction during BSFL rearing.

Environmental Impact Indicator	Feed Intake		Environmental Impact Reduction
	100%	90%	
Climate change (kg CO_2 eq)	944	856	9%
Fossil resources depletion (GJ)	17	15	10%
Land use (m².yr)	2179	1969	10%

4. Discussion

4.1. Impact of the Innovative Symbiosis Model Compared to That of the No-Symbiosis Model

This study contributed new data to the improvement of the environmental impact and sustainability of large-scale insect production by analyzing an industrial symbiosis model. The LCA results demonstrated that this symbiosis model is a game changer for the sustainability of industrial insect production with 80% reduction in CO_2 emissions (57 kt of CO_2 eq saved per year on the plant or 3.8 t of CO_2 eq saved per FU) and 83% reduction of fossil resources depletion (1170 TJ per year, which is equivalent to ~200,000 oil barrels) when compared to the no-symbiosis model. This symbiosis model addresses the key limitations previously acknowledged for the environmental sustainability of insect production, i.e., the input of raw materials for feeding insects and energy consumption. By using warm and wet agricultural by-products (wet wheat slurry) that are delivered via a pipeline linked to the starch manufacturer partner, the symbiosis model allowed (i) saving the drying energy and water that would otherwise need to be added to the substrate, (ii) reducing the greenhouse gases emissions associated with the transportation of the agricultural by-products and (iii) reducing the total energy needs of the production plant by capturing the calorific capacity of warm slurry. This first particularity of the symbiosis model resulted in saving 1422 kg CO_2 eq and 24 GJ per FU compared to the no-symbiosis model. Furthermore, the symbiosis model also enabled (i) using waste energy previously released to the atmosphere to heat the insect rearing facility (accounting for 53% of total energy consumption) and (ii) powering the entire insect production facility with renewable energy from a wood-based co-generated energy plant located next to it. This, in turn, resulted in a reduction of 2105 kg CO_2 eq and 51 GJ per FU, when compared to the no-symbiosis model.

Although the symbiosis model slightly underperformed compared to the no-symbiosis model in terms of land use (marginal increase of 3%), this was due to the forestry that is required to provide wood for the co-generation unit, as 20% of such wood is not waste wood (increase of 79 m^2.yr per FU). Hence, and depending on the category of environmental impact assessed, using wood-based co-generation is simultaneously responsible for the better and worse performances of the symbiosis model, highlighting the importance of a multiple impact analysis.

Several studies have confirmed IM and IO as reliable alternative ingredients to FM and VOs (soybean oil in most assessments), respectively, particularly regarding the nutritional demands and zootechnical performance of terrestrial and aquatic species e.g., [5–10,17]. In addition, insects have been acknowledged as sustainable sources of protein and oil [13–15,18–20]. Comparing the present results for the three indicators with those of previous LCAs, the lowest environmental impact values obtained for the symbiosis model are notable, regardless of insect species and production models (Table 3).

Table 3. Comparison of the environmental impact of producing 1 t IM using different insect species and production models.

Insect Species [Reference Source]	Indicators		
	Climate Change kg CO_2 eq	Fossil Resources Depletion GJ	Land Use m^2.yr
House fly larvae [21]	770	9.3	32
House fly larvae [22]	-	159.8–288.1	2790–5320
Mealworm larvae [23]	3500	44.3	4680
Mealworm larvae [24]	7100–7550	80.0–101.0	50
BSFL [25]	-	13.4–64.06	10–40
BSFL [26]	1240	1.5	-
BSFL [13]	2100	15.1	50
BSFL [18]	1360–15,100	21.2–99.6	32–7030
BSFL [present study]	536	9.4	1239

Although in terms of climate change and fossil resources depletion (536 vs. 770 kg CO_2 eq, 9.4 vs. 9.3 GJ, respectively) the results of the present study are similar to those for house fly larvae in the work of Van Zanten et al. [21], the data used by these authors were not obtained from a production unit, as it is the case of the present study, but from a hypothetical scenario extrapolated from research data results. The large difference in land use is easily explained by the exclusive use of pre-consumer food waste as larvae feeding material in the study by van Zanten et al. [21], which is difficult to rely on for large scale production of IM (further discussed below).

4.2. Impact Drivers and Scope for Improvement in the Symbiosis Model

The results obtained in the present A-LCA indicate that the largest contributing factor across all environmental impact indicators was insect feeding on wheat bran and wheat slurry (91%, 94%, and 96% of the total impact for climate change, fossil fuels depletion, and land use, respectively). The use of energy, particularly in the growth and reproduction phase, also contributed to the overall impact of the production process but to a much lower extent. These results agree with those of previous LCA studies; for example, the environmental impacts of larvae feeding and energy use were 55% and 38%, respectively, in Smetana et al., 2019 [15] and 75–80% and 15–19% in in Smetana et al., 2016 [18].

The higher impact from feed in the present study results from the usage of agricultural by-products, whereas the use of renewable energy drastically reduced the impact of energy use on the overall results. In contrast, the no-symbiosis model, energy consumption resulted in a substantial fraction of the climate change impact and fossil resources depletion accounting for respectively ~45% and ~54%. Smetana et al. [15] highlighted energy consumption as a major area for improvement that would enable decreasing the total impact of insect production by 25% just by switching to renewable energy sources. However, the authors foresaw this change as a long-term transition (10 years) due to the need of considerable investments. The results of the present study clearly demonstrate that co-locating insect plants with existing industrial players can accelerate this transition and lower the impact of energy consumption at the onset of insects' industrial production.

As for the environmental impact of raw materials, two impact sub-drivers are to be considered: The type of feed material used and the FCR of such materials by the insects. As discussed in previous studies, BSFL is a promising biomass transformer capable of consuming feed streams that are not suitable for other livestock [27]. Smetana et al. [18] assessed the impacts of feeding BSFL on different diets (base scenario with rye meal and wheat bran compared to 13 feeding variations of by-products and waste streams) and concluded that using low-value food processing by-products (distilled grains), as the ones used in the present study, was among the best strategies for sustainable feed production. To further improve the sustainability of insect-based feed ingredients, multiple authors have stated that the use of consumer food waste or manure (to which no environmental impact is allocated) could be beneficial to increase the sustainability of the production process [22,23,28–32]. However, relying on such streams as insect feed is illegal in some regions (e.g., manure is not allowed as insect feed in Europe). Moreover, it represents a challenge for large-scale production due to fluctuations in their availability and to variability in their composition and quality. Finding adequate by-products, with nutritional quality for insects and low environmental impact, will therefore be of strategic importance in the emergence of the insect production industry. The present study suggests that, in addition to the type of by-product selected as insect feed, the way to supply it also enables saving energy and significantly reducing the environmental impact of feed drying and transportation, as evidenced by the use of the direct pipeline, only possible due to the co-location of the insect production facility and starch manufacturer partner.

Larvae FCR is another impact driver with scope for improvement. The sensitivity analysis conducted on larvae feed intake reduction showed that changes in environmental impact were directly proportional to changes in FCR (10% decrease in feed intake led to 9–10% decrease in the impact values of all three indicators). The FCR of BSFL is significantly lower than that of other insects, being the main reason for most insect producers choosing this species. In fact, the FCR for BSFL was almost half the 2.2 kg/kg of live weight value obtained by Oonincx & de Boer [23] (data not shown), suggesting that the FCR of BSFL can be further optimized through the better stability of production systems [15] as well as by improving feed formulation, rearing conditions, and insect genetics thus improving the overall sustainability of insect-based ingredients' production.

Another area for improvement would be to increase the percentage of waste wood (the assumption used in the A-LCA was a waste wood minimum requirement of 80%) or biogas from bio-waste methanization in the mix used for energy generation to decrease land use without increasing the impact values of the other indicators.

4.3. Impact of IM and IO Compared to That of Conventional Feed Ingredients

Most previous studies on the environmental impact of insect production were conducted at laboratory or pilot industry scales, therefore hindering comparisons with the impacts of producing the conventional protein and oil sources, which occur at industrial scale. Moreover, most previous studies were based on partial or aggregated data, and not on data from a fully operational production facility. The present study, which is based on data from one of the first industrial scale insect production facilities worldwide, provides a basis for evaluating the environmental impact of novel insect-based ingredients (IM and IO) versus the conventional feed ingredients (FM and VOs) they can replace in aqua and monogastric feeds. The results of the present study confirmed the potential of IM and IO produced at industrial-scale as more sustainable than FM and VOs as suggested in previous small-scale studies [13–15,18–20]. Overall, replacing FM by the IM produced using the industrial symbiosis model can potentially decrease CO_2 emissions by 24 kt and fossil resources depletion by 336 TJ per year of operation of the insect production facility, which represent reductions by three- to four-fold. In addition, compared to the best alternative (soy oil without deforestation), IO production using the symbiosis model allowed saving 5.2 kt of CO_2 emissions, 64 TJ of fossil resources, and 1900 ha of land use per year of operation. Nevertheless, the better environmental performance of the IM and IO demonstrated here applies only to the ingredients produced using the symbiosis model and therefore cannot be generalized to all models of insect production at large-scale.

Although the A-LCA presented here provides a solid basis for comparing insect-based feed ingredients with conventional feed ingredients, there are some limitations. First, the lack of methodologic standards to assess the environmental impact of ingredients means that results from different studies are not directly comparable. Second, the FU selected for comparison will depend on the species the insect-based feed is intended for as well as on the specific formulation used by each market player. Finally, assessing the impacts of FM production on marine biodiversity, which were not included in the present assessment, would require an evolution in LCA to account for the threats to marine ecosystems [33].

5. Conclusions

This A-LCA of one of the first industrial-scale insect production facility in operation in the world demonstrates that the innovative symbiosis model implemented on the site drastically reduces the climate change and fossil resources impact of the production of insect ingredients. The symbiosis model which consists in the colocation of the insect facility with a feed manufacturer to directly supply by-products to feed the larvae and a renewable power plant to valorize waste energy to power the plant reduces CO_2 emissions by 80% and fossil resources depletion by 83% compared to a no-symbiosis model. This study further displays the precise environmental impact of IM and IO using the symbiosis model across climate change, fossil resources depletion and land use. The comparison of these results to the ones of alternatives (FM for IM and VOs for IO) demonstrates that IM and IO are both sustainable alternatives reducing CO_2 emissions by at least 51% and fossil resources depletion by 46%. However, these reductions in environmental footprint are only achieved when using a symbiosis model therefore outlining the importance of performing LCA to demonstrate the sustainability of other production models at industrial scale.

Author Contributions: C.P.V.P. and M.W. monitored the study with Quantis. C.R. supervised the study, M.L. and M.B. provided comments on the manuscript. All authors have read and agreed to the published version of the manuscript.

Acknowledgments: The authors acknowledge Miguel C. Leal and Joana Marques for comments on the manuscript.

References

1. FAO. *The State of World Fisheries and Aquaculture 2020. Sustainability in Action*; Food and Agriculture Organization of the United Nations: Rome, Italy, 2020.
2. Ritchie, H. Meat and Dairy Production. Available online: https://ourworldindata.org/meat-production (accessed on 8 December 2020).
3. Gasco, L.; Biancarosa, I.; Liland, N.S. From waste to feed: A review of recent knowledge on insects as producers of protein and fat for animal feeds. *Curr. Opin. Green Sustain. Chem.* **2020**, *23*, 67–69. [CrossRef]
4. FAO. Gateway to poultry production and products. Available online: http://www.fao.org/poultry-production-products/ (accessed on 8 December 2020).
5. Tschirner, M.; Kloas, W. Increasing the sustainability of aquaculture systems: Insects as alternative protein source for fish diets. *GAIA Ecol. Perspect. Sci. Soc.* **2017**, *26*, 332–340. [CrossRef]
6. Arru, B.; Furesi, R.; Gasco, L.; Madau, F.A.; Pulina, P. The introduction of insect meal into fish diet: The first economic analysis on European sea bass farming. *Sustainability* **2019**, *11*, 1697. [CrossRef]
7. Llagostera, P.F.; Kallas, Z.; Reig, L.; de Gea, D.A. The use of insect meal as a sustainable feeding alternative in aquaculture: Current situation, Spanish consumers' perceptions and willingness to pay. *J. Clean. Prod.* **2019**, *229*, 10–21. [CrossRef]
8. Schiavone, A.; Cullere, M.; De Marco, M.; Meneguz, M.; Biasato, I.; Bergagna, S.; Dezzutto, D.; Gai, F.; Dabbou, S.; Gasco, L.; et al. Partial or total replacement of soybean oil by black soldier fly larvae (*Hermetia illucens* L.) fat in broiler diets: Effect on growth performances, feed-choice, blood traits, carcass characteristics and meat quality. *Ital. J. Anim. Sci.* **2017**, *16*, 93–100. [CrossRef]
9. Sypniewski, J.; Kierończyk, B.; Benzertiha, A.; Mikołajczak, Z.; Pruszyńska-Oszmałek, E.; Kołodziejski, P.; Sassek, M.; Rawski, M.; Czekała, W.; Józefiak, D. Replacement of soybean oil by *Hermetia illucens* fat in turkey nutrition: Effect on performance, digestibility, microbial community, immune and physiological status and final product quality. *Br. Poult. Sci.* **2020**, *61*, 294–302. [CrossRef] [PubMed]
10. Cullere, M.; Schiavone, A.; Dabbou, S.; Gasco, L.; Dalle Zotte, A. Meat quality and sensory traits of finisher broiler chickens fed with black soldier fly (*Hermetia illucens* L.) larvae fat as alternative fat source. *Animals* **2019**, *9*, 140. [CrossRef]
11. Chia, S.Y.; Tanga, C.M.; van Loon, J.J.; Dicke, M. Insects for sustainable animal feed: Inclusive business models involving smallholder farmers. *Curr. Opin. Environ. Sustain.* **2019**, *41*, 23–30. [CrossRef]
12. Berggren, Å.; Jansson, A.; Low, M. Approaching ecological sustainability in the emerging insects-as-food industry. *Trends Ecol. Evol.* **2019**, *34*, 132–138. [CrossRef]
13. Salomone, R.; Saija, G.; Mondello, G.; Giannetto, A.; Fasulo, S.; Savastano, D. Environmental impact of food waste bioconversion by insects: Application of life cycle assessment to process using *Hermetia illucens*. *J. Clean. Prod.* **2017**, *140*, 890–905. [CrossRef]
14. Thévenot, A.; Rivera, J.L.; Wilfart, A.; Maillard, F.; Hassouna, M.; Senga-Kiesse, T.; Le Féon, S.; Aubin, J. Mealworm meal for animal feed: Environmental assessment and sensitivity analysis to guide future prospects. *J. Clean. Prod.* **2018**, *170*, 1260–1267. [CrossRef]
15. Smetana, S.; Schmitt, E.; Mathys, A. Sustainable use of *Hermetia illucens* insect biomass for feed and food: Attributional and consequential life cycle assessment. *Resour. Conserv. Recycl.* **2019**, *144*, 285–296. [CrossRef]
16. Jolliet, O.; Margni, M.; Charles, R.; Humbert, S.; Payet, J.; Rebitzer, G.; Rosenbaum, R. IMPACT 2002+: A new life cycle impact assessment methodology. *Int. J. Life Cycle Assess.* **2003**, *8*, 324. [CrossRef]
17. Li, S.; Ji, H.; Zhang, B.; Tian, J.; Zhou, J.; Yu, H. Influence of black soldier fly (*Hermetia illucens*) larvae oil on growth performance, body composition, tissue fatty acid composition and lipid deposition in juvenile Jian carp (*Cyprinus carpio* var. Jian). *Aquaculture* **2016**, *465*, 43–52. [CrossRef]
18. Smetana, S.; Palanisamy, M.; Mathys, A.; Heinz, V. Sustainability of insect use for feed and food: Life Cycle Assessment perspective. *J. Clean. Prod.* **2016**, *137*, 741–751. [CrossRef]

19.   Madau, F.A.; Arru, B.; Furesi, R.; Pulina, P. Insect Farming for Feed and Food Production from a Circular Business Model Perspective. *Sustainability* **2020**, *12*, 5418. [CrossRef]

20.   Cadinu, L.A.; Barra, P.; Torre, F.; Delogu, F.; Madau, F.A. Insect Rearing: Potential, Challenges, and Circularity. *Sustainability* **2020**, *12*, 4567. [CrossRef]

21.   Van Zanten, H.H.; Mollenhorst, H.; Oonincx, D.G.A.B.; Bikker, P.; Meerburg, B.G.; de Boer, I.J.M. From environmental nuisance to environmental opportunity: Housefly larvae convert waste to livestock feed. *J. Clean. Prod.* **2015**, *102*, 362–369. [CrossRef]

22.   Roffeis, M.; Muys, B.; Almeida, J.; Mathijs, E.; Achten, W.; Pastor, B.; Velásquez, Y.; Martinez-Sanchez, A.I.; Rojo, S. Pig manure treatment with housefly (*Musca domestica*) rearing–an environmental life cycle assessment. *J. Insects Food Feed* **2015**, *1*, 195–214. [CrossRef]

23.   Oonincx, D.G.A.B.; de Boer, I.J.M. Environmental impact of the production of mealworms as a protein source for humans–a life cycle assessment. *PLoS ONE* **2012**, *7*, e51145. [CrossRef]

24.   Smetana, S.; Mathys, A.; Knoch, A.; Heinz, V. Meat alternatives: Life cycle assessment of most known meat substitutes. *Int. J. Life Cycle Assess.* **2015**, *20*, 1254–1267. [CrossRef]

25.   Muys, B.; Roffeis, M. Generic Life Cycle Assessment of Proteins from Insects. In *Insects to Feed the World, Proceedings of the 1st International Conference, Wageningen, The Netherlands, 17 May 2014*; Ku Leuven: Leuven, Belgium, 2014.

26.   Komakech, A.J.; Sundberg, C.; Jönsson, H.; Vinnerås, B. Life cycle assessment of biodegradable waste treatment systems for sub-Saharan African cities. *Resour. Conserv. Recycl.* **2015**, *99*, 100–110. [CrossRef]

27.   Wang, Y.-S.; Shelomi, M. Review of black soldier fly (*Hermetia illucens*) as animal feed and human food. *Foods* **2017**, *6*, 91. [CrossRef] [PubMed]

28.   Diener, S.; Solano, N.M.S.; Gutiérrez, F.R.; Zurbrügg, C.; Tockner, K. Biological treatment of municipal organic waste using black soldier fly larvae. *Waste Biomass Valoriz.* **2011**, *2*, 357–363. [CrossRef]

29.   Diener, S.; Zurbrügg, C.; Tockner, K. Conversion of organic material by black soldier fly larvae: Establishing optimal feeding rates. *Waste Manag. Res.* **2009**, *27*, 603–610. [CrossRef]

30.   Li, Q.; Zheng, L.; Qiu, N.; Cai, H.; Tomberlin, J.K.; Yu, Z. Bioconversion of dairy manure by black soldier fly (Diptera: Stratiomyidae) for biodiesel and sugar production. *Waste Manag.* **2011**, *31*, 1316–1320. [CrossRef]

31.   Newton, L.; Sheppard, C.; Watson, D.W.; Burtle, G.; Dove, R. *Using the Black Soldier Fly, Hermetia Illucens, as a Value-Added Tool for the Management of Swine Manure*; Animal and Poultry Waste Management Center, North Carolina State University: Raleigh, NC, USA, 2005; Volume 17.

32.   Zhou, F.; Tomberlin, J.K.; Zheng, L.; Yu, Z.; Zhang, J. Developmental and waste reduction plasticity of three black soldier fly strains (Diptera: Stratiomyidae) raised on different livestock manures. *J. Med. Entomol.* **2013**, *50*, 1224–1230. [CrossRef]

33.   Woods, J.S.; Veltman, K.; Huijbregts, M.A.; Verones, F.; Hertwich, E.G. Towards a meaningful assessment of marine ecological impacts in life cycle assessment (LCA). *Environ. Int.* **2016**, *89*, 48–61. [CrossRef]

3

Inter-Organisational Coordination for Sustainable Local Governance: Public Safety Management in Poland

Barbara Kożuch [1,†] **and Katarzyna Sienkiewicz-Małyjurek** [2,*,†]

[1] Institute of Public Affairs, Jagiellonian University, Łojasiewicza 4 Str., Kraków 30-348, Poland; barbara.kozuch@uj.edu.pl

[2] Faculty of Organisation and Management, Silesian University of Technology, Roosevelta 26 Str., Zabrze 41-800, Poland

[*] Correspondence: katarzyna.sienkiewicz-malyjurek@polsl.pl.

[†] These authors contributed equally to this work.

Academic Editor: Adam Jabłoński

Abstract: The goal of this article is to examine the basic characteristics and factors that impact inter-organisational coordination in sustainable local governance to address: 1. What are the factors that effective inter-organisational coordination between independent units creating public safety system on local level in sustainable local governance depends on? 2. What are the principal features of inter-organisational coordination in the public safety management system studied in the context of sustainable local governance? The article's goal was reached using desk research analysis and empirical research. The desk research covers an analysis of international scientific publications. In turn, the empirical research was based on the example of public safety management. It covered interviews with practitioners dealing with public safety and a hermeneutic process within a focus group of scholars. As a result of the conducted research, interdependencies between coordination and other factors of inter-organisational collaboration were identified and the process of inter-organisational coordination during the emergency situations was characterised.

Keywords: inter-organisational coordination; sustainable local governance; sustainability; inter-organisational collaboration; public safety management; emergency; business model

1. Introduction

Civilisational development created goods that facilitate life and raise its standards. At the same time, an increase of hazards has taken place and side effects of technical advancement and space development have come into being [1,2]. Simultaneously the hazard of industrial calamities is growing, degradation of resources and natural resources is occurring, while biological and chemical pollution impacts public life. Moreover, polarisation of society, poverty and privation, terrorism, crime, and violence are expanding [3,4]. Spatial development is gaining significance in the perspective of social development, which to a large extent is characterised by lack of organisation and harmony [5].

The consequences of unlimited civilisational growth, globalisation, urbanisation, and an economic crisis have resulted in paying attention to durability and sustainable use of the possessed potential. Consequently, in the contemporary functioning of an organisation what gains more and more significance is the concept of sustainability, which consists in the realisation of rules of sustainable development and constructive confrontation of resources, goals, and strategic factors in order for the organisation to exist and develop [6].

In our times, the basic significance in assuring safety and sustainability in the public sector is attributed to regional and local development factors [7]. This is due to the fact that in the valid legislative solutions self-governments were given independence and freedom of decision making in the scope of realised tasks. Thanks to that, they have direct possibilities of creating safety and sustainability in the managed area. However, self-governments are able to realise the rules of safety and sustainability only by collaborating with other public and private entities and with the society [8]. This interaction is characterized by inter-organisational collaboration defined as "any joint activity by two or more agencies working together that is intended to increase public value by their working together rather than separately" [9] (p. 508). According to Arthur T. Himmelman, this collaboration includes exchange of information that is favourable to all parties (networking), with altering of activities (coordinating) and sharing of resources (cooperating) [10]. A similar perspective is presented by Richard C. Feiock, In Won Lee, and Hyung Jun Park who claim that coordination is a vital instrument of managing networks [11]. On the other hand Ranjay Gulati, Franz Wohlgezogen, and Pavel Zhelyazkov treat coordination as one of two indispensable facets of inter-organisational collaboration [12]. In our article we both agree with the allegation of the above-mentioned authors and in our analyses we assume a perspective that coordination is one of the principal elements of inter-organisational collaboration. This approach is based on the broadly known five Fayol's functions: planning, organising, command, coordination, and control. By treating coordination as one of the functions of management we present it in a broad scope, considering that it includes "the activities responsible to ensure the effectiveness of the collaborative work" [13] (p. 88). Consequently, in our approach coordination is a factor of collaboration, which refers to a decentralised approach to problem solving [14].

Despite a great deal of research in the public sector, inter-organisational collaboration is still a challenge. This results above all from decentralisation and narrowing of specialisation of each public organisation [15]. In public safety management problems without inter-organisational coordination may cause serious consequences and generate additional hazards, which was observed for example during Hurricane Katrina and the World Trade Center attacks [16–19]. Moreover, contemporary development trends focused on internationalisation and at the same time regionalisation combined with a strong and stable local governance are also a challenge for coordination. Problems in this scope may result from the overlapping nature of department jurisdictions [20]. There is also a research gap in the scope of the contextual variables in shaping collaborative efforts [21]. Moreover, despite the evident importance of coordinating actions during the time of threat, relatively little attention has been paid to it [22,23]. This means that there are theoretical and empirical gaps in the literature of the field. The necessity of theoretical justification of the sustainable approach to local governance and the lack of exhaustive analyses related to coordination generate the need to conduct research studies in this scope. Thus the goal of this publication is to examine the basic characteristics and factors that impact inter-organisational coordination in the public safety management system as a part of a sustainable local governance to address: 1. What are the factors that effective inter-organisational coordination between independent units creating public safety system on local level in sustainable local governance depends on? 2. What are the principal features of inter-organisational coordination in the public safety management system studied in the context of sustainable local governance?

The article's goal was reached using desk research analysis and empirical research. The desk research covers an analysis of international scientific publications. In turn, the empirical research was based on the example of public safety management in Poland.

In our article we refer our research to organisational coordination, since we have been studying the actions taken in order to harmonise and synchronise the enterprises of various organisations, which assumption is achieving of common goals and appropriate results [24]. Although we carry out our analyses in the public sector, we do not make any reference to the model of coordinating public policies. Our approach is close to the model of relational coordination [25,26] and decentralized intelligent adaptation [14].

The paper is organised as follows: First, we review sustainability in public safety management. Then, we discuss the general theory of coordination and explain the role of inter-organisational coordination in public safety management. In the part containing the research results we identified factors influencing and influenced by inter-organisational coordination. Next, we analyse the process and the features of inter-organisational coordination during emergency situations using the example of Polish circumstances. We emphasise that inter-organisational coordination is a central attribute of sustainable public safety management. Our results contribute to better understanding of coordination complexity in dynamic circumstances.

2. Methodology Research Method and Context

To achieve the purpose of the article, the desk research method and empirical investigations were carried out.

The desk research was based on the analysis of international scientific literature and it covered issues related to inter-organisational coordination and public safety management. Publications connected with the general coordination theory, inter-organisational coordination in the public sector and in dynamic context played a key role in this scope. We focused on foreign literature, indexed in generally acclaimed databases (Web of Science, Scopus) and works in English, in order to obtain a picture of inter-organisational coordination that would be as objective as possible. We have not covered academic achievements in the scope of coordinating in specific conditions of the private sector and within one organisation. We have focused on those publications dealing with inter-organisational coordination, which concern the problems of collaboration.

Moreover, based upon the research conducted so far [27], the relations occurring between coordination and other factors of effective inter-organisational collaboration were examined. These analyses were carried out within a hermeneutic process within a focus group of scholarsconducted in December 2014 within a four-person group of researchers actively involved into investigating inter-organisational collaboration. Two of them have been involved in research in this domain for over 10 years, and the remaining two—for over 5 years. Discussions within two sessions were held in 2014 on the grounds of practical instances and analyses of typical collaborative situations.

Empirical investigation was based on free-form interviews, which were conducted with 15 medium and lower level employees employed at police and fire brigade units and medical emergency stations in the area of the Silesian Province. They concerned the course of collaborative processes in public safety management. These interviews were conducted in September and October 2013. In the scope of coordination, this research covered the following issues:

(1)   coordinating actions taken within collaboration with other units prior to, during, and after the threat

(2)   enterprises in each unit within common action coordination

(3)   the course of the common action coordination process using a random example

In this article we presented the results and interpretation of the conducted analyses.

The research was conducted in Poland, where—in an organisational aspect—the authorities operate on two levels: government (central) and local government. The central level is responsible for the continuity of actions aiming at ensuring safety, it monitors and prevents hazards and their consequences. In turn the task of local governments is to identify hazards at the source, preventing them and eliminating their consequences. However, the decentralization of public authority ceded responsibility in the field of public safety onto each local government level *i.e.*, commune (Polish:

gmina), district and also province. Local governments fulfil their tasks independently, while the government administration has only a possibility to supervise their actions, which however, is limited and briefly specified by regulations.

The obligation to take action in case of the occurrence of a hazard is borne by the authority, which was first to receive information about it. This authority promptly informs about the event that has occurred the authorities of a higher and lower level respectively, presenting at the same time their assessment of the situation and information on the intended actions [28]. If the event's nature is supralocal, management of the action is taken over by the regional level. Similarly, in case of a supraregional hazard—management is taken over by the central authorities of state power.

Information on the necessity of taking action may be transferred directly from the hazard's location or by the 112 system, which operates in Poland on the local and provincial level. On the local level it is responsible for operating emergency numbers and organisation of emergency endeavours in a given action area by means of emergency call centres. In turn, the provincial level facilitates coordination of actions of a supralocal nature. All reports are registered in an ICT (Information and Communication Technologies) system and their transfer to an appropriate intervention and rescue unit depends on verification and justification of the report and disposing of the means of rescue entities [29].

An important issue in the operations of the public safety management system in Poland is the autonomy of the units participating in the actions. In a situation of hazard, these units operate autonomously, focusing on realising their statutory tasks and the scope of their cooperation results from the valid regulations. It is worth mentioning that a similar situation occurs in many places around the world, including in the scope of coordinating foreign aid during calamities. In other countries there are solutions that enable creation of inter-organisational teams [30–32]. That is why actions realised in the examined area in Poland are mainly based on the complementary roles and competences of many units, properly coordinated work, and effective communication. Taking the above into account, the basis of managing public safety is inter-organisational collaboration and the units taking part in it realise their tasks simultaneously, complementing each other.

Our research covers the context of conducting actions in public safety management, which is dependent on the type, nature, place, and range of the hazard's occurrence and course. During stabilisation, when routine action are carried out, the realisation of actions in the examined scope, including coordinating, is similar to other areas of local governance. General methods of coordination apply here. Situation changes during extreme events. Each hazard is an individual event, which is characterised by peculiar specifics of development and duration. The principal challenges are the following: high uncertainty, sudden and unexpected events; risk and possible mass casualty; increased time pressure and urgency, severe resource shortage, large-scale impact and damage, disruption of infrastructure support, multi-authority and massive people involvement, conflict of interest, and high demand for timely information [23]. Even the same type of hazard concerns a different location, which generates the need to take different actions. The differences in the duration of the hazard's occurrence are also significant. For example, a fire in the summer time, during the occurrence of drought, will carry a greater risk of occurrence of additional hazards compared with the winter time. Moreover, the victims of each hazard are different, which also generates the need to adapt actions to the needs. During extreme events the enterprises conducted in public safety management require proper preparation, and above all coordination of actions. Moreover, the operation of rescue units may seem similar, but in practice they differ by the level of organisation, they operate based on other standards and they are also characterised by a different organisational culture [19]. It is in line with the assumption of Arjen Boin and Paul 't Hart [33], according to which there is no unique and best form of organisation and in addition each emergency situation requires an individual approach that consists of (1) applying the general principles of organisational coordination; (2) lessons learned from experience coming from collaboration in similar situations; and (3) the specifics of a given event.

3. Theoretical Background

3.1. Sustainable Public Safety Management

Public safety is one of the principal foundations of a rich and well functioning society [34]. It constitutes an organised activity realised using personnel, financial, technical, information resources of many organisations, taken in order to minimise potential hazards, ensuring an undisturbed course of social life as well as protecting people's health, life, property, and the environment, which includes law observation and protection of order with focus on realizing the public interest [35]. Public safety management covers a large scope of research, which extends from social policy, through local and criminal policy, up to crisis management [36,37]. Its aim is to ensure the most favourable level of safety using the existing capabilities and limitations and taking into account the dynamics of the environment. The principal entities participating in public safety management include the following [38,39]:

- Local government
- Response and rescue units, including: a core unit where taking actions in response to a specific type of hazard fall into its competences; basic units which mostly respond collectively and mutually collaborate in public safety management; ancillary units which supplement actions taken by a core unit and basic units, and their knowledge and competences are critical in a specific situation
- Society: local communities and enterprises operating in a given territory
- Media: radio, television, press, Internet
- Non-governmental organisations
- Research and development units

The listed groups of entities constitute mutually complementary units, which include not only lawyers and experts on administrative sciences, but also specialists in the scope of management, sociology, economics, political sciences, technical sciences, environmentalists, *etc.* They form a public safety management system that constitutes a dynamic system of units, the aim of which is ensuring safe and sustainable conditions of operating to all entities in a given administrative area by using the possessed resources and within the valid formal rules and informal relations, characterised by the uniqueness and changeability of actions and constant adaptation to current conditions and arising needs [40].

In the stabilisation phase the local government plays the leading role in the public safety management system in a given administrative area, ensuring conditions of sustainable local development.   In this scope, preventing hazards achieved by education and building of resilience is of priority importance. These functions are realised above all by education, media, non-governmental organisations, and local governments within the formation of culture and national identity. Also the Police and State Fire Service prepare professional prevention programs aiming at excluding the occurrence of hazards. Local government fosters growth of the idea of inter-organisational collaboration.

However, the core of the system covers actions taken by the response and rescue units [41]. These units are appropriately prepared operation wise, they are trained and have appropriate skills and knowledge and they have at their disposal means and tools adequate to a given situation. Taking the above into account, during realisation the leading role is taken over by intervention and rescue units, while the local governments supervise their actions. Moreover, the principal function in realising intervention and rescue actions is fulfilled by: the Police, the State Fire Service, and medical rescuers. Most often these units participate in the actions in the first place. Depending on the type of hazard and the situation, other entities are engaged as well. The principal actions may be assisted by among other the Municipal Guard, Boarder Guard, Railway Guards, Road Transport Inspection, the army, or non-governmental organisations. In turn, the Environmental Protection Inspectorate, Sanitary Inspection, Construction Supervision Inspectorate, or social assistance workers may act as advisers and assist in decision making with their specialist knowledge. The type and degree of engagement of each unit depends on the level of complexity of a given situation [40].

In that context sustainability is the organisation's ability to continuously learn, adapt, and develop, and also revitalize, reconstruct, and reorientate in order to offer high value to recipients in a long period of time [42]. In the public sector it constitutes a tool which enables partner participation in making use of public goods taking into account limitations of resources.

From the analysed perspective sustainable local governance is defined as a process run by local governmental bodies aimed to socially and economically boost a specific region or locality, while respecting environmental protection and land development, being committed to sustainable management of the resources pool and tapping into cutting-edge public management tools, *i.e.*, coordination of inter-organisational collaboration [8] (p. 325). Its basis is a diagnosis of social needs, possessed resources, and condition of the environment, in which public services are offered. Based upon it, local development programs are created that serve sustaining of social life processes. Improvement of public institution actions, owing to collaboration, increases entrepreneurship and effectiveness of sustainable activities of local governments. As a result of this, the competitiveness of a given area grows, while the requiredenvironment quality standards are maintained.

Consequently, sustainability in public safety refers to efficient realisation of enterprises by taking actions that are appropriate to an existing need, without harm to society, economically justified and with the highest degree of care for the natural environment. Sustainable public safety management aims at well-balanced management of resources including local and natural ones as well as those possessed by each unit of the system being analysed. It constitutes a process realised by local response and rescue units within inter-organisational collaboration using modern public management tools, which aims at minimising potential hazards and ensuring most favourable level of public safety simultaneously respecting and ensuring of principal and integrated order. Taking into account the fact that it covers all orders of integrated development, it constitutes an interesting research area that is adequate to the issues being raised.

The characteristic features of public safety management make it an area of public governance, in which the need for coordination is especially visible. For that matter, it constitutes an interesting research area that is adequate to the issues being raised.

3.2. Coordination as a Factor of Inter-Organisational Collaboration

In local governance collaboration, which is one of the most important tasks of self-governmental sub-sector organisation, combining activities in favour of local development, is of key significance in this scope [43,44]. Local government units constitute collaborating institutions, which require appropriate coordination within co-governance. Based on the surveys and theoretical considerations, the literature state that collaboration between public sector organisations is one of several tools of local development management since it contributes to the growth of public services [45,46]. It is characterised by interdependence with simultaneous autonomy of functioning as well as settlement of collaboration rules by means of negotiation and based on organizational and legal factors. As it is emphasized by R. Lozano, collaboration constitutes a key element in running of the strategy of sustainability [47].

Inter-organisational collaboration includes sustainable relations, which join each organisation in realising their common goals. It is defined as a union of two or more organisations that is favourable to all parties and well-defined, which serves achieving of common goals [48] (p. 4). Among the causes of establishing inter-organisational collaboration one may distinguish the following: high levels of interdependence, need for resources and risk sharing, resource scarcity, previous history of efforts to collaborate, situation in which each partner has resources that other partners need, and complex issues [49]. Identified on the base of empirical evidence, the principal benefits in the scope of inter-organisational collaboration include among other [50–53]: consolidation of the resources of collaborating organisations, knowledge sharing, organisational learning, making use of the experience of other organisations, transfer of best practices, and creating innovative solutions. This is not a new concept, however it has enjoyed great interest only for about two decades [54]. Recently, more importance is given to the relational aspects.

The growing significance of inter-organisational collaboration in the activity of enterprises and public institutions results to a large extent from the dynamics of changes in the organisations' environment, seeking competitive advantage and the fact that at present it is not possible to act alone. Although the practice of collaboration between organisations is broadly applied, the presumptions of its implementation are generally known and it does not constitute a new phenomenon, it is a very difficult process [55]. The results of empirical and theoretical studies, presented in the literature, indicate that this is mainly due to its complexity, different approaches to realisation of mutual actions, potential disturbance in the course of collaboration processes, *etc.* [56,57]. Moreover, legal requirements or collaboration agreements do not constitute conditions sufficient enough to ensure sustainable inter-organisational collaboration. This is because its course is impacted by multiple factors with features that refer to both external and internal conditions, relational factors, and instruments of inter-organisational collaboration. They have a prerequisite nature. The most important one is coordination [27].

Coordination is defined as " … the act of managing interdependencies between activities performed to achieve a goal" [58] (p. 6). It is a relational process based on task interdependencies [59]. It originates from the need for simultaneous execution of activities falling under the powers of various organisations, and results from the specifics of their operations. From the traditional perspective, it refers to hierarchical control, whereas the organisational perspective pertains to centralised, dispersed coordination or a combination of two types at the organisational level [60]. Coordination is a continual process and a component of the organisation. It depends on the specifics of the entities involved, the circumstances as well as dynamics of change in the external environment in which the entities operate. It is assumed that good coordination is nearly invisible, only being noticed most clearly when it is lacking [61].

In the subject literature there are two levels of coordination: intra- and inter-organisational [62]. The former is related to coordination within an organisation, whereas the latter to coordination between organisations. In the subject literature one may also find many types of coordination between collaborating units, for example interim coordination, cross-agency coordination, relational coordination, network coordination, or network governance [63–66]. In all of the above-mentioned cases, the aim is to ensure sustainable inter-organisational collaboration by enhancing relations and task integration. This process is based on shared goals, shared knowledge, and mutual respect [26]. For the needs of this article, the term inter-organisational coordination was assumed.

Inter-organisational coordination is related to harmonising the actions of each unit in order to common and systematic rendering of specific services [63] (p. 118). It is defined as "the deliberate and orderly alignment or adjustment of partners' actions to achieve jointly determined goals" [12] (p. 12). It is based on such mechanisms as: partner-specific communication, rules and procedures, routines, liaison, and integration roles, interim authorities, *etc.* [59] (pp. 909–910). However, in order to realise common actions, it uses above all informal interactions and pays less attention to the valid procedures and organisational structures. These mechanisms, in particular, enable sustainable local governance through building durable relations between collaborating organisations. Key characteristics and differences of collaboration and coordination were presented in Table 1.

As it results from table 1 collaboration is a broader term than coordination. The subject literature emphasises that the priority significance of coordination in inter-organisational collaboration results from its role in the continuous synchronization of tasks and the contribution of collaborating organisations. It is because it constitutes a relational process, which covers managing correlation between tasks and between the entities that perform these tasks [63]. It manifests itself through systematic and reliable communication, which strengthens social relations in order for better integration of mutual enterprises. It emphasises the significance of the organisational structure, communication, and process management [12]. According to such concept, coordination enables going beyond rigid administrative structures and task centralisation towards greater freedom of action based on goodwill, trust, and commitment. It enables a more balanced management of resources and actions. Therefore, inter-organisational coordination indicates specific ways of implementing and conducting joint actions, owing to which it complements collaboration [12]. The notion of coordination is therefore related to operational activity, while collaboration concerns strategic decisions to a greater extent.

Table 1. Characteristics of collaboration and coordination.

Characteristics	Antecedents	Features	Modes
Collaboration	Interdependence; need for resources and risk sharing; resource scarcity; previous history of efforts to collaborate; situation in which each partner has resources that other partners need [49]; trust, trustworthiness [11]	Managing resource dependencies, sharing risk [12]; Conflict management [67]	Environment (history of collaboration, collaborative group seen as a legitimate leader in the community, favourable political and social climate); membership characteristics (mutual respect, understanding, trust, ability to compromise); process and structure (members share a stake in both process and outcome, multiple layers of participation, flexibility, development of clear roles and policy guideness, adaptability, appropriate pace of development); communication (open and frequent, established informal relationships and communication links); purpose (concrete , attainable goals and objectives, shared vision; resources (sufficient funds, staff, materials, and time, skilled leadership) [48]
Coordination	Information [11]; perception of common objects, communication, group decision-making [58]	Regulating and managing interdependencies [68]; managing uncertainties [12]; Goal decomposition [58]	Impersonal (plans, schedules, rules, procedures); personal (face-to-face communication); group (meetings) [69]; communication and decision procedures; mutual monitoring or supervisory hierarchy; group decision making; Mutual monitoring or property-rights sharing; programming; Hierarchical decision making; Integration and liaison roles; authority by expectation and residual arbitration [68]; formal (departmentalization or grouping of organizational units; centralization or decentralization of decision making; formalization and standardization; planning; output and behaviour control) and informal (lateral relations; informal communication; socialization) [70]

Source: own elaboration based on quoted literature.

A great number of research studies, information, and models in the scope of coordination causes that this area has been developing in various directions, depending on the conducted analyses. In some works its cognitive nature is emphasised, while in other the behavioural one, moreover it may be understood as a form of organizational control or team-based concertive control [67]. Attempts to model the interdependencies and level of coordination in specific fields are not consistent in the scope of coordination characteristics, but they point out which specific challenges are related to coordination [71]. For example, Henry Mintzberg's coordination model relates the coordination mechanisms to the organizational structure [72]. On the other hand, the model of Thomas W. Malone and Kevin Crowston is based on a concept of coordination as management of dependency between actions [61]. Moreover, on the one hand it is assumed that the problems of coordination may be solved by implementing appropriate mechanisms, of a general nature, which means that they may be applied in various organisational systems. On the other hand, there are opinions stating that one should identify in detail the nature of the environment in which an organisation operates in case of specific events and next develop appropriate procedures in relation to them [14]. We agree with the second approach and also the assumption that the higher the degrees of interdependency and the levels of tasks and environment uncertainty are, the more developed forms of coordination are required [12].These dependencies are especially visible in public safety management.

3.3. Basics of Inter-Organisational Coordination in Public Safety Management

According to Thomas E. Drabek [73], coordination is at the core of the practice of actions for safety. It is the philosopher's stone of public administration, and a central factor in poor performance during an response activities [74,75]. In actions for safety, coordination proceeds at diverse organisational levels [76]. It occurs in an intra-organisational dimension as coordination within specific organisations as well as an inter-organisation aspect as a regulator of external relations in an organisation. In this context, it is possible to talk about capabilities for effective resources administration in the form of inter-organisational teams, partnerships, alliances, *etc.* [77]. This capability is determined by the ability of specific organisations to adapt to dynamic conditions under which they operate, and to effective communication aimed at hammering out common agreements and a common stance regarding manners for conducting operations. At the core are both legal regulations as well as formal and informal relations emerging within collaborated organisations. Vertical coordination puts into place rigid principles as to the division of responsibility, the execution of activities and the control of outcomes. However, a new approach incorporating organisational connections gives priority to the mutual adaptation of entities and the integration of resources, authority and knowledge over formal mechanisms of authority [75,78].

Effective coordination is a necessary element of conducting action in public safety management. It is difficult to conduct in this area because it is connected with uncertainty, unexpected events, risk of hazards' accumulation, urgency, and infrastructure interdependency [23]. Apart from that, the situational complexity creates conditions, in which participation of various agencies is required and collaboration between them is necessary for realisation of actions. What is more, the higher the number of various organisations trying to achieve a common goal, the less probable that they will act in a coordinated way in order to achieve this goal [79]. In this connection, inter-organisational coordination in public safety management is a big challenge. The differences between the general theory of coordination and coordination between organisations in public safety management were presented in Table 2.

The principal difference between inter-organisational coordination in general and in public safety management lies in the nature of joint action. This influences all characteristics of coordination. It also causes that failures have more serious consequences and the intrinsic and extrinsic motivation, concerns, and results depend on the creativity and skills in making decisions in changeable and uncertain conditions, with limited pieces of information.

In the deliberations concerning inter-organisational coordination, we assume that its significance results from counterbalancing in the scope of actions and the level of participation of many independent organisations, taking into account social needs, natural environmental and spatial values as well as economic conditions. It facilitates achieving of the assumed goal avoiding excessive costs and damage. Consequently, inter-organisational coordination enables realisation of actions in changing, unsure, and dynamic conditions in accord with the philosophy of sustainability.

Table 2. General and specific approach to coordination.

Specification	General Theory of Coordination	Coordination in Public Safety Management
Substance of inter-organisational agreement	Ways of shaping interactions	Ways of shaping interactions between autonomous organizations
Motivation	More effectively managing task interdependencies and uncertainties	More effectively managing task interdependencies in order to identify and remove the sources and consequences of hazards
Concern/risks	Operational risk: inability to coordinate across organizational boundaries	Operational and situational risks: inability to coordinate joint actions of autonomous organisations in dynamic and uncertain circumstances
Typical positive results	Efficiency, effectiveness, flexibility/adaptiveness of joint action	Effectiveness, flexibility, adaptiveness of joint action in unique and rapidly changing situations
Typical failures	Omission, incompatibilities, misallocation	Inadvertent omissions leading to chaos, incompatibilities in rescue procedures, inadequate response, insufficient prevention of accumulation of hazards, increasing number of victims, additional damages
Remedies against failures	Hierarchies, authority, and formalisation; institutions and conventions; inter-personal linkages and liaisons	Changing hierarchical positions, integrated authority structures, improvement of rescue procedures, shared organising of training and simulations of events during the stabilisation phase, progressive adapting of regulations, advancing communication systems, creating good formal and informal relationships based on trust and organisational concern

Source: own elaboration based on [12] (p. 66).

4. Research Results

4.1. Relations between Coordination and other Instruments of Inter-Organisational Collaboration

Our previous research indicated that coordination is one of the key factors of inter-organisational collaboration [27]. These factors have a mutual impact on each other, which in effect influences both their role and the efficiency of collaboration itself. Taking this into consideration, we have decided to present our own reasoning based on chosen publications, which include the relations that characterise coordination and other factors of efficient inter-organisational collaboration. In our investigation a 3-level grade scale was applied to evaluate the impact of each factor, *i.e.*: 1—weak influence, 2—medium influence, and 3—strong influence. Whereas the relations between the factors were analysed in reference to the following grade scale: 0—lack of impact or minor impact, 1—significant impact, and 2—key impact.

Inter-organisational coordination was evaluated as a factor which has strong influence on the course of actions. This mainly results from specific and complementary competences of each organisation, task distribution, and responsibilities. These factors create the foundations of efficient realisation of actions. Taking this into account, inter-organisational coordination is of key importance to the course of collaboration.

Studying the relations occurring between inter-organisational coordination and other factors of efficient inter-organisational collaboration, our focus was directed to those factors that have a significant and key impact on the processes of action coordination between organisations. The relations, which were identified, are illustrated in Figure 1. It depicts those factors, which:

- only impact the course of inter-organizational coordination
- both impact and are a result of inter-organizational coordination
- are only a result of inter-organizational coordination

In figure 1 factors having a significant impact were indicated by a thinner arrow, while the key factors were indicated by a thicker one.

As it results from the verified connections, the key factors of inter-organizational collaboration, which influence inter-organisational coordination processes are:

- communication in inter-organisational working teams,

- constraints in inter-organisational collaboration,

- leadership with organisational and communication skills,

- organisation of collaborative work (e.g., time pressured, competitive, rapidly changing, stability),

- management of inter-organisational collaboration (e.g., styles, transparency of decisions and guidance),

- inter-organisational trust,

- professional communication between personnel from individual organisations.

These factors show that inter-organisational coordination depends mainly on organisational and relational conditions, which exist between collaborating units. Whereas, the key factors influenced by inter-organisational coordination include:

- organisation of collaborative work,

- support within collaborating organisations,

- adaptability to changing work requirements,

- flexibility and openness to changing circumstances of collaboration,

- performance of inter-organisational collaboration,

- self interest of individual organisations from collaboration.

These factors impact, above all, situation conditions in sustainable public safety management and the will to collaborate. The other analysed factors are also of significance, but they are not that important in inter-organisational coordination. Each of the said factors impacts the level of coordination sustainability. However, the significance of each one individually depends on the existence of other factors, which may mutually strengthen or weaken its influence. Moreover, the nature of relations taking place between inter-organisational coordination and other factors influencing and influenced by this process, is complex. This mainly results from the existing interdependency between all factors of effective collaboration and their mutual stimulating.

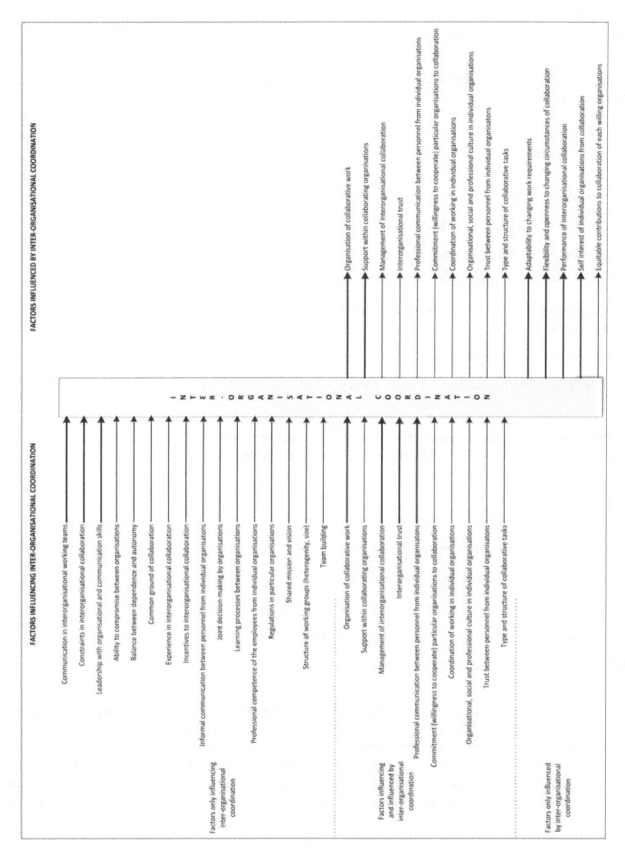

Figure 1. Factors influencing and influenced by inter-organizational coordination. Source: own elaboration based on [48,80–91].

4.2. Inter-Organisational Coordination during Emergency Situations

The process of managing public safety in terms of phases may be presented in the following cycle: actions taken prior to the hazard occurrence, during the hazard, after the hazard has been obviated [29]. Inter-organisational coordination takes place in all of the said phases, however its significance can be seen to the biggest degree in the phases in time and once the hazard has been obviated. Prior to the occurrence of the hazard, coordination is necessary in such action as preparing mutual enterprises, common training, and team building. However, these actions are conducted in stable conditions, in which considered modifications and changes are possible. The effect of turbulence and uncertainty of conditions in emergency situations is that inter-organisational coordination plays a key role in the phases prior to the occurrence and during the hazard.

The inter-organisational coordination of operations in emergency situations is executed by a single commander-in-chief. Our own empirical research showed that in Poland, responsibility for that is devolved on the Rescue Action Supervisor who is, in most cases, a fireman. Only in the event of a terrorist attack or demonstration command is taken over by a policeman with sufficient powers. Such inter-organisational coordination involves collecting, analysing, and verifying information, as well as assigning a sequence of operations performed and entities engaged. A classic example illustrating the coordination of operations in emergency management, is the flooding that took place in May and June of 2010 which engulfed the Czech Republic, Slovakia, Poland, Hungary, Ukraine, Austria, Germany, and Serbia. It was one of the largest floods in Poland in that during the period from 14 May to 30 June 2010, around 76,800 interventions related to relief and recovery actions were reported [92]. At that time, there was an increased demand for pumps with higher capacity than those the services already possessed. Efforts at the national level were launched, and firemen from other EU states took part in the operations. Persons charged with rescue actions in this event accomplished the following tasks based on communication processes:

(1)   prepare scenarios for potential situations, analyses, weather forecasts, collect information, anticipate demand;

(2)   calculate forces and resources, assess potential, analyse situations, prepare proposals for disposing forces depending on the demand, examine potential for requesting external forces;

(3)   contribute to the formulation of solutions intended to accomplish operations, raise forces, dislocate forces, put forces into operation, continue monitoring the situation and its reporting;

(4)   monitor the efficacy of the formulated solutions, participate in the work of military staff and teams, monitor the situation's progress, collaborate with commanders with regard to specific actions;

(5)   control efficacy of operations conducted by operational groups, verify information handed over, e.g., by phone, with the actual situation.

Another example of operations coordination and emergency management in Poland was the head-on collision of two high-speed passenger trains on 3 March 2012 near the town of Szczekociny. As a result, 16 people were killed and 57 passengers were injured. In the first train, an electric locomotive was destroyed and the first two carriages were derailed, while in the other train the locomotive and one carriage were derailed. Services from the national emergency management level and fire brigades from four provinces were used in the rescue action, including 450 rescuers and 400 policemen. The coordination process covered such operations as evacuation of the people affected, rendering first aid, searching destroyed carriages and the surrounding crash site, enabling access to trapped passengers, designating a temporary landing strip for helicopters of the Air Rescue Service, and securing the incident site. Coordination of basic operations did not pose a problem. However, contentious issues were exposed, and they referred to extra activities and details, e.g., places for tents. These examples confirm that both formal as well as posteriori relationships provide a basis for the coordination of operations during emergency situations. Moreover, they allow us to ascertain that organisational factors and organisational behaviours constitute the key determinants for improving communication and coordination in sustainable public safety management.

The quantity of information is essential for coordination and execution of effective operations in dynamically changing circumstances requires application of cutting-edge organisational and technical solutions. In addition, "some of the major challenges (...) include information mismanagement, resource allocation issues, and ineffective communication" [93] (p. 260). These challenges can lead to communication and consequently coordination breakdowns. To ensure efficacy of rescue actions and to streamline communication as well as coordination processes, there are emergency coordination centres established and they make up complex organisational and technical structures in line with administrative division at the local, regional, and national levels. Such centres also operate at the international level, e.g., Emergency Response Coordination Centre functions in the EU. It is a one-stop-shop providing an overview of the available civil protection assets and acts as a communication hub between the participating states, the affected country and dispatched field experts. The main purpose of its existence is to facilitate collaboration in civil protection interventions in the event of major emergencies, e.g., through pool resources that can be made available to help disaster-hit countries and share best practices in disaster management [94].

Emergency coordination centres are a support centre for those in charge of rescue actions. They handle information transfer as well as vertical and horizontal communication outside the incident site. They also oversee the course of action and if needed they bring and send extra resources to action. Thus, emergency coordination centres run the so-called "external coordination". The centres operate in line with a mutual substitution principle. It means that a report which cannot be received for any reason in a centre relevant for the caller's domicile will be automatically redirected to another Centre. For receiving the reports operators are employed, there may be also officers delegated, assigned from the police or fire brigade, employees in emergency management departments as well as municipal policemen. In Poland the tasks conferred on the centres include [95]:

(1) handle alarm reports, excluding fire signalisation systems,
(2) register and store data regarding alarm reports, including phone recordings with the complete alarm report, personal data of the reporting person and other persons indicated when receiving the report, information on the incident site and its type and shortened description of the event for the period of 3 years;
(3) conduct analyses related to functioning of the system in the area handled by the centre and producing statistics with regard to numbers, types, and response time for alarm reports;
(4) collaborate and exchange information with emergency coordination centres;
(5) exchange information and data, excluding personal data, for the purposes of analyses with the Police, National Fire Service, administrators of medical rescue teams, and entities which phone numbers are handled within the system.

In other countries, tasks accomplished by centres are essentially similar. For instance, in Sri Lanka they are as follows [96]:

(1) Maintaining and operating early warning towers and other early warning dissemination equipments
(2) Dissemination of early warning messages and ensuring reception at remote vulnerable villagers
(3) Coordination of donor assistance to strengthen capacity of technical agencies for early warning
(4) Initiating awareness on activities related to early warning among various agencies and the public
(5) Guiding district disaster management units in coordinating and implementing warning dissemination-related activities in the province, district, and local authority levels.

Emergency coordination centres collaborate with services statutorily appointed for security protection as well as social rescue organisations. Their operations enable to reduce the waiting time for assistance as well as time for rescue actions themselves, properly match forces and resources to the operations, bolster information transfer as well as create a consistent database for events [97].

Receipt of alarm reports in the centre by alarm number operators and dispatchers is carried out by means of information and communication technology systems. These systems ensure automatisation of receipt and registration of reports. They allow for identification of the phone number, location, and visualisation of the place from which the emergency call comes. Besides, it also enables overseeing the actual state of calls handled, elimination of hoax calls, and their selection [98–100].

An interesting example of the emergency coordination centre is the Integrated Security Centre operating in Ostrava in the Czech Republic since 2011. Its initial concept originated in the 1990s when the urgency for collaboration among rescue services was identified. It is currently a part of the Czech Integrated Rescue System which covers a connections system as well as principles guiding collaboration and emergency coordination of local and central authorities, as well as individuals and authorised persons when the necessity arises to undertake rescue or humanitarian actions and to prepare and conduct emergency operations. The Integrated Security Centre houses such units as: fire brigade, police, medical emergency, and municipal authorities. They form the mainstay of the system. An auxiliary role is played by: municipal police, military forces, ministry of health, ministry of interior, remaining rescue units, security companies, and non-governmental organisations. The unit responsible for response activities is the fire brigade across all levels of the state organisation depending on the scale of the event. However, the conditions for conducting the operations are determined by the public administration. The functioning of the Centre has helped to eliminate problems related to communication and operations coordination and to boost inter-organisational collaboration which through direct contacts and joint resolution of problems enables to continually improve collaboration principles within the system.

The analysis of the course of inter-organisational coordination during emergency situations enables stating that coordination constitutes a liaison which bonds actions taken in the scope of public safety management. Its significance results from the span of tasks that are realised, in which performance many entities are engaged, in each case in a different quantity and configuration. The conducted actions are based on collaboration between each of the partners, which separate and autonomous units and whose competences complement each other. This leads to a conclusion that inter-organisational coordination is a key factor of public safety management, which principal features are as follows:

- integrity of actions: the enterprises of each organisation are coherent and mutually complementary, while efficiency may be achieved only within mutual realisation of tasks;
- interdependence: each organisation is mutually dependent both in the scope of conducting actions, transferring information, as well as managing resources;
- mutuality: mutual enterprises are based on relations between each organisation;
- multiplicity: there are many possibilities of coordinating actions within one enterprise;
- adaptability: methods of coordination are adapted to existing conditions.

Moreover, inter-organisational coordination is a result of legal and organisational, social, and situational conditions. The first above-mentioned conditions are related to the existing legal regulations, procedures, and by-laws. They specify the rules of coordinating commonly conducted actions. In turn, the social conditions cover inter-organisational relations, which through shaping of appropriate behaviours, influence the enterprises' efficiency. Whereas, situational conditions specify the current context of actions' realisation. They cause that flexibility and agility is required of organisations participating in the actions. Both the factors and conditions of inter-organisational coordination impact the level of sustainable local governance. In principle, local governance is characterised by accountability, transparency, openness, and publicness. These features are favourable to improving sustainable local governance.

The analyses confirm the complexity of inter-organisational coordination and significance of relational aspects in the theory and practice of managing public safety.

5. Discussion and Conclusions

In this article we analyse inter-organisational coordination in the public safety management system. In our opinion the notion of collaboration is broader than coordination, which is consistent with the analyses conducted by Arthur T. Himmelman [10]. We also adapted the opinion of Richard C. Feiock, In Won Lee, and Hyung Jun Park [11] and we believe that coordination and collaboration are not points on a simple scale of service integration, but differ in their forms and structure. Starting from Fayol's understanding of coordination, we reinforce this notion as one of the key factors of collaboration. In our deliberations we also claim that in our research the context of realisation of actions is of significant importance, since the mechanism of coordination, which regulate the ways of effective collaboration, result from it [101]. According to Elodie Gardet and Caroline Mothe groups of representative mechanisms of coordination include the following [102]: exchange formalisation, trust, result division, guarantees against opportunistic behaviour, and conflict resolution. In turn, Jody Hoffer Gittell and Leigh Weiss on the base of a nine-hospital quantitative study of patient care coordination analysed such coordination mechanisms as [103]: routines, information systems, meetings, and boundary spanners. In our research we have demonstrated that in the Polish context of public safety management the formal mechanisms of coordination play the main role, which results from institutional arrangements. In the conditions of uncertainty and risk the formal decision-making structures constitute the foundation of conducting actions, although other mechanisms—such as trust, meetings, and routines—are also significant. To a greater extent these mechanisms are applied in the period of stabilisation, during action preparation. This proves that the priority significance of each coordination mechanism results from the situational context.

The analyses presented in this article are not free from limitations. These limitations result above all from the fact that the research is of a preliminary nature and it concerns a diagnosis of the level of inter-organisational coordination in public safety management in relation to factors of effective inter-organisational collaboration. In the future, we plan to expand these research studies in relation to enhanced inter-organisational coordination endeavours. Moreover, the research is located in the Polish context. Taking that into account, it is necessary to study the course of inter-organisational coordination in other social and political conditions. It is also recommended to comprehensively analyse the internal and external conditions of effective inter-organisational coordination, for which purpose the research on business models of public safety organisations may prove useful.

Despite these limitations we have been able to achieve the assumed goal of this publication. We argue that inter-organisational coordination as an instrument of collaboration between autonomous units is the key factor in sustainable public safety management. It binds the actions taken by each organisation, enables flexible adaptation of enterprises and possessed resources to the existing conditions, it configures the networks of public services' delivery and it maximises the usage of the possessed abilities. As a result of this, it increases the efficiency of public safety management.

In conclusion we claim that:

(1)   Inter-organisational coordination depends to a large extent on organisational and relational conditions, which occur between collaborating units. They include among other such factors as: communication in inter-organisational working teams, constraints in inter-organisational collaboration, leadership with organisational and communication skills, organisation of collaborative work (e.g., time pressured, competitive, rapidly changing, stability), management of inter-organisational collaboration (e.g., styles, transparency of decisions, and guidance), inter-organisational trust, and professional communication between personnel from individual organisations.

(2)   Coordination in public safety management is protean. During stabilization it is carried out by public administration and it involves determination of preventive operations. Some ways of that coordination can be applied in other areas of sustainable local government. However during the realisation phase the person in charge of rescue actions coordinates activities within

the incident site. Outside the incident site the coordination function is fulfilled by emergency coordination centres. This solution is the result of complexity embedded in the unique situation and efforts to be undertaken in face of hazard. Such coordination, particularly creation of formal and informal relationships based on trust and organisational concern, can be used in sheer inter-organisational collaboration.

(3) The principal features of inter-organisational coordination considered with regard to collaborated management are: integrity of actions, interdependence, mutuality, complexity, and adaptiveness to unique and rapidly changing situations. At the same time, inter-organisational coordination is a result of legal, organisational, social, and situational conditions. Features of inter-organisational coordination have a considerable impact on the level of sustainable public safety management.

Acknowledgments: Acknowledgments: The authors would like to thank an anonymous reviewers for constructive comments and suggestions. Empirical data were collected within the authors' own investigations carried out in 2013–2015 in the project entitled "Coordination, communication and trust as factors driving effective inter-organisational collaboration in the system of public safety management", financed by the Polish funds of the National Science Centre allocated on the basis of the decision No. DEC-2012/07/D/HS4/00537. Whereas, preparing of the publication was partly developed within the Statutory Research 2013–2016 of the Institute of Public Affairs of the Jagiellonian University in Cracow entitled "Managing Public Sector".

Author Contributions: Author Contributions: Barbara Kożuch and Katarzyna Sienkiewicz-Małyjurek worked together to conceived, designed and performed the research, analyzed the data and wrote the paper.

References

1. Van Wassenhove, L.N. Humanitarian aid logistics: Supply chain management in high gear. *J. Oper. Res. Soc.* **2006**, *57*, 475–489. [CrossRef]

2. Szymczak, M.; Sienkiewicz-Małyjurek, K. Information in the city traffic management system. The analysis of the use of information sources and the assessment in terms of their usefulness for city routes users. *LogForum* **2011**, *7*, 37–50.

3. Slabbert, A.D.; Ukpere, W.I. Poverty as a transient reality in a globalised world: An economic choice. *Int. J. Soc. Econ.* **2011**, *38*, 858–868. [CrossRef]

4. Smith, N. Economic inequality and poverty: Where do we go from here? *Int. J. Sociol. Soc. Policy* **2010**, *30*, 127–139. [CrossRef]

5. Sienkiewicz-Małyjurek, K. Spatial and organisational conditions of public safety in cities. In *Current Problems of Regional Development*, Proceedings of the International Scientific Conference on Hradec Economical Days 2008: A Strategy for Development of the Region and the State Location, University Hradec Kralove, Czech Republic, 5–6 February 2008; Jedlicka, P., Ed.; pp. 95–99.

6. Jabłoński, A. Wieloparadygmatyczność w zarządzaniu a trwałość modelu biznesu przedsiębiorstwa. *Studia i Prace Kolegium Zarządzania i Finansów Szkoły Głównej Handlowej w Warszawie* **2014**, *139*, 51–72. (In Polish)

7. Kozłowski, S. Polska droga do zrównoważonego rozwoju. In *Rozwój zrównoważony na szczeblu krajowym, regionalnym i lokalnym—doświadczenia polskie i możliwości ich zastosowania na Ukrainie*; Kozłowski, S., Haładyj, A., Eds.; KUL: Lublin, Poland, 2006; pp. 159–166. (In Polish)

8. Kożuch, B.; Sienkiewicz-Małyjurek, K. Collaborative networks as a basis for internal economic security in sustainable local governance. The case of Poland. In *The Economic Security of Business Transactions. Management in Business*; Raczkowski, K., Schneider, F., Eds.; Chartridge Books Oxford: Oxford, UK, 2013; pp. 313–328.

9. O'Leary, R.; Vij, N. Collaborative Public Management: Where Have We Been and Where Are We Going? *Am. Rev. Public Adm.* **2012**, *42*, 507–522. [CrossRef]

10. Himmelman, A.T. On coalitions and the transformation of power relations: Collaborative betterment and collaborative empowerment. *Am. J. Community Psychol.* **2001**, *29*, 277–284. [CrossRef] [PubMed]

11. Feiock, R.C.; Lee, I.W.; Park, H.J. Administrators' and Elected Officials' Collaboration Networks: Selecting Partners to Reduce Risk in Economic Development. *Public Adm. Rev.* **2012**, *72*, S58–S68. [CrossRef]

12. Gulati, R.; Wohlgezogen, F.; Zhelyazkov, P. The Two Facets of Collaboration: Cooperation and Coordination in Strategic Alliances. *Acad. Manag. Ann.* **2012**, *6*, 531–583. [CrossRef]

13.   Raposo, A.B.; Fuks, H. Defining Task Interdependencies and Coordination Mechanisms for Collaborative Systems. In *Cooperative Systems Design*; Blay-Fornarino, M., Pinna-Dery, A.M., Schmidt, K., Zaraté, P., Eds.; IOS Press: Amsterdam, The Netherlands, 2002; pp. 88–103.

14.   Leonard, H.B.; Howitt, A.M. Organising Response to Extreme Emergencies: The Victorian Bushfires of 2009. *Aust. J. Public Adm.* **2010**, *69*, 372–386. [CrossRef]

15.   Gregory, R. All the King's horses and all the King's men: Putting New Zealand's public sector back together again. *Int. Public Manag. Rev.* **2003**, *4*, 41–58.

16.   Comfort, L.K. Crisis Management in Hindsight: Cognition, Communication, Coordination, and Control. *Public Adm. Rev.* **2007**, *67*, 189–197. [CrossRef]

17.   Leonard, H.B.; Howitt, A.M. Katrina as prelude: Preparing for and responding to Katrina-Class Disturbances in the United States—Testimony to U.S. Senate Committee, 8 March 2006. *J. Homel. Secur. Emerg. Manag.* **2006**, *3*, 1547–7355. [CrossRef]

18.   Comfort, L.K.; Kapucu, N. Inter-organizational coordination in extreme events: The World Trade Center attacks, 11 September 2001. *Nat. Hazards* **2006**, *39*, 309–327. [CrossRef]

19.   Bharosa, N.; Lee, J.; Janssen, M. Challenges and obstacles in sharing and coordinating information during multi-agency disaster response: Propositions from field exercises. *Inf. Syst. Front.* **2010**, *12*, 49–65. [CrossRef]

20.   Panday, P.K. Policy implementation in urban Bangladesh: Role of intra-organizational coordination. *Public Organ. Rev.* **2007**, *7*, 237–259. [CrossRef]

21.   Meek, J.W. Nuances of Metropolitan Cooperative Networks. *Public Adm. Rev.* **2012**, *72*, S68–S69. [CrossRef]

22.   Chen, R.; Sharman, R.; Chakravarti, N.; Rao, H.R.; Upadhyaya, S.J. Emergency response information system interoperability: Development of chemical incident response data model. *J. Assoc. Inf. Syst.* **2008**, *9*, 1–54.

23.   Chen, R.; Sharman, R.; Rao, H.R.; Upadhyaya, S.J. Coordination In Emergency Response Management, Developing a framework to analyze coordination patterns occurring in the emergency response life cycle. *Commun. ACM* **2008**, *51*, 66–73. [CrossRef]

24.   Melin, U.; Axelsson, K. Understanding Organizational Coordination and Information Systems—Mintzberg's Coordination Mechanisms Revisited and Evaluated. Available online: http://aisel.aisnet.org/ecis2005/115/ (accessed on 18 December 2015).

25.   Gittell, J.H. Relationships between service providers and their impact on customers. *J. Sci. Res.* **2002**, *4*, 299–311. [CrossRef]

26.   Gittell, J.H. Relational coordination: coordinating work through relationships of shared goals, shared knowledge and mutual respect. In *Relational Perspectives in Organisational Studies: A Research Companion*; Kyriakidou, O., Özbilgin, M.F., Eds.; Edward Elgar Publishers: Cheltenham, UK, 2006; pp. 74–94.

27.   Kożuch, B.; Sienkiewcz-Małyjurek, K. Factors of effective inter-organisational collaboration: A framework for public management. Transylvanian Review of Administrative Sciences, forthcoming.

28.   Government Centre for Security. Act of 26 April 2007 on the Crisis Management. Available online: http://rcb.gov.pl/eng/wp-content/uploads/2011/03/ACT-on-Crisis-Management-final-version-31-12-2010.pdf (accessed on 25 January 2016).

29.   Kożuch, B.; Sienkiewicz-Małyjurek, K. Information sharing in complex systems: A case study on public safety management. *Procedia Soc. Behav. Sci.* **2015**, *213*, 722–727. [CrossRef]

30.   Waugh, W.L.; Streib, G. Collaboration and Leadership for Effective Emergency Management. *Public Adm. Rev.* **2006**, *66*, 131–140. [CrossRef]

31.   Kapucu, N.; Arslan, T.; Demiroz, F. Collaborative emergency management and national emergency management network. *Disaster Prev. Manag.* **2010**, *19*, 452–468. [CrossRef]

32.   Kapucu, N. Disaster and emergency management systems in urban areas. *Cities* **2012**, *29*, S41–S49. [CrossRef]

33.   Boin, A.; Hart, P. Organising for Effective Emergency Management: Lessons from Research. *Austr. J. Public Adm.* **2010**, *69*, 357–371. [CrossRef]

34.   Choenni, S.; Leertouwer, E. Public Safety Mashups to Support Policy Makers. In *Electronic Government and the Information Systems Perspective*, Proceedings of the First International Conference EGOVIS 2010, Bilbao, Spain, 31 August–2 September 2010; Andersen, K.M., Francesconi, E., van Engers, A.G.T.M., Eds.; Springer-Verlag: Berlin Heidelberg, Germany, 2010; pp. 234–248.

35.   Sienkiewicz-Małyjurek, K. Rola samorządów lokalnych w kształtowaniu bezpieczeństwa publicznego. *Samorz. Teryt.* **2010**, *7–8*, 123–139. (In Polish)

36. Tomasino, A.P. Public Safety Networks as a Type of Complex Adaptive System. In Unifying Themes in Complex Systems, Proceedings of the Eighth International Conference on Complex Systems, Volume VIII, Boston, MA, 26 June–1 July 2011; Sayama, H., Minai, A., Braha, D., Bar-Yam, Y., Eds.; New England Complex Systems Institute Series on Complexity, NECSI Knowledge Press: Cambridge, MA, USA, 2011; pp. 1350–1364.

37. Williams, C.B.; Dias, M.; Fedorowicz, J.; Jacobson, D.; Vilvovsky, S.; Sawyer, S.; Tyworth, M. The formation of inter-organizational information sharing networks in public safety: Cartographic insights on rational choice and institutional explanations. *Inf. Polity* **2009**, *14*, 13–29.

38. Kożuch, B.; Sienkiewicz-Małyjurek, K. Collaborative Performance In Public Safety Management Process. In *Transdisciplinary and Communicative Action*, Proceedings of the 5th International Conference Lumen 2014, Targoviste, Romania, 21–22 November 2014; Frunza, A., Ciulei, T., Sandu, A., Eds.; Medimond S.r.l.: Bologna, Italy, 2015; pp. 401–409.

39. Kożuch, B.; Sienkiewicz-Małyjurek, K. Mapowanie procesów współpracy międzyorganizacyjnej na przykładzie działań realizowanych w bezpieczeństwie publicznym. Zarządzanie Publiczne, 2015. forthcoming. (In Polish)

40. Sienkiewicz-Małyjurek, K.; Kożuch, B. System zarządzania bezpieczeństwem publicznym w ujęciu teorii złożoności. Opracowanie modelowe. *Bezpieczeństwo i Technika Pożarnicza* **2015**, *37*, 33–43. (In Polish)

41. Kożuch, B.; Sienkiewicz-Małyjurek, K. New Requirements for Managers of Public Safety Systems. *Procedia Soc. Behav. Sci.* **2014**, *149*, 472–478. [CrossRef]

42. Grudzewski, W.M.; Hejduk, I.K.; Sankowska, A.; Wańtuchowicz, M. *Sustainability w biznesie, czyli przedsiębiorstwo przyszłości, zmiany paradygmatów i koncepcji zarządzania*; Wydawnictwo Poltext: Warszawa, Poland, 2010. (In Polish)

43. Mah, D.N.; Hills, P. Collaborative governance for sustainable development: Wind resource assessment in Xinjiang and Guangdong Provinces, China. *Sustain. Dev.* **2012**, *20*, 85–97. [CrossRef]

44. Røiseland, A. Understanding local governance: Institutional forms of collaboration. *Public Adm.* **2011**, *89*, 879–893. [CrossRef]

45. Considine, M. Governance networks and the question of transformation. *Public Adm.* **2013**, *91*, 438–447. [CrossRef]

46. Lee, I.W.; Feiock, R.C.; Lee, Y. Competitors and Cooperators: A Micro-Level Analysis of Regional Economic Development Collaboration Networks. *Public Adm. Rev.* **2012**, *72*, 253–262. [CrossRef]

47. Lozano, R. Collaboration as a Pathway for Sustainability. *Sustain. Dev.* **2007**, *15*, 370–381. [CrossRef]

48. Mattessich, P.W.; Murray-Close, M.; Monsey, B.R. *Collaboration: What Makes It Work*; Amherst H. Wilder Foundation: Saint Paul, MN, USA, 2001.

49. Thomson, A.M.; Perry, J.L. Collaboration process: Inside the black box. *Public Adm. Rev.* **2006**, *66*, 20–32. [CrossRef]

50. Arya, B.; Lin, Z. Understanding collaboration outcomes from an extended resource-based view perspective: The roles of organizational characteristics, partner attributes, and network structures. *J. Manag.* **2007**, *33*, 697–723. [CrossRef]

51. Hansen, M.T.; Nohria, N. How to build collaborative advantage. *MIT Sloan Manag. Rev.* **2004**, *46*, 4–12.

52. Hardy, C.; Phillips, N.; Lawrence, T.B. Resources, Knowledge and Influence: The Organizational Effects of Interorganizational Collaboration. *J. Manag. Stud.* **2003**, *40*, 321–347. [CrossRef]

53. Powell, W.W.; Koput, K.W.; Smith-Doerr, L. Interorganizational collaboration and the locus of innovation: Networks of learning in biotechnology. *Adm. Sci. Q.* **1996**, *41*, 116–146. [CrossRef]

54. Berlin, J.M.; Carlström, E.D. Why is collaboration minimised at the accident scene? A critical study of a hidden phenomenon. *Disaster Prev. Manag.* **2011**, *20*, 159–171. [CrossRef]

55. Kaiser, F.M. *Interagency Collaborative Arrangements and Activities: Types, Rationales, Considerations*; Congressional Research Service: Washington, DC, USA, 2011.

56. McGuire, M. Collaborative Public Management: Assessing What We Know and How We Know It. *Public Adm. Rev.* **2006**, *66*, 33–43. [CrossRef]

57. Perrault, E.; McClelland, R.; Austin, C.; Sieppert, J. Working Together in Collaborations: Successful Process Factors for Community Collaboration. *Adm. Soc. Work* **2011**, *5*, 282–298. [CrossRef]

58. Malone, T.W.; Crowston, K. What is coordination theory and how can it help design cooperative work systems. In Proceedings of the Conference on Computer Supported Cooperative Work, Los Angeles, CA, USA, 7–10 October 1990.

59. Hartgerink, J.M.; Cramm, J.M.; Bakker, T.J.E.M.; van Eijsden, R.A.M.; Mackenbach, J.P.; Nieboer, A.P. The importance of relational coordination for integrated care delivery to older patients in the hospital. *J. Nurs. Manag.* **2014**, *22*, 248–256. [CrossRef] [PubMed]

60. Hossain, L.; Uddin, S. Design patterns: Coordination in complex and dynamic environments. *Disaster Prev. Manag.* **2012**, *21*, 336–350. [CrossRef]

61. Malone, T.W.; Crowston, K. The interdisciplinary study of coordination. *ACM Comput. Surv. (CSUR)* **1994**, *26*, 87–119. [CrossRef]

62. Lie, A. Coordination processes and outcomes in the public service: The challenge of inter-organizational food safety coordination in Norway. *Public Adm.* **2011**, *89*, 401–417. [CrossRef] [PubMed]

63. Bond, J.B.; Gittell, J.H. Cross-agency coordination of offender reentry: Testing collaboration outcomes. *J. Crim. Justice* **2010**, *38*, 118–129. [CrossRef]

64. Jones, C.; Hesterly, W.S.; Borgatti, S.P. A General Theory of Network Governance: Exchange Conditions and Social Mechanisms. *Acad. Manag. Rev.* **1997**, *22*, 911–945.

65. De Pablos Heredero, C.; Haider, S.; García Martínez, A. Relational coordination as an indicator of teamwork quality: Potential application to the success of e-learning at universities. *Int. J. Emerg. Technol. Learn.* **2015**, *10*, 4–8. [CrossRef]

66. Provan, K.G.; Kenis, P. Modes of Network Governance: Structure, Management, and Effectiveness. *J. Public Adm. Res. Theory* **2008**, *18*, 229–252. [CrossRef]

67. Carlson, E.J. Collaboration and Confrontation in Interorganizational Coordination: Preparing to Respond to Disasters. Available online: https://docs.google.com/viewer?url=https%3A%2F%2Fwww.ideals.illinois.edu%2Fbitstream%2Fhandle%2F2142%2F50617%2FElizabeth_Carlson.pdf%3Fsequence%3D1 (accessed on 11 January 2016).

68. Grandori, A. An Organizational Assessment of Interfirm Coordination Modes. *Organ. Stud.* **1997**, *18*, 897–925. [CrossRef]

69. Van De Ven, A.H.; Delbecq, A.L.; Koenig, R.J. Determinants of coordination modes within organizations. *Am. Sociol. Rev.* **1976**, *41*, 322–338.

70. Martinez, J.I.; Jarillo, J.C. The Evolution of Research on Coordination Mechanisms in Multinational Corporations. *J. Int. Bus. Stud.* **1989**, *20*, 489–514. [CrossRef]

71. Hossain, L.; Kuti, M. Disaster response preparedness coordination through social networks. *Disasters* **2010**, *34*, 755–786. [CrossRef] [PubMed]

72. Mintzberg, H. *The Structuring of Organizations*; Prentice-Hall: Englewood Cliffs, NJ, USA, 1979.

73. Drabek, T.E. Community Processes: Coordination. In *Handbook of Disaster Research*; Rodríguez, H., Quarantelli, E.L., Dynes, R.R., Eds.; Springer Science + Business Media: New York, NY, USA, 2007; pp. 217–233.

74. Abbasi, A.; Owen, C.; Hossain, L.; Hamra, J. Social connectedness and adaptive team coordination during fire events. *Fire Saf. J.* **2013**, *59*, 30–36. [CrossRef]

75. Morris, J.C.; Morris, E.D.; Jones, D.M. Reaching for the Philosopher's Stone: Contingent Coordination and the Military's Response to Hurricane Katrina. *Public Adm. Rev.* **2007**, *67*, 94–106. [CrossRef]

76. Comfort, L.; Dunn, M.; Johnson, D.; Skertich, R.; Zagorecki, A. Coordination in complex systems: Increasing efficiency in disaster mitigation and response. *Int. J. Emerg. Manag.* **2004**, *2*, 63–80. [CrossRef]

77. Kapucu, N. Interorganizational Coordination in Dynamic Context: Networks in Emergency Response Management. *Connections* **2005**, *26*, 33–48.

78. Wise, C.R. Organizing for Homeland Security after Katrina: Is Adaptive Management What's Missing? *Public Adm. Rev.* **2006**, *66*, 302–318. [CrossRef]

79. Bolland, J.M.; Wilson, J.V. Three Faces of Integrative Coordination: A Model of Interorganizational Relations in Community-Based Health and Human Services. *HSR Health Services Res.* **1994**, *29*, 341–366.

80. Leung, Z.C.S. Boundary Spanning in Interorganizational Collaboration. *Adm. Soc. Work* **2013**, *37*, 447–457. [CrossRef]

81. Patel, H.; Pettitt, M.; Wilson, J.R. Factors of collaborative working: A framework for a collaboration model. *Appl. Ergon.* **2012**, *43*, 1–26. [CrossRef] [PubMed]

82. Ales, M.W.; Rodrigues, S.B.; Snyder, R.; Conklin, M. Developing and Implementing an Effective Framework for Collaboration: The Experience of the CS2day Collaborative. *J. Contin. Educ. Health Prof.* **2011**, *31*, 13–20. [CrossRef] [PubMed]

83. Ansell, C.; Gash, A. Collaborative Governance in Theory and Practice. *J. Public Adm. Res. Theory* **2007**, *18*, 543–571. [CrossRef]
84. Chen, B. Antecedents or Processes? Determinants of Perceived Effectiveness of Interorganizational Collaborations for Public Service Delivery. *Int. Public Manag. J.* **2010**, *13*, 381–407. [CrossRef]
85. Daley, D.M. Interdisciplinary Problems and Agency Boundaries: Exploring Effective Cross-Agency Collaboration. *J. Public Adm. Res. Theory* **2009**, *19*, 477–493. [CrossRef]
86. Emerson, K.; Nabatchi, T.; Balogh, S. An integrative framework for collaborative governance. *J. Public Adm. Res. Theory* **2011**, *22*, 1–30. [CrossRef]
87. Fedorowicz, J.; Gogan, J.L.; Williams, C.B. A collaborative network for first responders: Lessons from the CapWIN case. *Gov. Inf. Q.* **2007**, *24*, 785–807. [CrossRef]
88. Franco, M. Determining factors in the success of strategic alliances: An empirical study performed in Portuguese firms. *Eur. J. Int. Manag.* **2011**, *5*, 608–632. [CrossRef]
89. Olson, C.A.; Balmer, J.T.; Mejicano, G.C. Factors Contributing to Successful Interorganizational Collaboration: The Case of CS2day. *J. Contin. Educ. Health Prof.* **2011**, *31*, 3–12. [CrossRef] [PubMed]
90. Raišienė, A.G. Sustainable Development of Inter-Organizational Relationships and Social Innovations. *J. Secur. Sustain. Issues* **2012**, *2*, 65–76. [CrossRef]
91. Ranade, W.; Hudson, B. Conceptual issues in inter-agency collaboration. *Local Gov. Stud.* **2003**, *29*, 32–50. [CrossRef]
92. The National Headquarters of the State Fire Service of Poland. Biuletyn Informacyjny Państwowej Straży Pożarnej za Rok 2010. Available online: http://www.straz.gov.pl/aktualnosci/biuletyn _roczny_psp_za_rok_2010 (accessed on 26 January 2016). (In Polish).
93. Reddy, M.C.; Paul, S.A.; Abraham, J.; McNeese, M.; DeFlitch, C.; Yen, J. Challenges to effective crisis management: Using information and communication technologies to coordinate emergency medical services and emergency department teams. *Int. J. Med. Inf.* **2009**, *78*, 259–269. [CrossRef] [PubMed]
94. European Commission; Humanitarian Aid and Civil Protection. Emergency Response Coordination Centre, ECHO Factsheet. Available online: http://ec.europa.eu/echo/files/aid/countries/factsheets/thematic/ERC_en.pdf (accessed on 20 September 2015).
95. Internetowy System Aktów Prawnych. *Ustawa z Dnia 22 Listopada 2013 r. o Systemie Powiadamiania Ratunkowego (Dz.U. 2013 poz. 1635)*; Available online: http://isap.sejm.gov.pl/DetailsServlet?id=WDU20130 001635 (accessed on 27 January 2016). (In Polish)
96. Asees, M.S. Tsunami Disaster Prevention in Sri Lanka. Available online: http://www. jamco.or.jp/en/ symposium/21/3/ (accessed on 28 September 2015).
97. Sienkiewicz-Małyjurek, K. The Flow of Information About the Actions Required in Emergency Situations: Issues in Urban Areas in Poland. *Int. J. Soc. Sustain. Econ. Soc. Cult. Context* **2013**, *8*, 61–71.
98. Aedo, I.; Díaz, P.; Carroll, J.M.; Convertino, G.; Rosson, M.B. End-user oriented strategies to facilitate multi-organizational adoption of emergency management information systems. *Inf. Process. Manag.* **2010**, *46*, 11–21. [CrossRef]
99. Lee, W.B.; Wang, Y.; Wang, W.M.; Cheung, C.F. An unstructured information management system (UIMS) for emergency management. *Expert Syst. Appl.* **2012**, *39*, 12743–12758. [CrossRef]
100. Juan, L.J.; Li, Q.; Liua, C.; Khana, S.U.; Ghani, N. Community-based collaborative information system for emergency management. *Comput. Oper. Res.* **2014**, *42*, 116–124.
101. Grandori, A.; Soda, G. Inter-firm networks: Antecedents, mechanisms and forms. *Organ. Stud.* **1995**, *16*, 183–214. [CrossRef]
102. Gardet, E.; Mothe, C. The dynamics of coordination in innovation networks. *Eur. Manag. Rev.* **2011**, *8*, 213–229. [CrossRef]
103. Gittell, J.H.; Weiss, L. Coordination Networks Within and Across Organizations: A Multi-level Framework. *J. Manag. Stud.* **2004**, *41*, 127–153. [CrossRef]

4

The Design of a Sustainable Location-Routing-Inventory Model Considering Consumer Environmental Behavior

Jinhuan Tang [1],*, Shoufeng Ji [2] and Liwen Jiang [2]

[1]   School of Economics and Management, Shenyang Aerospace University, Shenyang 110136, China
[2]   School of Business Administration, Northeast University, Shenyang 110169, China;
       sfji@mail.neu.edu.cn (S.J.); 1310514@stu.neu.edu.cn (L.J.)
*   Corresponding: jinhuan_tang@sau.edu.cn.

Academic Editors: Adam Jabłoński and Giuseppe Ioppolo

Abstract: Our aim is to design a sustainable supply chain (SSC) network, which takes into consideration consumer environmental behaviors (CEBs). CEBs not only affect consumers' demand for products with low carbon emissions, they also affect their willingness to pay premium prices for products with low carbon emissions. We incorporate CEBs into the SSC network model involving location, routing and inventory. Firstly, a multi-objective optimization model comprised of both the costs and the carbon emissions of a joint location-routing-inventory model is proposed and solved, using a multi-objective particle swarm optimization (MOPSO) algorithm. Then, a revenue function including CEBs is presented on the basis of a Pareto set of the trade-off between costs and carbon emissions. A computational experiment and sensitivity analysis are conducted, employing data from the China National Petroleum Corporation (CNPC). The results clearly indicate that our research can be applied to actual supply chain operations. In addition, some practical managerial insights for enterprises are offered.

Keywords: sustainable supply chain network; consumer environmental behaviors; location-routing-inventory; MOPSO

---

1. Introduction

Along with the heightened concerns over the past few decades relating to sustainable supply chains (SSC), governments, enterprises and consumers are becoming increasingly aware of the need to reduce carbon emissions. Governments have introduced a number of regulations, such as carbon taxes, cap-and-trade mechanisms and carbon constraints to mandate carbon emission reductions in SSC management [1]. In addition, a few socially responsible enterprises have engaged in voluntary emission reduction programs. Companies such as BP and Nike have taken actions to reduce emissions in order to improve their public image. Wal-Mart and Tesco require their suppliers to reveal their carbon emissions on product labels, where they can be seen by consumers and society. In addition, consumers with higher levels of environmental consciousness are willing to pay a premium price for low carbon products [2–5]. The demand for low carbon products has become greater and greater [6–8]. It can be safely assumed that low carbon products will become more competitively priced in the future. Clearly, the drive for environmental improvement is increasing.

Traditionally, a supply chain network design problem focuses on minimizing the fixed and operational costs that companies directly incur. Only recently, however, have some studies started taking carbon emissions into account [9–11]. Many studies indicate that there is a trade-off between the environment and economics in a supply chain [12–14]. However, it is possible to significantly reduce carbon emissions without greatly increasing costs, using proper supply chain operations [15,16]. In general, there is a paradox between cost and carbon emissions in SSC management.

Companies are never going to reduce their carbon emissions until factors such as cost, profits, brand awareness and consumer pressure are involved. Currently, the main drive for carbon emission reduction can be classified into two categories. The first is mandatory emission reductions, which includes features such as carbon taxes and carbon cap policies [17]. This approach to carbon emissions is punitive. The alternative method is to encourage enterprises to voluntarily reduce their carbon emissions. This encouragement, in turn, can take the form of two types of motivation. One type is through policies such as carbon allowances and cap-and-trade mechanisms. The second type takes on board market considerations. For example, studies have shown that green products have the marketing potential to endow an enterprise with a good public image, which in turn can improve the relevant products' pricing structure or increase consumer demand [8,18]. Looking further into the future, the effects of exploiting the marketing potential of products with low carbon emissions will increase substantially. Creating a SSC network is both a challenge and an opportunity. Presumably, the information already available to society at large has made consumers more environmentally mature, and these mature consumers would like to purchase products with smaller carbon footprints. In this study, we propose the design of a SSC network from a market-driven perspective. Specifically, the purpose of this study is to optimize the profitability of a company through CEB. We decide on the design of the SSC network after considering the number and location of warehouses, the routes from manufacturers to warehouses and from warehouses to retailers, and the inventory polices of the various facilities. Firstly, a multi-objective model is constructed to create a trade-off between cost and carbon emissions. Then, a general revenue objective factoring in CEBs is modeled, based on the relationship between cost and carbon emissions. This study allows us to achieve the best of both worlds, *i.e.*, maximizing the profits of companies, while reducing carbon emissions as much as possible. These achievements also represent the main points of innovation in this paper.

The remainder of the paper is organized as follows: Section 2 reviews the relevant literature. Problem descriptions and assumptions are presented in Section 3. Section 4 describes the multi-objective model that creates the trade-off between cost and carbon emissions, and then constructs the general revenue objective function taking CEBs into consideration. The approach used as a solution for the model is given in Section 5. Results of the computational experiment and a sensitivity analysis are conducted in Section 6; the managerial insights are also illustrated in this section. Finally, our conclusions are presented in Section 7.

2. Literature Review

A key driver of any supply chain is its distribution network. This network, however, is generally also the main source of carbon emissions. The operations of a supply chain network consist of three major components, namely location, routing and inventory (LRI). However, most existing literature integrates only any two of the above, *i.e.*, location-routing problems [19], inventory-routing problems [20], and location-inventory problems [21], as their target topics. Ahmadi-Javid and Azad [22] presented for the first time a model to simultaneously optimize location, routing and inventory decisions in a supply chain network. Ahmadi-Javid and Seddighi [23] studied a ternary integration problem that incorporated location, routing and inventory decisions in designing a multi-source distribution network. They then solved the model using a three-phase heuristic. On the whole, very few researchers have studied the ternary integration LRI problem, and fewer still have incorporated carbon emissions into an LRI problem when designing a supply chain network. This is a very important issue, which has unfortunately been largely ignored.

Numerous studies concentrate on the trade-off between the environment and the economy in supply chain management [12,24]. According to the most recent papers, three types of research have been conducted and corresponding suggestions made: (i) Translate carbon emissions into cost by introducing carbon regulations, such as a carbon tax, cap-and-trade mechanisms, *etc*. Kroes *et al.* [25]

investigated the relationship between a firm's environmental performance compliance and their marketing success in the context of stringent cap-and-trade regulations. Benjaafar et al. [12] presented a cost optimization model via translating carbon emissions into unit costs by carbon price. The two studies proved that there is a close relationship between economic costs and carbon emissions. Similar research was conducted by Hua et al. [24], which studied managing carbon footprints in an inventory system under a carbon emission trading mechanism. (ii) A mandatory carbon cap is used to reduce emissions. This policy specifically prohibits companies from emitting any carbon emissions in excess of their carbon cap. Diabat et al. [26] proposed a mixed-integer program model with carbon cap constraints when designing a supply chain network. A carbon-constraint economic order quantity (EOQ) model was provided to reduce emissions by properly adjusting order quantities [16]. The effects of carbon-constraint measures are significant. However, it is relatively difficult to implement such policies, as they are currently unacceptable to many companies. Businesses, which are profit-driven, lack the motivation to participate in this non-profitable activity. (iii) Provide a set of Pareto solutions, which shows the trade-off between cost and carbon emissions. The advantage of this method is that it can give a set of non-dominated solutions. In addition, the decision makers can choose their preferred configuration. Wygonik and Goodchild [27] presented trade-offs between cost, service quality and the carbon emissions of an urban delivery system. Wang et al. [28] provided a bi-objective optimization model for a green supply chain network design. One of the two objectives was cost minimization; the other was to minimize carbon emissions. The Pareto results showed that the bi-objective model is an effective tool for solving this kind of problem. However, the terminal decision will be made by managers, and thus, personal preferences will inevitably be involved.

The worldwide reduction framework would involve drawing more companies into carbon reduction activities and also into assuming social responsibilities. In order to determine how to make enterprises voluntarily reduce emissions in the context of an earnings-dominated market, it is first necessary to learn how best to improve the potential motivation for corporations to reduce their carbon emissions. The use of carbon labeling is an effective means to encourage consumers to buy environmentally friendly products. There is, however, a definite need to better understand consumers' responses to eco-labels [28]. Consumers' willingness to pay a premium price for products with lower carbon emissions has been shown to be increasing [4,29]. Vanclay et al. [30] defined three levels of carbon labeling (from low to high) as green, yellow and black. They then found that after labeling, the black-labeled (highest carbon emission) product sales decreased by six percent, while green-labeled product sales increased by four percent, when all other conditions were basically unchanged. These results imply that the potential effectiveness of carbon labels in emission reductions is significant. However, green products usually cost more than conventional products, which in turn makes green goods more expensive [3].The key issue is whether consumers will be willing to pay a premium price for the green goods. If not, governments may have to subsidize producers who manufacture green products [5]. Some studies have shown that the higher the CEBs, the higher the price consumers are willing to pay for environmentally friendly products [2].

Economic globalization and rapid high-tech development have intensified market competition to unprecedented levels. New patterns of product competition will emerge over the next few years, and the manufacture of green products as part of that competition is an irresistible trend. Conrad [3] studied the effects of consumer environmental concerns on price, choice of product and market share in the context of duopoly. Liu et al. [8] proved that, as consumers' environmental awareness increases, retailers and manufacturers with superior eco-friendly operations will benefit in the long run. A model considering the effect of environmental conscious consumers on firms' adoption of cleaner technologies showed that, as pollution intensifies, consumers play a much more positive role in the companies' environmental activities. The consumers' attitudes encourage firms to reduce carbon emissions, even in the absence of emission regulations [7]. However, many studies focus on emission reduction through governmental regulations, and rarely through market forces [31]. Actually, consumer response and preference for greener products, as well as market competition, combine to strongly encourage companies to adopt environmentally friendly operations.

By reviewing previous studies, we find that very little research has been conducted on LRI optimization as a means to minimize carbon emissions. Fewer still have incorporated CEBs into a revenue model. Indeed, most studies fail to properly integrate market-driven factors—in particular CEBs—and LRI operations and revenue objectives with cost-environment trade off. In this paper, we make the following contributions: (i) The concept of consumer environmental behaviors (CEBs) was proposed and incorporated into a revenue function. CEBs not only affect consumers' demand for low carbon emission products, but also their willingness to pay a premium price for low carbon emission products. (ii) A multi-objective mixed-integer formulation for the trade-off between cost and carbon emissions was presented first. The solution was then found using the multi-objective particle swarm optimization (MOPSO). Hence, a set of distributed Pareto optimal solutions can be obtained. On this basis, revenue function can be maximized. (iii) We conduct a computational experiment based on data from the China National Petroleum Corporation (CNPC) to test the presented models. Then, the Pareto solutions are presented. In addition, a number of sensitivity analyses are implemented on multiple variables. Hence, we obtain interesting managerial insights that may be of use to logistics service firms.

3. Description and Assumptions

3.1. Problem Description

For a supply chain network consisting of manufacturers (M), warehouses (W) and retailers (R), the location of warehouses is potentially significant. In addition, each warehouse has a specific capacity level, which makes the supply chain network more realistic. The goals of our model are to choose and allocate warehouses, schedule vehicle routes and determine an inventory policy to meet retailers' demands taking into consideration CEBs. The framework of the problem is depicted in Figure 1.

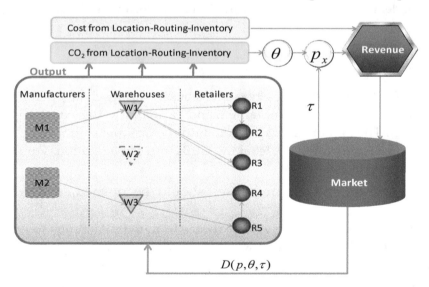

Figure 1. The framework of supply chain network.

In Figure 1, the operations generate cost and CO_2 in a supply chain network involving location, routing and inventory. θ is the green level coefficient of products, which is decided by the CO_2 emissions from the LRI operations, which can in turn be calculated by Equation (14); τ is the consumer environmental behaviors (CEBs), and a larger τ indicates that consumers are willing to pay a higher premium for greener products. CEBs can be calculated as $\tau = \int_{\underline{g}}^{\overline{g}} \tau(g)\beta$, where $\tau(g)$ is the CEBs of consumer group g, β is a correction factor of CEBs over time. We assume $\beta \geqslant 1$, because CEBs would not decrease over time; $\underline{g}$ is the consumer group with the worst CEBs, and $\overline{g}$ is the consumer group with the best CEBs. p is the price of the product, which is decided by θ and the CEBs τ. The market demand of a product depends on p, θ and τ. Conversely, operation-induced emissions and cost will be influenced by the market, which is important, especially in a situation of oversupply. To maximize profits, supply chain enterprises will certainly endeavor to meet consumers' preferences, so as to improve their businesses' performance.

3.2. Assumptions

We assume that the consumers are under symmetric information regarding products' carbon emissions. With the preferences displayed by CEBs, we aim to find the optimal supply chain network design and operational strategy.

(i) In this paper, the CEB choices focus on the carbon emissions from the LRI, including sourcing, production and/or recovery. It is reasonable to choose supply chain services as the study object, as they represent a major source of carbon emissions.

(ii) There is no difference among delivery routes, and the road conditions are nearly the same. In other words, the carbon emissions and costs are only affected by the distance travelled.

(iii) Each warehouse is assumed to follow a (Q, R) inventory policy. That is, when the inventory of a warehouse reaches the reorder point R, a fixed quantity Q is ordered from the upper stream plant.

(iv) The discussed products/services are in an oversupplied market. CEBs are in positive correlation with market demand. We assume the consumer demand function is expressed as:

$$D(p_x, \theta, \tau) = D_0 - \lambda_1 p_x + \frac{1}{2}\lambda_2 \tau \theta \tag{1}$$

where D_0 is the initial demand without considering CEBs or a premium for greener products, λ_1 is the market inverse demand coefficient, λ_2 is the attraction coefficient with the environmentally friendly level of products, and τ is the consumers' environmental preference for low carbon products. Obviously, the market demand is a decreasing function of price, and an increasing function of θ and τ.

4. The Model

4.1. A Multi-Objective Model for Cost and Carbon Emissions

There is a trade-off between cost and carbon emissions in supply chain operations. Generally, a set of optimal Pareto solutions (c_x, e_x) can be obtained, and particularly, the extreme values on the Pareto curve are $(\underline{c}, \bar{e})$ and $(\bar{c}, \underline{e})$. The aim of this paper is to find the optimal solution $(c_x{}^*, e_x{}^*)$ in the supply chain; one which will maximize profits while taking CEBs into consideration. For these operations, we should make the following decisions:

(i) Location decisions—how many warehouses should be opened, and where to locate the opened warehouses.

(ii) Routing decisions—how to assign the vehicle routes from manufacturers to warehouses (M-to-W) and from warehouses to Retailers (W-to-R).

(iii) Inventory decisions—what is the order quantity, and how many safety stocks should be maintained?

(iv) What is the most appropriate level of green to choose?

Thus, the decision variables can be denoted as

$$y_j = \begin{cases} 1, & \text{if warehouse } j \text{ is opened} \\ 0, & \text{otherwise} \end{cases}, \; j \in J$$

$$x_{ji}^r = \begin{cases} 1, & \text{if retailer } i \text{ is assigned to warehouse } j \\ 0, & \text{otherwise} \end{cases}, \; i \in I, j \in J$$

$$x_{kj}^p = \begin{cases} 1, & \text{if warehouse } j \text{ is assigned to manufacture } k \\ 0, & \text{otherwise} \end{cases} \quad , j \in J, k \in K$$

$$z_{miv} = \begin{cases} 1, & \text{if } m \text{ precedes } i \text{ in the route of vehicle } v \\ 0, & \text{otherwise} \end{cases} \quad , \forall m \in (I \cup J), i \in I.$$

Q_j is the order quantity of warehouse j.

The multi-objective function includes cost and carbon emissions from location, routing and inventory. First, the cost is composed using the following terms:

(i) Location cost. The cost of warehouse location is $\sum_{j \in J} f_j y_j$, where f_j is the single cost of opening warehouse j.

(ii) Routing cost occurs in the distribution from M-to-W and from warehouse to retailer (W-to-R), which are $\sum_{k \in K} \sum_{j \in J} t_1 d_{kj} x_{kj}^p$ and $\sum_{j \in J} \sum_{i \in I} \sum_{m \in (I \cup J)} t_2 d_{mi} z_{miv}$, respectively, where t_1 is the M-to-W routing cost per distance; d_{kj} is the distance from manufacturer k to warehouse j; t_2 is W-to-R routing cost per distance; and d_{mi} is the distance from warehouse j (or retailer k k) to retailer k'

(iii) Inventory cost. Working inventory is $\sum_{j \in J} \sum_{i \in I} (h_o \frac{\sum_{i \in I} \mu_i x_{ij}^r}{Q_j} + h_j \frac{Q_j}{2})$, and safety stock is $\sum_{j \in J} h_j z_\alpha \sqrt{L_j \sum_{i \in I} \sigma_i^2 x_{ji}^r}$ [22], where h_o is the ordering cost, μ_i is the demand by retailer i, h_j is the hold cost per unit; L_j is the lead time of DC j; z_α is left α-percentile of standard normal random variable Z, i.e., $P(Z \leqslant z_\alpha) = \alpha$ (α is the desired percentage of retailers' orders that should be satisfied); σ_i^2 is the variance of demand from retailer i.

The carbon emissions are composed of the following terms:

(i) Carbon emissions from facilities. The carbon emissions of a warehouse location can be denoted as $\sum_{j \in J} \hat{f}_j y_j$, where $\hat{f}_j$ is the carbon emissions of building warehouse j.

(ii) Carbon emissions from routing. The routing emissions from the M-to-W and W-to-R transportations are denoted as $\sum_{k \in K} \sum_{j \in J} \hat{t}_1 d_{kj} x_{kj}^p$ and $\sum_{j \in J} \sum_{i \in I} \sum_{m \in (I \cup J)} \hat{t}_2 d_{mi} z_{miv}$, respectively, where $\hat{t}_1$ is the M-to-W carbon emissions per distance, and $\hat{t}_2$ is the carbon emissions per distance from warehouse j (or retailer k) to retailer k'.

(iii) Carbon emissions from inventory. The inventory emissions come from the working inventory and safety stock, which are $\sum_{j \in J} \sum_{i \in I} \hat{h}_j \frac{Q_j}{2}$ and $\sum_{j \in J} \hat{h}_j z_\alpha \sqrt{L_j \sum_{i \in I} \sigma_i^2 x_{ji}^r}$, respectively, where $\hat{h}_j$ is the carbon emissions per holding inventory. It is worth mentioning that carbon emissions from inventory mainly refer to the energy consumption and product emissions during storage.

(iv) Other emissions, including emissions from purchasing, production and recovery. The purchasing emission is $Pur'.\sum_{i \in I} \mu_i$, where Pur' is carbon emissions from purchase per unit. The production emission is $Pn'.\sum_{i \in I} \mu_i$, where Pn' is carbon emissions from production per unit. The recovery emission is $Rcy'.\sum_{i \in I} \mu_i$, where Rcy' is carbon emissions from recovery per unit.

The multi-objective problem is formulated as follows:

$$\min c_x = (\sum_{j \in J} f_j y_j + \sum_{k \in K} \sum_{j \in J} t_1 d_{kj} x_{kj}^p + \sum_{j \in J} \sum_{i \in I} \sum_{m \in (I \cup J)} t_2 d_{mi} z_{miv} + \sum_{j \in J} \sum_{i \in I} (h_o \frac{\sum_{i \in I} \mu_i x_{ji}^r}{Q_j}$$

$$+ h_j \frac{Q_j}{2}) + \sum_{j \in J} h_j z_\alpha \sqrt{L_j \sum_{i \in I} \sigma_i^2 x_{ji}^r}) / \sum_{i \in I} \mu_i$$

(2)

$$\min e_x = \left(\sum_{j\in J} \hat{f}_j y_j + \sum_{k\in K}\sum_{j\in J} \hat{t}_1 d_{kj} x^p_{kj} + \sum_{j\in J}\sum_{i\in I}\sum_{m\in(I\cup J)} \hat{t}_2 d_{mi} z_{miv} + \sum_{j\in J}\sum_{i\in I} \hat{h}_j \frac{Q_j}{2}\right. \tag{3}$$

$$\left. + \sum_{j\in J} \hat{h}_j z_\alpha \sqrt{L_j \sum_{i\in I} \sigma_i^2 x^r_{ji}}\right)/\sum_{i\in I}\mu_i$$

$$\text{s.t. } Q_j + z_\alpha \sqrt{L_j \sum_{i\in I}\sigma_i^2 x^r_{ji}} \leq N_j, \ \forall j\in J \tag{4}$$

$$\sum_{i\in I}\sum_{m\in(I\cup J)} \mu_i z_{miv} \leq V^c, \ \forall m\in(I\cup J) \tag{5}$$

$$\sum_{v\in V}\sum_{m\in(I\cup J)} z_{miv} = 1, \ \forall i\in I \tag{6}$$

$$\sum_{j\in J}\sum_{i\in I} z_{jiv} \leq 1, \ \forall v\in V \tag{7}$$

$$\sum_{m\in(I\cup J)} z_{miv} - \sum_{m\in(I\cup J)} z_{imv} = 0, \ \forall i\in I, \ \forall v\in V, \ \forall m\in(I\cup J) \tag{8}$$

$$R_{iv} - R_{mv} + (n_r \times z_{miv}) \leq n_r - 1, \ \forall i\in I, \ \forall m\in(I\cup J), \ \forall v\in V \tag{9}$$

$$y_j = \{0,1\}, \ \forall j\in J, \ \forall n\in N_j \tag{10}$$

$$x^p_{kj} = \{0,1\}, \ \forall k\in K, \ \forall j\in J \tag{11}$$

$$x^r_{ji} = \{0,1\}, \ \forall j\in J, \ \forall i\in I \tag{12}$$

$$z_{miv} = \{0,1\}, \ \forall m\in(I\cup J), \ i\in I, \ \forall v\in V. \tag{13}$$

Equation (2) minimizes the cost of the CLRIP, where the first three terms are the fixed location cost, inventory cost, and routing cost, respectively. Equation (3) minimizes the carbon emissions. Equation (4) restricts the inventory in warehouse j to remain within its capacity N_j. Equation (5) restricts the load of each vehicle to within its capacity V^c. Equation (6) ensures one and only one vehicle serves any retailer. Equation (7) requires that each vehicle serves no more than one warehouse. The flow conservation Equation (8) states that a vehicle entering a node must also leave the node, so as to ensure the route is circular. The sub-tour elimination Equation (9) guarantees that each tour contains a warehouse, from which the tour originates and some retailers [32], where R_{iv} is an auxiliary variable defined for retailer i for sub-tour elimination in the route of vehicle v, n_r is the number of retailers. Equations (10)–(13) enforce the decision variables to remain within their respective domains.

4.2. The Revenue Model Considering CEBs

This study focuses on the effects of CEBs on the task of designing a supply chain network, which includes making LRI decisions. CEBs not only affect consumers' willingness to pay premium prices for greener products, but they also affect the market demand for such products. This willingness to pay varies greatly across industries and consumer groups and also changes in intensity over time [4]. If anything, carbon emissions due to logistics operations have been a concern for a considerable length of time, as these operations are a major source of emissions. We are interested in determining how to maximize earnings, as well as how to improve competition, through the influence of CEBs in three supply chain network structures which include location, routing and inventory considerations.

As non-green products have already been in circulation for many years, the general optimal decision is based on cost minimization. In this study, however, in addition to cost, we also consider carbon emissions as a benchmark. There is a terminal consumer group with an average CEB in the market. The green level θ is closely related to the carbon emissions from the supply chain. It has been proven that the carbon emissions and cost are in negative correlation, and thus, we assume that the optimal cost corresponds to a poor performance in relation to carbon emissions, and vice versa. Specifically, with an operation map, we can connect inputs $[\underline{c}, \bar{c}]$ to corresponding outputs $[\bar{e}, \underline{e}]$. Then θ can be denoted as

$$\theta = \bar{e}/e_x \tag{14}$$

where e_x is the actual carbon emission, and thus $(\theta - 1)$ is the carbon abatement ratio. p is the price of non-green products, $(\underline{c}, \bar{e})$ represents the cost and carbon emissions, and p_x is the price with (c_x, e_x). As we know, the marginal cost of carbon reduction increases by degrees. The "low hanging fruit" effect also indicates that initial basic improvement is easier, but the cleanup is harder. Thus, the above situation is considered, and the price of a product with green level θ is

$$p_x = p\theta^2 \tag{15}$$

It is worth noting that product price is a quadratic function of θ, since the environmental improvement has an increasing marginal cost, and production price is worked out to the costing. The quadratic function is commonly used to describe the cost related to the product's environmental improvement. That is, each additional increment of emissions reduction is more difficult, and hence costlier to achieve [8]. Also, from the market's perspective, consumers with CEBs are willing to pay a premium price for green products. The greener the product, the more expensive it will be. In addition, for an advanced green product, too, even a small improvement will result in a significant price increase. This increase is deemed to be reasonable.

The aim is to find an optimal portfolio (c_x, e_x) under this context. The basic profit function can be defined as

$$\prod = (p_x - c_x - c_0)D - \varepsilon \tag{16}$$

where constant c_0 is the unit cost of raw materials, and ε is other expenditure, which can be ignored in most cases.

Substituting Equations (1)–(15) into Equation (16), then:

$$\prod = (p\theta^2 - c_x - c_0)(D_0 - \lambda_1 p\theta^2 + \frac{1}{2}\lambda_2 \tau \theta) \tag{17}$$

Based on Equation (17), if there is no CEB, the enterprise loses the motivation to reduce carbon emissions, which is consistent with the traditional model. We assume the traditional model has revenue of $\prod^C$, with the only measure being the cost, and we mark it as model PC. In this condition, $\theta = 1$, $\tau = 0$, thus:

$$\prod^C = (p - \underline{c} - c_0)(D_0 - \lambda_1 p) \tag{18}$$

Enterprises have an incentive to join in carbon reduction practices only when $\prod - \prod^c > 0$. c_0 is the same constant in $\prod$ and $\prod^c$, and thus can be ignored. Then, enterprises will participate in carbon emissions when $(p\theta^2 - c_x)(D_0 - \lambda_1 p\theta^2 + \frac{1}{2}\lambda_2 \tau \theta) > (p - \underline{c})(D_0 - \lambda_1 p)$, and thus $c_x < p\theta^2 - \dfrac{(p - \underline{c})(D_0 - \lambda_1 p)}{D_0 - \lambda_1 p\theta^2 + \dfrac{1}{2}\lambda_2 \tau \theta}$. Actually, θ is a function of e_x; the relationship between c_x and e_x is important, and it will be solved in the next section.

5. Solving Approach

5.1. Particle Swarm Optimization Algorithm

The particle swarm optimization (PSO) algorithm was first proposed by Kennedy and Eberhart [32]. It is a population-based optimization technique and is becoming very popular, due mainly to its simplicity of implementation and ability to quickly converge to a reasonably good solution [33]. It has been extensively applied to many complex network optimization problems. In the PSO heuristic procedure, a swarm of particles is retained in the search process. Each particle follows a specific trajectory in the search space, and each step of the particle determines a trial solution. Each particle has knowledge of its previous best experience, as well as the best global experience of the entire swarm. The current best fitness of, *i.e.*, the best solution found so far by particle p is represented by $\mathbf{x}_{pbest_p}$, while the global best fitness among all particles is represented by $\mathbf{x}_{gbest}$. The velocity and position of particle p at iteration (time) t in dimension d are represented by $v_{pd}(t)$ and $x_{pd}(t)$, respectively. Each particle updates its direction at time t according to Equation (19) in the following [32]:

$$v_{pd}(t) = \omega v_{pd}(t-1) + c_1 r_1(t)(\mathbf{x}_{pbest_{pd}} - \mathbf{x}_{pd}(t)) + c_2 r_2(t)(\mathbf{x}_{gbest} - \mathbf{x}_{pd}(t)) \qquad (19)$$

where ω is the inertia influencing the local and global ability of the particle; usually a value between 0.2 to 0.6 is recommended; c_1 and c_2 are cognitive and social learning rates, respectively, and $r_1(t)$ and $r_2(t)$ are two uniform random numbers such that $r_1, r_2 \in [0, 1]$.

The position of particle p is then updated according to Equation (20) in the following

$$x_{pd}(t) = x_{pd}(t-1) + v_{pd}(t) \qquad (20)$$

The update of velocity and the position process is repeated for every dimension and for all particles in the swarm. Eventually the swarm as a whole, like a flock of birds collectively foraging for food, is likely to move close to an optimum of the fitness function [33].

5.2. The Hybrid PSO

The multi-objective model contains location and routing assignments involving binary decisions. Multi-objective programming problems with binary variables cannot be directly processed using the Multi-objective Particle Swarm Optimization (MOPSO) heuristic procedure. Following Shankar *et al.* [33], the velocity of a particle should be modified if x_d is binary. The modified velocity can be updated as:

$$v_{pd}(t) = v_{pd}(t-1) + r_1(t)(\mathbf{x}_{pbest_{pd}} - x_{pd}(t-1)) + r_2(t)(\mathbf{x}_{gbest} - x_{pd}(t-1)) \qquad (21)$$

where $r_1(t)$ and $r_2(t)$ are two random numbers. The position of particle p can be updated as:

$$x_{pd}(t) = \begin{cases} 0, & \text{If } \rho_{pd} < s(v_{pd}(t)) \\ 1, & \text{If } \rho_{pd} \geqslant s(v_{pd}(t)) \end{cases} \qquad (22)$$

where ρ_{pd} is a uniformly distributed random number such that $\rho_{pd} \in [0, 1]$ and $s(v_{pd}(t))$ is the probability threshold given by $s(v_{pd}) = \dfrac{1}{1 + \exp(-v_{pd}(t))}$. In the MOPSO heuristic procedure, the velocity and positions of the continuous particles are updated according to Equations (19) and (20), respectively, while those of the binary variables are updated according to Equations (21) and (22), respectively.

5.3. An Improved Constraint of the MOPSO

In order to improve the ability of the heuristic procedure to search the edges crossing unconnected parts of the feasible region, and also to obtain global non-dominated solutions, some infeasible solutions that are near the feasible solutions are retained in the swarm at the beginning of the search process. A constraint that restricts the infeasibility degree of the constraints is used. At the end of the solution process, all particles retained in the swarm must be feasible. Any infeasible particles will be deleted from the external file gradually, throughout the progress of the search process. A dynamic self-adapting process is needed to control the infeasibility degree in the heuristic procedure. In the multi-objective programming model, the ℓth inequality constraint can be written as $g_\ell(\mathbf{x}) \leqslant 0$ and the ℓ'th equality constraint can be written as $h_{\ell'}(\mathbf{x}) - \delta = 0$. The infeasibility of a trail solution $\mathbf{x}$ can be quantized as follows:

$$C(\mathbf{x}) = \sum_{\ell} \max(g_\ell(\mathbf{x}), 0) + \sum_{\ell'} \max(|h_{\ell'}(\mathbf{x}) - \delta|, 0) \tag{23}$$

In Equation (23), δ is a permissible deviation, such that $\delta > 0$ and is very small. If $\mathbf{x} \in X$, $C(\mathbf{x}) = 0$. A dynamic infeasibility threshold ε is used that guarantees the final solutions are all feasible. This threshold is defined as:

$$\varepsilon = \begin{cases} \varepsilon_0 \times (1 - 5t/4T), & \text{if } t \leqslant 0.8T \\ 0, & \text{if } t > 0.8T \end{cases} \tag{24}$$

where ε_0 is the initial allowable deviation of all the constraints. Obviously, ε decreases with the increase in the number of evolutionary generations. In the searching process, the solution $\mathbf{x}$ is retained if $C(\mathbf{x}) \leqslant \varepsilon$; otherwise it is discarded.

5.4. Selecting the Optimal Particles

The solution of the MOPSO optimization problem is different from a single objective optimization problem. With a single objective problem, it is easy to know which particles are the personal best (pbest) and global best (gbest). With the MOPSO, however, it is difficult to judge which particles are pbest and gbest, because the particles are often non-dominate solutions. However, it is important to pick suitable pbest and gbest particles, since each particle must change its position, as guided by pbest and gbest. Each particle moves toward the non-dominated frontier during the search process [34].

The selection for pbest is relatively simple compared to gbest. A method called Prandom is used in this study, according to which a single pbest is maintained. Pbest is replaced if a new value < pbest, or else, if the new value is found to be mutually non-dominating with pbest, one of the two is randomly selected to be the new best [35]. Before the selection for gbest, there are still some works to illustrate. In the MOPSO algorithm, we usually store the non-dominate solutions in archive, and the archive has a limited capacity. Thus, in order to maintain the archive, the crowding distance should be measured as a base for reserving or discarding non-dominate solutions. The crowding distance dt_{ij} can be calculated as:

$$dt_{ij} = \sqrt{\sum_{l=1}^{k} f_l(X_i) - f_l(X_j)^2} \tag{25}$$

where $f_l(X)$ denotes the objective functions in the dimension l. According to Equation (25), the crowding distance matrix can be indicated as:

$$DT = \begin{bmatrix} dt_{11} & dt_{12} & \cdots & dt_{1n} \\ dt_{21} & dt_{22} & \cdots & dt_{2n} \\ \vdots & \vdots & \vdots & \vdots \\ dt_{n1} & dt_{n2} & \cdots & dt_{nn} \end{bmatrix} \tag{26}$$

where n is the number of non-dominate solutions in the archive. Set S and A represents the populations with particles and archive storing, non-dominate solutions. The particles in S can be divided into two types. One set (S1) is comprised of particles that are dominated by at least one of the non-dominate solutions in A. The other set (S2) is comprised of particles that are not dominated by any one solution in A. $S = S1 \cup S2$. In the same way, archive A can also be divided into three types. Set A1 is the non-dominate solutions, which dominate at least one of the particles in S. Set A2 is the non-dominate solutions which have the same position with the particles in S. Set A3 is comprised of the other non-dominate solutions. $A = A1 \cup A2 \cup A3$. Figure 2 shows the mapping relations of S and A.

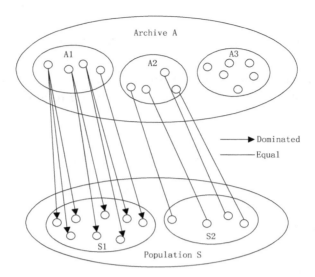

Figure 2. The mapping relationship of archive A and population S.

For the MOPSO algorithm, the diversity and convergence of population are contradictory issues. One contradiction is the diversity, which guarantees the global best while avoiding the local optimal. The other is the convergence, which promotes particles approaching the Pareto frontier as far as possible. Hence, for particles in S1, if we select non-dominate solutions in A1, which dominate the particles as gbest, the search engines would speed up. However, this can lead to a premature problem. For particles in S2, the global best selection strategy would lead those particles moving to less crowded regions to improve the capability of a global search.

Regardless, each non-dominate solution in the archive has its unique feature. To maintain the diversity of an algorithm, each should have a chance to become a global guide. When paired with these factors, two properties, f_{ri} and f_{pi}, are given for non-dominate solutions in the archive. f_{ri} denotes how often the non-dominate solution is selected as gbest, and f_{pi} denotes how many particles in the current population select the non-dominate solution as gbest. Generally, the size of f_{pi} should be restricted. If one gbest is selected by too many particles, the result would be particles converging to a limited region. Based on our experience, we use $f_{pi} \leqslant 0.05N$, where N is the number of particles [36].

Putting the above pieces together, the global best can be selected as follows:

(i)   For each particle in S1, we select a non-dominate solution that randomly dominates the particle from A1 as gbest, but $f_{pi} \leqslant 0.05N$ is necessary. If no solution is found, the gbest should be selected from the A1 with greater crowding distance and smaller f_{ri}.

(ii) For each particle in S2, a random probability model is employed to select gbest from the A2 with greater crowding distance and smaller f_{ri}.

The pseudo-code of MOPSO algorithm depicting the entire process is given as follows:

(1)   Initialize positions and velocities of all particles.
(2)   Set the current particle position as Pbest.
(3)   While (iter_count < T)
(4)   for each particle (i = 1:n)
(5)   Select a gbest from the archive.
(6)   Update velocity and position.
(7)   Evaluate the fitness values of the current particle i.
(8)   Update the pbest of each particle by comparison criteria.
(9)   End for
(10) Update archive by non-dominate solutions.
(11) For each particle in archive

(12) If $f_{pi} \leqslant 0.05N$

(13) Select a dominate solution with greater crowding distance and smaller f_{ri} from archive as gbest randomly.

(14) End if

(15) End for

(16) Output

(17) End while

6. Computational Experiment

In this section, we evaluate the presented model using a set of numerical data from a real case. The problem is solved by the MOPSO method with Matlab 7.01 on a PC with Intel core i5 and 2.4 GHz. Then, the effects of CEBs and green levels on the decision process are comprehensively analyzed. Finally, some managerial insights are presented.

6.1. Case Study

We consider the experiment based on a case study from the petrochemical industry. Specifically, data from the Northeast Chemical Sales Company of the China National Petroleum Corporation (CNPC) (Beijing, China) was studied. CNPC is a large group, and its supply chain network is responsible for transporting petrochemicals from plants, via warehouses, to retailers. This transportation operation involves location, routing and inventory decisions, as well as the creation of considerable carbon emissions. In this paper, a section of the operational data was analyzed. Specifically, this case study involves two plants, five potential warehouses with retailing functions and eight retailers. Each trajectory is relative to a routing cost and the amount of carbon emission. The routings and distances are shown in Figure 3. The parameters of the warehouses and retailers are listed in Tables 1–3. In addition, the market inverse demand coefficient is set as 5500, and the attraction coefficient with the environment level of products is set as 5000. CEB is 1, and the routing cost per distance of M-to-W and W-to-R are all equal to q. The order cost is 500, and the capacity of each vehicle is 1500. In addition, $\hat{f}_j^A = 29.3N_j$, the carbon emissions per distance are 0.17, and the carbon emissions per inventory are 0.00276.

Table 1. The parameters of potential warehouses.

	Beijing	Tianjin	Cangzhou	Jinan	Zhengzhou
Lead time(days)	3	5	6	4	8
Demand variance	12	14	9	11	8
Service level	95%	95%	95%	95%	95%

Table 2. The area and fixed location cost of potential DC.

	Area of Location (m^2)	Fixed Location Cost (¥)	Hold Cost (¥/ton Day)
Beijing	3000	2,000,000	0.3
Tianjin	3600	1,800,000	0.25
Cangzhou	4000	1,120,000	0.3
Jinnan	4200	1,560,000	0.25
Zhengzhou	5000	1,870,000	0.3

Table 3. The parameters of retailers.

	Beijing	Tianjin	Baoding	Cangzhou	Shijiazhuang	Jinan	Liaocheng	Linyi	Qingdao	Xinyang	Zhengzhou	Taiyuan	Yuncheng
Initial demand	430	416	463	577	506	509	522	439	536	696	589	554	694
Service level	92%	91%	95%	95%	90%	98%	91%	94%	95%	95%	95%	95%	90%
Demand variance	9	12	7	8	14	6	6	9	9	11	9	7	9

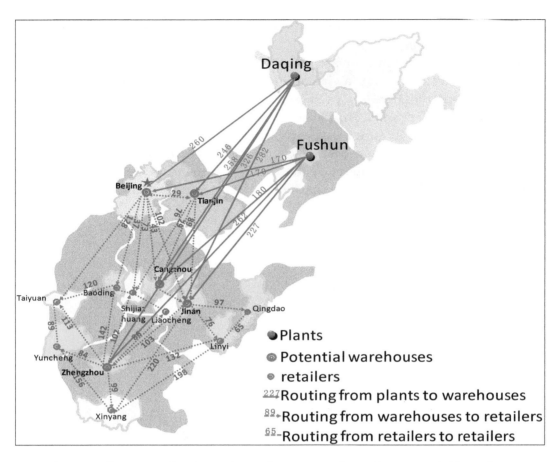

Figure 3. The network of two plants, five potential warehouses and 14 retailers.

6.2. Numerical Analysis

According to the above data and the approach used to solve the question in Section 5, the trade-off between cost and carbon emissions can be shown as Figure 4. The result provides decision makers with decidedly indifferent choices. In conclusion, all the points on the Pareto line are the solutions, but the managers themselves cannot directly decide. If CEBs are incorporated, the optimal solution is unique (Figure 5). Clearly, revenue first increases and then decreases with increasing carbon emissions. The increasing gradient is greater than the decreasing gradient. This result illustrates that a proper carbon reduction policy can improve corporate revenue, but excessive carbon reduction activities would have a negative impact. Figure 5 shows that the maximum attainable revenue is ¥601,230,000. The optimal configuration can be shown as follows: The location decision is to open Cangzhou, Jinan, and Zhengzhou. The routing decision is divided into two parts. (i) As regards the routing from plants to warehouses, the first decision is that Daqing serves Cangzhou and Jinan, while Fushun serves Zhengzhou. (ii) Considering transportation from warehouses to retailers, the routing schedule of the Cangzhou warehouse is Cangzhou-Tianjin-Beijing-Baoding-Cangzhou-Shijiazhuang-Taiyuan-Cangzhou. The routing schedule for the Jinan warehouse is Jinan-Liaocheng-Linyi-Qingdao-Jinan, and the routing schedule for the Zhengzhou warehouse is Zhengzhou-Xinyang-Yuncheng-Zhengzhou. The order quantities of the three warehouses are 4792, 3156 and 2834 tons, respectively.

We are interested in how CEBs affect companies' decision making. As we know, CEBs mainly affect demand. The effect of consumers' environmental preference on demand for products with different carbon emissions is shown in Figure 6. We vary the CEBs from 1 to 1.8 and obtain a series of demand *vs.* carbon emissions. Clearly, the curves move from left to right as the coefficient increases from 1 to 1.8, which implies that with the same carbon emission levels, larger CEBs lead to greater demand. This is due to the fact that when consumers pay closer attention to environmental protection, enterprises are more likely to take actions that will improve their environmental protection levels. Then, consumers with greater environmental awareness will buy more products from those enterprises with superior eco-friendly operations. This is a virtuous cycle. However, the marginal cost of implementing environmental improvements increases by degrees. As we know, the ultimate goal of enterprise management is to maximize benefits. Similarly, we adjust the carbon emissions variable to analyze the effect of CEBs on revenue (Figure 7). Clearly, revenue increases as the CEBs move from 1 to 1.8. However, the degree of revenue growth is clearly slower than the increasing CEBs. That is to say, the initial improvement brought about by the CEBs greatly affects the operation of supply chain enterprises, but this effect will weaken because of the high costs associated with further reductions of carbon emissions.

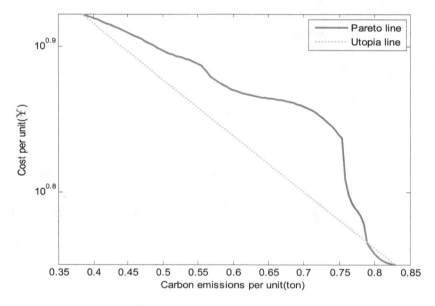

Figure 4. Pareto optimal curve between cost and carbon emissions.

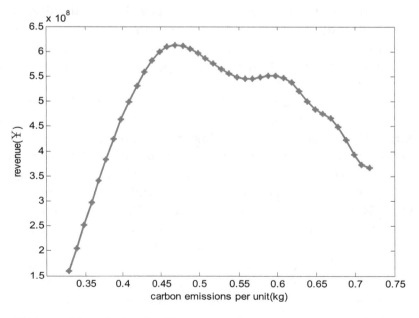

Figure 5. The relationship between carbon emissions and revenue.

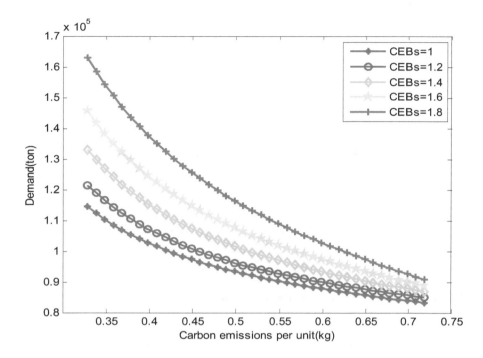

Figure 6. The demand in different consumer environmental preferences varying with carbon emissions.

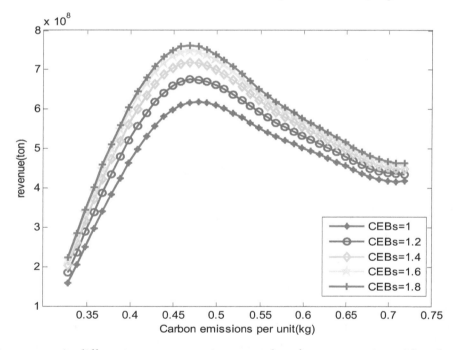

Figure 7. The revenue in different consumer environmental preferences varying with carbon emissions.

We assume that product pricing is a function of carbon emissions. However, it is not a hard and absolute fact that pricing is the single, key factor. Our analysis (Figure 8) shows that higher prices generate greater revenue. What is important is that the higher the price of a product, the bigger the revenue will be obtained with lower carbon emissions. This illustrates that a higher price for green products can stimulate a reduction in carbon emissions, but that higher price can also curb product demand (Figure 9). Clearly, product pricing is increasing with a reduction in carbon emissions. When the price increases, the product demand decreases. In this case, the consumer's willingness to pay is the most important factor. Hence, the enterprise should encourage consumers to improve their CEBs, and pay closer attention to purchasing green products.

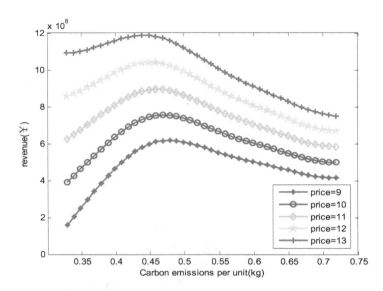

Figure 8. The revenue *vs.* carbon emissions in different product pricing.

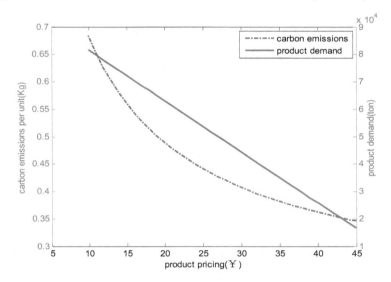

Figure 9. The relationship between product pricing -carbon emissions, and product pricing-product demand.

6.3. Managerial Insights

In the current business climate, enterprises and consumers have gradually come to recognize the importance of environmental protection. Both businesses and consumers are more inclined to make an effort to reduce carbon emissions. In particular, consumers with greater environmental awareness are happy to pay a premium price for low carbon emission products. This willingness, which is based on increased environmental awareness, provides an opportunity for logistics enterprises. Our study is consistent with the work of Liu *et al.* [8], which found that, with consumers' greater environmental awareness, more of them are willing to pay higher prices for low carbon emission products. In turn, the enterprises that produce those products can earn greater revenue.

In addition, the companies that produce low carbon emissions should also make a concerted marketing effort to shift consumers' traditional purchasing decision criteria and transform those buyers into a group with a preference for low carbon emission products and services. This study indicates that the returns can be substantial if consumers who are currently not interested in purchasing environmentally friendly products make even a little progress. Moreover, the results show that low carbon emission operations cost more than the operations that do not consider carbon emissions.

However, when the CEBs are positive, an optimal degree of carbon reduction will maximize revenue. Sadly, the unavoidable fact is that most consumers loathe paying to pay premium prices for low carbon emission products. If enterprises are going to implement sustainable decisions, they must be certain of CEBs.

7. Conclusions

This paper discussed the effects of consumer environmental behaviors (CEBs) on the design of a sustainable supply chain. CEBs not only affect consumers' willingness to pay premium prices for low carbon emission products, but also the overall demand for low carbon emission products. We introduced a sustainable supply chain network model based on the joint optimization of location, routing and inventory, taking carbon emissions into consideration. The distinguishing feature of our model is its consideration of the CEBs, which affect both carbon emission decisions and product demand.

First, a multi-objective model is constructed, which provides a trade-off between costs and carbon emissions. The MOPSO algorithm is used to solve the model, and then a Pareto optimal set can be obtained. After that, we model the revenue function based on the Pareto solutions. In the computational experiments, we test the model by the data from the Northeast Chemical Sales Company of CNPC. We first obtain the Pareto optimal curve, which provides a portfolio of configurations for decision makers. Then, we can use the same technique to obtain the revenue curves from different carbon emissions. Hence, the unique optimal revenue levels and the relevant decisions can be acquired. Finally, the sensitivity of the case study was analyzed. We are interested in the effects of CEBs on the demand and revenue in a three-level supply chain. The results show that more positive CEBs result in greater demand and higher revenue. We also observe that the pricing of low carbon operations is critical. Therefore, enterprises should make marketing efforts to strengthen consumers' environmental preferences. Companies should support their claims to consumers and ensure the degree of CEBs before implementing their carbon emission reduction policies.

Further research is required to determine more specific factors pertaining to CEBs in a supply chain (e.g., the decision makers' appetite for risk, the expectations of market development and the effects of government intervention via carbon emission reduction policies and legislation), so that the model will be more adaptive to real-life scenarios.

Acknowledgments: The authors would like to express our sincere thanks to the anonymous referees and editors for their time and patience devoted to the review of this paper. This work is supported by NSFC Grant (No. 71572031).

Author Contributions: Jinhuan Tang proposed the model, write and revise the whole paper. Shoufeng Ji contributes to join the research and give many valuable suggestions. Liwen Jiang is responsible for the solving method, especially in the game theory, she made an enormous contribution.

References

1. Hufbauer, G.C.; Charnovitz, S.; Kim, J. *Global Warming and the World Trading System*; Peterson Institute for International Economics: Washington, DC, USA, 2009.
2. Chistra, K. In search of the green consumers: A perceptual study. *J. Serv. Res.* **2007**, *7*, 173–191.
3. Conrad, K. Price competition and product differentiation when consumers care for the environment. *Environ. Resour. Econ.* **2005**, *31*, 1–19. [CrossRef]
4. Laroche, M.; Bergeron, J.; Barbaro-Forleo, G. Targeting consumers who are willing to pay more for environmentally friendly products. *J. Consum. Market.* **2001**, *18*, 503–520. [CrossRef]
5. Moon, W.; Florkowski, W.J.; Brückner, B.; Schonhof, I. Willing to pay for environmental practices: Implications for eco-labeling. *Land Econ.* **2002**, *78*, 88–102. [CrossRef]
6. Ghosh, D.; Shah, J. A comparative analysis of greening policies across supply chain structures. *Int. J. Prod. Econ.* **2012**, *135*, 568–583. [CrossRef]

7.   Gil-Moltó, M.J.; Varvarigos, D. Emission taxes and the adoption of cleaner technologies: The case of environmentally conscious consumers. *Resour. Energy Econ.* **2013**, *35*, 486–504. [CrossRef]

8.   Liu, Z.L.; Anderson, T.D.; Cruz, J.M. Consumer environmental awareness and competition in two-stage supply chains. *Eur. J. Oper. Res.* **2012**, *218*, 602–613. [CrossRef]

9.   Elhedhli, S.; Merrick, R. Green supply chain network design to reduce carbon emissions. *Transp. Res. Part D* **2012**, *17*, 370–379. [CrossRef]

10.   Paksoy, T.; Özceylan, E.; Weber, G.W.; Barsoum, N.; Weber, G.W.; Vasant, P. A multi objective model for optimization of a green supply chain network. *Glob. J. Technol. Optim.* **2011**, *2*, 84–96.

11.   Paksoy, T.; Özceylan, E. Environmentally conscious optimization of supply chain networks. *J. Oper. Res. Soc.* **2013**, *65*, 855–872. [CrossRef]

12.   Benjaafar, S.; Li, Y.; Daskin, M. Carbon footprint and the management of supply chains: Insights from simple models. *IEEE Trans. Autom. Sci. Eng.* **2013**, *10*, 99–115. [CrossRef]

13.   Kim, N.S.; Janic, M.; Van Wee, B. Trade-off between carbon dioxide emissions and logistics costs based on multiobjective optimization. *Transp. Res. Rec. J. Transp. Res. Board* **2009**, *2139*, 107–116. [CrossRef]

14.   Wang, F.; Lai, X.F.; Shi, N. A multi-objective optimization for green supply chain network design. *Decis. Support Syst.* **2011**, *51*, 262–269. [CrossRef]

15.   Chaabane, A.; Ramudhin, A.; Paquet, M. Design of sustainable supply chains under the emission trading scheme. *Int. J. Prod. Econ.* **2012**, *135*, 37–49. [CrossRef]

16.   Chen, X.; Benjaafar, S.; Elomri, A. The carbon-constrained EOQ. *Oper. Res. Lett.* **2013**, *41*, 172–179. [CrossRef]

17.   Babiker, M.H.; Criqui, P.; Ellerman, A.D.; Reilly, J.M.; Viguier, L.L. Assessing the impact of carbon tax differentiation in the European Union. *Environ. Model. Assess.* **2003**, *8*, 187–197. [CrossRef]

18.   Jabali, O.; Woensel, T.V.; de Kok, A.G. Analysis of Travel Times and CO_2 Emissions in Time-Dependent Vehicle Routing. *Prod. Oper. Manag.* **2012**, *21*, 1060–1074. [CrossRef]

19.   Nagy, G.; Salhi, S. Location-routing: Issues, models and methods. *Eur. J. Oper. Res.* **2007**, *177*, 649–672. [CrossRef]

20.   Dror, M.; Ball, M. Inventory/routing: Reduction from an annual to a short-period problem. *Naval Res. Logist. (NRL)* **1987**, *34*, 891–905. [CrossRef]

21.   Shen, Z.J.M.; Coullard, C.; Daskin, M.S. A joint location-inventory model. *Transp. Sci.* **2003**, *37*, 40–55. [CrossRef]

22.   AhmadiJavid, A.; Azad, N. Incorporating location, routing and inventory decisions in supply chain network design. *Transp. Res. Part E Logist. Transp. Rev.* **2010**, *46*, 582–597. [CrossRef]

23.   Ahmadi-Javid, A.; Seddighi, A.H. A location-routing-inventory model for designing multisource distribution networks. *Eng. Optim.* **2012**, *44*, 637–656. [CrossRef]

24.   Hua, G.W.; Cheng, T.C.E.; Wang, S.Y. Managing carbon footprints in inventory management. *Int. J. Prod. Econ.* **2011**, *132*, 178–185. [CrossRef]

25.   Kroes, J.; Subramanian, R.; Subramanyam, R. Operational compliance levers, environmental performance, and firm performance under cap and trade regulation. *Manuf. Serv. Oper. Manag.* **2012**, *14*, 186–201. [CrossRef]

26.   Diabat, A.; David, S. A Carbon-Capped Supply Chain Network Problem. In Proceedings of the IEEE International Conference on Industrial Engineering and Engineering Management, Hong Kong, China, 8–11 December 2009; IEEE press: Piscataway, NJ, USA, 2010; pp. 523–527.

27.   Wygonik, E.; GooDChild, A. Evaluating CO_2 emissions, cost and service quality trade-offs in an urban delivery system case study. *IATSS Res.* **2011**, *35*, 7–15. [CrossRef]

28.   Thøgersen, J. Promoting Green Consumer Behavior with Eco-Labels. In *New Tools for Environmental Protection: Education, Information, and Voluntary Measures*; Dietz, T., Stern, P., Eds.; National Academy Press: Washington, DC, USA, 2002; pp. 83–104.

29.   Young, W.; Hwang, K.; McDonald, S.; Oates, C.J. Sustainable consumption: Green consumer behaviour when purchasing products. *Sustain. Dev.* **2010**, *18*, 20–31. [CrossRef]

30.   Vanclay, J.K.; Shortiss, J.; Aulsebrook, A.; Gillespie, A.M.; Howell, B.C.; Johanni, R.; Maher, M.J.; Mitchell, K.M. Customer response to carbon labeling of groceries. *J. Consum. Policy* **2011**, *34*, 153–160. [CrossRef]

31.   Tang, C.S.; Zhou, S. Research advances in environmentally and socially sustainable operations. *Eur. J. Oper. Res.* **2012**, *223*, 585–594. [CrossRef]

32. Desrochers, M.; Laporte, G. Improvements and extensions to the Miller-Tucker-Zemlin subtour elimination constraints. *Oper. Res. Lett.* **1991**, *10*, 27–36. [CrossRef]

33. Kennedy, J.; Eberhart, R. Particle swarm optimization. In Proceedings of the IEEE International Conference on Neural Networks, Perth, Australia, 27 November–1 December 1995; pp. 1942–1948.

34. Shankar, B.L.; Basavarajappa, S.; Chen, J.C.; Kadadevaramath, R.S. Location and allocation decisions for multi-echelon supply chain network–a multi-objective evolutionary approach. *Expert Syst. Appl.* **2013**, *40*, 551–562. [CrossRef]

35. Everson, R.M.; Fieldsend, J.E.; Singh, S. Full Elite Sets for Multi-Objective Optimisation. In *Adaptive Computing in Design and Manufacture V*; Springer: London, UK, 2002; pp. 343–354.

36. Ling, H.F.; Zhou, X.Z.; Jiang, X.L.; Xiao, Y.H. Improved constrained multi-objective particle optimization algorithm. *J. Comput. Appl.* **2012**, *32*, 1320–1324.

5

The Effect of the Internal Side of Social Responsibility on Firm Competitive Success in the Business Services Industry

M. Isabel Sánchez-Hernández [1], Dolores Gallardo-Vázquez [2], Agnieszka Barcik [3] and Piotr Dziwiński [4,*]

[1]   Business Administration and Sociology Department, School of Economics, University of Extremadura, Ave. Elvas s/n, Badajoz 06006, Spain; isanchez@unex.es

[2]   Financial Economics and Accountancy Department, School of Economics, University of Extremadura, Ave. Elvas s/n, Badajoz 06006, Spain; dgallard@unex.es

[3]   Department of Management and Transport, University of Bielsko-Biała, Willowa 2, Bielsko-Biala 43-309, Poland; abarcik@ath.bielsko.pl

[4]   Department of Law and Administration, The University of Dąbrowa Górnicza, Cieplaka 1c, Dąbrowa Górnicza 43-300, Poland

*   Correspondence: pdziwinski@wsb.edu.pl.

Academic Editor: Adam Jabłoński

Abstract: This work focuses on the internal side of social responsibility of organizations in a regional context. Through a survey of 590 managers in classical business services (human-capital intensive) and representative of the productive economy of the Region of Extremadura (Spain), an empirical analysis is conducted. First, a factor analysis is conducted to explore the main dimensions of the internal face of Social Responsibility and second, a structural equations model is developed to look for a relationship with business competitiveness. Business performance and innovation are also considered in the model. The main contribution of the article is the establishment of a set of indicators that will help to build an ongoing and meaningful dialogue with employees improving their quality of life at work that will also serve as important guidance for the increasing of the firm's competitiveness through responsible human resources practices. Some suggestions for a research agenda emerge from this first attempt to approach the internal side of responsibility in business.

Keywords: human recources management (HRM); internal social responsibility (ISR); service sector; social responsibility (SR)

1. Introduction

The rise of service economy has been the predominant pattern over the last few years [1–3]. We know a great deal about the organization and management of Social Responsibility (SR) and the link with Human Resources Management (HRM), but comparatively little about how applicable this is to the service sector. In this work, we identify the components of the internal side of Social Responsibility in the services industry.

Freeman [4] gave a broad definition of stakeholders as any group or individual who can affect or is affected by the achievement of the organization's objectives. This author also highlights how *stakeholders* are simply constituents within and outside the organization, who have a stake in an organization's functioning and outcomes. The well-known *Stakeholder Theory* offers an instrumental value in providing a framework for guiding the actions of organizational members to ensure that the relationships that contribute to their financial viability are managed responsibly [5,6]. Some authors refer to the moral claim on the actions of the firms to define the stakeholders [7] such as consumers, employees, competitors, suppliers, government, as well as other actors in society. It is evident that the firm responds to multiple *stakeholders* for different reasons and in various ways [8,9].

According to the *Stakeholder Theory*, it is generally recognized that Social Responsibility (SR) has two dimensions: the external dimension and the internal one. On the one hand, the external dimension of SR is reflected in a large relationship of organizations with their communities. Companies interact with their external stakeholders when they provide business operations by guaranteeing economic activity, tax revenues, investing in the local economic system, concluding contracts with the local distributors, respecting human rights, and encouraging protection activities on environment by considering environmental concerns in business operations. On the other hand, the understudied internal side of SR has the emphasis on employees. Mason and Simmons [10] say that employees expect SR values similar to other stakeholders, arguing that employees seek functional, economic, psychological, and ethical benefits from their employing organizations. In this sense, if employers provide challenging, stimulating and fulfilling work, some functional benefits will be obtained and it will also be perceived as indicative of a socially responsible employer and a main driver of Internal Social Responsibility (ISR) practices [11,12].

In general terms, SR has been considered to be "an organization's obligation to maximize its positive impact on stakeholders and to minimize its negative impact" [13]. However, the heterogeneity of definitions has been highlighted by Matten and Moon [14], (p.405) when they said "SR is an umbrella term overlapping with some, and being synonymous with other, conceptions of business-society relation". According to the renewed definition by the European Commission, SR is the responsibility of enterprises for their impacts on society with reference to collaborate with stakeholders "to integrate social, environmental and ethical concerns, respect for human rights and consumer concerns into their business operations and their core strategy" [15] (p.7). Taking into account that classical organizational boundaries have become obsolete because "what once was 'outside' the organization is now 'inside' and *vice versa*" [16] (p.449) we found in this fact a fundamental reason for the emergence of the internal face of SR. Nowadays, the external side of SR and the internal one are more related than ever showing higher interconnectivity as have been shown by Sánchez-Hernández and Grayson [17]. According to this work, companies should discover the social and environmental potential of employees in order to integrate their interests and skills into the overall SR efforts. This will be the way to internalize a Social Responsible Strategy within the organization creating dynamic capabilities likely to lead to competitive advantages. The interaction of Strategy and HRM issues [18] explains how employees are important to a firm's success. According to the *Resource-Based Theory* (RBT) of the firm, human capital is a key factor explaining performance differences across firms [19]. In this respect, Crook [20] has pointed out the importance of "specific" employees, referring to the best and brightest human capital available in the labor market, to achieve high performance. Shoemaker [16] argued that treating HRM and SR separately is an outdated approach because organizations develop towards open systems where cooperative action is based on the willingness of employees to bring in and expand their talents as part of communities of work.

Despite the huge academic literature devoted to SR, literature about ISR is surprisingly scarce and empirical studies are inexistent as far as we know. However, the need for real improvement in organizational capability for doing well, and also for doing well in respect to stakeholders, as a basis for competitive strategy and competitive advantage, has received widespread attention in the academic and professional management literature [21]. In addition, competitive advantage is increasingly achieved through the mobilization of the accumulated know-how of individual employees to create value through processes that are not easily imitable [22]. Consequently, ISR has to be analyzed for one important reason: because employees are stakeholders able to create social value for the company mediating between the company and the consumers.

Worried about the under-studied internal side of SR, this work focuses upon regional businesses in Extremadura (Autonomous Region in the southwest of Spain) interacting with the local community by investing in the regional economic system, contracting with the local distributors, taking into account environmental concerns (external side of SR) and also recruiting employees, guaranteeing jobs, wages, training, and employees quality of life (the internal one).

The paper exposes what could be considered socially responsible management of human resources, called sustainable HRM—what actions related to human capital any organization could perform to state that employees' management is sustainable. In previous work, the authors have developed and empirically validated an SR scale in the regional context of study [23]. Now, we address internal practices considered sustainable in academic management literature by isolating the internal aspects of the general scale mentioned. For the definition of indicators that reflect these actions, we have covered several areas. All of them include some determinants of pleasant working conditions, and are oriented to the pursuit of social welfare [24–29].

There are many different areas that could be addressed. Thus, we start to refer to the actions devoted to support the employment of people at risk of social exclusion [30,31] and, at the same time, the fact that the company values the contribution of disabled people to the business world [32–34]. Moreover, the interest in the employee's quality of life [29,35], the importance of payments of wages above the industry average and the existence of pension plans [36,37], or the fact that employee compensation will be related to their skills and results [38,39], are aspects that determine a responsible management into the organization. We can add the standards of health and safety beyond the legal minimum (because every company has to fulfill the law) [40], the commitment with the job creation [41] and the training and development programs for employees [32,42]. In addition, it is important to consider the conciliation of professional and personal lives [43,44] and the equal opportunities for all employees [32,42,45–47]. In the line of social commitment, the participation of the organization in social projects [48,49] and the organization of volunteer activities in collaboration with NGOs [49,50], define new responsible actions in management.

Moreover, to be responsible, the organization must have dynamic mechanisms of dialogue with employees. In this respect, Preuss and others [51] conclude after some case study analyses that dialogue with employee representatives and trade unions could play an active role in SR and, in some cases, even a pivotal one. While the company is doing SR actions, it must raise awareness and inform employees on SR and the actions committed. Finally, the fact that the organization was an active member of any association that promotes the implementation of SR, as could be the case of the United Nations Global Compact for instance, is considered very important [52].

After this theoretical introduction, employees could be considered the center of any responsible business. European firms pursue SR for concerns of stakeholders such as government, regulatory bodies, customers or pressure groups. This is the external SR orientation. However, the aim of this paper is to study the ISR of organizations. In this sense, we say that SR behavior and values should also include internal aspects of management related to intra-organizational elements, organizational capabilities and HRM. As follows, through a survey of managers, we first carry on a factor analysis to explore the main dimensions of the ISR. Once the multidimensionality of this new construct is empirically determined, interpreted, and understood, the empirical analysis continues by looking for a relationship between ISR and business competitiveness. The work finishes with conclusions, limitations of the study, and lines of research for the near future.

2. Method

2.1. Sample and Procedure

The information for this investigation was collected from business services managers in the Autonomous Community of Extremadura, in southwestern Spain. The broad argument to choose services in this work is that the match between HRM and SR strategy should be greater in services than in manufacturing, highlighting the internal side of SR. According to Legge [53], services are competing in the knowledge-based economy. Services are used to characterize high skilled people and high cost industry. In this context, it is likely to adopt HRM policies very well linked to SR strategy that treat employees as an asset that enables the company to create added-value.

To justify the selected region, we have to say that, since 2010, a special plan for the promotion of SR exists in the Region. The main pillars for building a responsible culture in the region are: The *Law of SR in Extremadura* (15/2010 of 9 December) and the *Decree* (110/2013 of 2 July) for the establishment of the Autonomous Council for the promotion of Social Responsibility of Extremadura, the Office of Corporate Social Responsibility, and the Procedure for qualification and registration of socially responsible companies. At this point, it is important to highlight that the special plan for the promotion of SR in the Region is enhancing both the external and the internal side of SR. Table 1 presents the study's technical data sheet.

Table 1. Technical data sheet.

Data Sheet	
Geographical Scope	Region of Extremadura (Spain)
Universe	SMEs (Small and medium–sized enterprises) Business Services—Source: Spain's Central Enterprise Directory 2009
Method of information collection	Phone contact
Emitted calls	14,580
Population	5332 contacted firms
Final sample	590 SMEs
Index of participation	11.07%
Measurement error	3.3%
Trust level	95% z = 1.96 p = q = 0.5
Sampling method	Simple random
Average duration of the interview	14:35 (minutes:seconds)

Source: Own work.

The representative sample of regional business services comprised 590 SMEs (Small and medium-sized enterprises) with their corresponding predetermined substitute firms to control the non-response index. The objective universe was drawn from Spain's Central Enterprise Directory (SCED). Before beginning the study, we calibrated the representativeness of the sample of firms that were to participate in the survey. To this end, weighting coefficients were established according to the defined strata of the firms in the sample. Possible biases relative to the characteristics of the total population of the Directory were checked for using statistical tests, comparing the structure of the sample with the total population of the SCED. The results justified the validity of the sample for the purposes of the study. A pilot test was also carried out in order to check that the survey would be appropriately interpreted by the respondent. The administration of one *ad hoc* questionnaire was by telephone interviews with business services managers. They were carried out using the Computer Aided Telephone Interviewing (CATI) system. The participation index was 11.07%, corresponding to the percentage of firms in which a valid interlocutor agreed to participate in the study. A total of 590 completed surveys were collected, which resulted in a response rate of 11.07%.

2.2. The Measurement Instrument

An *ad hoc* questionnaire was provided to inquire into the manager's perceptions with responses on a 10-point Likert scale. These responses went from "0: totally in disagreement" to "10: totally in agreement" for the ISR items, and from "0: far below the competition" to "10: far above the competition" for the items corresponding to the rest of the constructs. With this instrument, we analyze the ISR as a first attempt to standardize it aligned with the "Guidance on Social Responsibility" published for the International Organization for Standardization (ISO 26000) in 2010. The aim is to assist companies to expand their responsible behavior from external actions to internal actions looking for synergies and better performance. Thus, and according to previous work [23,32,54], the selected indicators reflecting ISR actions are shown in Table 2 (from INTR1 to INTR18) selectively supported by Turker [42], Agudo-Valiente *et al.* [45], Lu *et al.* [47] and Pérez *et al.* [46]. All indicators are considered internal activities related to ISR rather than external activities because, in these actions, we can observe how employees mediate the relationship between the company and the society.

Table 2. Selected indicators about the internal dimension of social responsibility (SR).

Indicators	
INTR1	We support the employment of people at risk of social exclusion
INTR2	We value the contribution of disabled people to the business world
INTR3	We are aware of the employees' quality of life
INTR4	We pay wages above the industry average
INTR5	Employees compensation is related to their skills and their results
INTR6	We have standards of health and safety beyond the legal minimum
INTR7	We are committed to job creation (fellowships, creation of job opportunities, …)
INTR8	We foster our employees' training and development
INTR9	We have human resource policies aimed at facilitating the conciliation of employees' professional and personal lives
INTR10	Employees' initiatives are taken seriously into account in management decisions
INTR11	Equal opportunities exist for all employees
INTR12	We participate in social projects to the community
INTR13	We encourage employees to participate in volunteer activities or in collaboration with NGOs
INTR14	We have dynamic mechanisms of dialogue with employees
INTR15	We understand the importance of pension plans for employees
INTR16	We put into practice specific actions to raise awareness, to educate, and to inform employees on the principles and actions related to SR
INTR17	The values related to SR are present in the vision and strategy of the firm
INTR18	We are active members of organizations, businesses, or professional association or discussion groups that promote the implementation of SR

Source: Own work.

2.3. Factor Analysis

We observe that the selected indicators from the formulated domain of the internal side of SR offered in Table 2 are measures or variables related to ISR. However, we wonder whether they could be correlated with each other. In this case, it means that scores on each variable share information contained in the others [55]. In general, factor analysis is a collection of methods to explain the correlations among variables in terms of more fundamental elements called factors. Specifically, and according to Jolliffe [56], the central idea of a principal component analysis is to reduce the dimensionality of a data set in which there is a large number of interrelated variables, as is the case of the first approximation to ISR shown in Table 2, while retaining as much as possible of the variation present in the data set. This reduction is achieved by transforming the factors or principal components to a new set of variables, which are uncorrelated, and which are ordered so that the first few retain most of the variation present in all of the original variables. In addition, and considering that in the factor analysis literature attention has been given to the issue of sample size, it is important to remark that our sample ($N = 590$) is good enough. Taking into account the recommendations given by Mundfrom *et al.* [57] even under the worst imaginable conditions of low communities and a larger number of weakly determined factors, the very large required sample is over 500.

In this research, a factor analysis is used as a method for grouping the proposed variables related to ISR according to a similar correlation pattern in order to discover the main factors for this construct. An exploratory principal components factor analysis has allowed us to check the factorial composition and validity. Thus, the initial 18-item instrument is performed to determine the structure of ISR. In our analysis, the value of the Kaiser–Meyer–Olkin measure of sampling adequacy (KMO = 0.873) and the Bartlett sphericity test showed the existence of good correlations between the variables, so that we could continue with the factorial analysis. The principal components factor analysis with varimax rotation has produced five factors (Table 3).

We can observe how the eigenvalues and explained variance decline following the extraction of the first factor. The factors extracted explained 61% of the total variance. To validate the exploratory factor analysis, we took two random sub-samples. The validity of the factor analysis was confirmed since the communities of the sub-samples were found to be similar in value to those of the initial sample, the total explained variance was also similar, and the factor loadings after varimax rotation were also close to the initial sample. While the values of Cronbach's alpha is always lie between 0 and 1, the values calculated are all well in excess of the generally accepted rule-of-thumb lower limit of 0.60 to be acceptable [58]. Cronbach's alpha are good for the first three factors ($\alpha_1 = 0.813$; $\alpha_2 = 0.735$; $\alpha_3 = 0.711$) and acceptable for the others ($\alpha_4 = 0.64$; $\alpha_5 = 0.67$). This result is good enough because Cronbach's alpha has a positive relationship with the number of items in the scale and the questionnaire contained only 18 items. The magnitude of the alpha values obtained is an evidence for the internal consistency of the items forming the scales.

Table 3. Factor analysis.

Items	Factor 1	Factor 2	Factor 3	Factor 4	Factor 5
INTR10	0.754	0.106	0.137	0.105	0.122
INTR14	0.747	−0.010	0.248	0.081	0.171
INTR11	0.737	0.031	0.145	0.206	0.103
INTR9	0.659	0.153	0.100	0.136	−0.014
INTR8	0.656	0.276	0.031	0.278	0.074
INTR7	0.433	0.315	0.014	0.244	0.113
INTR18	0.059	0.785	0.126	0.045	0.049
INTR17	0.179	0.729	0.262	0.005	0.163
INTR16	0.160	0.708	0.230	0.176	0.003
INTR13	0.115	0.144	0835	0.086	0.015
INTR12	0.107	0.199	0.775	0.111	0.101
INTR15	0.266	0.231	0.599	0.052	−0.008
INTR4	0.128	0.048	0.104	0.798	0.087
INTR5	0.288	−0.031	0.136	0.708	0.085
INTR6	0.225	0.263	0.016	0.622	0.032
INTR1	0.068	0.122	0.093	0.018	0.836
INTR2	0.158	0.044	−0.010	0.103	0.835
INTR3	0.461	0.052	0.042	0.362	0.483
% of standard deviation	31.133	10.315	7.640	6.228	5.687
Accumulated %	31.133	41.448	49.088	55.316	61.003

Notes: Determinant of the correlation matrix = 0.003; Kaiser-Meyer-Olkin Index = 0.873; Barlett Test (Chi-squared; sf) = 4335 (153); Signification level = 0.000. *Source:* Own work.

Another aspect of construct validity is the ability of factors to reflect the theoretical dimensions or those argued by academic literature accurately. The individual factors contributing to the ISR model and their theoretical explanation are the following:

- Factor one—*Responsible HR (RHR)* (31.1% of explained variance): This factor can be described and interpreted as representing the responsiveness of HRM policies in respect to employees' needs and wants. This first factor is aligned with previous work in Internal Marketing [17,59] where employees are considered clients, internal clients, and a very important stakeholder to attend. Job creation, training, conciliation and equal opportunities and dynamic mechanisms of employees' participation in management decisions fostering dialogue form part of this composite factor.

- Factor two—*Responsible Organizational Culture (ROC)* (10.3% of explained variance): Internalization of SR principles and values into the vision and strategy of the business, relationship with associations promoting SR, and the effort to communicate SR aspects to employees internally form the essential elements of a culture of responsibility and form this second factor in the analysis.

In this respect, some authors have highlighted the importance of the culture of responsibility as the first step to become a responsible business [17,60].

- Factor three—*HR and Social Issues (HRSI)* (7.6% of explained variance): This factor can be best described as representing the link between internal HRM practices and the external side of SR in their relationship with the community in any effort for attending social issues. Being aware of problems in society including pension plans for retirement and fostering corporate volunteering are included in this factor and theoretically defended before in the same context [49] and previously in others [61,62].
- Factor four—*Responsible Compensation (RC)* (6.2% of explained variance): Aligned to previous studies [63,64], going beyond the legal minimum and beyond the average in the sector in human resources tools such as wages, health and safety and linking employees' compensation to their performance, form the essential elements of this factor.
- Factor five—*Employees Quality of Life (EQL)* (5.6% of explained variance): The essential element of this final factor forming ISR, also previously analyzed [29], is the aim to improve employees' quality of life including the disabled and people in risk of social exclusion.

These five factors were perceived as ISR dimensions for the purposes of our study, and their compatibility with the following step in this research is indicative of the validity of the study. In addition, the requirement of discriminant validity to demonstrate that any indicator should correlate more highly with another construct than with the construct it intends to measure [65] is also satisfactory in all factors in the analysis. Once the five dimensions have been found and described, the path analysis to test the relationship between ISR and competitive success is carried out in the following session.

2.4. Path Analysis

Structural equations modeling (SEM) has been used, considering it is very suitable for our research interests, because the construct under study, ISR, is relatively new and the theoretical model and their measures are not well formed [66]. According to literature review, when companies are involved in SR activities, the internal dimension determines relations with their internal stakeholders, especially their employees, and higher competitive success could be expected. Business performance and innovation have also been considered in the developed structural model. The relationship between performance and competitive success has been noted in business strategy fieldwork by Porter [67,68]) and other authors [69,70], and previous work has demonstrated the mediation role of innovation between SR and competitive success [32]. Innovation that is intrinsically about identifying and using opportunities to create new products, services, or work practices [71] is also identified in the model as a mediator variable when considering ISR because it is theoretically and widely accepted that improvements to HRM have a positive impact on innovation [72,73]. According to Cano and Cano [74], certain HR practices such as goal recognition or reward for achievement, have a positive effect on innovation performance in the company. In fact, these HR improvements promote the ability to innovate because they first improve the ability to deal with complexity [75]. In addition, academic literature on HRM has demonstrated how better HR practices are also linked to firm performance [76]. Finally, the link of these previous variables to competitive success is the soul of the *Resource-Based Theory* of the firm [5,6] previously exposed. The focus of management on sustainable HRM is the key to enhance employee commitment and satisfaction, which, in turn, increases the service innovation and performance, and will ultimately generate better overall competitive success [77]. The model shown in Figure 1 includes four related latent variables that make up the proposed relationships defined in the following hypotheses.

Hypothesis 1—There is a direct and positive relationship between the ISR and business performance.

Hypothesis 2—There is a direct and positive relationship between business performance and competitive success.

Hypothesis 3—There is a direct and positive relationship between the ISR and innovation.

Hypothesis 4—There is a direct and positive relationship between innovation and competitive success.

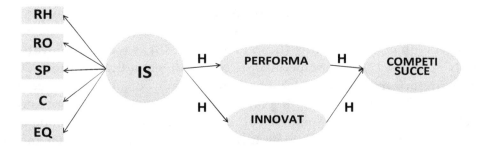

Figure 1. The structural model. Source: own work.

To measure ISR, we have considered the five dimensions found in the previous factor analysis (with the sort names RHR, ROC, HRSI, RC and EQL). Consequently, ISR has been defined as a second order construct. Indicators for each dependent variable are shown in Table 4.

Table 4. Original Indicators for performance, innovation and competitive success.

	Indicators for Performance (PER), Innovation (INV) and Competitive Success (COM)
PER1	Level of before-tax profits
PER2	Level of profitability
PER3	Increase in sales
PER4	Profit margin
PER5	Market share for our products and/or services
PER6	Level of customer satisfaction and loyalty
PER7	Satisfaction and retention of the best employees
PER8	Market positioning, image, and reputation
INV1	We try to carry out R&D projects
INV2	We have put new products or services on the market
INV3	We have introduced new practices to foster entry into new national markets
INV4	We have introduced new practices to foster entry into new international markets
INV5	We are aware of the importance of working as a network, and we have created new alliances or associations
INV6	We have put into place improvements in our production and/or distribution process or techniques
INV7	We have intensified our information and communication technologies
INV8	We have increased our presence on the Internet
INV9	We have initiated changes in the marketing area (design, packaging, prices, ...)
INV10	Our firm has introduced new methods with a view to satisfying the norms of certification
INV11	We have implemented internal or external employee training in order to improve knowledge and creativity within the firm
INV12	We have implemented new managerial practices related to the organization of work and the corporate structure
INV13	We have introduced standards of production or customer management that take social and environmental aspects into account
COM1	Quality in our human resource management
COM2	The levels of training and empowerment of our personnel
COM3	The leadership capabilities of our managers
COM4	Our capabilities in the field of marketing
COM5	Quality of our products and services
COM6	The levels of organizational and administrative management quality
COM7	Technological resources and information systems
COM8	Transparency of our financial management
COM9	The cohesion of our corporate values and culture
COM10	Market knowledge, know-how, and accumulated experience

Source: Own work.

To measure performance, innovation and competitive success, we have considered scales previously used by Gallardo-Vázquez and Sánchez-Hernández [32]. Performance is considered a reflective construct with eight indicators (from PER1 to PER8) as well as innovation with thirteen indicators (from INV1 to INV13) and competitive success with ten indicators (from COM1 to COM10). At this point, it is important to distinguish performance from competitive success in the model. Performance considers firm results going beyond short-term financial performance and pursuing sustainable development. Instead, competitive success considers aspects of competition. Firms have competitive success when they are able to attain favorable positions in the market and obtain superior results, while avoiding the need to have recourse to an extremely poor retribution of the factors of production. Consequently, competitive success implies getting better positions than your competitors because of "something more" than performance.

For the measurement of performance, this construct was taken to be multi-dimensional in accordance with the literature and basing the dimensions considered on a combination of the contribution of Wiklund and Shepherd [78] with that of Pelham and Wilson [79] to include growth in market share and sales. In addition, we consider a very broad conception of innovation. The construct is conceived as the adoption of new idea or practice capable of leading to new products or services [80] to enter new markets [81] or to the generation of new organizational or administrative processes [82].

With respect to the last dependent variable in the model, a firm was taken to have competitive success when it is able to attain a favorable position in the market and obtain superior results, while avoiding the need to have recourse to an extremely poor retribution of the factors of production. To measure competitive success, we used indicators previously considered in academic literature [83,84].

Once the model and related constructs have been described, the first statistical step was to analyze whether the theoretical concepts where properly measured by the observed indicators. This analysis was carried out for the two attributes *validity* (measuring what one really wanted to measure) and *reliability* (whether the process is stable and consistent). To this end, we calculate the individual item reliability, the internal consistency or reliability of the scales, the average variances extracted (AVE), and the discriminant validity. Results are shown in Table 5.

Table 5. Results from the measurement model.

Constructs	Reliable Indicators	Loadings (λ)	AVE	Crombach's Alpha	Composite Reliability
ISR	RHR	0.671	0.5167	0.6943	0.8097
	ROC	0.728			
	RC	0.671			
	EQL	0.675			
Performance	D6	0.892	0.7514	0.8327	0.9004
	D7	0.906			
	D8	0.798			
Innovation	INV5	0.717	0.5336	0.8747	0.9012
	INV6	0.678			
	INV7	0.768			
	INV8	0.698			
	INV9	0.721			
	INV11	0.772			
	INV12	0.785			
	INV13	0.695			

Table 5. *Cont.*

Constructs	Reliable Indicators	Loadings (λ)	AVE	Crombach's Alpha	Composite Reliability
Competitive Success	COM1	0.761	0.5768	0.8530	0.8909
	COM2	0.784			
	COM3	0.768			
	COM5	0.800			
	COM6	0.744			
	COM8	0.708			

Source: Own work.

The most remarkable result in this step is the confirmation of four of the five dimensions found in ISR. The dimension linking HRM and Social Issues, factor three, has been removed from the model, as we have kept only factor loadings greater than 0.67 on ISR construct, which implies more shared variance between ISR and its four items than error variance [85].

The second step of the analysis of the structural model consisted of the estimation of the assumed linear relationships among exogenous and endogenous latent constructs. The correlations among study variables are shown in Table 6. Correlations indicate that the managers' perceptions regarding the ISR of their company were positively related to competitive success, innovation and performance, providing preliminary support for hypotheses.

Table 6. Inter-correlations matrix.

Variable	1	2	3	4
1. ISR	1			
2. Innovation	0.505	1		
3. Performance	0.242	0.161	1	
4. Competitive Success	0.394	0.312	0.575	1

Source: Own work.

The hypotheses have been tested by examining the magnitude of the standardized parameters estimated between constructs with the corresponding *t*-values that indicate the level of significance. We employ the bootstrap routine [66], a non-parametric re-sampling technique that offers the *t*-statistic values. All hypotheses were verified as it is shown in Table 7.

Table 7. Hypotheses testing.

HYPOTHESIS/Structural Relation A → B	Original Path Coefficients (β)	Mean of Sub-Sample Path Coefficients	*Standard Error*	*t*-Value
H_1: ISR →Performance	0.2425	0.2453	0.0729	3.32 ***
H_2: Performance → Competitive Success	0.5394	0.5504	0.0530	10.17 ***
H_3: ISR →Innovation	0.5054	0.5133	0.0550	9.16 ***
H_4: Innovation → Competitive Success	0.2249	0.2242	0.0542	4.14 ***

Source: Own work.

Finally, to measure the relevance of the dependent construct's prediction, PLS (Partial Least Squares) uses the Q^2 index from Stone–Geisser as a criterion, which is calculated based on the redundancies that result from the product of communities (λ^2) with the AVE indicator and is also cross-validated. According to Chin [86], the Stone–Geisser criterion Q^2 values have been obtained from running a blindfolding procedure and range above the threshold level of zero (0.48 for performance; 0.40 for innovation; 0.45 for competitive success), indicating that the exogenous constructs have predictive relevance for the endogenous construct under consideration.

3. Results and Discussion

While acknowledging that the regional context of the study puts limits on the generalization of our findings, we nonetheless see a number of interesting conclusions. The main contribution of the article is the establishment of a set of indicators that define ISR as a result of a dynamic process that provides information about a firm's actions in responsible HRM. This article argues in favor of a stronger focus upon the management of ISR policies and practices in enterprises. Our results show the main factors determining the ISR structure as they have been perceived by a big sample of services business managers in the region under study. The obtained empirical evidence is a contribution to the SR research where there is a lack in studies devoted to the internal side. Therefore, this study contributes to the generation of knowledge on internal responsible behavior of companies. As demonstrated, ISR in service business, which is more influenced by human resources practices, is defined by five well-delimited dimensions such as: responsible human resources practices; organizational culture of responsibility; social projects promotion; significant compensation policies and employee quality of life. A point of interest that needs to be highlighted is the important role that HRM could play in the SR strategy of any business, an aspect that has been analyzed with the developed structural equation model.

It has been demonstrated empirically that ISR has an effect on increasing the firm's competitiveness. The conceptual model has been tested empirically confirming the four hypotheses H_1, H_2, H_3 and H_4. Consequently, the model has been validated where innovation and performance have the role of mediator variables between ISR and competitive success in accordance with previous work in general SR [23,32], where ISR was not isolated from the holistic construct of firm responsibility.

4. Conclusions

Although an abundance of research exists on the general topic of SR, little has been run toward identifying, or perhaps more importantly, measuring its internal aspects in business services. This investigation provides ample foundation for further research on this topic and contributes to a better appreciation and understanding of the role of responsible HRM practices.

To conclude, it should be noted that results from the analysis should be interpreted for SMEs, overcoming the limitations coming from the regional context of study and also from the selection of the sample limited to the service sector, and limited to a single Spanish Autonomous Community. Consequently, our results are not directly extrapolated to other environments that differed greatly in their defining variables. However, since the predominance of business services and the predominance of SMEs are characteristic for the whole Spanish territory, and even the whole European Union, we can accept the results satisfactorily. We believe that our study represents a substantial contribution to the knowledge of ISR, but, in the near future, qualitative and quantitative research should be done on the topic. Managers have to be aware that one of the most important stakeholders the company has is the employee. Employees have to be considered an internal client [59,87] and, consequently, SR should start inside the company. In fact, we question whether there is sufficient focus upon investment in employees, which could be regarded as an important driver of external SR practice [88].

Some suggestions for a research agenda emerge from this attempt to approach the internal side of responsibility in business. First, new studies in the same direction but in other sectors and regions have to be addressed, and second, and related to SR and internal management, we suggest an analysis of the theoretical and hypothetical relationship between the internal and the external side of SR in order to determine the direct effect in external SR fostered by responsible HR policies internally. In line with other authors [59,89], we remark on the importance of internal marketing as a way to sell the responsible company culture internally to employees to somehow help external SR to develop at the same time that companies improve their competitive success. The more important the concept and practice of ISR becomes, the more likely the companies will improve their competitive advantage. It should be taken as an important opportunity for the responsible reinvention of management.

In conclusion, ISR and HRM are interrelated concepts influencing the business competitive success, and their effectiveness depends on responsible practices inside the spheres of the company.

Acknowledgments: Acknowledgments: The authors are grateful to all the managers in business services who participated in the survey and contributed to the paper.

Author Contributions: Author Contributions: M. Isabel Sánchez-Hernandez designed the research, analyzed the data and wrote the manuscript, Dolores Gallardo-Vázquez collected data and performed research, Agnieszka Barcik analyzed the data and revised the research and paper, and Piotr Dziwiński analyzed the data, revised the research and corrected the final version of manuscript.

References

1. Peneder, M.; Kaniovski, S.; Dachs, B. What follows tertiarisation? Structural change and the role of knowledge-based services. *Serv. Ind. J.* **2003**, *23*, 47–66. [CrossRef]
2. Ehret, M.; Wirtz, J. Division of labor between firms: Business services, non-ownership-value and the rise of the service economy. *Serv. Sci.* **2010**, *2*, 136–145. [CrossRef]
3. Buera, F.J.; Kaboski, J.P. Scale and the origins of structural change. *J. Econ. Theory* **2012**, *147*, 684–712. [CrossRef]
4. Freeman, R.E. *Strategic Management: A Stakeholder Approach*, 1st ed.; Harpercollins College Div., Pitman Series: Marshfield, MA, USA, 1994.
5. Donaldson, T.; Preston, L. The Stakeholder Theory of the Corporation: Concepts, Evidence, and Implications. *Acad. Manag. Rev.* **1995**, *1*, 65–91.
6. Freeman, R.E.; Harrison, J.E.; Wicks, A.C. *Managing for Stakeholders: Survival, Reputation, and Success*; Yale University Press: New Haven, CT, USA, 2007.
7. Kaler, J. Evaluating stakeholder theory. *J. Bus. Eth.* **2006**, *69*, 249–268. [CrossRef]
8. Berrone, P.; Surroca, J.; Tribo, J.A. Corporate ethical identity as a determinant of firm performance: A test of the mediating role of stakeholder satisfaction. *J. Bus. Eth.* **2007**, *76*, 35–53. [CrossRef]
9. Verbeke, A.; Tung, V. The Future of Stakeholder Management Theory: A Temporal Perspective. *J. Bus. Eth.* **2013**, *112*, 529–543. [CrossRef]
10. Mason, C.; Simmons, J. Embedding Corporate Social Responsibility in Corporate Governance: A Stakeholder Systems Approach. *J. Bus. Eth.* **2013**, *119*, 77–86. [CrossRef]
11. Mont, O.; Leire, C. Socially responsible purchasing in supply chains: Drivers and barriers in Sweden. *Soc. Responsib. J.* **2009**, *5*, 389–407. [CrossRef]
12. Barcik, A.; Dziwiński, P. Relations with employees in CSR strategies at Polish enterprises with regard to compliance mechanism. *Responsib. Sustain.* **2015**, *3*, 13–26.
13. Ferrell, O.C.; Fraedrich, J.; Ferrell, L. *Business Ethics: Ethical Decision Making and Cases*; Houghton Mifflin: Boston, MA, USA, 2008.
14. Matten, D.; Moon, M. "Implicit" and "explicit" CSR: A conceptual framework for a comparative understanding of Corporate Social Responsibility. *Acad. Manag. Rev.* **2008**, *33*, 404–424. [CrossRef]
15. Commission of the European Communities, COM. Communication from the Commission to the European Parliament, the Council, the European Economic and Social Committee and the Committee of the Regions. Available online: http://eur-lex.europa.eu/legal-content/EN/TXT/?uri=CELEX%3A52011DC0681 (accessed on 17 February 2016).
16. Schoemaker, M.; Nijhof, A.; Jonker, J. Human value management. The influence of the contemporary developments of corporate social responsibility and social capital on HRM. *Manag. Rev.* **2006**, *17*, 448–465.
17. Sánchez-Hernández, M.I.; Grayson, D. Internal marketing for engaging employees on the corporate responsibility journey. *Intang. Cap.* **2012**, *8*, 275–307. [CrossRef]
18. Barney, J. Firm resources and sustained competitive advantage. *J. Manag.* **1991**, *17*, 99–120. [CrossRef]
19. Acedo, F.J.; Barroso, C.; Galán, J.L. The resource-based theory: Dissemination and main trends. *Strateg. Manag. J.* **2006**, *27*, 621–636. [CrossRef]
20. Crook, T.R.; Todd, S.Y.; Combs, J.G.; Woehr, D.J.; Ketchen, D.J., Jr. Does human capital matter? A meta-analysis of the relationship between human capital and firm performance. *J. Appl. Psychol.* **2011**, *96*, 443–456. [CrossRef] [PubMed]

21. Porter, M.E.; Kramer, M.R. The link between competitive advantage and corporate social responsibility. *Harv. Bus. Rev.* **2006**, *84*, 78–92. [PubMed]

22. Varey, R.J. Internal marketing: A review and some interdisciplinary research challenges. *Int. J. Serv. Ind. Manag.* **1995**, *6*, 40–63. [CrossRef]

23. Gallardo-Vázquez, D.; Sánchez-Hernández, M.I. Measuring Corporate Social Responsibility for competitive success at a regional level. *J. Clean. Prod.* **2014**, *72*, 14–22. [CrossRef]

24. Carroll, A. A three-dimensional conceptual model of corporate performance. *Acad. Manag. Rev.* **1979**, *4*, 497–505.

25. Aupperle, K.; Carroll, A.B.; Hatfield, J. An empirical examination of the relationship between corporate social responsibility and profitability. *Acad. Manag. J.* **1985**, *28*, 446–463. [CrossRef]

26. Wood, D.J.; Jones, R.E. Stakeholder mismatching: A theoretical problem in empirical research on corporate social performance. *Int. J. Organ. Anal.* **1995**, *3*, 229–267. [CrossRef]

27. Quazi, A.M.; O'Brien, D. An empirical test of a cross-national model of corporate social responsibility. *J. Bus. Eth.* **2000**, *25*, 33–51. [CrossRef]

28. Maignan, I.; Ferrell, O.C. Measuring Corporate Citizenship in Two Countries: The Case of the United States and France. *J. Bus. Eth.* **2000**, *23*, 283–297. [CrossRef]

29. Sánchez-Hernández, M.I.; García-Míguelez, M.P. Improving Employees Quality of Life. In *Best Practices in Marketing and Their Impact on Quality of Life*; Alves, H., Vázquez, J.L., Eds.; Springer Dordrecht Heidelberg: New York, NY, USA; London, UK, 2013; pp. 241–254.

30. Zinn, J.O. Introduction: Risk, social inclusion and the life course. *Soc. Policy Soc.* **2013**, *12*, 253–264. [CrossRef]

31. Hayman, L.W.; McIntyre, R.B.; Abbey, A. The bad taste of social ostracism: The effects of exclusion on the eating behaviors of African-American women. *Psychol. Health* **2014**, *3*, 1–16. [CrossRef] [PubMed]

32. Gallardo-Vázquez, D.; Sánchez-Hernández, M.I. *Corporate Social Responsibility in Extremadura*; Fundación Obra Social La Caixa: Badajoz, Spain, 2012. (In Spanish)

33. Bruyére, S.; Filiberto, D. The green economy and job creation: Inclusion of people with disabilities in the USA. *Int. J. Green Econ.* **2013**, *7*, 257–275. [CrossRef]

34. Kulkarni, M.; Rodrigues, C. Engagerment with disability: Analysis of annual reports of Indian organizations. *Int. J. Human Resour. Manag.* **2014**, *25*, 1547–1566. [CrossRef]

35. Cullinane, S.J.; Bosak, J.; Flood, P.C.; Demerouti, E. Job design under lean manufacturing and the quality of working life: A job demands and resources perspective. *Int. J. Human Resour. Manag.* **2014**, *25*, 2996–3015. [CrossRef]

36. Amstrong, M. Amstrong's Handbook of Reward Management Practice. In *Improving Performance through Reward*, 4th ed.; Kogan Page: London, UK, 2012.

37. Esping-Andersen, G. *The Three Worlds of Welfare Capitalism*; John Wiley & Sons: Chichester, UK, 2013.

38. Cohen, E. *CSR for HR: A Necessary Partnership for Advancing Responsible Business Practices*; Greenleaf Publishing Limited: Sheffield, UK, 2010.

39. Long, C.S.; Perumal, P. Examining the impact of human resource management practices on employees' turnover intention. *Int. J. Bus. Soc.* **2014**, *15*, 111–126.

40. Lozano, R.; Huisingh, D. Inter-linking issues and dimensions in sustainability reporting. *J. Clean. Prod.* **2011**, *19*, 99–107. [CrossRef]

41. Bischoff, C.; Wood, G. Micro and small enterprises and employment creation: A case study of manufacturing micro and small enterprises in South Africa. *Dev. South. Afr.* **2013**, *30*, 564–579. [CrossRef]

42. Turker, D. Measuring Corporate Social Responsibility: A Scale Development Study. *J. Bus. Eth.* **2009**, *85*, 411–427. [CrossRef]

43. Vázquez-Carrasco, R.; López-Pérez, M.E.; Centeno, E. A qualitative approach to the challengues for women in management: Are they really starting in the 21st century? *Qual. Quant.* **2012**, *46*, 1337–1357. [CrossRef]

44. Tato-Jiménez, J.L.; Bañegil-Palacios, T.M. Effects of formal and informal practices of reconciling work and life on the performance of Spanish listed companies. *Res. J. Bus. Manag.* **2015**, *9*, 391–403. [CrossRef]

45. Agudo-Valiente, J.M.; Garcés-Ayerbe, C.; Salvador-Figueras, M. Social responsibility practices and evaluation of corporate social performance. *J. Cleaner Prod.* **2012**, *35*, 25–38. [CrossRef]

46. Pérez, A.; Martínez, P. Rodríguez del Bosque, I. The development of a stakeholder-based scale for measuring corporate social responsibility in the banking industry. *Serv. Bus.* **2012**, *7*, 459–481. [CrossRef]

47.　Lu, R.X.A.; Lee, P.K.C.; Cheng, T.C. Socially responsible supplier development: Construct development and measurement validation. *Int. J. Prod. Econ.* **2012**, *140*, 160–167. [CrossRef]

48.　Hillman, A.J.; Keim, G.D. Shareholder value, stakeholder management, and social issues: What's the bottom line? *Strateg. Manag. J.* **2001**, *22*, 125–139. [CrossRef]

49.　Sanchez-Hernandez, M.I.; Gallardo-Vázquez, D. Approaching corporate volunteering in Spain. *Corpor. Gov.* **2013**, *13*, 397–411. [CrossRef]

50.　Knutsen, W.L.; Chan, Y. The Phenomenon of Staff Volunteering: How Far Can You Stretch the Psychological Contract in a Nonprofit Organization? *VOLUNTAS Int. J. Volunt. Nonprofit Organ.* **2015**, *26*, 1–22. [CrossRef]

51.　Preuss, L.; Haunschild, A.; Matten, D. The rise of CSR: Implications for HRM and employee representation. *Int. J. Hum. Resour. Manag.* **2009**, *20*, 953–973. [CrossRef]

52.　Cetindamar, D. Corporate social responsibility practices and environmentally responsible behavior: The case of the United Nations Global Compact. *J. Bus. Eth.* **2007**, *76*, 163–176. [CrossRef]

53.　Legge, K. Human Resource Management: Rhetorics and Realities. MacMillan Press: London, UK, 1995.

54.　Gallardo-Vázquez, D.; Sánchez-Hernández, M.I. Structural analysis of the strategic orientation to environmental protection in SME's. *BQR—Bus. Res. Q.* **2014**, *17*, 115–128. [CrossRef]

55.　Cudeck, R. Exploratory Factor Analysis. In *Handbook of Applied Multivariate Statistics and Mathematical Modeling*; Tinsley, H., Brown, S., Eds.; Academic Press: San Diego, CA, USA, 2000; pp. 265–296.

56.　Jolliffe, I. *Principal Component Analysis*; John Wiley & Sons: Chichester, UK, 2005.

57.　Mundfrom, D.J.; Shaw, D.G.; Ke, T.L. Minimum sample size recommendations for conducting factor analyses. *Int. J. Test.* **2005**, *5*, 159–168. [CrossRef]

58.　Nunnally, J.C.; Bernstein, I.H. *Psychometric Theory*, 3rd ed.; McGraw Hill: New York, NY, USA, 1994.

59.　Sánchez-Hernández, M.I.; Miranda, F.J. Linking internal market orientation and new service performance. *Eur. J. Innov. Manag.* **2011**, *14*, 207–226. [CrossRef]

60.　Pohl, M. Corporate Culture and CSR-How They Interrelate and Consequences for Successful Implementation. In *The ICCA Handbook on Corporate Social Responsibility*; Hennigfeld, J., Pohl, M., Tolhurst, N., Eds.; John Wiley & Sons: Chichester, UK, 2006.

61.　Muthuri, J.N.; Matten, D.; Moon, J. Employee volunteering and social capital: Contributions to corporate social responsibility. *Br. J. Manag.* **2009**, *20*, 75–89. [CrossRef]

62.　Kim, H.R.; Lee, M.; Lee, H.T.; Kim, N.M. Corporate social responsibility and employee–company identification. *J. Bus. Eth.* **2010**, *95*, 557–569. [CrossRef]

63.　Mahoney, L.S.; Thorne, L. Corporate social responsibility and long-term compensation: Evidence from Canada. *J. Bus. Eth.* **2005**, *57*, 241–253. [CrossRef]

64.　Collier, J.; Esteban, R. Corporate social responsibility and employee commitment. *Bus. Eth. A Eur. Rev.* **2007**, *16*, 19–33. [CrossRef]

65.　Barclay, D.; Higgins, C.; Thompson, R. The partial least squares (PLS) approach to causal modeling: Personal computer adoption and use as an illustration. *Technol. Stud.* **1995**, *2*, 285–309.

66.　Chin, W. Issues and Opinion on Structural Equation Modelling. *MIS Q.* **1998**, *2*, vii–xv.

67.　Porter, M.E. *Competitive Strategy: Techniques for Analyzing Industries and Competitors*; The Free Press: New York, NY, USA, 1980.

68.　Porter, M.E. Towards a dynamic theory of strategy. *Strateg. Manag. J.* **1991**, *12*, 95–117. [CrossRef]

69.　Spanos, Y.E.; Lioukas, S. An Examination into the Causal Logic of Rent Generation: Contrasting Porter's Competitive Strategy Framework and the Resource Based Perspective. *Strateg. Manag. J.* **2001**, *22*, 907–934. [CrossRef]

70.　Wagner, M.; Schaltegger, S. Introduction: How Does Sustainability Performance Relate to Business Competitiveness? *Greener Manag. Int.* **2003**, *44*, 5–16. [CrossRef]

71.　Van de Ven, A.H. Central problems in the management of innovation. *Manag. Sci.* **1986**, *32*, 590–660. [CrossRef]

72.　Sánchez-Hernández, M.I.; Gallardo-Vazquez, D.; Dziwiński, P.; Barcik, A. Innovation through corporate social responsibility—Insights from Spain and Poland. In *Handbook of Research on Internationalization of Entrepreneurial Innovation in the Global Economy*; IGI Global: Hershey, PA, USA, 2015; pp. 313–328.

73.　Subramaniam, M.; Youndt, M.A. The influence of intellectual capital on the types of innovative capabilities. *Acad. Manag. J.* **2005**, *48*, 450–463. [CrossRef]

74. Cano, C.P.; Cano, P.Q. Human resources management and its impact on innovation performance in companies. *Int. J. Technol. Manag.* **2006**, *35*, 11–28. [CrossRef]

75. Lund Vinding, A. Absorptive capacity and innovative performance: A human capital approach. *Econ. Innov. New Technol.* **2006**, *15*, 507–517. [CrossRef]

76. Mavondo, F.T.; Chimhanzi, J.; Stewart, J. Learning orientation and market orientation: Relationship with innovation, human resource practices and performance. *Eur. J. Mark.* **2005**, *39*, 1235–1263. [CrossRef]

77. Little, M.M.; Dean, A.M. Links between service climate, employee commitment and employees' service quality capability. *Manag. Serv. Qual. Int. J.* **2006**, *16*, 460–476. [CrossRef]

78. Wiklund, J.; Shepperd, D. Knowledge-based resources, entrepreneurial orientation and the performance of small and medium-sized businesses. *Strateg. Manag. J.* **2003**, *24*, 1307–1314. [CrossRef]

79. Pelham, A.; Wilson, D. A longitudinal study of the impact of market structure, firm structure, strategy, and market orientation culture on dimensions of small-firm performance. *Am. Mark. Assoc.* **1996**, *24*, 27–43. [CrossRef]

80. Yalcinkaya, G.; Calantone, R.J.; Griffith, D.A. An examination of exploration and exploitation capabilities: Implications for product innovation and market performance. *J. Int. Mark.* **2007**, *15*, 63–93. [CrossRef]

81. Medrano-Sáez, N.; Olarte-Pascual, M.C. Marketing Innovation as an Opportunity in a Situation of Uncertainty: The Spanish Case, 327–341. In *Soft Computing in Management and Business Economics*; Springer: Berlin Heidelberg, Germany, 2012.

82. Carmona-Lavado, A.; Cuevas-Rodríguez, G.; Cabello-Medina, C. Social and organizational capital: Building the context for innovation. *Ind. Mark. Manag.* **2010**, *39*, 681–690. [CrossRef]

83. Hughes, M.; Ireland, R.D.; Morgan, R.E. Stimulating dynamic value: Social capital and business incubation as a pathway to competitive success. *Long Range Plan.* **2007**, *40*, 154–177. [CrossRef]

84. Abraham, S.C. *Strategic Planning: A Practical Guide for Competitive Success*; Emerald Group Publishing: Bingley, UK, 2012.

85. Carmines, E.G.; Richard, A.Z. *Reliability and Validity Assessment*; Sage Publications: Beverly Hills, CA, USA, 1979.

86. Chin, W.W. Issues and opinion on structural equation modeling. *MIS Q.* **1988**, *22*, vii–xvi.

87. Ahmed, P.K.; Rafiq, M. *Internal Marketing—Tools and Concepts for Customer-Focused Management*; Butterworth-Heinemann Publications: Oxford, UK, 2002.

88. Bansal, H.S.; Mendelson, M.B.; Sharma, B. The impact of internal marketing activities on external marketing outcomes. *J. Qual. Manag.* **2001**, *6*, 61–76. [CrossRef]

89. Ariza-Montes, J.A.; Muniz, R.N.M.; Leal-Rodríguez, A.L.; Leal-Millán, A.G. Workplace bullying among managers: A multifactorial perspective and understanding. *Int. J. Environ. Res. Public Health* **2014**, *11*, 2657–2682. [CrossRef] [PubMed]

6

Development of a Novel Co-Creative Framework for Redesigning Product Service Systems

Tuananh Tran and Joon Young Park *

Department of Industrial and Systems Engineering, Dongguk University, Pil-dong, Jung-gu, Seoul 100715, Korea; meslab.org@gmail.com
* Correspondence: jypark@dgu.edu.

Academic Editor: Adam Jabłoński

Abstract: Product service systems (PSS) have been researched in academia and implemented in industry for more than a decade, and they bring plenty of benefits to various stakeholders, such as: customers, PSS providers, the environment, as well as society. However, the adoption of PSS in industry so far is limited compared to its potentials. One of the reasons leading to this limitation is that PSS design is tricky. So far, there are several methods to design PSS, but each of them has certain limitations. This paper proposes a co-creative framework, which is constructed using the concept of user co-creation. This novel framework allows designers to design PSS effectively in terms of users' perception of PSS value, design quality and evaluation. The authors also introduce a case study to demonstrate and validate the proposed framework.

Keywords: product service system; PSS; PSS design; co-creation; PSS redesign; PSS business model

---

1. Introduction

1.1. Product Service System

Before the 2000s, consumers were familiar with the paradigm in which companies sell tangible products to the market. For instance: Nokia provided mobile phones; Electrolux provided washing machines; HP provided printers, *etc.* Nowadays, the demands of customers become more and more diversified, and the business environment becomes more and more competitive. This leads to the fact that companies are having a difficult time competing with the conventional business model of selling purely tangible products [1,2]. There is a need for finding new ways to enhance competitiveness, to attract new customers, as well as to keep existing ones. This need is fulfilled by incorporating the concept of product service systems (PSS) [3–5]. These PSS are a form of servitization in which a combination of a tangible product and an intangible service, called a "PSS offering" or simply "PSS", is provided to the customers [6].

There are several examples of PSS in reality. According to Goedkoop *et al.* [7], PSS is "a marketable set of products and services capable of jointly fulfilling a user's needs". By this definition, the offering of an iPhone and the Appstore from Apple Inc. can be considered as a PSS. In the same manner, a car-sharing service, where the users check in and pick up a car at a station, use and return the car at another station, check out and pay per use, is also a PSS. In the car-sharing example, users do not buy the car; they buy the "mobility" or the use of the car. This new concept of buying is similar to a "functional economy" [8], where customers are interested in "hiring products to get jobs done" [3,9,10]. Baines *et al.* also introduced a well-known example of a PSS, which is the "document management solution" [11]. In this example, the customer does not buy a photocopier. Instead, the customer only buys its use. The company still owns the product and takes care of refilling, maintenance, replacing parts, *etc.*

Since the very first work by Goedkoop *et al.* nearly two decades ago, PSS has gone a long way with various research having been carried out by various researchers. The pioneering works also include the ones by Mont [8] and Morelli [12]. So far, PSS is classified into several types. According to Tukker [13], there are three types of PSS: product-oriented PSS, use-oriented PSS and result-oriented PSS.

1.2. Adoption of PSS in Industry

PSS brings benefits to various stakeholders, as studied in the literature [5,11]. For the customers, PSS provides flexible services with a higher level of personalization, better and continuously-improved quality and, finally, total satisfaction. For companies, thanks to the implementation of PSS, they gain the loyalty of customers, as well as better control of product quality, continuous improvement, chances for reducing costs, increasing knowledge and innovation. For society and the environment, PSS is also beneficial in terms of reducing materials' consumption through sharing their use, increasing the responsibility of manufacturers, expanding the lifecycle of the products and creating more jobs in the service sector.

PSS is now adopted more and more in industry. In order to promote the adoption of PSS, several challenges need to be resolved. These challenges were mentioned in various works by Mont [8], Baines *et al.* [11] and Beuren *et al.* [5]. The first challenge is that "ownerless consumption" is not familiar to the vast majority of customers. They are familiar with the concept of paying and getting "physical" items. Another challenge is for the manufacturers. They might have difficulties when making decisions on pricing, managing risks and changing the organization due to a changing business model. The major challenge for expanding PSS adoption is "PSS design". This is not an easy task, because PSS is a complicated system. In PSS, besides products and services, there are also other elements, such as the delivery network, stakeholders, value proposition, *etc.*

In order to design PSS, several methods have been introduced. Vasantha *et al.* reviewed eight well-known PSS design methods that have been implemented widely so far [6]. As will be analyzed in Section 2, there is still a lack of an effective method to design PSS collaboratively and practically. This lack somehow limits the expansion of PSS adoption in industry.

1.3. Motivation for This Work and Research Goal

This research is motivated by the following real-world scenario: Mulenserv is a company that provides various engineering services to customers in the industrial market. One of Mulenserv's services is a PSS, which leases technical manuals and books together with supporting services (lectures, application workshops, technical contests, *etc.*). Their target customers are engineering individuals, as well as small technical companies. This is a niche market, and the PSS is highly customized due to the diversified demands of various customers. After six months of the initial release, the response of the market was limited: acceptance of potential customers, as well as satisfaction of customers who purchased the PSS were lower than expected. The company needs to redesign to improve the PSS, so that the acceptance rate and customer satisfaction can be improved and the sales can be increased sustainably. In order to achieve this goal, they need an effective customer-centric framework to improve the PSS design, *i.e.,* redesign the new PSS starting from the existing one. According to Vezzoli *et al.* [14], most of the successful cases of PSS applications are from the B2B (business to business) sector, not B2C (business to consumer). Mulenserv is a typical B2C case, and a design solution is needed to help its PSS survive when being launched.

Since customer acceptance and satisfaction with the PSS is of critical importance to its success and this acceptance strongly depends on the perception of the users of the provided service [14], this paper aims to develop a co-creative framework that allows companies to redesign a PSS in order to improve the design of the PSS in terms of users' perception of its value, design quality and evaluation and, thus, leading to increasing customer acceptance and, therefore, increasing its success. In this work, we set the scope of the framework in a B2C environment. We construct this framework by incorporating the concept of user co-creation.

The next parts of this paper are organized as follows: Section 2 reviews existing literature that is related to the research topic. Section 3 analyzes solutions and proposes the framework. Section 4 introduces the case study, the experimental implementation, results and discussions. Section 5 draws concluding remarks and suggests future work.

2. Literature Review

2.1. Existing Methods to Design and Redesign PSS

PSS providers need tools, techniques and methods to design and enhance their PSS to satisfy their customers. There has been much research conducted to propose PSS design methodologies with similar intentions and different ideas [15].

Several methods for designing PSS have been introduced so far [1,2,11]. Beside case-specific methods, which were developed to design very specific PSSs [16,17], there are several generic methods that can be used to design various cases of PSS. These methods were summarized by Vasantha *et al.* [6]. Although being well known and widely implemented, these methods have limitations. One of them is the lack of user co-creation in the design processes [6]. These methods do not mention in detail the importance of co-creation, and there are no clear definitions of the roles of customers in the PSS design process.

More recently, Pezzotta *et al.* [18] proposed a framework to design and assess PSS from a service engineering approach. This framework utilizes computer-aided modeling tool for service design. It starts with functional analysis and the identification of customer needs, simulating and testing various scenarios to find out the best solution. Although being well structured, this method has little involvement in co-creation, and the case study provided in the work [18] is more like a B2B case.

Morelli [19] commented that design methods should identify who is involved in the design process and their roles, as well as possible scenarios that could occur. The need for implementing customer co-creation is also raised in the work of Beuren *et al.* [5]. Vezzoli *et al.* [14] implied that a design method should include details of where and when to involve stakeholders (producer/provider, customer, *etc.*) and to allow customers to customize a PSS according to their preferences.

Beside the lack of co-creation, existing PSS design methods provide little practical guidelines for practitioners (*i.e.*, companies) [2]. Incorporating incremental steps in a path or practice is necessary for a design method [14]. There is a lack of illustrating cases that can demonstrate and give insights into how PSS design methods work in various situations. This explains why existing methods are not effective in terms of practical implementation. Furthermore, Qu *et al.* [15] suggested that more quantitative works need to be conducted in the literature because these works are more objective and persuasive.

In summary, existing design methodologies have not considerably included co-creation in the design processes and are not effective enough to act as practical guidelines for practitioners. In this sense, the involvement of each stakeholder in the design phases is not clarified in detail, and the representation of PSS itself is complicated. There is a need for a new method that is co-creative with user involvement in the design process, better defined roles and responsibilities of stakeholders and a simpler PSS representation and that can provide practical guidelines. This method also need to be evaluable.

2.2. Value Perception

In a service-oriented system, like a PSS, value perception is a critical issue to decide the buying potential of customers, because the service part in PSS is intangible and its value is difficult to measure and estimate [9,11,12]. In order to increase the value perception of PSS, the value of the PSS needs to be visualized. One of the methods to visualize PSS value is communicating and demonstrating PSS to the customers [20]. The importance of PSS value and value proposition has been mentioned in several works [21–23]. In one of the PSS design methods reviewed by Vasantha *et al.* [6], the value proposition is considered as an important dimension that forms the PSS [24]. Value is claimed to be the differentiating factor that enables the success of a PSS, and new methods are needed to understand value perception in order to evaluate PSS performance [11].

There are also several notable works on PSS value visualization. The value proposition was emphasized in the PSS design method proposed by Morelli [12]. Several tools that support value visualization have been introduced, including the "PSS board" [9] and color-coded CAD models [25]. A framework to enhance value visualization and perception has also been proposed by Kowalkowski and Kindstrom [20]. The above works focus on either value perception of the company (instead of the customers) [9,12,25] or value perception particularly in industrial markets [20].

Vezzoli *et al.* [14] commented that because of the lack of understanding about PSS and the deep perception of its value, customers are not eager to adopt PSS solutions. This is a barrier for PSS application at the industrial scale. There is a need for new strategies and approaches to make consumers accept this new model of consumption.

In order to increase users' acceptance of PSS offerings, designers must find ways to increase users' perception of PSS value, and thus, the visualization of PSS becomes critical. In Section 3, the authors of this work propose a method to represent and present PSS to enhance the communication of PSS value to the users and enable user participation in co-creation.

2.3. Co-Creation in the Design Improvement and Evaluation of PSS

Steen *et al.* [26] identified three types of benefits of co-creation for the design project, the customers and the PSS provider. They did this by reviewing the literature and observing three service design projects. In that work, experimental results were not reported in terms of numerical data, and they also implied that there was a need for conducting another experiment and performing a numerical analysis to validate the effectiveness of user involvement in a service-oriented design project.

The design and development of PSS is a participatory process, and thus, co-creation has been mentioned in the literature as one of the success enabling factors for PSS [6,11]. Co-creation refers to the participation of customers or users in various phases of its lifecycle, such as ideation, design, development and implementation (*i.e.*, use), *etc.* The role of user participation is critical to the success because of the importance of users in a PSS model. Users are among the most important stakeholders, and because of the presence of the "service" part in which users only buy or hire things that help them to get jobs done [3,9], users' voices deserve a deep consideration. As pointed out by Vansantha *et al.*, to improve PSS design, co-creation is employed limitedly in existing PSS design methods [6].

PSS evaluation is an essential issue that has been mentioned by various researchers [9,27–30]. Especially, evaluation at the development stage can help companies to reduce the risks of PSS launching. Existing PSS design methods do not consider co-creation deep enough [6,11].

There are several works that dealt briefly with the evaluation issue in PSS design. A "lifecycle simulation" model was proposed by Komoto and Tomiyama [30] and was demonstrated with a maintenance service. The evaluation of PSS was also considered in the tool developed by Lim *et al.* [9]. Another approach to PSS evaluation through prototyping was proposed [28]. These works [9,28,30] focused on the evaluation of PSS mostly for companies, not for customers.

Customers can be used as a source of innovation by involving them in the PSS design process [1,11,31]. A PSS design process in which the participation of customers is used for evaluation was proposed by Shih *et al.* [27]. In other work, an algorithm for PSS evaluation was proposed by Yoon *et al.* [28]. However, still, in these works [27,28], customers are not the main drive for making a difference in the effectiveness of the evaluation result.

We aim to develop a novel co-creative framework that uses the co-creation of customers (*i.e.*, users), has detailed defined roles, responsibilities and activities of stakeholders throughout the design process and includes a simple and clear PSS representation. This proposed framework is used to enhance the value perception, evaluation and design quality of PSS. It starts with the existing PSS or initial PSS conceptual idea and produces an improved PSS design as the outcome. The PSS that is developed using the proposed framework can be better accepted by customers. This leads to the success of PSS and encourage the application of PSS in industry.

3. Methodology

Figure 1 shows the research procedure of this paper. This explains how we construct this research. The authors analyze solutions to implement user co-creation and PSS representation. Based on those analyses and the sequence of co-creative design activities, the authors propose the framework. This framework is explained in detail and implemented in a case study as an experiment. The results were collected, analyzed and validated to evaluate the framework.

3.1. Implementation of the Co-Creation Concept

The co-creation of customers/users in the PSS design process can be enabled by the participation of users in various design activities. Previous research pointed out that allowing users to participate in the design process might make significant changes [32]. Users can participate in proposing ideas, suggesting design corrections or even generating new concepts.

As pointed out in a previous work [33], to make user participation become easy and effective, the co-creation tasks need to be clarified and simplified. In order to achieve this, we carefully train the participants about each task in which they are involved. We also use simplified PSS representation so that the users can contribute their innovation properly and systematically.

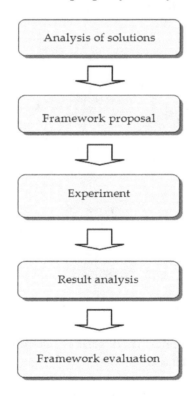

Figure 1. The research procedure.

3.2. Simplified PSS Representation

In order to simplify co-creation activity and maximize effective participation, we break down PSS into basic elements so that the representation of PSS can be in the simplest form. When being shown to the participants, the PSS will be represented as a combination of the following elements:

- Product: The tangible part of a PSS, for instance an iPhone.
- Service: The intangible part of PSS, for instance the Appstore

- Process: Serial and parallel activities happen inside a PSS. This describes the process of how a PSS is served to the customer.
- Parameters: The metrics of product and service features. For example: how long is the service time; how much is the charge per mile for a car sharing service, *etc.*
- Network: The infrastructure of PSS showing the interactions of products, services, users, *etc.* For example, to deliver technical support services to PC (personal computer) buyers, the company may use email, telephone, on-site, *etc.*
- Stakeholders: Companies, customers, suppliers, *etc.*
- Value proposition: Model that explains how PSS provides value to a customer, a company and other stakeholders.

A PSS can be represented in a simple form using a set of the above elements. Each representation is called a "PSS configuration" or "PSS design" in this work. The purpose of this simplification is to briefly represent a PSS as a combination of various "specifications", and thus, it allows users to suggest PSS designs easily by filling in the form with their favorite inputs for those specifications. We would like to note that this is for the convenience of user participation, and this simplification is used only within this work.

3.3. The Proposed Framework

Based on the analysis of solutions and the PSS design process, we propose a framework to enhance the value perception, evaluation and design quality of PSS. The proposed framework is shown in Figure 2.

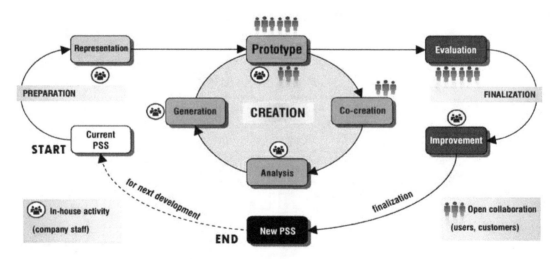

Figure 2. The proposed framework.

The proposed framework can be generally described as follows: The company wants to improve their current PSS by redesigning it with user co-creation. To do that, they first invite a group of users (Group 1) to participate. In order to make these users understand the PSS, the company represents the PSS in a simple form, and then, they prototype the PSS so that the users can actually see and experience the PSS. After that, these users co-create by suggesting various PSS options that they think might meet their needs. The company collects inputs from users, analyzes those inputs and produces new possible PSS designs. After new PSS designs are produced, the company invites another group of users (Group 2) to participate in prototyping and evaluating the newly-created designs. The designs will be evaluated by scoring along various criteria, and the one that gains the highest score will be selected as the winning design. The company will try to improve this design, if possible, and finally, they have a new PSS that is improved compare to the previous version. The detailed explanation of the proposed framework, its phases and corresponding methods can be found in Table 1.

Table 1. Working mechanism of the proposed framework.

Step	Tasks	Method	Implementation of Method
Preparation phase			
0	**Start** *Description*: The company has a PSS to be redesigned or a PSS idea to design further. *Purpose*: This step is the kickoff of the process.	N/A	N/A
1	**Representation** *Description*: The company breaks down a complex PSS into basic elements and prepares to communicate to users so that they can understand. *Purpose*: This step is the preparation for prototyping and user co-creation in the next phase.	*Method*: Simplified PSS presentation (Section 3.2) *Purpose*: This method is used to make users understand the PSS well, so that they can contribute their ideas effectively (Section 3.1).	A PSS is represented as a combination of elements, and the representation is summarized in a table (see Table 2 below).
Creation phase			
2	**Prototype #1** *Description*: The company demonstrates the prototype to a group of users. The users see and experience how the PSS works. This prototype can be presented in the form of a working prototype, such as: participatory prototyping or in the form of a storyboard, a simulation or any media-based illustration, depending on the type and characteristics of the PSS. *Purpose*: This step makes users (user Group 1) clearly understand what the PSS is like and how it might be provided. By understanding this, they can experience the PSS to some extent, and this allows them to contribute ideas more properly.	*Method*: Storyboard and participatory game *Purpose*: The storyboard explains briefly the PSS structure and mechanism, as well as elements and parameters, while the participatory game actually allows users to experience the PSS themselves by playing roles in the PSS process.	The PSS is introduced to the users firstly in the form of a storyboard, which explains what is included and how the PSS is provided (process, parameters, *etc.*). After that, the users are invited to participate in the participatory simulation of the PSS by playing roles.
3	**Co-creation** *Description*: The users participate actively to propose their own "PSS configurations" and customize the PSS design according to their own preferences. This can be done by inviting users, hosting participatory games or crowdsourcing. *Purpose*: This step allows users to contribute their ideas by directly inputting their desired parameters.	*Method*: User submission forms *Purpose*: These are forms that are created especially for collecting user inputs. The pre-defined forms helps to simplify the task for user submission and, thus, ensure effective contribution.	Users are asked to fill in a form with their desired parameters for the PSS. They are also asked to give comments and suggestions for the existing PSS, which was previously demonstrated in the "Prototype #1" step.
4	**Analysis** *Description*: The company analyzes user-generated PSS configurations and identifies the "favorite" configurations. *Purpose*: This step summarizes user inputs and analyzes how various alternatives of PSS options are favored by users. From this analysis, new PSS concepts might emerge.	*Method*: Simple statistical analysis *Purpose*: This method allows designers to collect and classify options to find "patterns".	Designers collect user input options and parameters, cluster them into segments of closely equivalent values, count frequencies and figure out the "favorite" configurations.

Table 1. *Cont.*

Step	Tasks	Method	Implementation of Method
Creation phase			
5	**Generation** *Description*: Based on the "favorite configurations" above, the company builds new PSS concepts, *i.e.*, "user-generated concepts". *Purpose*: This step makes new PSS concepts from users' favorite options and parameters.	*Method*: Concept generation *Purpose*: This method helps to generate various concepts or alternatives by combining various favorite options and parameters.	Designers combine various options and generate several alternatives that can be considered as user-generated concepts.
6	**Prototype #2** *Description*: The company demonstrates the prototypes of newly-generated concepts to a group of users so that they can evaluate them. *Purpose*: This step ensures that the users (user Group 2) understand the PSS thoroughly as, well as experience the PSS themselves, so that they can give a precise and proper evaluation.	*Method*: Storyboard and participatory game *Purpose*: The storyboard explains briefly the PSS structure and mechanism, as well as the elements and parameters, while the participatory game actually allows users to experience the PSS themselves by playing roles in the PSS process.	The PSS is introduced to the users firstly in the form of a storyboard that explains what is included and how the PSS is provided (process, parameters, *etc.*). After that, the users are invited to participate in the participatory simulation of the PSS by playing roles.
Finalization phase			
7	**Evaluation** *Description*: The evaluation criteria are explained to the users, and the users score to evaluate various concepts. Based on the evaluation results, the company can select the winning (*i.e.*, the best) concept. *Purpose*: This step collects the evaluation of users (user Group 2) for the newly-designed PSS, as well as the existing PSS, so that the performances of alternatives can be compared quantitatively.	*Method*: Multi-criteria scoring *Purpose*: This method allows users to evaluate the PSS along various criteria, and thus, a comprehensive evaluation can be achieved to give deeper insights and a precise comparison.	A list of criteria is proposed (Table 5) and a scoring scale of 1 to 5 is used to score PSS concepts. Scores are collected and calculated, and the results will be used to compare concepts to identify the best one.
8	**Improvement** *Description*: The company can improve the winning concept by selecting strong aspects of other concepts and implementing these aspects in the winning concept to achieve an "improved concept". *Purpose*: This step helps designers to exploit the best aspects of each concept to ensure that there is no waste of innovation.	*Method*: Manual improvement	Designers try to find strong aspects of low scored concepts and try to implement those aspects in the winning concept.
9	**End** The company achieves a new PSS design that is improved compared to the initial idea or the previous design.	N/A	N/A

Section 4 introduces a case study that is used to explain how the proposed framework can be used and validated.

4. Case Study and Validation of the Framework

4.1. Introduction to the Case

In Section 1, we mentioned Mulenserv and its PSS briefly. Mulenserv has a PSS called "N-Handbook", which is a book plus additional services for individuals and enterprises to learn new product development (NPD) at a professional level. The N-Handbook is a complex PSS offering, as shown in Table 2.

Table 2. Elements of the N-Handbook.

Element	Content
Product	• A printed book • Optional additions: USB/DVD for lecture video storage, wooden box for keeping the book and accessories
Service	• Lecture videos (YouTube channel) • Offline lectures • Additional documentation (tutorials, case studies, exercises, *etc.*, on closed discussion boards) • Questions and Answers (QnAs) • Offline seminars, examination and certification, project guidance, consulting
Process	• Online/offline announcement • Customer consulting • Customer purchase + delivery • Customers use • Provide services • Feedback and prepare for next version
Parameters	• Forms of support • Number of offline lectures • Length of each offline lecture • Availability of online lectures • Length of project practice • Availability of examination and certification • Recommendation for job seeking • Annual update frequency • Number of offline seminars/best practices • Renewal fee for new release • Price of the package
Network	• Existing web systems of Mulenserv, social network, email, *etc.*, for delivering services • Offline network for delivering products (shops, post offices)
Stakeholders	• The company (designers, staff) • Users • Suppliers (print shops, network providers) • Others
Value proposition	• Bringing long-term benefits with flexible costs • Users make the most of the N-Handbook

4.2. Experimental Implementation of the Proposed Framework

In order to demonstrate, as well as to validate the proposed framework, we conduct an experiment with user participation. In this experiment, a group of users is asked to comment, suggest, give feedback to the existing design of the N-Handbook and to further ideate their own configuration of the N-Handbook. Details are as follows:

Step 0: Start

The company starts with the existing design of the N-Handbook, which is currently offered to customers. This design is denoted as D_0.

Step 1: Representation

The PSS is represented using a simplified representation.

In this experiment, assuming that the process, network, stakeholders and value proposition elements are fixed, the existing N-Handbook can be described as in Table 3.

Table 3. Details of the existing N-Handbook.

Element	Content
Product	• A printed book: black and white
Service	• Lecture videos: YouTube channel • Offline lectures: Yes • Additional documentation (tutorials, case studies, exercises, *etc.*, on closed discussion boards): Yes • QnAs: Yes • Offline seminars: Yes
Process	• Online/offline announcement • Customer consulting • Customer purchase + delivery • Customers use • Provide services • Feedback and prepare for next version
Parameters	• Forms of support (FOS): No • Number of offline lectures (NOL): 12 • Length of each offline lecture (LEL): 2 h • Availability of online lectures (AOL): Yes • Length of project practice (LPP): not available (N/A) • Availability of examination and certification (AEE): No • Recommendation for job seeking (RJS): No • Annual update frequency (AUF): 1 per year • Number of offline seminars/best practices (NOS): 1 per year • Renewal fee for new release (RFR): 50% discount (DC) • Price of the package (POP): 210 USD
Network	• Existing web systems of Mulenserv, social network, email, *etc.*, for delivering services • Offline network for delivering products (shops, post offices)
Stakeholders	• The company (designers, staff) • Users • Suppliers (print shops, network providers) • Others
Value proposition	• Bringing long-term benefits with flexible costs • Users make the most of the N-Handbook

Step 2: Prototype

The company communicates about the printed books and shows media about the additional services and explains the process, network, value proposition, parameters, *etc.*, of the N-Handbook in detail to a group of 21 participants (Group 1). These participants are selected from the database of individuals who showed interest in the N-Handbook, including the persons who asked for information and the persons who actually purchased. This is to ensure that the selected participants are enthusiastic enough about the future PSS and that we can keep them in the loop of participation.

Step 3: Co-creation

The participants are asked to give comments and suggestions for improving the existing design. The participants are also asked to propose their own preferences for the N-Handbook offering, including product, service and parameters. This is done by direct input to a pre-defined form.

Step 4: Analysis

The feedback (comments, suggestions) from the participants are collected and applied to improve the design of the existing N-Handbook.

The proposed preferences of the participants are collected and analyzed to find "favorite patterns" or the favorite PSS configurations. This is done manually by the designers by counting each and every proposed preference and making detailed statistics.

Step 5: Generation

The designers generate "new PSS designs" in this step. The design that is the result of implementing participants' comments and suggestions is called D_{0X}. There are three "favorite patterns" from participants' proposed preferences, and thus, the designers produce three more "new PSS designs", which are called D_1, D_2 and D_3. The details of D_{0X}, D_1, D_2 and D_3 can be found in Table 4 below.

Table 4. Comparison of various new N-Handbook designs.

Element	Content of N-Handbook Designs			
	D_{0X}	D_1	D_2	D_3
Product	Color printed book	Black and white printed book Wooden box USB DVD	Color printed book Wooden box DVD	Black and white printed book DVD
Service	YouTube channel Offline lecture Additional documentation QnAs Offline seminars	Offline lecture Additional documentation QnAs Offline seminars	Offline lecture Additional documentation QnAs Offline seminars	YouTube channel Offline lecture Additional documentation QnAs Offline seminars
Process	• Online/offline announcement • Customer consulting • Customer purchase + delivery • Customers use • Provide services • Feedback and prepare for next version			
Parameters	FOS: No NOL: 12 LEL: 2 h AOL: Yes LPP: 3 months AEE: Yes RJS: Yes AUF: 2 per year NOS: 2 per year RFR: 70% DC POP: 210 USD	FOS: Facebook NOL: 4 LEL: 2 h AOL: Yes LPP: 3 months AEE: Yes RJS: Yes AUF: 1 per year NOS: 4 per year RFR: 70% DC POP: 200 USD	FOS: Multi [*] NOL: 12 LEL: 2 h AOL: No LPP: 3 months AEE: Yes RJS: Yes AUF: 3 per year NOS: 3 per year RFR: 70% DC POP: 230 USD (*): Facebook, Boards, email, Mobile apps	FOS: Multi [*] NOL: 8 LEL: 2 h AOL: No LPP: 2 months AEE: Yes RJS: Yes AUF: 3 per year NOS: 2 per year RFR: 80% DC POP: 190 USD (*): Boards, email
Network	• Existing web systems of Mulenserv, social network, email, *etc.*, for delivering services • Offline network for delivering products (shops, post offices)			
Stakeholders	• The company (designers, staff) • Users • Suppliers (print shops, network providers) • Others			
Value proposition	• Bringing long term benefits with flexible costs • Users make the most of the N-Handbook			

Step 6: Prototype

The company demonstrates the prototypes of the PSS concepts to a new group of 65 participants (Group 2) who are selected from the database of individuals who showed interest in the N-Handbook, including the persons who asked for information and the persons who actually purchased.

Step 7: Evaluation

After explaining the four designs (*i.e.*, D_{0X}, D_1, D_2 and D_3) thoroughly, the participants are asked to score each design along various criteria on a one to five scale. The scoring criteria are retrieved from the survey result from both groups of users before their participation. These are the most agreeable criteria to be used to evaluate the designed PSS among the participants. Details of the scoring criteria are provided below (Table 5).

Table 5. Scoring criteria.

Criteria	Description
Ease of access	How easily can the users access, use and leverage the package?
Applicability	Is this package applicable to the users' job?
Affordability	Is the price of the offering affordable (considering its content)?
Desirability	Do the users want to buy the package?
Necessity	Is this package necessary for the users' job?
Acceptance	If the users are offered this package, would they accept the offering?

Various designs are scored along the above criteria, and the results are recorded for further analysis. The analyzed results are shown in Section 4.3.

Step 8: Improvement

After scoring, the best design is identified, and the designers would try to improve it by trying to implement the strong aspects of other designs into it.

Step 9: End

The company achieves an improved PSS design with higher quality, user acceptance and satisfaction.

4.3. Experimental Results

After collecting the scores from participants, we calculate the mean values of scores for all 65 participants, as shown in Table 6.

Table 6. Mean values of scores for various designs along various criteria.

Criteria	Mean Value of Scores for Various Designs			
	D_{0X}	D_1	D_2	D_3
Ease of access	3.21	3.80	3.98	3.72
Applicability	3.18	3.74	3.90	3.97
Affordability	2.74	3.20	2.87	3.75
Desirability	2.70	3.13	3.38	3.44
Necessity	3.28	3.72	3.85	3.75
Acceptance	3.02	3.54	3.98	3.66

Figure 3 shows the data in Table 6 graphically.

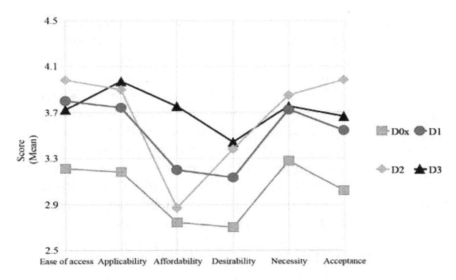

Figure 3. Visualized data showing the scores of various designs along various criteria.

Figure 3 shows that, for all criteria, designs that were suggested by users (*i.e.*, D_1, D_2 and D_3) perform better than the design that was developed solely by Mulenserv's designers (*i.e.*, D_{0X}, represented by the line with square points), especially in terms of "ease of access", "applicability" and "acceptance". This shows the outperformance of user-suggested designs, and thus, it shows the benefits of user co-creation and the use of the proposed framework.

4.4. Result Analysis and Validation

In order to validate the significance of experimental results to draw conclusions on the advantage of the proposed framework, the authors perform a *t*-test on the collected data of D_{0X} and D_2. The dataset for this *t*-test is collected from scoring results by all participants. This means that we use the result of the experiment performed at Mulenserv in the case study for this validation. The analysis results, which are rounded, are shown in Table 7.

Table 7. *t*-test analysis results.

Value	Ease of Access	Applicability	Affordability	Desirability	Necessity	Acceptance
Pearson correlation coefficients	0.257	0.317	0.403	0.391	0.390	0.0314
t-statistic	4.387	5.068	0.798	4.128	3.879	5.030
P (T ⩽ t) one-tailed	2.191×10^{-5}	1.833×10^{-6}	0.214	5.399×10^{-5}	1.250×10^{-4}	2.111×10^{-6}
P (T ⩽ t) two-tailed	4.382×10^{-5}	3.667×10^{-6}	0.428	1.080×10^{-4}	2.501×10^{-4}	4.221×10^{-6}

The reason why we choose D_2 to compare to D_{0X} is that D_2 performs the highest among the three user-suggested designs in terms of "acceptance", which is the most important criteria for a PSS.

Table 7 shows that, for almost all criteria, the differences between D_2 and D_{0X} are large enough to confirm the significance of the collected data because of the *t*-test result, $P (T \leqslant t) < 0.05$ for both one-tailed and two-tailed tests. There is only one exception for "affordability". For this criterion, the *t*-test result cannot ensure the real difference between D_2 and D_{0X}. Another *t*-test result shows that, in terms of "affordability", D_3, which was also suggested by the users, significantly outperforms D_{0X}. In order to improve D_2 to become even better, Mulenserv can consider applying D_3's pricing strategy to enhance D_2's "affordability".

Eventually, we can say that the experimental data are significant, the results are validated and the user-suggested designs perform better than the design that was solely developed by Mulenserv's team. This confirms the advantage of the proposed framework.

The key to successful implementation of this framework is user co-creation throughout the process. Users understand what they need the most and would be ready to accept offerings that are tailored to their needs. Two other important factors are the simplification of PSS configurations using elements and the demonstration of PSS prototypes so that the users can experience and understand the PSS before co-creation. The proposed framework is structured regarding all of those factors.

There are several issues when adopting the design process of conventional NPD (new product development) to the PSS context. In NPD, the company designs and develops products according to the requirements that were retrieved from customer needs and the results of competitive benchmarking. In some cases, the communication of customer needs to the design team is not done properly, and that leads to ineffective products. When being applied to PSS design, where user emotion, behavior and preferences are highly significant, conventional NPD processes may not work properly. These cases of designing PSS need a new approach, such as our proposed framework. On the other hand, if the design requires technical skills, such as engineering, drafting, manufacturing, *etc.*, the co-creation task may become difficult for users to participate in, and the model may not be applied effectively. In summary, the proposed framework can effectively deal with the designing of user-sensitive components, such as consumer PSS in a B2C environment (not industrial PSS in a B2B environment).

After proposing the framework and conducting the experiment, we gained more insights and experience of how users are actually involved in a co-creative design process. To gain the expected result for implementation, several guidelines can be found below:

- Prepare the scenario of implementing the framework in the case, and communicate necessary activities during the process to all design team members.
- Prototypes of PSS are very important. The prototypes help users to fully understand how the PSS works, allowing them to experience it so that they can generate and evaluate the PSS in a correct way.
- Representing of the PSS is also important. PSS representation needs to be simple, but thorough enough to cover all possible PSS elements and parameters. This allows users to co-create effectively in terms of quantity and quality.
- Selection of the right participants is essential. Since the participation to co-create in this process is time consuming and requires plenty of effort, only users who are enthusiastic enough can ensure effective participation.

4.5. Managerial Implications

As shown by the validation of the experimental data, proper implementation of the proposed framework can lead to better performance of the PSS. This suggests that the concept of co-creation and user involvement can be implemented to bring innovation and breakthroughs to PSS development. The proposed framework can also be used to estimate the response of potential users (buyers) to the "to be launched" PSS. Companies can customize the proposed framework for their specific PSS design projects while keeping the basic principles: the right users; simple representation; thorough prototypes; easy input forms; and comprehensive evaluation.

In the case study of this paper, we use an on-site participatory design for invited users. Other methods of involving users can also be used, such as crowdsourcing. In this case, we can use a website where we upload a call for participation, demonstrations of the PSS, guidelines for each and every step, *etc.* This is another option for PSS projects. As suggested in the "Tasks" column of each step (Table 1), companies can choose various tools to perform tasks in the process of the proposed framework.

5. Conclusions

In this work, the authors propose a co-creative framework for redesigning a PSS. For the first time, a framework for user co-creation in PSS design has been proposed, detailed and evaluated with experimental implementation.

Our work provides a practical guideline for developers in designing and redesigning PSS. It enhances the value perception, evaluation and design quality of PSS. The experimental implementation with the case study and the analysis of the experimental results shows that the proposed framework is valid.

The proposed framework can effectively deal with the designing of user-sensitive components, such as consumer PSS in a B2C environment. In cases that requires a high level of technical skills and knowledge or cases with complicated service processes, such as industrial PSS (in a B2B environment), this framework might not work effectively.

Whether PSS can lead to achieving sustainability depends on how the technical design and the business model are developed to address sustainable development criteria. One limitation of this work is that, due to its focus, there is a lack of such consideration. Therefore, this work cannot claim the possibility of achieving sustainability through PSS. In our following work, where the focus is more appropriate, we would consider this issue as a separate research topic.

Furthermore, for future work, in order to prove the advantages of the proposed framework, a comparison between its implementation results and those of other existing methods will be carried out. Furthermore, an architecture of a computer program (or a mobile application) that employs this framework as the backbone can be developed. This program can assist design teams to design PSS collaboratively within their own team and with innovative customers.

Acknowledgments: This research was supported by the Basic Research Program through the National Research Foundation of Korea (NRF) funded by the Ministry of Education (No. 2013R1A1A2013649).

Author Contributions: Tuananh Tran conceived of, designed and performed the experiments; Joon Young Park proposed and Tuananh Tran performed the analysis of the experimental data. Tuananh Tran wrote the initial manuscript. Joon Young Park corrected and revised the final writing.

References

1. Weber, C.; Steinbach, M.; Botta, C.; Deubel, T. Modeling of product–Service systems (PSS) based on the PDD approach. In Proceedings of the International Design Conference, Dubrovnik, Croatia, 18–21 May 2004; pp. 547–554.
2. Aurich, J.C.; Mannweiler, C.; Schweitzer, E. How to design and offer service successfully. *CIRP J. Manuf. Sci. Technol.* **2010**, *2*, 136–143. [CrossRef]
3. Bettencourt, L.A.; Ulwick, A.W. The customer—Centered innovation map. *Harv. Bus. Rev.* **2008**, *5*, 109–114.
4. Sakao, T.; Birkhofer, H.; Panshef, V.; Dorsam, E. An effective and efficient method to design services: Empirical study for services by an investment machine manufacturer. *Int. J. Internet Manuf. Serv.* **2009**, *2*, 95–110. [CrossRef]
5. Beuren, F.H.; Ferreira, M.G.G.; Miguel, P.A.C. Product-service systems: A literature review on integrated products and services. *J. Clean. Prod.* **2013**, *47*, 222–231. [CrossRef]
6. Vasantha, G.V.A.; Roy, R.; Lelah, A.; Brissaud, D. A review of product-service systems design methodologies. *J. Eng. Des.* **2012**, *23*, 635–659. [CrossRef]
7. Goedkoop, M.J.; van Halen, C.J.G.; te Riele, H.R.M.; Rommens, P.J.M. Product Service Systems, Ecological and Economic Basis. Report to Ministry of Housing, Spatial Planning and the Environment Communications Directorate, The Hague, The Netherlands. 1999. Available online: http://docplayer.net/334668-Product-service-systems-ecological-and-economic-basics.html (accessed on 29 April 2016).
8. Mont, O.K. Clarifying the concept of product-service system. *J. Clean. Prod.* **2002**, *10*, 237–245. [CrossRef]
9. Lim, C.H.; Kim, K.J.; Hong, Y.S.; Park, K.T. PSS Board: A structured tool for product-service system process visualization. *J. Clean. Prod.* **2012**, *37*, 42–55. [CrossRef]
10. Hussain, R.; Lockett, H.; Vasantha, G.V.A. A framework to inform PSS conceptual design by using system–in–use data. *Comput. Ind.* **2012**, *63*, 319–327. [CrossRef]
11. Baines, T.S.; Lightfoot, H.; Steve, E.; Neely, A.; Greenough, R.; Peppard, J.; Roy, R.; Shehab, E.; Braganza, A.; Tiwari, A.; *et al.* State-of-the-art in product service systems. *Proc. Inst. Mech. Eng. Part B* **2007**, *221*, 1543–1552. [CrossRef]
12. Morelli, N. The design of product/service systems from a designer's perspective. *Common Ground (Lond.)* **2002**, *18*, 3–17.

13. Tukker, A. Eight types of product-service system: Eight ways to sustainability? Experiences from SusProNet. *Bus. Strategy Environ* **2004**, *13*, 246–260. [CrossRef]

14. Vezzoli, C.; Ceschin, F.; Diehl, J.C.; Kohtala, C. New design challenges to widely implement 'Sustainable Product–Service Systems'. *J. Clean. Prod.* **2015**, *97*, 1–12. [CrossRef]

15. Qu, M.; Yu, S.; Chen, D.; Chu, J.; Tian, B. State-of-the-art of design, evaluation, and operation methodologies in product service systems. *Comput. Ind.* **2016**, *77*, 1–14. [CrossRef]

16. Luiten, H.; Knot, M.; van der Host, T. Sustainable product service systems: The kathalys method. In Proceedings of the 2nd International Symposium on Environmentally Conscious Design and Inverse Manufacturing, Tokyo, Japan, 11–15 December 2001; pp. 190–197.

17. Manzini, E.; Vezolli, C. A strategic design approach to develop sustainable product service systems: Examples taken from the "environmental friendly innovation" Italian prize. *J. Clean. Prod.* **2003**, *11*, 851–857. [CrossRef]

18. Pezzotta, G.; Pirola, F.; Pinto, R.; Akasaka, F.; Shimomura, Y. A Service Engineering framework to design and assess an integrated product-service. *Mechatronics* **2015**, *31*, 169–179. [CrossRef]

19. Morelli, N. Developing new product service systems (PSS): Methodologies and operational tools. *J. Clean. Prod.* **2006**, *14*, 1495–1501. [CrossRef]

20. Kowalkowski, C.; Kindström, D. Value visualization strategies for PSS Development. In *Introduction to Product/Service-System Design*; Sakao, T., Lindahl, M., Eds.; Springer: London, UK, 2009; pp. 159–182.

21. Sakao, T.; Shimomura, Y. Service Engineering: A Novel Engineering Discipline for Producers to Increase Value Combining Service and Product. *J. Clean. Prod.* **2007**, *15*, 590–604. [CrossRef]

22. Kim, Y.S.; Wang, E.; Lee, S.W.; Choi, Y.C. A Product-Service System Representation and Its Application in a Concept Design Scenario. In Proceedings of the 1st CIRP Industrial Product Service Systems (IPS2) Conference, Cranfield University, England, UK, 1–2 April 2009; pp. 32–39.

23. Maussang, N.; Zwolinski, P.; Brissaud, D. Product-service system design methodology: From the PSS architecture design to the products specifications. *J. Eng. Des.* **2009**, *20*, 349–366. [CrossRef]

24. Tan, A.R.; Matzen, D.; McAloone, T.; Evans, S. Strategies for Designing and Developing Services for Manufacturing Firms. *CIRP J. Manuf. Sci. Technol.* **2010**, *3*, 90–97. [CrossRef]

25. Bertoni, A.; Bertoni, M.; Isaksson, O. Communicating the Value of PSS Design Alternatives using Color-Coded CAD Models. In Proceedings of the 3rd CIRP International Conference on Industrial Product Service Systems, Braunschweig, Germany, 5–6 May 2011.

26. Steen, M.; Manschot, M.; De Koning, N. Benefits of co-design in service design projects. *Int. J. Des.* **2011**, *5*, 53–60.

27. Shih, L.H.; Hu, A.H.; Lin, S.L.; Chen, J.L.; Tu, J.C. ; Kuo T.C. An Integrated Approach for Product Service System Development: II. Evaluation Phase. *J. Environ. Eng. Manag.* **2009**, *19*, 343–356.

28. Yoon, B.; Kim, S.; Rhee, J. An evaluation method for designing a new product-service system. *Expert Syst. Appl.* **2012**, *39*, 3100–3108. [CrossRef]

29. Exner, K.; Lindow, K.; Buchholz, C.; Stark, R. Validation of Product-Service Systems-A Prototyping Approach. *Procedia CIRP* **2014**, *16*, 68–73. [CrossRef]

30. Komoto, H.; Tomiyama, T. Design of Competitive Maintenance Service for Durable and Capital Goods using Life Cycle Simulation. *Int. J. Autom. Technol.* **2009**, *3*, 63–70.

31. Dorst, K. The core of 'design thinking' and its application. *Des. Stud.* **2011**, *32*, 521–532. [CrossRef]

32. Kleemann, F. Un(der)paid Innovators: The Commercial Utilization of Consumer Work through Crowdsourcing Science. *Technol. Innov. Stud.* **2008**, *4*, 5–26.

33. Tran, T.; Park, J.Y. Crowd Participation Pattern in the Phases of a Product Development Process that Utilizes Crowdsourcing. *Ind. Eng. Manag. Syst.* **2012**, *11*, 266–275. [CrossRef]

7

Development of an Innovation Model based on a Service-Oriented Product Service System (PSS)

Seungkyum Kim [1], Changho Son [2], Byungun Yoon [3] and Yongtae Park [1,*]

[1] Department of Industrial Engineering, Seoul National University, 1 Gwanak-ro, Gwanak-gu, Seoul 151-742, Korea; hdglace8@snu.ac.kr

[2] Department of Weapon System Engineering, Korea Army Academy at Yeong-Cheon, 135-1 Changhari, Young-Cheon, Gyeongbuk 770-849, Korea; c13981@snu.ac.kr

[3] Department of Industrial & Systems Engineering, Dongguk University, Seoul 04620, Korea; postman3@dongguk.edu

* Author to whom correspondence should be addressed; parkyt1@snu.ac.kr.

Academic Editor: Adam Jabłoński

Abstract: Recently, there have been many attempts to cope with increasingly-diversified and ever-changing customer needs by combining products and services that are critical components of innovation models. Although not only manufacturers, but also service providers, try to integrate products and services, most of the previous studies on Product Service System (PSS) development deal with how to effectively integrate services into products from the product-centric point of view. Services provided by manufacturers' PSSes, such as delivery services, training services, disposal services, and so on, offer customers ancillary value, whereas products of service providers' PSSes enrich core value by enhancing the functionality and quality of the service. Thus, designing an effective PSS development process from the service-centric point of view is an important research topic. Accordingly, the purpose of this paper is to propose a service-oriented PSS development process, which consists of four stages: (1) strategic planning; (2) idea generation and selection; (3) service design; and (4) product development. In the proposed approach, the PSS development project is initiated and led by a service provider from a service-centric point of view. From the perspective of methodology, customer needs are converted into product functions according to Quality Function Deployment (QFD), while Analytic Hierarchy Process (AHP) is employed to prioritize the functions. Additionally, this paper illustrates a service-oriented PSS development that demonstrates the application of the proposed process. The proposed process and illustration are expected to serve as a foundation for research on service-oriented PSS development and as a useful guideline for service providers who are considering the development of a service-oriented PSS.

Keywords: Product Service System (PSS); service-oriented PSS development process; English education; Analytic Hierarchy Process (AHP); Quality Function Deployment (QFD)

---

1. Introduction

Recently, customer needs have become increasingly diversified and ever-changing. Under this circumstance, because it is very difficult to fulfill sophisticated customer needs by product innovation alone, many attempts to overcome this problem have involved combining products and services. In practice, companies, such as General Electric, Xerox, Canon, and Parkersell, have shown a considerable increase in sales and profits from services since the mid-1990s [1]. Although such companies had originally made profits by only selling products, they have maintained growth by integrating services into their products. These attempts can be regarded as Product Service Systems

(PSS), which are firstly defined as a set of products and services that fulfills customer needs and has lower environmental impact [2]. Most of the early studies on PSS focused on the environmental aspect. However, the scope and concept of PSS have been expanded, as various studies on PSS have been actively conducted. Nowadays, PSS is regarded as an integrated system of products and services to provide customers with functions and value that they need [3]. Thus, it is one of the critical components of innovation models that can create value on existing and new businesses.

Most of the previous studies on PSS are based on the viewpoint of manufacturers [4–11]. Particularly, studies on PSS development deal with how to effectively integrate services into products from the product-centric point of view, and they focus on a specific phase, not the whole development process. Low *et al.* [4] suggested an idea generation method using theory of solving inventive problem (TRIZ) methodology, while Uchihira *et al.* [8] proposed a method that identifies PSS opportunities along with product usage. Aurich *et al.* [6] and Yang *et al.* [11] utilized product life-cycle data for idea generation and design of PSSes. In summary, there is a lack of research on PSS development covering the whole development process, and it is rare to find PSS research conducted from the service-centric point of view. However, service providers are also making attempts to integrate products into their services for effective service deliveries and differentiated customer value. Amazon's Kindle is an example of this case. PSSes developed by manufacturers and service providers have different characteristics in terms of customer value. Services of manufacturers' PSSes, such as delivery services, training services, disposal services, and so on, offer customers ancillary value instead of core value that customers recognize when consuming the product, whereas products of service providers' PSSes ensure that core value is enriched by enhancing functionality and quality of the service. In the case of Kindle, e-book contents are instantly delivered with lower cost, easier access, and easier payment; therefore, Kindle enriches the core value that Amazon has offered customers as an online bookstore. Thus, a different approach for developing a service-centric PSS is required. Therefore, designing an effective PSS development process from the service-centric point of view is an important research topic.

Accordingly, this paper proposes a service-oriented PSS development process in which the PSS development project is initiated and led by a service provider from a service-centric viewpoint to generate a new innovation model. In contrast to a single product or service development, PSS development is carried out by multiple actors, including manufacturers and service providers; hence, the role of each actor should be defined clearly. In the proposed process, which consists of four stages, the actor and its role are specified for each stage. Additionally, this paper introduces a real PSS development case from the education industry sector, which demonstrates the application of the proposed process and discusses the practical issues that can occur during the PSS development project. The fact that the proposed process was applied to real business practices has practical significance and, furthermore, this research could serve as a useful guideline for service providers to develop a service-oriented PSS.

The remainder of this paper is organized as follows. In the next section, the previous studies on PSS development are reviewed, which build a foundation for the proposed approach. In Section 3, a service-oriented PSS development process is proposed including the concept, framework, and detailed processes. Section 4 introduces the case of service-oriented PSS development in detail. Finally, this research ends with conclusions that include contributions, limitations and directions for future research.

2. Literature Review

2.1. Definition of PSS

Recently, PSS has received much attention from both industry and academia. Accordingly, active research regarding PSS is underway. Goedkoop *et al.* [2] initially suggested the PSS concept, which is defined as "a system of products, services, networks of players, and supporting infrastructure that continuously strives to be competitive, satisfy customer needs and have a lower environmental impact than traditional innovation models" [2]. On the other hand, Wong [12] defined PSS as follows; "Product Service-Systems (PSS) may be defined as a solution offered for sale that involves both a product and a service element, to deliver the required functionality", which was not limited to the environmental impact. Although many researchers have since proposed different definitions of PSS, it has generally been considered as "product(s) and service(s) combined in a system to enable new innovation models aiming to fulfill customer needs" [2,3,13,14].

2.2. Characteristics of PSS

The main characteristics of PSS, in comparison with pure products or services, are threefold. First, firms can improve the level of interaction with their customers through PSS. In terms of customer relationships, the products, and services offered through PSS play a complementary role in satisfying the customers' requirements. For instance, if a company that sells washing machines also provides laundry service to its customers, the interaction with customers will be increased because of the characteristics of this add-on service. Second, there are a variety of types of payment and ownership of PSS [15]. This is because PSS is an integrated model of ownable and tangible products and non-owned and intangible services. Accordingly, most PSS providers have ownership of their PSS and sell the usage rights or results. Tukker [15] suggested three main categories of PSS, including product-oriented services, use-oriented services, and result-oriented services. In case of use-oriented services and result-oriented services, the payment reference is not for the product, but a payment per unit time or unit use, and so on. The product stays in ownership with the provider in the above cases, whereas products are mainly sold and some extra services are added in product-oriented services. Here, there is no pre-determined product involved for result-oriented services.

Lastly, stakeholders creating PSS value are very diverse [16,17], including PSS providers and customers. A representative example where integrated products and services are provided through collaboration among several firms is Apple's AppStore.

2.3. Types of PSS

The most widely accepted of the proposed PSS types is the work by Tukker [15]. The three main categories are as follows: product-oriented PSS, use-oriented PSS, and result-oriented PSS. First, the product-oriented PSS is the most similar to the concept of the traditional product, since the value is achieved by selling the product. However, this is accompanied by additional services such as after-sales services to guarantee the functionality of the product. Second, use-oriented PSS basically sells the "use" of a product, not the product itself. What is delivered to the customer is a function that the customer wants, for example, leasing or sharing services. Finally, result-oriented PSS sells a result or capability instead of a product. The customer pays only for the provision of agreed results. Selling laundered clothes instead of a washing machine is a good example of result-oriented PSS [3,15].

2.4. Research on PSS Development Process

Most studies of the PSS development process have been based on the development process of products or services and consist of three main phases: analysis, idea generation, and selection, and implementation [17]. The first phase, analysis, includes environmental analysis, SWOT analysis, and so on, which has been treated as a small part of PSS development research. Nevertheless, some methodologies have been developed and employed in the analysis phase. The "Innovation Scan" was developed for analyzing and forecasting the relationship between customer needs and product functions [18], while the product-service integrated roadmap was proposed for the strategic planning of product-service integrated offerings [19]. The next phase, idea generation and selection, has been the most actively studied. Lee and Kim [20] classified PSS by function and developed PSS ideas using a combination of products and services. Low et al. [4], Chen and Huang [21], and Chen and Li [22] utilized TRIZ for idea generation. The TRIZ method stands for "Teoriya Resheniya Izobretatelskikh

Zadatch" in Russian which means theory of inventive problem solving [23,24]. This method solves technical problems and offers innovative product structures by employing a knowledge base built from the analyses of approximately 2.5 million patents, primarily on mechanical design [25]. TRIZ consists of three basic tools: (1) 40 principles to resolve conflicts effectively; (2) a knowledge database system that consists of physical, chemical, and geometrical effects and rules for problem solving; and (3) modeling a technological problem.

Uhlmann and Stelzer [26] suggested seven dimensions to determine PSS ideas through a case study. The seven dimensions are composed of customer skills, customer will to build up skills, property rights, human resources, outsourcing of product, existing network of suppliers, and process monitoring to determine PSS ideas through a case study.

Meiner and Kroll [27] proposed an approach to creating a new PSS model based on service processes. In addition, many tools, such as extended service blueprint [10], system map, interaction storyboard, stakeholder motivation matrix [28], modified IDEF0 [29], and many others to design PSSes using generated and selected new ideas have been developed. Finally, in the implementation phase, Schuh and Gudergan [30] suggested a framework using QFD (Quality Function Deployment) and Yang et al. [11] provided a methodology for the realization of PSSes through the utilization of product life-cycle data. The QFD has been widely used since Akao suggested it in 1990. The tool that has been used most frequently in QFD is a matrix called the House Of Quality (HOQ), which is utilized for the aim of converting market information into product strategies for business [31].

As we have explained, most previous research on PSS development has focused on a specific phase, not the whole development process. In particular, these studies have been mainly conducted from the product-centric point of view. In other words, previous studies of PSS development dealt with products and relevant supporting services, but the converse was not the case. While the term, "service-oriented product" was utilized in some studies [32,33], it represented use-oriented PSS rather than service-supporting products. Therefore, research on the entire development process for service-oriented PSS is still the domain of a few pioneers.

3. Service-Oriented PSS Development

3.1. Concept

This research proposes the service-oriented PSS development process for developing a new innovation model. The term, "service-oriented PSS" stands for a PSS in which a product is integrated into a service as a supporting tool to make the existing service more competitive. The distinctive characteristics of the service-oriented PSS are twofold. First, customer needs for the existing service are the starting point of service-oriented PSS development, whereas product-centric PSS development begins with the needs for the product itself or the context of product usage. After customer needs for the service are investigated, the product functions to fulfill these needs are derived from the investigation result. Subsequently, new services are developed by combining the existing service with the new product. Where a single service cannot meet customer needs without a product, it can be complemented by the integration of the service and product. That is to say, functions required for the product are derived from customer needs for the service, and the product makes the service more competitive. The integration of the service and product constitutes the service-oriented PSS, which can provide greater competitiveness and value than a stand-alone service.

Second, in service-oriented PSS development, the role of the product manufacturer should receive greater emphasis than that of the service provider in product-centric PSS development. Most previous studies on PSS development considered services as the means to offer customers ancillary value in order to raise lock-in effects and sales from the manufacturers' viewpoint, and manufacturers introduce and operate their own services in many cases [7]. On the other hand, it is hard for service providers to develop and produce products. In a relative sense, products are dependent on technologies, equipment, and facilities, whereas services are dependent on humans. Thus, service providers should establish strong partnerships with manufacturers to develop service-oriented PSSes and closely collaborate with partners on product and service developments. In these regards, service-oriented PSS development differs from product-centric PSS development.

3.2. Framework

The service-oriented PSS development process proposed in this research is derived from the product development process of Cooper *et al.* [34,35], the service development process of Brügemann [36], and several cases of PSS development projects summarized by Tukker and Tischner [17]. The product development process of Cooper *et al.* [34,35] is represented by the stage-gate process which comprises a five-stage (scoping, build business case, development, testing and validation, and launch), five gate (idea screen, second screen, go to development, go to testing, and go to launch) process incorporating a discovery stage and a post-launch review, whereas the service development process of Brügemann [36] is composed of eight stages: "situation analysis", "objectives", "strategy", "idea finding", "generation of requirements", "development", "implementation", and "delivery of service". Tukker and Tischner [17] investigated PSS development methods used in PSS development projects and grouped them into three phases, "analysis", "idea generation and selection", and "implementation". Based on these references, we made the service-oriented PSS development process by grouping similar stages and excluding stages related to marketing, distribution, and use in order to focus on development. The result consists of four stages, "strategic planning", "idea generation and selection", "service design", and "product development". Between every stage, an intermediate evaluation and back-loop scheme using the results of intermediate evaluation is applied like Cooper *et al.*'s five gates. Contrary to the previous sequential processes, the proposed process is a hybrid of sequential and parallel processes, because PSS development includes product development as well as service development. The planning and idea generation for PSS development are carried out sequentially and service design proceeds in parallel with product development.

As shown in Figure 1, the service-oriented PSS development process has two layers, a service provider layer and product partner (manufacturer) layer, which show the participants for each stage. Service-oriented PSS development is initiated by the service provider, hence the first stage, "strategic planning" is carried out by the service provider alone. The next stage, "idea generation and selection" is performed by the service provider and the product partner selected in the previous stage. Together they generate detailed ideas for planned PSS development. Subsequently, the third and fourth stages, "service design" and "product development", are conducted concurrently by the service provider and the product partner, respectively. At this time, the key aspect to successful PSS development is to achieve consensus on the service and product through effective communication and interaction between the two actors. To this end, the results of service design should be delivered to the product partner in order to verify the technical feasibility of the required service functions, and the pilot product should also be delivered to the service provider in order to judge the suitability of the design and functions. These collaborations are expressed as arrows between "service design" and "product development" in Figure 1. Here, a service-oriented PSS can be developed from the open innovation concept of Chesbrough [37]. From a service-centered point of view, product partners can be considered as external; *i.e.*, the use of purposive inflows and outflows of knowledge is to accelerate internal innovation and expand the markets for external use of innovation. Actors and key features for each stage of the service-oriented PSS development process are summarized in Table 1.

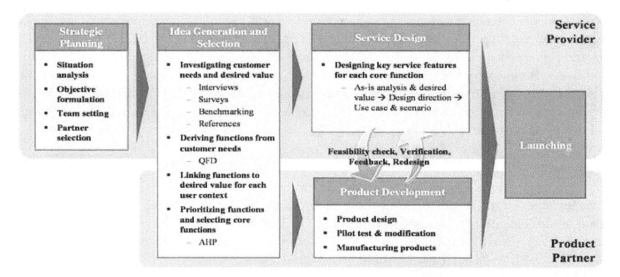

Figure 1. Service-oriented PSS development process.

Table 1. Actors and key features for each stage of the service-oriented PSS development process.

Stage		Actor	Key Feature
Strategic Planning		Service Provider	The service-oriented PSS development is initiated by the service provider, and a product partner is selected.
Idea Generation and Selection		Service Provider & Product Partner	During this stage, there is a preliminary check of the feasibility of the ideas and consensus on the detailed PSS concept is achieved through collaboration between the two actors.
PSS Development	Service Design	Service Provider	Detailed service features and product functions are verified and redesigned based on feedback. Finally, the final service-oriented PSS is developed.
	Product Development	Product Partner	
Launching		Service Provider & Product Partner	The service-oriented PSS is launched in the market.

3.3. Detailed Process

3.3.1. Strategic Planning

A service-oriented PSS development project is initiated by the service provider and the first stage is strategic planning. First, the service provider determines what to develop. In the case that services, alone, are provided, the service provider builds a general concept of PSS development that combines the existing services and product in order to increase competitiveness and customer satisfaction as well as add new value for customers. Thereafter, the service provider conducts situation analyses, including market analysis, competence analysis, competitor analysis, and so on. Subsequently, the concrete objectives of the PSS development project and the team that will lead it are formulated. Lastly, the product partner that will cover the product development is selected. The selection of a product partner to develop the service-oriented PSS can be accomplished through a variety of methods. Among them, an emergent theory of partner selection through collaboration, similar to that produced by Emden *et al.* [38], is utilized. The model is composed of three broad phases: (1) technological alignment; (2) strategic alignment; and (3) relational alignment. Technological capability, resource complementarity, and overlapping knowledge bases are considered in the first phase. Then, motivation and goal correspondence are checked in the second phase. Finally, compatible cultures, propensity to change, and long-term orientation are screened in the third phase.

3.3.2. Idea Generation and Selection

The second stage is idea generation and selection, which are conducted by the service provider and the product partner selected in the previous stage. In this stage, it is essential to investigate customer needs for the existing service and derive product functions from these needs. To this end, expected user groups are firstly selected, and each group's needs for the existing service are investigated thoroughly. At this point, not only customer needs but also their desired requirements *i.e.*, what they ultimately want from the service, should be identified. Interviews and surveys are the most useful and representative methods for this purpose. Particularly, in-depth interviews with customers and related experts are an effective means to figure out the ideal service scenarios and product functions required when the service is combined with the product. In addition, reviews in relevant professional publications and reports, and benchmarking of existing relevant services and products can provide the implications of success and failure factors that help derive product functions.

The next step is to derive product functions based on prior investigations of customer needs. At this point, customer needs are converted into product functions in a similar manner to QFD, which transforms customer needs into engineering/process requirements. Subsequently, additional functions can be added from the benchmarking results. Eventually, the customer needs generated from the service are analyzed and converted into product functions.

The following step is to match up functions with desired requirements using QFD. The desired requirements can be varied according to the purpose and situation of each user group. Thus, the functions that will be provided should differ in accordance with user groups. To deal with this problem, the actors in this stage should analyze the user context and derive desired requirements according to each user group's context based on the results of the investigation conducted previously. Subsequently, actors match every function with certain desired requirements and user groups. Consequently, the results can show a user group and its desired requirements provided by a specific function, functions needed by a specific user group, and functions that fulfill certain desired requirements. An exemplified outcome of this task is illustrated in Figure 2.

Lastly, functions are prioritized by the Analytic Hierarchy Process (AHP) method and core functions are selected as the final outcome of this stage. The AHP is a decision-aiding method developed by Saaty [39–41]. It is one of the most widely used multi-criteria decision-making tools and is an Eigenvalue approach to pair-wise comparisons. It also provides a methodology to calibrate the numeric scale for the measurement of both quantitative and qualitative performances [42]. The number of core functions can vary according to constraints such as project schedule and financial budget, and the remaining functions can be developed and added to the next version of the PSS. Through the previous steps such as investigating customer needs and desired requirements, deriving functions, and linking functions with desired requirements, participants in this stage can be regarded as experts who have sufficient knowledge about the desired requirements and the necessary functions. Thus, they can evaluate the relative importance between two functions based on their experiences when using the AHP method.

User group 1									
User context & DR*	Context 1			Context 2			Context 3		...
Functions	DR 1-1	DR 1-2	...	DR 2-1	DR 2-2	...	DR 3-1	DR 3-2	...	...
Function 1	O	O			O					
Function 2				O			O			
Function 3				O			O	O		
Function 4	O			O						
⋮										

* DR: desired requirement

Figure 2. An example of a matrix for linking functions to desired requirements for each user context.

3.3.3. Service Design

The service design stage and the product development stage proceed in parallel under the respective guidance of the service provider and product partner after the second stage, idea generation and selection. In the service design stage, the service provider designs services in detail, which can be realized with the product functions derived in the previous stage.

Service dominant logic is comprised of five steps as follows: (1) as-is analysis; (2) setting service design direction; (3) creating service use-cases; (4) making service scenarios; and (5) checking feasibility. First, the service provider conducts the "as-is analysis", which analyzes the current situation of services offered without a product. The deficiencies in current services that are contrary to the ideal services and desired requirements are derived from "as-is analysis". Thereafter, the service provider establishes the direction of the service design for overcoming the gap between the current services and the ideal ones via integration with product functions. Subsequently, the service provider develops use-cases based on the design direction, which includes elements such as actors (users, service providers, and so on), product, and infrastructure (systems, networks, and so on.) as well as the relationships between elements such as information input/output and physical materials. After all the use cases have been developed, service scenarios for each user group can be created by aggregating them. During these tasks, modeling methods such as IDEF0 which is a compound acronym Icam DEFinition for Function Modeling, where "ICAM" is an acronym for Integrated Computer Aided Manufacturing and service blueprint [29] can be exploited. After the use cases and service scenarios have been developed, they are delivered to the product partner to verify the technical feasibility. Then, the service provider receives feedback on the technical feasibility of the service, and redesigns services based on this. Furthermore, the service provider should give feedback on the pilot product to the product partner.

3.3.4. Product Development

In this stage, the product partner develops the product. The product partner develops the basic design, architecture, and product specifications, and realizes the functions derived from the idea generation and selection. Once the pilot product is created, the product partner should deliver it to the service provider and modify its design, functions, and so on, according to the feedback from the service provider. In addition, once the product partner receives the use cases and service scenarios from the service provider, the product partner checks the feasibility to determine whether it is possible to realize the product functions required by the service or not. If there is a function that is impossible to realize, the product partner sends feedback so that the relevant service can be redesigned. Otherwise, the product partner modifies the functions, architecture, or specifications of the product according to the use cases and service scenarios. Effective and efficient interaction between the service provider and product partner is critical to develop a successful PSS. Thus, various iterations of feasibility checks, verifications, feedback and redesigns are inevitable while jointly developing the service and product. Once the final consensus on the service and product is achieved through these processes, the product partner manufactures the products. Finally, service-oriented PSS development is finished and launched. There are many factors to take into account when launching a service-oriented PSS. The launching stage needs to address some basic issues such as launch goal and strategy, major player and stakeholders, target customers, current market environment, and so on [43]. It is critical to carefully design a launch plan and prepare internally before a public launch. This internal preparation will address issues such as testing and validation, pricing, documentation, warranty, demos, sales tools, training for sale/channels/service/support, and so on.

4. Illustration: T Smart Learning

4.1. Introduction to the Case Companies and the PSS Development Project

The illustration in this paper is derived from a PSS development project undertaken by S Telecom in collaboration with C Learning. S Telecom is a mobile service provider in Korea, with 50.6% market share as of 2010. Since its launch on 29 March 1984 S Telecom has evolved from a first-generation analog cellular system, to a second-generation CDMA provider, and then to the world's first third-generation synchronized IMT-2000 cellular system. S Telecom also became the world's first company to commercialize HSDPA in May 2006. S Telecom provides not only mobile telecommunication services but also convergence services including media, social networking, content delivery, location-based service, platform, commerce, and a host of other options. Recently, S Telecom has been actively seeking new business opportunities to cope with B2C market saturation by developing B2B innovation models in various industry sectors, including the education industry.

C Learning is a language institute located in Korea and Canada. C Learning was founded in 1998 and offers ESL (English as a Second Language) learning services by combining self-developed programs and native English-speaking instructors. C Learning provides more than 60,000 students with unique programs based on critical thinking and cognitive language development. This is made possible by more than 1300 instructors, 390 corporate employees, and its ESL R-and-D center. Recently, the company has reached saturation in terms of the number of students it can teach due to physical space constraints. Thus, an innovative method for continuous growth is required. Additionally, the Korean Education Ministry unveiled a plan to introduce a new English aptitude test—NEAT (National English Ability Test)—that focuses on tests of speaking and writing ability, and will replace the English section of the standardized college entrance examination. Therefore, new coursework and classes to prepare for the NEAT will have to be created.

Under this background, S Telecom and C Learning signed a memorandum of understanding on developing an English learning system that uses wireless communications networks to allow students to study anywhere and anytime, keep parents up to date with students' progress, and to increase communication between the teacher and students within the classroom. The characteristics of this system as a PSS are as follows. It consists of actors (students, parents, and instructors), contents, learning-support devices, and network infrastructures. From its inception, the project considered English learning services and learning-support devices (products) simultaneously in order to create a successful PSS that can raise the effectiveness and efficiency of learning. Accordingly, many stakeholders' needs were investigated and incorporated during the development process. Furthermore, this system will only be meaningful if customer needs are fulfilled by the services or functions offered via the product. Thus, product possession itself has no meaning. In particular, product functions were developed in order to fulfill customer needs and desired requirements that were derived and analyzed from existing English learning services. These characteristics made this English learning system a service-oriented PSS.

4.2. Strategic Planning

To begin, S Telecom and C Learning analyzed the global trend and potential of the English education market, the state of affairs of the major IT players (Apple, Intel, and so on) in the education sector, and local cases of device-based learning services by mobile service providers. These analyses produced the following results: (1) English education is experiencing high growth in the global market and Asia is the most promising region; (2) the focus of English education is moving toward improving fundamental listening, speaking, reading, and writing abilities, instead of grammar and reading comprehension; and (3) key success factors for a device-based learning system involve not only fine contents but also specialized functions increase the effectiveness of education. Consequently, S Telecom and C Learning set up an objective to develop a PSS that combines an English learning service and a mobile device. The first target service was the NEAT coursework, which had already been made by the R-and-D center of C Learning. The target product was a tablet PC-like device, which supports wireless data communication and provides specialized functions for effectively improving listening, speaking, reading, and writing English abilities. In addition, they made a plan to gradually expand the target market by adding other coursework and subjects and entering global education markets such as China and Southeast Asian countries.

Next, S Telecom and C Learning set up an exclusive TFT (Task Force Team) for developing the product. After establishing the team setting, the TFT searched for various device manufacturers and software developers in order to select product partners, and contacted them based on considerations of technological competency and quality, as well as cost. Finally, the hardware and software-product partners were selected and members from these product partners joined the TFT.

4.3. Idea Generation and Selection

For idea generation and selection, the TFT thoroughly investigated customer needs and desired requirements in English education. The TFT conducted in-depth interviews with more than 20 students and parents, and 20 experts in English education such as English teachers, directors of language institutes, and coursework developers so that users' and teachers' needs for existing English learning services and ideal methods of learning English were investigated. Additionally, the TFT reviewed eight books about the theory of English learning and 11 autobiographies by people who were successful in learning English. They also benchmarked 52 on/offline learning services and 36 learning-support devices. This broad and deep investigation enabled the TFT to achieve a full understanding of the existing English education services. It is very important to devote sufficient time and effort to this kind of task, since it serves as the foundation of the following tasks.

After extensive investigations, the TFT derived device functions based on the investigation results. The needs were converted into functions via QFD methodology, and other functions were added based on the benchmarking results. In this process, there was a preliminary check of the feasibilities of the functions, especially by TFT members who joined from product partners. For example, the "eyeball tracking" function was excluded due to technical problems and cost. Finally, 149 functions were derived. Examples of customer needs and relevant functions are summarized in Table 2.

Table 2. Examples of customer needs and relevant functions.

User Group	Need	Function
Student	"Although I cannot understand what is said in class, I hesitate to ask a question." "I want learning to be more interesting." "I want more exposure to English."	Evaluating the current level, Daily test, Learning history, Learning game, Role-play, Avatar, Online community, Push contents, and *etc.*
Teacher	"I want to arouse students' interest with teaching materials made of multimedia contents such as movies, sitcoms, news, and pop songs." "In the class, it takes too much time to correct each student's speaking and writing." "I want to check homework and score exams more efficiently."	Coursework generator, Multimedia contents library, Speaking evaluation, Writing evaluation, Auto-grading, Class planner, Student profile management, and *etc.*
Parent	"I wonder my child follows the coursework well." "I want to know how much my child's achievement level is improving."	Informing of diagnosis results, Informing of progress, Informing of attitude in class, and *etc.*

The following step involves matching functions with desired requirements as well as the user context for each user group using QFD. This task was conducted through a one-day workshop attended by all members of the TFT, whereas previous tasks such as interviews, benchmarking, and function derivation were assigned to groups composed of two or three members. The TFT divided users into three groups: student, teacher and parent. For each group, the TFT analyzed user context and derived desired requirements in each context based on the investigation results (see Figures 3 and 4). Finally, 34 function sets were derived by grouping similar functions among 149 functions.

Student											
User context & DR* \ Functions	...	Speaking					Listening			...	
	...	Mimicking /shadowing	Imitation/ reproduction	Present- ation	Debate	...	Recog- nizing	Skim- ming	Scan- ning	...	...
Text-to-speech		O					O	O	O		
Record and play			O	O							
Partial repeat		O					O				
Memo				O	O			O	O		
⋮											

* DR: desired requirement

Figure 3. The partial outcome of linking functions to desired requirements for students' context.

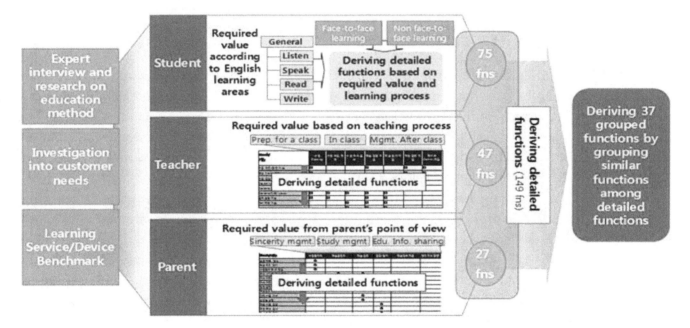

Figure 4. The partial outcome of linking functions to desired requirements for students' context.

Lastly, the TFT prioritized the function sets by the AHP method, and selected the core function sets. Since too many functions were derived, it was not reasonable to develop them all together in view of time-to-market, development cost, and quality. Thus, the TFT needed to select functions that would be developed for the first version of T Smart Learning, and the AHP method was employed for this aim. In addition, all members took an entire day to prioritize function sets as a group. The criteria for AHP were determined through discussion as follows: (1) effectiveness of learning; (2) personalized learning; and (3) competitiveness. After obtaining the weights for all criteria by pairwise comparisons, the TFT conducted pairwise comparisons between function sets for each criterion. Eventually, all function sets were prioritized and all consistency ratios were below 0.1, which means that all comparisons were consistent (see Table 3). Based on the priorities, five function sets for students were selected as core function sets. Additionally, the function sets for teachers and parents were selected as core function sets in order to cover all user groups, even though these priorities were ranked below the other function sets. In the final outcome (see Appendix 5), the core function sets included: (1) listening-specialized function set; (2) speaking-specialized function set; (3) reading-specialized function set; (4) writing-specialized function set; (5) personal care function set; (6) teacher-support function set; and (7) parent-support function set. Other function sets will be developed and added in the next version of T Smart Learning.

In this step, the AHP method was an effective means to reach a consensus on which functions would be developed first. During pairwise comparisons, the members of TFT discussed the relative importance between functions and, consequently, the consensus was built spontaneously. Thus, the AHP method served as a tool for not only prioritizing functions but also for building a consensus among TFT members.

Table 3. Priority of criteria and consistency ratio.

Criteria	Priority	Consistency Ratio for Function Sets Evaluation
Effectiveness of learning	0.5438	0.05066
Personalized learning	0.1103	0.02724
Competitiveness	0.3460	0.03084

4.4. Service Design

The TFT (excluding members from product partners) designed services in detail, which can be realized by utilizing the core functions derived in the previous stage. First, the TFT analyzed the deficiencies of the current English education services offered without a product, and derived the service design direction for each function set to compensate for the gap between the current situation and desired requirements investigated previously. Thereafter, the TFT created the service use-cases based on the design directions and developed service scenarios by aggregating use-cases.

The case of the speaking-specialized function set is as follows. The requirements for learning how to speak English are mimicking, imitation, reproduction, presentation, debate, self-check, and evaluation. In detail, students should listen to the native speaker's pronunciation and imitate it at the beginning. The next step is to practice various expressions that have similar meanings. Subsequently, it is necessary to improve the ability to organize the contents of what will be said. Finally, students will be able to make a presentation and participate in a debate with their own thoughts and opinions. In all these processes, self-check and evaluation can make learning more effective. However, there is little or no chance to speak English in reality. Moreover, students cannot find self-learning methods or receive instant feedback on their speaking abilities. Thus, the TFT established the design direction as follows: (1) providing various expressions recorded in a native speaker's pronunciation in order to allow self-practice; (2) giving instant feedback on speaking ability; and (3) offering a virtual place to communicate with colleagues via telepresence. According to these design directions, the TFT designed service use cases such as "speaking English by watching one's face via a camera in the device", "comparing one's pronunciation with a native speaker's by a record and play function", "providing a role-play service through which one can communicate with virtual characters through the device", and "providing a group discussion service via telepresence and giving instant feedback based on STT (Speech-to-Text) technology". The TFT delivered these outcomes to the product partners and received feedback from them. Subsequently, the use-cases were redesigned based on the feedback. For example, the software product partner recommended that the TFT change "giving instant feedback based on STT technology" because of the low accuracy of current STT technology. Thus, the TFT changed the concept of the feedback service from automated instant feedback to semi-automated not-instant feedback, in which manual correction by a teacher is included. The use-case of the feedback service is shown in Figure 5.

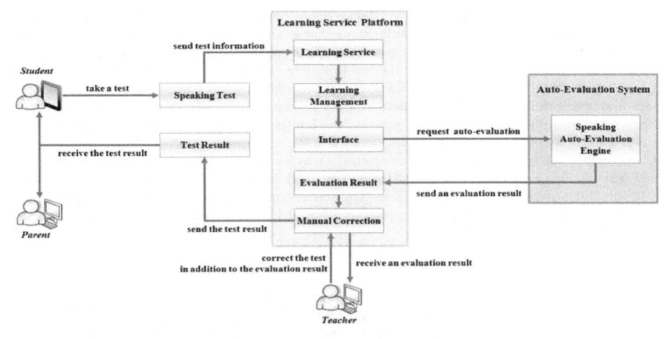

Figure 5. The use-case of the feedback service.

Finally, the TFT developed the service scenario for each user group by aggregating the service use-cases, and the partial outcome of the service scenario for the students is illustrated in Figure 6. The service scenarios were also confirmed by the product partners.

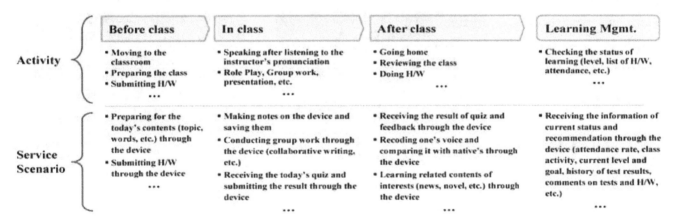

Figure 6. The partial outcome of the service scenario for the student.

4.5. Product Development

The respective hardware and software-product partners developed the hardware and software products that could realize the core functions derived in the idea generation and selection stage. During the development process, the product partners received service use-cases and scenarios from the TFT and incorporated them into the product development. Furthermore, the product partners communicated with the TFT continuously to receive feedback on the intermediate outcomes, and modified the products accordingly. The hardware product partner intended to develop a new device that specialized in learning, and the software product partner intended to develop a new software platform and related applications for the device based on Android open-source software.

However, it was hard to complete the hardware product development before the scheduled date. When considering the quality, cost, and release timing, the TFT and product partners decided to apply an existing tablet PC for the first version. Accordingly, the TFT and the hardware product partner consented to develop a learning-specialized device based on a long-term plan, whereas the software product partner developed the application launcher that would make an Android OS-based tablet PC operate as a new learning device. In this case, the application launcher can be regarded as another OS operating on top of the Android OS. While developing the software product, the software product partner improved the user interface and functions according to feedback from the TFT. Although the shape and specifications of the device are identical with the existing general-purpose tablet PC, the device with the launcher can provide an entirely new English-learning experience. In addition to the launcher, the software product partner developed a system comprised of the architecture, platform, and servers, which is indispensable for operating a service based on a mobile network and device (see Figure 7). Finally, S Telecom and C Learning launched a service-oriented PSS, T Smart Learning, on 18 July 2011, after a one month pilot test. The actual appearance of T Smart Learning is shown in Figure 8. The left figure is the main screen of T Smart Learning and the right one is the screen studying English.

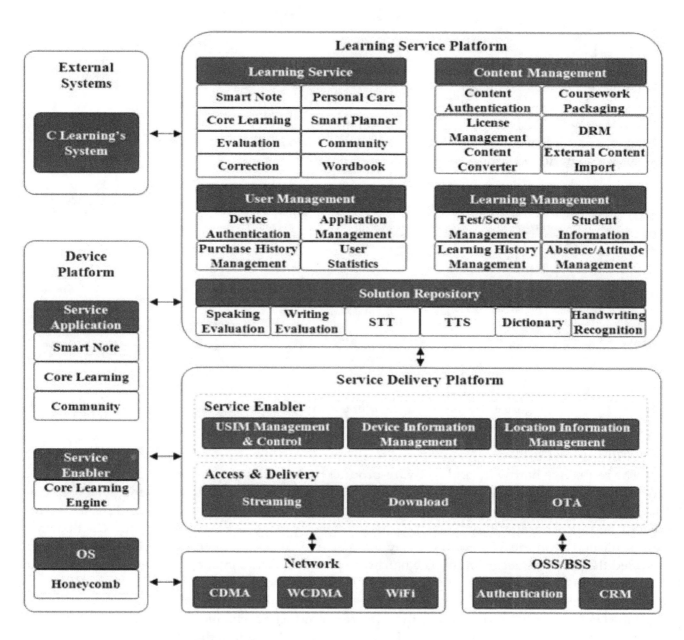

Figure 7. System architecture of T Smart Learning.

Figure 8. Actual appearance of T Smart Learning.

4.6. Discussions and Implications

The proposed framework was validated by applying it to a practical case in the illustration part. Although many cases can be utilized for complete validation, this paper performed an in-depth analysis in the T Smart Learning case to investigate the details of the framework. Consequently, the systematic approach to develop a service-oriented PSS enabled us to successfully generate creative ideas, design a service, and develop a PSS by reflecting the interaction between service providers and product partners. The most important part in the validation is how much users are satisfied with the practicality of the suggested approach. The TFT members in the aforementioned case highlighted the usefulness of four stages and techniques in each stage such as QFD and scenario analysis. In addition, active feedbacks among stakeholders could facilitate the process of developing the PSS.

However, several critical points should be considered to elevate the quality of application of the proposed approach. In the idea generation and selection stage of our case study, the TFT members of service providers had difficulty defining functions and judging their development potential. They also had difficulty separating them into hardware and software products because of the lack of knowledge and product development experience. At this time, the TFT members of the product partners played a key role in checking the feasibility of the functions and classifying them. On the contrary, the members of product partners who had a rudimentary understanding of the service gained a deeper understanding through the steps of deriving functions and conducting the AHP method, and this positively influenced the development of the requisite product in service-oriented PSS. Thus, it is definitely necessary to involve the product partners in the idea generation and selection stage.

The service providers and product partners should communicate and interact during the service design and product development stages. Through efficient and effective communication feedback is exchanged and incorporated into service design and product development. If miscommunication occurs at this point, the project team will not achieve satisfactory results. In our case, all TFT members got together and shared the progress of service design and product development once every two weeks. In spite of that, the project schedule was actually delayed due to miscommunication. Thus, it is necessary to execute more research on a systematic method for effective communication between the service design and product development teams. In this regard, Kleinsmann *et al.* [44] found factors that influence the creation of a shared understanding in collaborative new product development, and they also identified four collaboration types and their mechanisms. A similar study of PSS development would provide valuable findings and implications.

It is not easy to develop a new hardware product for service-oriented PSS. In our case, a general-purpose tablet PC was employed, contrary to the initial objective, although the hardware product partner still aimed to develop a new device that specialized in English education. Since the development of a new hardware product is highly risky in terms of cost and time, the service provider should consider customizing a general-purpose hardware product from its inception. Thus, the decision-making step on whether to develop or customize should be included in future research on the service-oriented PSS development process.

5. Conclusions

This paper proposes a service-oriented PSS development process in which the PSS development project is initiated and led by a service provider from a service-centric point of view. The proposed process, which is based on the product development process, service development process, and cases of PSS development projects, consists of four stages: (1) strategic planning; (2) idea generation and selection; (3) service design; and (4) product development. For each stage, actors and detailed procedures, including key features and useful methods, are suggested. Additionally, the real PSS development case of an English education service is introduced in detail as a demonstration of the application of the proposed process.

The contribution of this paper is that it expands the current scope of PSS research by suggesting the concept and development process of service-oriented PSS from the service provider's viewpoint, contrary to the manufacturer's viewpoint of existing studies. This can establish a foundation for research on service-oriented PSS development. Moreover, the proposed process and illustration are expected to serve as a useful guideline when service providers develop a service-oriented PSS.

However, this paper has some limitations. Firstly, the majority of the proposed process covers qualitative aspects. If more quantitative methods are added to the process, the proposed process can be made more systematic. Thus, the systematic and quantitative approach to partner selection, idea generation, service design, and collaboration with product partners are future research topics. Secondly, the case presented in this paper covers only specific industry sectors. Numerous case studies of broad industry sectors can provide us with worthwhile implications for service-oriented PSS development. In particular, cases of proven market success could confirm the validity of the proposed process. Therefore, in-depth case studies of various industries including successful cases could be another line of future research. Thirdly, since this research focuses on the PSS development process, subsequent processes such as a launching and operating process were not dealt with in this paper. Unique characteristics of PSS can be reflected to implement the details of the launching and operating processes. Thus, future research can present a complete framework of service-oriented PSS development from planning to operation by including the launching and operating process.

Acknowledgments: This work was supported by the National Research Foundation of Korea Grant funded by the Korean Government (NRF-2014R1A1A2054892).

Author Contributions: Seungkyum Kim designed the study, outlined the methodology, analyzed the data, interpreted the results and wrote the manuscript. Changho Son analyzed the data and wrote the manuscript. Byungun Yoon designed the study and wrote the manuscript. Yongtae Park implemented the research, designed the study, outlined the methodology, and helped complete the draft of this research. All authors have read and approved the final manuscript.

Appendix

Table A1. 34 Function sets and AHP results.

User Group	Function Sets	AHP Results				Note
		Effectiveness of Learning	Personalized Learning	Competitiveness	Overall Priority	
student	writing-specialized	0.05249	0.05220	0.08347	0.06317	core function
student	speaking-specialized	0.05517	0.05220	0.05839	0.05596	core function
student	listening-specialized	0.05438	0.05220	0.05839	0.05553	core function
student	reading-specialized	0.05431	0.05220	0.05839	0.05549	core function
student	personal care	0.05309	0.05220	0.05839	0.05482	core function
teacher	interaction in class	0.03939	0.05986	0.06446	0.05032	core function (teacher-support)
teacher	auto-correction	0.05693	0.04637	0.03691	0.04884	core function (teacher-support)
student	dictionary	0.05161	0.04637	0.03691	0.04595	
teacher	auto-grading	0.04297	0.04402	0.03739	0.04116	core function (teacher-support)
student	note	0.04175	0.02700	0.03615	0.03819	
student	planner	0.04283	0.01653	0.02806	0.03482	
student	diagnosis	0.02942	0.03376	0.03715	0.03258	
student	push contents	0.03615	0.01263	0.01679	0.02686	
student	contents library	0.02209	0.02926	0.03220	0.02638	
student	game	0.02837	0.03330	0.02007	0.02604	
teacher	checking homework	0.02182	0.03009	0.03117	0.02597	core function (teacher-support)
teacher	making tests	0.02755	0.01008	0.01998	0.02300	core function (teacher-support)
teacher	making teaching material	0.01824	0.03138	0.02745	0.02288	core function (teacher-support)
student	communication	0.02073	0.01957	0.02633	0.02254	
student	search	0.03144	0.01354	0.01139	0.02253	
parent	informing of diagnosis results	0.02337	0.01279	0.01139	0.01806	core function (parent-support)
parent	informing of progress	0.01537	0.02573	0.01967	0.01800	core function (parent-support)
student	counseling	0.01593	0.01276	0.02117	0.01739	
teacher	class/student management	0.01538	0.01974	0.01211	0.01473	core function (teacher-support)
teacher	communication with parents	0.01499	0.01974	0.01211	0.01452	
parent	informing of attitude in class	0.01394	0.02704	0.01072	0.01427	core function (parent-support)
parent	intimacy	0.01190	0.02276	0.01160	0.01300	core function (parent-support)
parent	education-related information	0.01226	0.01660	0.01215	0.01270	core function (parent-support)
student	synchronization	0.01073	0.01974	0.01211	0.01220	
teacher	other teacher-support	0.00889	0.02055	0.01160	0.01112	
student	help	0.01079	0.01092	0.01008	0.01056	
teacher	student control	0.00920	0.00852	0.01095	0.00973	
student	timer	0.00789	0.01206	0.01160	0.00964	
parent	nurture-related information	0.00696	0.01014	0.01139	0.00885	core function (parent-support)

References

1. Martinez, V.; Bastl, M.; Kingston, J.; Evans, S. Challenges in transforming manufacturing organizations into product-service providers. *J. Manuf. Technol. Manag.* **2010**, *21*, 449–469.

2. Goedkoop, M.J.; van Halen, C.J.G.; te Riele, H.R.M.; Rommens, P.J.M. *Product Service Systems, Ecological and Economic Basis*; Technical Report; Pre Consultants: Amersfoort, The Netherlands, 1999.

3. Baines, T.S.; Lightfoot, H.W.; Evans, S.; Neely, A.; Greenough, R.; Peppard, J.; Roy, R.; Shehab, E.; Braganza, A.; Tiwari, A.; *et al.* State-of-the-art in product-service systems. *Proc. Inst. Mech. Eng. Part B* **2007**, *221*, 1543–1552. [CrossRef]

4. Low, M.K.; Lamvik, T.; Walsh, K.; Myklebust, O. Manufacturing a green service: Engaging the TRIZ model of innovation. *IEEE Trans. Electron. Packag. Manuf.* **2001**, *24*, 10–17.

5. Alonso-Rasgado, T.; Thompson, G. A rapid design process for Total Care Product creation. *J. Eng. Des.* **2006**, *17*, 509–531. [CrossRef]

6. Aurich, J.C.; Fuchs, C.; Wagenknecht, C. Life cycle oriented design of technical Product-Service Systems. *J. Clean. Prod.* **2006**, *14*, 1480–1494. [CrossRef]

7. Tan, A.R.; McAloone, T.C.; Gall, C. Product/service-system development—An explorative case study in a manufacturing company. In Proceedings of the International Conference on Engineering Design 2007, Paris, France, 28–31 August 2007.

8. Uchihira, N.; Kyoya, Y.; Kim, S.; Maeda, K.; Ozawa, M.; Ishii, K. Analysis and Design Methodology for Recognizing Opportunities and Difficulties for Product-based Services. In Proceedings of the PICMET 2007, Portland, OR, USA, 5–9 August 2007.

9. Sakao, T.; Sandström, G.Ö.; Matzen, D. Framing research for service orientation of manufacturers through PSS approaches. *J. Manuf. Technol. Manag.* **2009**, *20*, 754–778.

10. Shimomura, Y.; Hara, T.; Arai, T. A unified representation scheme for effective PSS development. *CIRP Ann.-Manuf. Technol.* **2009**, *58*, 379–382. [CrossRef]

11. Yang, X.; Moore, P.; Pu, J.; Wong, C. A practical methodology for realizing product service systems for consumer products. *Comput. Ind. Eng.* **2009**, *56*, 224–235. [CrossRef]

12. Wong, M. Implementation of innovative product service-systems in the consumer goods industry. Ph.D. Thesis, University of Cambridge, Department of Engineering, Cambridge, UK, 2004.

13. Mont, O. Clarifying the concept of product-service system. *J. Clean. Prod.* **2002**, *10*, 237–245. [CrossRef]

14. Manzini, E.; Vezzoli, C. A strategic design approach to develop sustainable product service systems: Examples taken from the "environmentally friendly innovation" Italian prize. *J. Clean. Prod.* **2003**, *11*, 851–857. [CrossRef]

15. Tukker, A. Eight types of product service system: Eight ways to sustainability experiences from SusProNet. *Bus. Strateg. Environ.* **2004**, *13*, 246–260. [CrossRef]

16. Krucken, L.; Meroni, A. Building stakeholder networks to develop and deliver product-service-systems: Practical experiences on elaborating pro-active materials for communication. *J. Clean. Prod.* **2006**, *14*, 1502–1508. [CrossRef]

17. Tukker, A.; Tischner, U. *New Business for Old Europe: Product-Service Development, Competitiveness and Sustainability*; Greenleaf Publishing: Sheffield, UK, 2006.

18. Tukker, A.; van Halen, C. *Innovation Scan for Product Service Systems: Manual*; TNO: Delft, The Netherlands; PricewaterhouseCoopers: Utrecht, The Netherlands, 2003.

19. Suh, J.; Park, S. Service-oriented Technology Roadmap (SoTRM) using patent map for R&D strategy of service industry. *Expert Syst. Appl.* **2009**, *36*, 6754–6772.

20. Lee, S.; Kim, Y. A product-service system design method integrating service function and service activity and case studies. In Proceedings of the 2nd CIRP IPS2 Conference, Linköping, Sweden, 14–15 April 2010.

21. Chen, J.; Huang, C. A TRIZ based eco-innovation method for PSS. In Proceedings of the 16th CIRP International Conference on Life Cycle Engineering, LCE 2009, Cairo, Egypt, 4–6 May 2009.

22. Chen, J.; Li, H. Innovative design method of product service system by using case study and TRIZ model. In Proceedings of the 2nd CIRP IPS2 Conference, Linköping, Sweden, 14–15 April 2010.

23. Genrich, A.; Shulyak, L. *And Suddenly the Inventor Appeared: TRIZ, the Theory of Inventive Problem Solving*; Technical Innovation Center, Inc.: Worcester, UK, 1996.

24. Domb, E. QFD and TIPS/TRIZ. Available online: http://www.trizjournal.com/archives/1998/06/c/index.htm (accessed on 23 October 2015).

25. Yamashina, H.; Ito, T.; Kawada, H. Innovative product development process by integrating QFD and TRIZ. *Int. J. Prod. Res.* **2002**, *40*, 1031–1050. [CrossRef]

26. Uhlmann, E.; Stelzer, C. Identifiaction of the IPS2 business model in the early stage of creation. In Proceedings of the 2nd CIRP IPS2 Conference, Linköping, Sweden, 14–15 April 2010.

27. Meier, H.; Kroll, M. From products to solutions-IPS2 as a means for creating customer value. In Proceedings of the 16th CIRP International Conference on Life Cycle Engineering, LCE 2009, Cairo, Egypt, 4–6 May 2009.

28. Manzini, E.; Collina, L.; Evans, S. *Solution Oriented Partnership: How to Design Industrialised Sustainable Solutions*; Cranfield University: Cranfield, UK, 2004.

29. Morelli, N. Developing new product service systems (PSS): Methodologies and operational tools. *J. Clean. Prod.* **2006**, *14*, 145–1501. [CrossRef]

30. Schuh, G.; Gudergan, G. Service engineering as an approach to designing industrial product service systems. In Proceedings of the 1st CIRP Industrial Product-Service Systems (IPS2) Conference, Cranfield, UK, 1–2 April 2009.

31. Hauser, J.R.; Clausing, D. The house of quality. *Harvard Business Review*, May 1988; 63–73.

32. Umeda, Y.; Tsutsumida, M.; Tomiyama, T.; Tamura, T.; Fujimoto, J. Study on feasibility of service-oriented products using life cycle simulation. *J. Jpn. Soc. Des. Eng.* **2001**, *36*, 517–526.

33. Fujimoto, J.; Umeda, Y.; Tamura, T.; Tomiyama, T.; Kimura, F. Development of service-oriented products based on the inverse manufacturing concept. *Environ. Sci. Technol.* **2003**, *37*, 5398–5406. [CrossRef] [PubMed]

34. Cooper, R.G.; Edgett, S.J.; Kleinschmidt, E.J. Optimizing the stage-gate process: What best-practice companies do—I. *Res. Technol. Manag.* **2002**, *45*, 21–27.

35. Cooper, R.G.; Edgett, S.J.; Kleinschmidt, E.J. Optimizing the stage-gate process: What best-practice companies do—II. *Res. Technol. Manag.* **2002**, *45*, 43–49.

36. Brügemann, L.M. Innovation of an Eco-efficient Product-Service Combination. Master's thesis, Delft University of Technology, Delft, The Netherlands, 2000.

37. Chesbrough, H. Open innovation: Where we've been and where we're going. *Res. Technol. Manag.* **2012**, *55*, 20–27. [CrossRef]

38. Emden, Z.; Calantone, R.J.; Droge, C. Collaborating for new product development: Selecting the partner with maximum potential to create value. *J. Prod. Innov. Manag.* **2006**, *23*, 330–341. [CrossRef]

39. Saaty, T.L. *The Analytic (Hierarchy) Process*; McGraw-Hill: New York, NY, USA, 1980.

40. Saaty, T.L. Decision making for leaders. *IEEE Trans. Syst. Man Cybern.* **1985**, *15*, 450–452. [CrossRef]

41. Saaty, T.L. How to make a decision: The analytic hierarchy process. *Eur. J. Oper. Res.* **1990**, *48*, 9–26. [CrossRef]

42. Vaidya, O.S.; Kumar, S. Analytic hierarchy process: An overview of applications. *Eur. J. Oper. Res.* **2006**, *169*, 1–29. [CrossRef]

43. Soni, A.; Cohen, H. Successfully launching your product: Getting it right. *Handb. Bus. Strateg.* **2004**, *5*, 263–268. [CrossRef]

44. Kleinsmann, M.; Buijs, J.; Valkenburg, R. Understanding the complexity of knowledge integration in collaborative new product development teams: A case study. *J. Eng. Technol. Manag.* **2010**, *27*, 20–32. [CrossRef]

8

A New Systematic Approach to Vulnerability Assessment of Innovation Capability of Construction Enterprises

Jingxiao Zhang [1],*, Haiyan Xie [2], Klaus Schmidt [2] and Hui Li [1],*

[1]   Institution of Construction Economics, Chang'an University; NO.161, Chang'an Road, Xi'an 710061, China

[2]   Department of Technology, Illinois State University; Normal, IL 61790, USA; hxie@ilstu.edu (H.X.); kschmid@ilstu.edu (K.S.)

*   Correspondence: zhangjingxiao@chd.edu.cn (J.Z.); lihui9922@chd.edu.cn (H.L.);

Academic Editor: Adam Jabłoński

Abstract: The purpose of this research is to study the vulnerability of construction enterprises' innovation capabilities (CEIC) and their respective primary influencing factors. This paper proposed a vulnerability system framework of CEIC, designed two comprehensive assessments for analysis, namely the entropy and set pair analysis method (E-SPA) and the principle cluster analysis and SPA method (P-SPA), and compared grades to verify the vulnerability assessments. Further, the paper quantitatively assessed the major influencing factors in facilitating management, reducing vulnerability, and improving the ability of construction enterprises to respond to changes in the construction industry. The results showed that vulnerability could be effectively and systematically evaluated using E-SPA. However, managing or reducing entrepreneurial sensitivity and improving the ability to respond was critical to supporting sustainable CEIC. The case studies included in this paper suggested that in ensuring sustainable CEIC, companies should concentrate on highly educated human resources, R&D investments, intellectual property related innovations, and government support. This research provided a practical framework and established a sustainable strategy for companies to manage their vulnerability in developing innovation capability. In addition, this research presented an innovative and effective way to quantitatively analyze vulnerability which offered a foundation to signify a new paradigm shift in construction sustainable development.

Keywords: construction enterprise; innovation capability; vulnerability assessment; innovation uncertainty; sustainable development

1. Introduction

As a critical driver of the sustainable development of a nation, a region, an industry, or an enterprise, innovation can provide a continual basis for sustainable socio-economic development and growth. Construction innovation, as a sustainable driver and a crucial condition, represents the pulse of construction economic development of any nation [1–3]. The innovative capabilities of construction enterprises thus hold a key position in advancing industrial and national development [4,5]. The current innovation status of the construction industry reflects the complex features of the industry [6]. As any nation or region will have demand for continued construction, statistics related to this construction make up a major portion of an economy's well-being. The innovation accomplishments of construction enterprises are affected by the innovation efforts of other firms, and are achieved through the continuing cooperation among industries for breakthroughs in products, processes, and designs. These breakthroughs reflect the strength and innovative desires and interests of construction companies. However, compared to other industries, there is a lack of focus on the diffusion rates of innovation in different sectors of construction, such as building and civil infrastructure. Depending on the developmental level of an economy, the need for civil infrastructure may vary. However, innovation is needed at all levels of economic development [7]. Civil infrastructure companies are large in size and have potential for radical innovations, while residential construction companies are usually small and give limited consideration as to how to effectively convert new research and development into innovation. Often, large companies do not invest sufficiently in innovation as they already dominate a major portion of the existing market. Smaller companies on the other hand need to demonstrate higher degrees of innovation in order to enter or even stay in the market [8]. A similar observation was made by Hultgren and Tantawi [9] in the study of potential radical innovation in large firms.

However, researchers recently noticed that sustainable economic development has its vulnerability, which was considered as a new paradigm shift in the analysis of uncertainty in economic studies of system sensitivity and response capability. Vulnerability research has a wide range of applications, including climate change prediction, natural disaster prevention, food security, and public health improvement [10–21]. Generally, innovation vulnerability relates to the risk or uncertainty of a company's innovation capability. Therefore, eliminating risks or identifying weaknesses is perhaps a preferred method of overcoming vulnerability. Elimination should, however, not simply lead to the avoidance of uncertainty when studying innovation capability, because uncertainty can sense or trace new directions or paths of economic development and thereby represents an innovative strength [18,19]. This new cognitive reasoning requires firms to treat uncertainty as part of innovation capability and develop a strategy to overcome it, or manage uncertainty instead of eliminating it. Construction entrepreneurs should consider the opportunities stemming from uncertainties as well. With this understanding, it is a crucial prerequisite for successful promotion of construction enterprise's innovation capability (CEIC) to develop and implement a strategy when managing the uncertainty that is part of CEIC. However, there is still a lack of quantitative research to assess the uncertainty involved in innovation, particularly in relation to estimating innovation capability at a firm, industrial, or national level [22,23]. A similar discussion can be found in Costanza *et al.* [24] "to say that we should not do valuation of ecosystems is to deny the reality that we already do, always have and cannot avoid doing so in the future". The research by Costanza *et al.* [24] emphasized the importance of quantifying ecosystem values for the support of policy decisions or influencing public opinions. This research stressed the necessity for quantitative research in innovation uncertainty. This research was based on an inverse perspective of the relationship between uncertainty and innovation capability. Furthermore, it studied the vulnerability of CEIC and worked to build a system approach to assess the vulnerability of CEIC [11,13,15–17,20,21,25–27]. This new approach aimed to manage and reduce the vulnerability of CEIC and to support the sustainable improvement of CEIC.

In order to assess the vulnerability of CEIC, this research quantitatively analyzed the individual vulnerabilities of the major influence factors of CEIC with the objective to manage and improve their responsive abilities. In order to achieve this goal, this research constructed a framework of vulnerability of CEIC, using two comprehensive methods of vulnerability assessment in socio-economic research. The two methods were the entropy and set pair analysis method (E-SPA) and the principle cluster analysis and SPA method (P-SPA). This research also implemented these methods in eight construction enterprises to analyze their CEIC, and compared the respective results. The results demonstrated the functions of the vulnerability framework in the uncertainty analysis of construction innovation. The results are applicable to other industries too.

This research expands the field of innovation functions of a company to enhance its competitiveness and sustainable development from an inverse perspective when managing innovation risks. It identified new areas of economic growth with potential broad impact on multiple industries. At an industrial level, the research may help governments, industrial associations, and other organizations implement targeted incentives for innovation planning, to reduce uncertainty and risk, to respond to an innovation-driven service economy, and to promote regional and national innovation. In the long run, the research can help to enhance the positions of industries and facilitate national innovation strategies for economic development and restructuring.

The rest of the paper is structured as follows. Section 2 focuses on the review of literature, links of analysis levels, and the research agenda. Section 3 provides the research methods. Section 4 builds the vulnerability framework based on the selected theories and methods and implements the research procedure and measurements to analyze the vulnerability of CEIC. Section 5 presents the research results, summarizes the conclusions, and highlights the implications of vulnerability assessment for innovation capability in enterprises, and at industrial and national levels.

2. Literature Review

2.1. Innovation and Uncertainty

Enterprises are becoming more specialized than ever before. Based on the technological know-how of a company, competition may lead to additional challenges with respect to innovation and handling uncertainty. Adaptability paired with innovation therefore becomes a key factor to advance technological diversity and the willingness to experiment with new products and services. According to Bell and Pavitt [27], firms rarely fail because of an inability to master a new field of technology, but because of the lack of adaptability and responsiveness to new industry demands and the inability to proactively embrace and discover new technological opportunities [28].

Companies are vulnerable to external factors if they are not well prepared or not strategically aligned with the new innovative technologies. Companies need to be willing to take risks in order to succeed in the competitive construction industries. Finding the right approach to balancing risk *versus* a company's vulnerability and its innovative capability is key to success. Facing constant competition in the advancement of any industry for new technology separates company strategies that are sustainable from those that are not. Major differences in this approach seem to exist between larger and smaller companies in the same industries since key challenges for the strategic management of technology depend on a company's size and its core business: small firms must focus on defining and defending their product niche while large firms focus on building and exploiting competences based on R&D or on complex production or information systems. Companies require continuous learning, the capacity to integrate specialists, and a willingness both to break down established functional and divisional boundaries and to take a view to the long term [29].

Among a multitude of research, Schumpeter's concept of long waves, a theory of technical innovation and structural change, shows that the successful diffusion of this technology depends on a wide variety of institutional changes. Freeman *et al.* points to a number of policies including flexible working hours, training and less restrictive macroeconomic demand policies which would help to generate higher levels of innovation [30]. This concept could certainly be extended to the sustainability of an innovation friendly company environment. Innovation does not lead to success just by itself if it is not supported by progressive and flexible federal, regional, and company specific policies. Otherwise, potential risk factors or the perception of uncertainty will hinder the advancement and sustainability of a progressive innovative environment.

Nevertheless, innovation processes are often criticized because they do not accurately portray the process of industry movement, in which there were uncertain and dynamic interactions among knowledge, resources, and environments [31]. Therefore, striving to remove uncertainty might lead to the risk of hindering or even completely impeding innovation rather than promoting it. Despite much success in overcoming uncertainty, it has become clear that uncertainties can never be completely removed. Instead, uncertainty keeps emerging in new forms accompanying complex scientific processes, organization structures, and technical systems. Strategies should be prepared at different levels of acceptance of uncertainty and be utilized to benefit social-economic developments [18]. Uncertainty is not a deficiency, but a structural feature embedded in any entrepreneurial entity.

Likewise, uncertainty is not strictly a shortcoming, rather an important factor that can lead to growth. The endeavor to eliminate uncertainty holds the risk of jeopardizing rather than promoting innovation.

Dealing with uncertainty is a continuous process for construction innovation. The concept of coping with uncertainty, as opposed to removing it through planning and control, was presented and substantiated by Bohle [32]. This new cognitive approach to manage uncertainty in innovation processes is not just wishful thinking. For example, Bohle [32] proposed approaches such as experience-led and subject-based actions in project management. They provided new ways of dealing with uncertainty in project management. However, these methods have barely been further developed into quantitative instruments for systematic promotion of innovation processes [32]. This paper developed a new system with quantitative methods to manage the uncertainty in construction innovation. Meanwhile, the system has the ability to react and overcome uncertainty with countermeasures, instead of eliminating uncertainty which might weaken the power of innovation.

2.2. Vulnerability

As an emerging area, systematic studies of vulnerability began with research on natural disasters, with the purpose to achieve sustainable development of the environment through reducing uncertainty, sensitivity, and vulnerability [10]. At present, scholars widely use the methodologies of vulnerability research to explore economic domains, such as financial vulnerability and household vulnerability [10, 21,33–35]. For example, Dominitz and Manski [17] first discussed the vulnerability of a country's economic system. United Nations Development Programme (UNDP) [35] defined the concept of economic vulnerability as the capability to suffer the damage due to the impact of unanticipated events in the process of economic development. Vulnerability relates to the sensitivity to disturbance inside and outside of a system and the lack of capability to respond to make necessary changes to the system's structure and functions. In addition, sensitivity and adaptability are key components of the evaluation of the vulnerability of a system [14,16,21,33,34,36–39].

Vulnerability management includes the assessment of a system's sensitivity and adaptability by managing or restricting the potential hazards to realize the systematic promotion in the political, social, economic, or environmental fields. In recent years, examples of systems for which vulnerability assessments were performed include, but are not limited to, climate changes, natural disasters, ecological crises, food security, and public health. The research methods used include composite index method, fuzzy method, scenario analysis, and input-output method [14,16,21,25,33,34,36–39]. Such assessments were conducted on behalf of a range of different organizations, from small businesses to large enterprises. For example, Gnangnon [25] endowed different weights to various economic growth-indicators to calculate economic vulnerability indices in developing countries. Turner et al. [21] proposed a framework of factors and linkages to study the potential effects of the vulnerability of a couple of human–environment systems which was also related to the sensitivity and resilience of the system.

However, innovation capability is an important driver of any economic system, and the assessment of the vulnerability of innovation capability has not drawn enough attention, especially in regards to CEIC. Therefore, it is urgent to study how to measure the level of vulnerability, select indices, and manage index information to conduct a vulnerability assessment of CEIC. In this research, the authors first selected indices of vulnerability by using the entropy method. The entropy method is a common method to generate the objective weight of index system [40,41]. The next method used in this research is Set Pair Analysis (SPA), which is a novel method to target the uncertainty in a system [42,43]. The core thought of set pair analysis was to treat the confirmed uncertainty of the object to be studied as a confirmed uncertainty system, and to analyze and study the connection and conversion of the research objects for the similarities and differences. The core concept of set pair analysis was the set pair and the connection degree [42]. Another comparison method of principle cluster analysis (PCA) was also used to assess vulnerability. PCA assessment is usually used for the vulnerability assessment of tourism economic systems or city economic systems [38,44–47]. Using Entropy SPA (E-SPA) and PCA-SPA (P-SPA), the authors analyzed cases of large construction companies to reveal their vulnerability levels.

2.3. Construction Enterprise's Innovation Capability (CEIC)

From a system point of view, construction innovation capabilities at firm, regional, and national levels are three closely related categories, which support and influence each other, characterized by general factors to realize the overall achievement of sustainable innovation. In innovation systems, the national, regional or industrial technical changes and economic growth are the outcomes of the innovation activities that take place among all firms. However, the changes are not simply the summation of firm-level innovation capabilities, but the result of their interactions at national, regional or industrial levels instead. At national or regional levels, innovation measurements are calculated by agencies such as European Innovation Scoreboard [48], OECD STI Outlook [49], Nordic Innovation Monitor [50], UNCTAD indicators [51] and World Bank indicators [52]. The measured innovation efficiencies refer to innovation input and output, innovation activity, innovation environment, *etc.* with relevant indicators.

CEIC can be used as an important carrier for national and regional innovation strategies. It is usually implemented at a micro level to foster, form, and upgrade innovation capabilities [3,23,53–58], such as innovation environments, innovation investment capabilities, cooperative innovation capabilities, intellectual property capabilities, and change-innovation capabilities [1]. Innovation capabilities enable construction enterprises to create, deploy, and maintain advantageous business performance in the long run. The representations of innovation capabilities, such as distinct skills, processes, procedures, organizational structures, decision rules, and disciplines, undergird enterprise-level sensing, seizing, and reconfiguring capacities.

At the enterprise-level, there are three main types of studies that focused on construction innovation capability. The first type of studies concentrated on analyzing and evaluating the major changes in overall innovation capability and specified the current status and history of innovation capability, e.g., international comparative study [59–61]. The second type of studies focused on the evaluations of enterprise innovation capabilities in key sectors (or areas), a.k.a. primary businesses' innovation. For example, equipment manufacturing, strategic approaches for emerging markets, and process plant construction are considered as business innovation [1,2,4,62–65]. The third type focused on evaluating and comparing the different types and sizes of CEIC [53,66–71], such as domestic and foreign-funded enterprises, large, small-and-medium and micro enterprises, or state-owned and private enterprises.

In terms of types of constitution, CEIC refers to industrial innovation, technological innovation, system innovation, organizational innovation, and collaborative innovation [1,3,72,73]. The participants of CEIC involve government, business, universities, individuals, and community groups. The input factors of CEIC include capital investment, intellectual property, training, human resources (HR), *etc.* Researchers noticed that CEIC contributed to the enhancement of national competitive advantage, optimization of industrial resource allocation and the employment market, reduction of energy dissipation and pollution, and improvement of social welfare [3]. The systematic framework of CEIC gradually transited from individual and closed-end efforts into open-ended and multilateral cooperative processes. The multilateral interactions help to form the cooperative effects to improve the efficiency of labor, information, knowledge, technology, management and capital to implement CEIC strategies [4,74,75]. Even though the above studies focused on product capability, technology patents, knowledge transfer, university–industry–government cooperation, or output efficiency, there is still deficiency in holistic understanding of the social and organizational aspects of innovations. For example, as an important innovation resource, HR and the associated working conditions become key enablers and central factors of innovations. So, instead of studying the individual parameters of production, technology, and organization *etc.*, this research studied CEICs systematically in a framework. Additionally, the generic innovation models [71,76] put forward that the frameworks with successful innovation outcomes were built by considering the focus of innovation, contextual factors, organizational capabilities and innovation processes. The links between the key concepts used in this research are shown in Figure 1. With the adoption of the extensions of generic innovation models, the framework of CEIC included the following items:

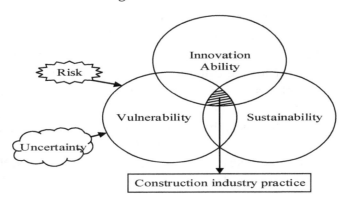

Figure 1. Links between key concepts.

(A) An ideal environment for innovation capability. The environment of CEIC should be at a high level of economic development, enterprise information management, and human resource access, and with the support from government and social sectors to create an accessible and sustainable environment [77,78].

(B) Adequate resources for innovation capability. Without an innovation resource pool, it is difficult for CEIC to carry out innovation activities, such as management innovation, technology innovation, and product innovation [79,80]. CEIC is the carrier of a national and regional innovation strategy. The cooperation among university, industry, and society, together with the alliance of capital, market demands and human resource (HR) pools for business innovation, are key to complying with CEIC [81–84].

(C) Progressive innovation activities. CEIC is important to the foundation of the entire innovation in an economic society. It also contributes to product innovation, process innovation, marketing innovation and organizational innovation. Resources, technology, and knowledge (tangible and intangible) are bundled, linked and incorporated for innovation activities, which then would be converted and organized into routines and systems to formalize innovation capabilities and lead to production competencies and performance [85,86]. In order to strengthen innovation activities, construction enterprises should actively and continuously promote the innovation investments in human and financial resources, pay good attention to integration and absorption of external technologies, and sustain the creation and ownership of intellectual properties.

(D) Emerging innovation output. As a measurement of the CEIC levels, innovation output includes the number of patents registered, technical trading expansion, and brand building promotion efforts [2,66,87]. Innovation in the area of high-tech and knowledge-intensive service helps the optimization of production and service structure at the industrial level; meanwhile, the new production or service methods enable enterprises to further optimize the product structure. This reciprocal process is an important aspect of innovation outputs [88–91].

(E) Improved economic efficiency. The economic efficiency of CEIC includes the efficiencies of labor input, capital investment, and energy investment, which contribute to sustainable development of business environments [92–95]. The construction enterprises with strong dynamic capabilities are highly entrepreneurial, with innovation-capability uncertainty, and are highly vulnerable to innovation environments. From a system uncertainty perspective, this uncertainty or dynamic feature is mainly due to the sensitivity of CEIC to internal and external system disturbances. In addition, the lack of responsiveness of CEIC hinders the sustainable development of those companies. The theoretical framework in this research quantitatively evaluated the vulnerability of CEIC to improve innovation capability. The analysis of the vulnerability or uncertainty of CEIC helps to promote the sustainability of innovation capability.

2.4. Analysis Level and Framework

Items A to E in the aforementioned framework of CEIC can be summarized in the following Table 1. Table 1 shows that there are three implications for CEIC. The implications are reflected in the following aspects. (a) Innovation capability is inherently unstable. (b) Innovation capability is sensitive to the interferences and changes from the outside world. (c) CEIC is vulnerable to risk. Thus, the vulnerability of CEIC is a comprehensive system affected by sensitivity and adaptability. Sensitivity is the degree of susceptibility to external shocks, or ability to deal with innovation uncertainty and risk [77,83–86]. If a system has weak sensitivity, it would be less susceptible and demonstrate stronger resistance than one with strong sensitivity. Adaptability is the ability to quickly adjust from a risky or uncertain situation to a stable or sustainable situation. It also demonstrates the ability of a system to maintain itself. Adaptability has a direct relationship with the innovation self-maintenance capability of a system.

Table 1. Analysis level.

Topic	Innovation and uncertainty	Innovation capability	Vulnerability
Literature summary	Managing uncertainty is absolutely necessary from the perspective of construction innovation. There will always be something unforeseeable. Flexibility and creativity are important features of a successful innovation strategy.	System dynamics and uncertainty are likely affected by product, technology, organization, and people. The current influence factors and measurement methods are not industry specific.	Uncertainty threats are studied using system sensitivity and adaptability to analysis the vulnerability in political, social, economic fields. Comprehensive methods or mixed method such as E-SPA, PCA, and SPA were used to assess economic vulnerability.
Major trends in research	Systematical description or linkage to deal with uncertainty with quantitative methods to promote innovation process.	Uncertainty measurement of CEIC with generic influence factors	Exploratory implementation of the measurements and verification of innovation vulnerability.
Research Focus	This research constructed the vulnerability-assessment framework, implemented the corresponding indices, and verified CEIC using common comprehensive methods from economic vulnerability areas.		

In summary, the vulnerability indicator (X) of CEIC could be expressed in Equation (1).

$$X = f(S, A) \tag{1}$$

Letter S represents sensitivity. Letter A represents adaptability. Large value of X indicates the tendency towards exposure to risk and uncertainty. It also means that CEIC will be slowed down to return to a sustainable state. Thus, the framework of Equation (1) is used to analyze vulnerability from two aspects, namely system sensitivity and adaptability. This research extracted data from 2013 National Innovation Index Reprot [96] to build the vulnerability indices in Table 2. In Table 2, the target layers include Innovation Input Capability (IIC), Cooperative Innovation Capability of Enterprise (CICE), Intellectual Property Capability (IPC), Change Innovation Capability (CIC), and Innovation Environment (IE). Each target layer is further divided into sensitivity indices and adaptability indices. The explanations of both sensitivity and adaptability indices in Table 2 include their indicators, measurement units, descriptions, and tropisms. For sensitive and adaptive indicators, a positive tropism (+) indicates a direct relationship between the index and the sensitivity or adaptability; a negative tropism (−) indicates an inverse relationship between the index and the sensitivity or adaptability.

Table 2. Vulnerability-assessment framework and indices of construction enterprise's innovation capability (CEIC).

Target layer	Sensitivity (S)	Indicators	Sensitive indicator description and its tropism	Adaptability (A)	Indicators	Adaptive indicator description and its tropism
Innovation Input Capability (IIC)	IICS$_1$	Innovative funding accounted for the main business revenue/%	It reflects the strength of innovation funding (−)	IICA$_1$	R&D expenditure accounts for the main business revenue	It reflects R & D expenditure intensity (+)
	IICS$_2$	The proportion of R & D types of HR employed/%	It reflects the intensity of R & D personnel investment (−)	IICA$_2$	The proportion of PhD graduates in HR of a corporate	It reflects the structure of highly educated personnel in an enterprise (+)
	IICS$_3$	The funding of R & D specific sector accounted for corporate R & D expenditure/%	It reflects the state of the R & D funding of a specific sector (−)	IICA$_3$	The personnel R & D investment of a specific sector accounted for that of corporate R & D /%	It reflects the manpower situation of R & D institutions (+)
Cooperative Innovation Capability of Enterprise (CICE)	CICES$_1$	Cooperation Project accounted for the whole research project/%	It reflects the cooperative scope of the enterprise (+)	CICEA$_1$	The R & D expenditure proportion of universities and research institutions in whole corporate R&D expenditures/%	It reflect R & D cooperation with universities and research institutions (+)
	CICES$_2$	The ratio of technology import expenditure accounted for the whole R & D funding	It reflects the introduction status of technology with respect to independent research (+)	CICEA$_2$	The ratio of digestion and absorption funds accounted for technology import funds	It reflects the absorption and re-innovation status for the introduction technology (−)
	CICES$_3$	The proportion of cooperation innovative project accounted for the whole enterprise project/%	It reflects the innovation state of the business cooperation with external institutions (−)	CICEA$_3$	The proportion of cooperation patent accounted the total patent application/%	It reflects the cooperation scale of technological inventions (+)
Intellectual Property Capability (IPC)	IPCS$_1$	The percent of enterprise invention patent applications accounted for the whole patent applications/%	It reflects patent application levels. (−)	IPCA$_1$	100,000 RMB R & D funding per invention patent applications/(No./100,000 RMB)	It reflects the patents output efficiency (+)
	IPCS$_2$	The patent-owned project accounted for the whole enterprises' projects/%	It reflects the patent protection awareness of enterprises (−)	IPCA$_2$	10,000 patents-owned of enterprise employees/(piece /10,000 employees)	It reflects the size of enterprise patent pool (+)
	IPCS$_3$	# of implementations of invention patents accounted for overall implemented patents/%	It reflects the transformation and application status of invention patents (−)	IPCA$_3$	The ratio of patent licensing and transfer income accounted for new product sales revenue	It reflects the ratio of patent assets income and new product sales revenue (+)
Change Innovation Capability (CIC)	CICS$_1$	New product marketing expenses accounted for all marketing costs/%	It reflects the marketing strength of new-investment products (−)	CICA$_1$	New product sales revenue accounted for the main business revenue/%	Reflects the impact of business activities on the entire production of innovative activities(+)
	CICS$_2$	PCT applications accounted for the whole patent applications/%	It reflects the potential technology inventions an enterprise in the international market (−)	CICA$_2$	Income from patented project accounted for the entire project income of an enterprise/%	It reflects the corporate innovation competitiveness (+)
	CICS$_3$	Labor productivity/(RMB/person)	It reflects the innovation impact on labor productivity (−)	CICA$_3$	Comprehensive energy output/%	It reflects social performance of corporate energy consuming (−)
Innovation Environment (IE)	IEGS$_1$	Direct government support (GS)extent/%	The ratio of direct government support accounted for the whole R & D expenses (+)	IEGS$_2$	Indirect government support(GS) extent/%	The ratio of indirect government support accounted for the whole R & D expenses (−)
	IESS$_1$	The extent of Social capital to support (SS) R&D/%	The ratio of financial institutions support R&D accounted for the whole R & D expenses (+)	IESS$_2$	The extent Social capital to support (SS) project development/%	The ratio of social-capital development projects accounted for the total capital of enterprises (−)

Note 1: Indices from 2013 National Innovation Index Report [96]; Note 2: For sensitive and adaptive indicators, a positive tropism (+) indicates a direct relationship between the index and the sensitivity or adaptability; a negative tropism (−) indicates an inverse relationship between the index and the sensitivity or adaptability.

The authors designed the research steps and framework as per Figure 2. This research used the common mixed methods of E-SPA and P-SPA to analyze the vulnerability of CEIC. Particularly, Zhao's grade standards [97] were used as SPA method of the inventor to grade the vulnerabilities of selected cases. In addition, the major influencing factors of response capability were ranked to manage the vulnerability of CEIC.

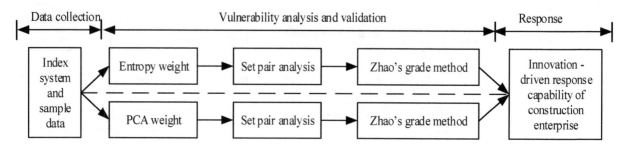

Figure 2. Research steps and framework.

3. Research Method

3.1. Entropy and SPA (E-SPA) Method

3.1.1. Entropy Weight

Many generic evaluation models rely on subjective weighting methods to determine the weights of indices in their evaluations. Entropy method [41] is an objective empowerment approach used to reflect the disorder degree of information in information theories, which now has been expanded to social and economic areas [40,41,47,98,99]. The weights of individual indicators are determined by calculating the entropy and entropy weight of each of them. The greater the entropy is, the smaller the corresponding entropy weight will be for any indicator. If an entropy weight is zero, the indicator provides no useful information to decision-makers. That indicator may be removed in the evaluation process. The amount of useful information that an indicator provides to a decision-maker is objective. So, using the entropy method to determine index weights could provide realistic and objective insight into the CEIC vulnerability system. The four main steps [41,44] taken are as follows.

Step 1: The formation of the evaluation matrix (Table S1).

Suppose there are m units and n indicators to be evaluated to establish the original data matrix in Equation (2).

$$R = (r_{st})_{m \times n}(s = 1, 2, ..., m; t = 1, 2, ..., n) \tag{2}$$

where r_{st} represents the actual value of the tth index of sth unit.

Step 2: The standardization of the evaluation matrix.

The following equation is used to normalize the matrix B,

$$B = (b_{st})_{m \times n}(s = 1, 2, ..., m; t = 1, 2, ..., n) \text{ with } b_{st} = \frac{r_{st} - r_{min}}{r_{max} - r_{min}} \tag{3}$$

where r_{max} and r_{min} represent the maximum and minimum values, respectively, for the evaluation unit.

If indicator is the positive tropism (+)

$$b_{st} = \frac{r_{st} - r_{min}}{r_{max} - r_{min}} \tag{3a}$$

If indicator is the negative tropism (−)

$$b_{st} = \frac{r_{max} - r_{st}}{r_{max} - r_{min}} \tag{3b}$$

Step 3: The calculation of the entropy

The entropy of the system can be defined by using the following calculations:

$$H_t = -\left(\sum_{s=1}^{m} f_{st}\ln f_{st}\right) / \ln m \ (s = 1,2,...,m; t = 1,2,...,n) \tag{4}$$

where $f_{st} = b_{st} / \sum_{s=1}^{m} b_{st}$; if $f_{st} = 0$, redefine the f_{st} as

$$f_{st} = (1 + b_{st}) / \sum_{s=1}^{m} (1+b_{st}) \tag{5}$$

Step 4: The calculation of the entropy weight

$$w = (\omega_t)_{1 \times n}, \ \omega_t = (1 - H_t) / \left(n - \sum_{t=1}^{n} H_t\right) \text{ with } \sum_{t=1}^{n} \omega_t = 1 \tag{6}$$

3.1.2. Set Pair Analysis (SPA)

Given two sets v and u, the set pair is expressed as $H = (v,u)$. Equation (7) calculates the connection degree of the two sets:

$$\mu = \frac{S}{N} + \frac{F}{N}i + \frac{P}{N}j = a + bi + cj, \text{ where } a + b + c = 1 \tag{7}$$

In Equation (7), N is the total number of characteristics of a set pair; S is the number of characteristics of two sets; P is the number of opposite characteristics of two sets; F is the number of characteristics of two sets, which are independent to each other. The ratio $\frac{S}{N}$ is the similarity degree of two sets; $\frac{F}{N}$ is the difference degree of two sets; $\frac{P}{N}$ is the opposite degree of two sets.

In summary, a in Equation (7) is the coefficient of similarity degree; c is the coefficient of opposite degree. i and j are the coefficients of the difference and the opposite degrees. i takes the uncertain value in the section $[-1, 1]$ according to different situations; j takes the value of -1 in general situations to indicate that $\frac{P}{N}$ is the opposite to the similarity degree $\frac{S}{N}$.

3.1.3. E-SPA Vulnerability Method

(1) The formation of vulnerability evaluation matrix of CEIC

Given that vulnerability system of CEIC is $Q = \{E, G, W, D\}$, the m evaluation unit is $E = \{e_1, e_2 \cdots e_m\}$, the n indices of each unit is $G = \{g_1, g_2 \cdots g_n\}$, the index weight is $W = \{w_1, w_2 \cdots w_n\}$ (see also Equation (6)), the index evaluation is d_{kp} $(k = 1, 2, \cdots, m; p = 1, 2, \cdots, n)$, then the evaluation matrix D of vulnerability system of CEIC is shown in Equation (8).

$$D = \begin{bmatrix} d_{11} & d_{12} & \cdots & d_{1n} \\ d_{21} & d_{22} & \cdots & d_{2n} \\ \cdots & \cdots & \cdots & \cdots \\ d_{m1} & d_{m2} & \cdots & d_{mn} \end{bmatrix} \tag{8}$$

(2) Identification of similarity and opposite degree

Identify the maximum index set $U = \{u_1, u_2, \cdots u_n\}$ and the minimum index set $V = \{v_1, v_2, \cdots v_n\}$ in the evaluation unit to generate the similarity degree a_{kp} and opposite degree c_{kp} of d_{kp} in the evaluation matrix D on basis of the set $\{v_p, u_p\}$.

If d_{kp} is a positive tropism (+),

$$\begin{cases} a_{kp} = \dfrac{d_{kp}}{u_p + v_p} \\ c_{kp} = \dfrac{u_p v_p}{d_{kp}\,(u_p + v_p)} \end{cases} \tag{9a}$$

If d_{kp} is a negative tropism (−),

$$\begin{cases} a_{kp} = \dfrac{u_p v_p}{d_{kp}\,(u_p + v_p)} \\ c_{kp} = \dfrac{d_{kp}}{u_p + v_p} \end{cases} \tag{9b}$$

(3) The connection degree of vulnerability

The connection degree μ of set pairs $\{E_k, U\}$ in $[V, U]$ is shown in Equation (10).

$$\begin{cases} \mu_{(E_k, U)} = a_k + b_{ki} + c_{kj} \\ a_k = \sum \omega_p a_{kp} \\ c_k = \sum \omega_p c_{kp} \end{cases} \tag{10}$$

(4) The vulnerability indicator X of CEIC

Given x_k represents the connection degree between evaluation unit E_k and the max index set $U = \{u_1, u_2, \cdots u_n\}$ for the Kth construction enterprise, which is shown in Equation (10), the larger x_k is or the closer vulnerability to the max value, the more vulnerable and uncertain the CEIC, and *vice versa.*

$$x_k = \frac{a_k}{a_k + c_k} \tag{11}$$

3.2. PCA and SPA (P-SPA) Method

The PCA Score process is shown in the following seven steps [100,101].

Step 1: Using SPSS 22 software to implement the factor analysis to extract the principal component $F_1, F_2, \ldots, F_n$.

Step 2: Calculating the loading of F_1 score. Factor scores were generated and standardized through loadings. The F_1 loading was divided by the square root of the corresponding eigenvalues of F_1, to generate its orthogonal eigenvectors. N indicators were given as $a_1, a_2, \ldots, a_N$.

Step 3: Calculating F_1 score (f_1) with Equation (12). In Equation (12), $x_1, x_2, ..., x_N$ were the standardized data of N items with the first sample.

$$f_1 = a_1 \times x_1 + a_2 \times x_2 \cdots \cdots a_N \times x_N \tag{12}$$

Step 4: Repeating the steps to calculate F_2, F_3 and F_n scores ($f_2, f_3, \cdots, f_N$) in the first sample.

Step 5: According to the variance % ($v_1, v_2, v_3, \cdots v_n\%$) and cumulative variance % ($cv\%$) of Initial eigenvalues, the weighted sum score Fs was calculated by Equation (13) in the first sample.

$$Fs = (v_1 f_1 + v_2 f_2 + v_3 f_3 + \cdots + v_n f_n)/cv \tag{13}$$

Step 6: Repeating the process on other samples. Then, N indicators were normalized score to calculate the weight, and the weight set WP,

$$WP = [wp_1, wp_2, \cdots, wp_n] \tag{14}$$

Step 7: Constructing the P-SPA Vulnerability method. After using Equations (8) and (14) to alternate the entropy weight, the authors followed the analogy steps of E-SPA method to analysis the vulnerability of CEIC.

4. Empirical Analysis

4.1. Data Collection

In order to verify the vulnerability method of CEIC, comprehensive, accurate, and representative data were retrieved from the "E01Civil Construction Industry Classification Guideline of the Chinese Securities Regulatory Commission (CSRC)", which included a total of 51 public construction companies (E01 and E05 Building Decoration Classification Guideline) in the Shanghai stock exchange and the Shenzhen stock exchange, P.R. China in 2014. A set of these enterprises was identified and used to test the vulnerability framework. Enterprises from the CSRC list are usually large-scale, global competitors and ideal for CEIC analysis. The annual reports of the CSRC provide the enterprise specific information. The authors carefully cleansed the data using the following criteria. (1) The company is listed in the CSRC list for at least eight consecutive years; and (2) there must be an accurate business description. After data cleansing, there were eight enterprises that fit the criteria and were used in the model construction.

On average, researchers used between five and 25 companies with time durations of one to four consecutive years for validation or verification in research projects [92–98]. Additional data were collected from internal sources such as HR, intellectual property, government support, enterprise, innovation investment, management reports, secretarial files, and electronic records. All of the selected companies produced and maintained such information for their day-to-day managerial and operational use. In other words, these data were secondary in nature and were readily available within the business organizations.

The selected companies are listed in Table 3, and the corresponding data are listed in Table 4a,b. The eight companies included in Table 3 are large construction enterprises. The following framework does not contain any parameters that would be affected by the company size of a sample. In addition, the assessment method and framework are applicable to small and medium enterprises (SMEs).

Table 3. Selected samples of the eight construction enterprises.

ID	The Listed Time	Domain Business Area	Research Time Span	The Code
A	2007	Construction of structural steel, Industrial construction	2007–2014	1
B	2001	Railway Engineering and other engineering construction, real estate projects, sales	2007–2014	2
C	1994	Industrial construction, commercial construction, real estate, food service, design and consulting, and facility rental (since 2008)	2007–2014	3
D	2004	Road and bridge construction, asphalt concrete sales, environmental protection business	2005–2014	4
E	1997	Project contracting, cement production and sales, civil explosive, hydroelectric power construction, management of expressways, real estate	2004–2014	5
F	2006	Construction, real estate development	2006–2014	6
G	2005	Installation of cement production lines, manufacturing of machinery and equipment, design and technology transfer, supervision	2007–2014	7
H	2005	Civil construction, Industrial construction, public facilities construction, building decoration, sales of building materials	2005–2014	8

Table 4. Sensitivity data of vulnerability of CEIC.

	Innovation Input capability			Cooperation Innovation Capability			Intellectual Property Capability			Innovation Change Capability			Innovation Environment	
	$IICS_1$	$IICS_2$	$IICS_3$	$CICES_1$	$CICES_2$	$CICES_3$	$IPCS_1$	$IPCS_2$	$IPCS_3$	$CICS_1$	$CICS_2$	$CICS_3$	$IEGS_1$	$IESS_1$
A	9.15%	30.8%	40.98%	0.9%	1.692	24.2%	12.37%	9.89%	40.0%	4.0%	12.95%	267879	21.57%	3.41%
B	8.78%	30.5%	37.29%	1.17%	1.12	24.4%	12.49%	10.59%	38.7%	5.8%	10.54%	254396	26.62%	4.05%
C	9.17%	28.9%	44.22%	0.97%	1.43	25.7%	11.92%	13.66%	42.9%	3.9%	12.62%	266902	19.89%	3.92%
D	7.98%	30.9%	39.89%	1.50%	0.99	22.8%	12.51%	10.79%	32.6%	3.3%	14.55%	267983	23.09%	2.97%
E	8.46%	27.3%	42.25%	1.32%	1.01	23.9%	13.05%	14.82%	45.5%	4.9%	13.21%	259987	20.99%	3.38%
F	9.22%	28.4%	43.77%	0.73%	1.73	23.1%	13.58%	13.37%	36.1%	3.1%	12.74%	269808	19.72%	3.02%
G	9.01%	29.1%	39.83%	0.68%	1.66	25.5%	11.47%	9.52%	39.9%	2.9%	13.09%	270002	21.03%	3.96%
H	8.69%	31.0%	40.17%	1.01%	1.59	24.9%	12.06%	12.22%	40.8%	3.7%	13.11%	268147	20.76%	3.55%

4.2. E-SPA Result

4.2.1. Entropy Weight of Indices

The authors constructed the evaluation matrix and matrix standardization with Equations (2) and (3). They then used Equations (4)–(6) to deal with the standardization data in Tables 4 and 5. The results of entropy weights of indices are shown in Table 6. The corresponding calculation process in this research could be seen in the Supplementary Materials.

Table 5. Adaptability data of vulnerability of CEIC.

	Innovation Input capability			Cooperation Innovation Capability			Intellectual Property Capability			Innovation Change Capability			Innovation Environment	
	$IICA_1$	$IICA_2$	$IICA_3$	$CICEA_1$	$CICEA_2$	$CICEA_3$	$IPCA_1$	$IPCA_2$	$IPCA_3$	$CICA_1$	$CICA_2$	$CICA_3$	$IEGS_2$	$IESS_2$
A	9.15%	3.31%	11.35%	44.19%	0.139	21.84%	0.231	993	13.9%	52.99%	10%	27.0%	36.9%	6.8%
B	10.27%	1.49%	10.98%	42.97%	0.152	21.55%	0.301	899	15.3%	53.73%	9.77%	26.3%	40.3%	10.7%
C	8.96%	2.99%	11.77%	43.58%	0.144	24.31%	0.240	967	15.1%	52.92%	9.31%	27.9%	39.6%	8.9%
D	9.39%	4.01%	11.09%	45.76%	0.098	17.67%	0.229	952	14.7%	53.88%	10.34%	25.4%	43.3%	9.7%
E	7.29%	4.21%	12.03%	44.62%	0.101	18.23%	0.206	1007	13.6%	51.64%	9.69%	25.9%	39.8%	9.5%
F	8.98%	3.13%	10.84%	40.88%	0.127	19.71%	0.200	981	14.2%	53.01%	10.51%	27.3%	38.1%	8.4%
G	9.37%	3.47%	9.96%	41.47%	0.130	16.89%	0.236	1017	13.7%	52.68%	9.98%	28.5%	39.9%	10.6%
H	9.59%	3.00%	10.38%	43.51%	0.136	19.01%	0.219	977	15.0%	53.03%	10.01%	27.2%	40.4%	10.9%

4.2.2. Identification of Vulnerability

The author constructed the assessment matrix using Equation (8) with indices data to generate the similarity and opposition degrees. In step 1, the authors identified the maximum data set U and minimum data set V as shown in Table 7.

In step 2, the authors used the Equations (9a) and (9b) to generate the similarity a_{kp} and opposition degree c_{kp} in the d_{kp} of Equation (8).

In step 3, the authors used Equation (10) to deal with index weight, the similarity a_{kp}, and opposition degree c_{kp}. The calculations generated the similarity a and opposition degree c of vulnerability of enterprise innovation capability in Table 8. The authors used Equation (11), the similarity a, and opposition degree c to calculate the vulnerability indicator X in Table 8.

In step 4, the authors used the analogy process to deal with sensitivity and adaptability data respectively, the similarity a, opposition degree c, and vulnerability indicator X of enterprise' sensitivity. The data of adaptability of innovation capability were also generated as shown in Table 8.

Table 6. Entropy weight and PCA weight of indices.

Index	IICS₁	IICS₂	IICS₃	CICES₁	CICES₂	CICES₃	IPCS₁	IPCS₂	IPCS₃	CICS₁	CICS₂	CICS₃	IEGS₁	IESS₁
Entropy Weig	0.0432038	0.049067048	0.035248156	0.03877084	0.053206164	0.040532366	0.028819682	0.038867465	0.029726585	0.030631336	0.024660397	0.04749291	0.039519158	0.04478313
PCA Weig	0.106823571	0.01461821	0.027886806	0.047262562	0.003170126	0.265283625	0.185939536	0.014947161	0.163610376	0.125805123	0.185006011	0.108780112	0.048122622	0.278513069

Index	IICA₁	IICA₂	IICA₃	CICEA₁	CICEA₂	CICEA₃	IPCA₁	IPCA₂	IPCA₃	CICA₁	CICA₂	CICA₃	IEGS₂	IESS₂
Entropy Weig	0.02301168	0.025365134	0.033259383	0.033075712	0.041265951	0.037907817	0.033785378	0.026661727	0.048286338	0.026045051	0.028806943	0.033478911	0.024799668	0.04062169
PCA Weig	0.090782332	0.185267733	0.014451584	0.036046266	0.219449805	0.185363984	0.185020389	0.099616493	0.174176412	0.005760201	0.261574165	0.136289993	0.005362125	0.110553235

Table 7. The max data set U and min data set V.

V	0.0922	0.31	0.4422	0.0068	0.99	0.257	0.1358	0.1482	0.058	0.1455	270002	0.1972	0.0297
U	0.0798	0.273	0.3729	0.015	1.73	0.228	0.1147	0.0952	0.029	0.1054	254396	0.2662	0.0405
Sign.	−1	−1	−1	1	1	−1	−1	−1	−1	−1	−1	1	1
V	0.0729	0.0149	0.0996	0.4088	0.152	0.1689	0.2	0.136	0.5164	0.0931	0.285	0.433	0.109
U	0.1027	0.0421	0.1203	0.4576	0.098	0.2431	0.301	0.153	0.5388	0.1051	0.254	0.369	0.068
Sign.	1	1	1	1	−1	1	1	1	1	1	−1	−1	−1

Table 8. a, c and X of vulnerability framework of CEIC.

		Sensitivity			Adaptability			Vulnerability		
		a_s	c_s	X_s	a_a	c_a	X_a	a_v	c_v	X_V
A	E-SPA	0.498155954	0.89206403	0.50453205	0.512365605	0.477439407	0.517642969	0.504628	0.4838469	0.5105117
A	P-SPA	0.491235713	0.492601156	0.499306062	0.45408915	0.556627269	0.449274536	0.471400152	0.526789897	0.47225491
B	E-SPA	0.503231366	0.487123778	0.508132228	0.482450401	0.515158926	0.483606546	0.4937662	0.499893	0.4969171
B	P-SPA	0.459289356	0.541436498	0.458956221	0.595191645	0.39944844	0.598399013	0.531858619	0.465617555	0.533204334
C	E-SPA	0.481693552	0.503798343	0.488784894	0.499736677	0.488092023	0.505894066	0.4899117	0.466446	0.4965877
C	P-SPA	0.487313981	0.504576976	0.491297937	0.49295145	0.525135707	0.484193761	0.490324286	0.515554954	0.487458401
D	E-SPA	0.503713135	0.491682509	0.506043138	0.512686689	0.481130567	0.51587622	0.5078003	0.4868764	0.510518
D	P-SPA	0.546644712	0.443842588	0.551894721	0.424835683	0.568083583	0.427865284	0.4816099	0.51018494	0.485589657
E	E-SPA	0.471534032	0.520072564	0.475525308	0.503390354	0.492286234	0.505576168	0.860437	0.5074167	0.4892431
E	P-SPA	0.441540415	0.547433388	0.46463207	0.372700497	0.615243849	0.377248474	0.404781199	0.5836429	0.409521783
F	E-SPA	0.47024256	0.507239244	0.48983419	0.491055936	0.496107288	0.497441481	0.488606	0.502169	0.4932856
F	P-SPA	0.544361307	0.451137158	0.546822849	0.409052674	0.601814228	0.404655324	0.47210905	0.531595876	0.470366378
G	E-SPA	0.511031793	0.485367578	0.512878479	0.477164652	0.513768697	0.481530521	0.4956063	0.4983035	0.4986431
G	P-SPA	0.572003164	0.424703054	0.573893444	0.364723594	0.642851229	0.361981647	0.461319784	0.54119007	0.460164838
H	E-SPA	0.493845236	0.491114037	0.501386452	0.480387508	0.508383974	0.485842803	0.4877156	0.49898	0.4942919
H	P-SPA	0.493941132	0.491211171	0.501385553	0.413605743	0.605142191	0.405994191	0.451043552	0.552048191	0.449653339

Note: (a) a_s, c_s and X_s refer to the similarity, opposition and vulnerability in the single sensitivity system of CEIC. (b) a_a, c_a and X_a refer to the similarity, opposition and vulnerability in the single adaptability system of CEIC. (c) a_v, c_v and X_V refer to the similarity, opposition and vulnerability in the whole vulnerability system of CEIC.

According to Table 9, the comparison of X_v indicates that companies A and D had the most vulnerability and company F had the least vulnerability of CEIC. At the same time, the ranking of vulnerabilities of CEIC in the eight companies was E, F, H, C, B, G, A and D, in an ascending order. By comparing the X_s of sensitivity, it was found that G, B, D are the three most sensitive companies. E is the least sensitive. By comparing the X_a of adaptability, it was found that A, D and C are the three most adaptable companies. E is the least adaptable.

Therefore, the less sensitive a company is, the better the vulnerability of their CEIC is managed. The more sensitive and adaptable they are, the more likely it is that vulnerability of their CEIC is increased. For the sustainable development of CEIC, it is a pertinent practical solution to manage and reduce sensitivity and promote adaptability. Not only should attention be given to adaptability, sensitivity is important to address in examining the linkage between innovation capability and vulnerability factors.

4.3. P-SPA Result and Validation

Using Equation (14), the weights of indices of the PCA method were generated as shown in Table 6. Further, the authors used the weight indices of PCA method to alternate the entropy weight in Equation (8) in order to calculate the vulnerability of CEIC. The results are shown in Table 8.

Following the steps in Section 3.2, the authors extracted the six principal components from F1 to F6 and their variances (%) in Table 9 to build Equation (15). The weighted sum scores of Fs are shown in Equation (15).

$$\text{Fs} = (0.30251f_1 + 0.25894f_2 + 0.18625f_3 + 0.10871f_4 + 0.07236f_5 + 0.05256f_6)/0.98133 \tag{15}$$

Table 9. Total variance explained of original questionnaire.

Component	Initial Eigenvalues			Extraction Sums of Squared Loadings		
	Total	% of Variance	Cumulative %	Total	% of Variance	total %
1	8.470	30.251	30.251	8.470	30.251	30.251
2	7.250	25.894	56.145	7.250	25.894	56.145
3	5.215	18.625	74.770	5.215	18.625	74.770
4	3.044	10.871	85.641	3.044	10.871	85.641
5	2.026	7.236	92.877	2.026	7.236	92.877
6	1.472	5.256	98.133	1.472	5.256	98.133
7	0.523	1.867	100.000			

Extraction Method: Principal Component Analysis.

Using PCA and SPA (P-SPA) methods, the authors found that company B had the greatest vulnerability X_v and company E had the least vulnerability X_v of CEIC. At the same time, the companies with the ascending vulnerability X_v of CEIC were E, H, G, F, A, D, C and B.

With the results of P-SPA method in Tables 7 and 8 through comparing the X_s and X_a of sensitivity and adaptability, the authors found that companies E and F both had lower vulnerability X_v, lower sensitivity, and higher adaptability correspondingly. The calculation results of P-SPA validate the vulnerability system discussed in Section 4.2. While companies A and D both had higher vulnerability X_v, the higher sensitivity X_s and lower adaptability X_a correspondingly. The findings help to develop CEIC by promoting adaptability and managing sensitivity simultaneously.

4.4. Vulnerability Grade

The authors used Zhao's grade standard [97] to calculate indicators for the SPA method. The calculation of the SPA classic grade method is shown in the following three evaluation conditions.

If $\max[a, b, c] = b$, it is grade 2; If $\max[a, b, c] = a$, and $a + b \geqslant 0.7$, it is grade 1, otherwise it is grade 2; If $\max[a, b, c] = c$, and $b + c \geqslant 0.7$, it is grade 3, otherwise it is grade 2.

Grade 1 indicates that the vulnerability of innovation capability is high. A company needs to reduce risk in the system and manage its CEIC. Grade 2 indicates that the vulnerability is satisfactory. A company needs to be more active in managing the uncertainty of its innovation capability. Grade 3 indicates that the vulnerability is low. It is recommended to continue current operations to maintain innovation capability.

The calculations of the vulnerability grades of both the E-SPA and P-SPA methods are based on Equation (7) and Table 8, with further comparison shown in Table 10. The samples are at level 2 from the calculations of both the E-SPA method and P-SPA method. These companies were in a good position to manage risk or uncertainty of innovation capability. The results show that the P-SPA method effectively validates the E-SPA method to assess the vulnerability and its grade of CEIC.

Table 10. The vulnerability grade of innovation capability.

Code	A	B	C	D	E	F	G	H
E-SPA method	2	2	2	2	2	2	2	2
P-SPA validation	2	2	2	2	2	2	2	2

4.5. Response with Major Influencing Factors

The vulnerability X_v of CEIC comes from the combined effects of sensitivity and adaptability. The authors constructed a vulnerability matrix of CEIC using the horizontal axis with low and high sensitivity and the vertical axis with low and high adaptability. The high sensitivity and low adaptability interval is an ideal area for CEIC. It shows an effective path to improve the adaptability and management or to reduce sensitivity. With low sensitivity and high adaptability, it helps to reduce the vulnerability of CEIC. Thus, an innovation strategy might look for the major influencing factors and compose a targeted solution to improve the adaptability of CEIC to maintain this sustainable path. This research used the major impact index formula [14,20,102] to generate and compare the impact extent of the adaptable indices, which are shown in Equation (16) and Table 11.

$$A_i = \omega_i d_i / \sum_{i=1}^{n} \omega_i d_i \times 100\% \tag{16}$$

A_i represents the impact extents of indices. ω_i represents the entropy weight of an index. d_i represents the standardization value of an index. n represents the index number in the adaptability system of CEIC. This research used $Ai \geqslant 5\%$ [14,20,102] to evaluate the extent of impacts of indices and compared their frequencies. The indices were then placed in descending order of their frequencies. The top frequencies were the major influencing factors of the adaptability system in the vulnerability of CEIC.

Table 11. Major influence factors in the adaptability system.

	IICA$_1$	IICA$_2$	IICA$_3$	CICEA$_1$	CICEA$_2$	CICEA$_3$	IPCA$_1$	IPCA$_2$	IPCA$_3$	CICA$_1$	CICA$_2$	CICA$_3$	IEGS$_2$	IESS$_2$
A	5.4254	6.4111	8.208	8.4744	3.7526	9.5526	3.9171	8.0228	3.2187	5.9293	6.2568	6.1192	9.3678	15.344
B	9.9312	0	6.8815	6.1135	0	10.274	14.580	0	20.8391	10.487	4.7657	10.253	5.017	0.8552
C	5.2773	5.7243	11.578	7.4888	2.5018	15.512	5.4755	6.2874	17.435	6.0904	0	2.6517	5.8671	8.1089
D	5.6946	8.2524	6.2032	11.615	14.491	1.3994	3.4066	4.2053	10.971	9.1461	8.6829	11.756	0	4.1751
E	0	11.532	14.713	11.525	17.720	3.1127	0.9126	11.095	0	0	4.1477	12.766	6.1665	6.3067
F	6.104	7.1534	6.4344	0	8.9359	6.7386	0	8.666	7.9712	7.4507	13.474	6.0616	9.4247	11.585
G	11.374	13.076	0	2.832	11.906	0	8.5283	18.881	2.0115	8.5637	11.390	0	9.3303	2.105
H	8.8239	6.996	3.262	8.8562	6.0746	5.381	3.1576	8.7559	19.756	8.0296	8.3486	6.9752	5.583	0
Freq.	7	7	6	6	5	5	3	6	5	7	5	6	7	4
Freq.%	0.875	0.875	0.75	0.75	0.625	0.625	0.375	0.75	0.625	0.875	0.625	0.75	0.875	0.5

The largest frequency (0.875%) indices in the adaptability system of CEIC were IICA$_1$, IICA$_2$, CICA$_1$ and IEGS$_2$. Table 11 also shows that the major influencing factors (0.875%) for CEIC mainly focus on (a) investment, especially R&D expenditure and the proportion of highly educated employees [103]; (b) innovation and change, especially the impact of new service or innovation activities on the market [78]; (c) government support, for example, large program support and taxation exemptions for application of certain innovation technologies [3,56,60,104–106].

The second-tier factors (0.75%) are $IICA_3$, $CICEA_1$, $IPCA_2$ and $CICA_3$. They emphasize the key roles of HR investment and innovation in change, referring to the amount of HR of R&D institutions and the management of corporate energy consumption. In addition, cooperative innovation of enterprise and IP capability played major roles in sustainable CEIC, such as the enterprise investment in university–industry cooperative innovation and the size of enterprise patent pools [69,84,107].

However, much attention should be given to output performance of IP capability ($IPCA_1$, 0.375%) to promote IP marketing and to solve IP transformation problems [108,109]. The lack of social capital [3,110] support given to corporate total capital ($IESS_2$, 0.5%) also leads to inadequate investment in CEIC.

4.6. Discussion

As discussed in this paper, CEIC is vulnerable, and this vulnerability can be measured. The researchers applied and confirmed a quantitative system approach to address the vulnerability of an enterprise's innovation efforts. Vulnerability research, as a new paradigm of sustainable development, uncertainty and risk, sheds light on how to best analyze the uncertainty of innovation capability. As an innovative method, SPA focuses on uncertainty and is widely applied in the economic and social fields [11,12,18,26,111–114], and is combined with some common comprehensive methods, such as E-SPA and P-SPA [44,100–102]. Innovation capability is an important driver of economic development and is closely linked to uncertainty and risk. However, within the new paradigm of reducing uncertainty, very little research exists to develop a systematic approach to assessing the vulnerability of innovation capability [22,23].

In order to extend a generic model of construction innovation [71,76], this new vulnerability framework of CEIC focuses on the extent of innovation investment, IP capability, cooperative innovation, change innovation and the overall environment to foster companies' innovation. Further, this research used the corresponding index in the 2013 National Innovation Survey System of MOST, China to match and test the proposed framework (see also Section 2.4) of the vulnerability system of CEIC, which contained two subsystems referred to as the sensitivity and adaptability of a systematic approach and includes the above five criteria and 28 indicators.

Meanwhile, this paper applied the E-SPA as the main method to analyze the case data to evaluate levels of vulnerability, comparing the results of P-SPA to confirm the empirical results. The authors used the E-SPA and P-SPA measurements regarding the vulnerability and uncertainty of innovation capability and quantitatively bridged the gap in system assessments of vulnerability of CEIC. More importantly, this research justified the necessity for a new approach to examining construction innovation uncertainty and built a foundation for overcoming construction innovation uncertainty, with a view to provide a basis for further research on this topic.

For two subsystems of CEIC, sensitivity referred to the ability of the system to withstand external or internal interferences or pressures. The less the sensitivity, the greater a system's resilience, and vice versa. Adaptability refers to the ability to respond to change which embodies an uncertain state or crisis situations. In other words, the greater the adaptability of a company, the stronger will be the ability of a company to respond to those challenges, and vice versa.

In this research, case studies showed that the sustainable CEIC needed to increase the innovation investment capability such as to enhance HR funding for highly skilled or talented individuals and R&D expenditure for individuals that show the greatest potential for innovation. Much attention seems to be given to the collaboration innovation between universities and research institutions, with the objective to impact business and marketing strategies that already demonstrate a high level performance of intellectual property, which could increase social recognition and capital support, in order to obtain more government assistance [104,115–118]. Thus, at the policy planning or strategic levels, positive industrial and corporate environments may lead to an optimization of an enterprise's innovation efforts and may attract sustainable government support. Furthermore, well established policy and strategic planning may encourage investment in corporate innovation. Topics for further research may include how to implement a practical strategy and operation of a market-oriented university–industry cooperative innovation approach, and how to strengthen and improve the innovation performance of intellectual property capabilities.

5. Conclusions

This study discussed the vulnerability framework of CEIC, and attempts to quantify an evaluation system for CEIC. It opened doors to future research in the theory and application areas in this field. This study proposed a new systematic approach to supplement the quantitative framework and methods in examining the uncertainty regarding a company's ability to innovate applied to the case of construction enterprises. Uncertainty regarding CEIC should not simply be ignored. Rather, it should be managed intelligently and, in an ideal world, help to develop an environment conducive to ongoing innovation. Vulnerability, and the management thereof, is a new domain in the large field of socioeconomic research. This research built a vulnerability framework for CEIC, which examines the subsystems of sensitivity and adaptability and a number of factors including innovation investment capability, cooperation innovation capability, intellectual property capability, change innovation capability, and innovation environment. Further, this research assessed the vulnerability of CEIC, using the comparative results of E-SPA and P-SPA methods for confirmation. It analyzed the major influencing factors in promoting sustainable CEIC.

Case studies showed that the two comparative methods confirm the same grade level of vulnerability of CEIC. We identified a stronger practical approach to reduce the vulnerability of CEIC by managing or reducing sensitivity and strengthening adaptability to respond to new economic environments. The major influencing factors of CEIC are focused on (a) the highly educated HR innovation team, (b) R&D investment intensity, (c) substantial market-led corporate–university–industry cooperation on intellectual property performance, (d) government support and social capital support, and (e) change innovation in construction energy consumption.

In summary, this research provided a theoretical framework and an application method to assess and evaluate both the vulnerability and uncertainty involved in innovation. This research can be implemented to evaluate and grade the vulnerability of CEIC at national, industrial or enterprise levels with the corresponding sequential data and indices. A limitation of this research may result due to the sequential data boundary, *i.e.*, at industrial or national levels, in conducting a systematic analysis to conceptualize innovation capability. A possible future research project may be to expand the dynamic data collection to analyze the vulnerability of construction innovation at both the macro and industrial levels.

Acknowledgments: Acknowledgments: This research is supported by the National Nature Science Foundation of China (NO.71301013), Humanity and Social Science Program Foundation of Ministry of Education of China (NO.13YJA790150), China ASC Fund (NO. asc-kt2014022 and asc-kt2014023), China scholarship council, Shaanxi Nature Science Fund (NO.2014JM2-7140), Shaanxi Social Science Fund (NO.2014HQ10, NO. 2015Z071 and NO. 2015Z075), Xi'an Science Technology Burea Fund(NO.CXY1512(2)), and Special Fund for Basic Scientific Research of Central College (Humanities and Social Sciences), Chang'an University (NO.0009-2014 G 6285048 and NO. 310828155031).

Author Contributions: Author Contributions: Prof. Zhang and Prof. Li analyzed the data and contributed to drafting the paper. Prof. Zhang and Prof. Li contributed to the concept and design of the paper. Prof. Xie and Prof. Schmidt contributed useful advice and modified the paper. Prof. Zhang is in charge of the final version of the paper.

Abbreviations

The following abbreviations are used in this manuscript:

CEIC: Construction enterprises' innovation capabilities
E-SPA: The entropy and set pair analysis method
P-SPA: The principle cluster analysis and SPA method
R&D: Research and development
UNCTAD: United Nations Conference on Trade and Development
UNDP: United Nations Development Programme
OECD: Organization for Economic Co-operation and Development
OECD STI: OECD Science, Technology and Innovation
MOST, China: Ministry of Science and Technology of the People's Republic of China

References

1. Akintoye, A.; Goulding, J.; Zawdie, G. *Construction Innovation and Process Improvement*; Wiley-Blackwell: Hoboken, NJ, USA, 2012.
2. Brochner, J. Construction contractors as service innovators. *Build. Res. Inf.* **2010**, *38*, 235–246. [CrossRef]
3. Castro-Lacouture, D.; Irizarry, J.; Ashuri, B.; American Society of Civil Engineers; Construction Institute. Construction research congress 2014 construction in a global network. In Proceedings of the 2014 Construction Research Congress, Atlanta, GA, USA, 19–21 May 2014; American Society of Civil Engineers: Reston, VA, USA, 2014.
4. Forbes, L.H.; Ahmed, S.M.; Ebooks Corporation. Modern construction lean project delivery and integrated practices. In *Industrial Innovation Series*; CRC Press: Boca Raton, FL, USA, 2011.
5. Goh, B.; Tjoa, A.; Xu, L.; Chaudhry, S. Intelligent enterprises for construction: Bridging the technology and knowledge gaps through innovation and education. *Res. Pract. Issues Enterp. Inf. Syst.* **2006**, *205*, 119–131.
6. Blayse, A.M.; Manley, K. Key influences on construction innovation. *Constr. Innov.* **2004**, *4*, 143–154. [CrossRef]
7. Suprun, E.V.; Stewart, R.A. Construction innovation diffusion in the Russian Federation. *Constr. Innov.* **2015**, *3*, 278–312. [CrossRef]
8. Kulatunga, U.; Amaratunga, R.; Haigh, R. Construction Innovation: A Literature Review on Current Research. 2006. Available online: http://usir.salford.ac.uk/9886/1/205_Kulatunga_KJ_et_al_CONSTRUCTION_INNOVATION_A_LITERATURE_REVIEW_ON_CURRENT_RESEARCH_2006.pdf (accessed on 21 December 2015).
9. Hultgren, A.; Tantawi, A. *Front-End Idea Screening of Potential Radical Innovation in Large Firms: A Holistic Framework for the Volvo Group*; Chalmers University of Technology: Göteborg, Sweden, 2014.
10. Baker, S.M. Vulnerability and resilience in natural disasters: A marketing and public policy perspective. *J. Public Policy Mark.* **2009**, *28*, 114–123. [CrossRef]
11. Le Breton-Miller, I.; Miller, D. The paradox of resource vulnerability: Considerations for organizational curatorship. *Strat. Manag. J.* **2015**, *36*, 397–415. [CrossRef]
12. Dabla-Norris, E.; Gündüz, B.Y. Exogenous shocks and growth crises in low-income countries: A vulnerability index. *World Dev.* **2014**, *59*, 360–378. [CrossRef]
13. Dass, M.; Kumar, P.; Peev, P.P. Brand vulnerability to product assortments and prices. *J. Mark. Manag.* **2013**, *29*, 735–754. [CrossRef]
14. Li, F.; Wan, N.Q.; Shi, B.L.; Liu, X.M.; Guo, Z.J. The vulnerability measure of tourism industry based on the perspective of "environment-structure" integration a case study of 31 provinces in mainland China. *Geogr. Res.* **2014**, *33*, 569–581.
15. Herceg, I.; Nesti, D. A new cluster-based financial vulnerability indicator and its application to household stress testing in Croatia. *Emerg. Markets Finance Trade* **2014**, *50*, 60–77.
16. Holand, I.S.; Lujala, P.; Rød, J.K. Social vulnerability assessment for Norway: A quantitative approach. *Nor. J. Geogr.* **2011**, *65*, 1–17. [CrossRef]
17. Rodríguez-Núñez, E.; García-Palomares, J.C. Measuring the vulnerability of public transport networks. *J. Transp. Geogr.* **2014**, *35*, 50–63. [CrossRef]

18. Rossignol, N.; Delvenne, P.; Turcanu, C. Rethinking vulnerability analysis and governance with emphasis on a participatory approach. *Risk Anal. Int. J.* **2015**, *35*, 129–141. [CrossRef] [PubMed]

19. Springer, N.P.; Garbach, K.; Guillozet, K.; Haden, V.R.; Hedao, P.; Hollander, A.D.; Huber, P.R.; Ingersoll, C.; Langner, M.; Lipari, G.; *et al.* Sustainable sourcing of global agricultural raw materials: Assessing gaps in key impact and vulnerability issues and indicators. *PLoS ONE* **2015**, *10*, 1–22. [CrossRef] [PubMed]

20. Hong, T.; Jian, Z. Regional vulnerability evaluation index system of environmental emergencies in petrochemical industry. *Adv. Mater. Res.* **2014**, *1073–1076*, 400–404.

21. Turner, B.L.; Kasperson, R.E.; Matson, P.A.; McCarthy, J.J.; Corell, R.W.; Christensen, L.; Eckley, N.; Kasperson, J.X.; Luers, A.; Martello, M.L.; *et al.* A framework for vulnerability analysis in sustainability science. *PNAS* **2003**, *100*, 8074–8079. [CrossRef] [PubMed]

22. Dassen-Housen, P. Management of uncertainty—A contradiction in itself? In *Enabling Innovation: Innovative Capability—German and International Views*; Jeschke, S., Isenhardt, I., Hees, F., Trantow, S., Eds.; Springer-Verlag: Berlin, Germany, 2011; pp. 30–33.

23. Trantow, S.; Hees, F.; Jeschke, S. Innovative capability. In *Enabling Innovation: Innovative Capability —German and International Views*; Jeschke, S., Isenhardt, I., Hees, F., Trantow, S., Eds.; Springer-Verlag: Berlin, Germany, 2011; pp. 1–13.

24. Costanza, R.; d'Arge, R.; Groot, R.D.; Farber, S.; Grasso, M.; Hannon, B.; Limburg, K.; Naeem, S.; O'Neill, R.V.; Paruelo, J.; *et al.* The value of ecosystem services: putting the issues in perspective. *Ecol. Econ.* **1998**, *25*, 67–72. [CrossRef]

25. Gnangnon, S.K. Does structural economic vulnerability matter for public indebtedness in developing countries? *J. Econ. Stud.* **2014**, *41*, 644–671. [CrossRef]

26. Pérez Agúndez, J.A.; Yimam, E.; Raux, P.; Rey-Valette, H.; Girard, S. Modeling economic vulnerability: As applied to microbiological contamination on the Thau Lagoon shellfish farming industry. *Mar. Policy* **2014**, *46*, 143–151. [CrossRef]

27. Ransbotham, S.; Mitra, S.; Ramsey, J. Are markets for vulnerabilities effective? *MIS Q.* **2012**, *36*, 43–64.

28. Bell, M.; Pavitt, K. Technological accumulation and industrial growth: Contrasts between developed and developing countries. *Ind. Corp. Change* **1993**, *2*, 157. [CrossRef]

29. Pavitt, K. What we know about the strategic management of technology. *Calif. Manag. Rev.* **1990**, *32*, 17–26. [CrossRef]

30. Freeman, C. The 'national system of innovation' in historical perspective. *Camb. J. Econ.* **1995**, *19*, 5–24.

31. OECD. *Proposed Guidelines for Collecting and Interpreting Technological Innovation Data: Oslo Manual*; OECD Publication Services: Paris, France, 1997.

32. Böhle, F. Management of uncertainty–A blind spot in the promotion of innovations. In *Enabling Innovation–German and International Views*, 1st ed.; Al, S.J.E., Ed.; Springer-Verlag: Berlin, Germany, 2011; pp. 17–29.

33. Dominitz, J.; Manski, C.F. *Perceptions of Economic Vulnerability: First Evidence from the Survey of Economic Expectations/Jeff Dominitz and Charles f. Manski*; Institute for Research on Poverty, University of Wisconsin-Madison: Madison, WI, USA, 1995.

34. Berry, P.M.; Rounsevell, M.D.A.; Harrison, P.A.; Audsley, E. Assessing the vulnerability of agricultural land use and species to climate change and the role of policy in facilitating adaptation. *Environ. Sci. Policy* **2006**, *9*, 189–204. [CrossRef]

35. UNDP. *Human Development Report 1999*; Oxford University Press: Oxford, UK, 1999.

36. Erol, O.; Sauser, B.; Mansouri, M. A framework for investigation into extended enterprise resilience. *Enterp. Inf. Syst.* **2010**, *4*, 111–136. [CrossRef]

37. Prewitt, K. The federal statistical system: Its vulnerability matters more than you think—Section four: Strengthening the statistical system: Future of innovation in the federal statistical system. 2010. Available online: https://us.sagepub.com/en-us/nam/the-federal-statistical-system-its-vulnerability-matters-more-than-you-think/book235999 (accessed on 22 December 2015).

38. Han, R.; Tong, L.; Tong, W.; Yu, J. Research on vulnerability assessment of human-land system of Anshan city based on set pair analysis. *Progr. Geogr.* **2012**, *31*, 344–351.

39. Reed, M.S.; Podesta, G.; Fazey, I.; Geeson, N.; Hessel, R.; Hubacek, K.; Letson, D.; Nainggolan, D.; Prell, C.; Rickenbach, M.G.; *et al.* Surveys: Combining analytical frameworks to assess livelihood vulnerability to climate change and analyse adaptation options. *Ecol. Econ.* **2013**, *94*, 66–77. [CrossRef] [PubMed]

40. Aldana-Bobadilla, E.; Kuri-Morales, A. A clustering method based on the maximum entropy principle. *Entropy* **2015**, *17*, 151–180. [CrossRef]
41. Benedetto, F.; Giunta, G.; Mastroeni, L. A maximum entropy method to assess the predictability of financial and commodity prices. *Dig. Signal Process.* **2015**, *46*, 19–31. [CrossRef]
42. Zou, Q.; Zhou, J.Z.; Zhou, C.; Song, L.X.; Guo, J. Comprehensive flood risk assessment based on set pair analysis-variable fuzzy sets model and fuzzy AHP. *Stochast. Environ. Res. Risk Assess.* **2013**, *27*, 525–546. [CrossRef]
43. Xia, C.; Yi, M.; Wei, W.; Yu, Z. Discussion of annual runoff dry-wet classification based on set pair analysis. *Yangze River* **2015**, *46*, 21–24.
44. Su, M.R.; Yang, Z.F.; Chen, B. Set pair analysis for urban ecosystem health assessment based on emergy-vitality index. *China Environ. Sci.* **2009**, *29*, 892–896.
45. Meng, X.M.; Hu, H.P. Application of set pair analysis model based on entropy weight to comprehensive evaluation of water quality. *J. Hydraul. Eng.* **2009**, *40*, 257–262.
46. Sun, B.; Wang, H. Inventory Evaluation Model and Application of Shipbuilding Enterprise Based on the Method of Optimal Combination. *Int. J. U- E-Serv. Sci. Technol.* **2015**, *8*, 175–184. [CrossRef]
47. Li, B.; Yang, Z.; Su, F. Measurement of vulnerability in human-sea economic system based on set pair analysis: A case study of Dalian city. *Geogr. Res.* **2015**, *34*, 967–976.
48. Gobble, M.M. The 2009 European innovation scoreboard: EU lags us & Japan while China closing gap with EU. *Res. Technol. Manag.* **2010**, *53*, 2–4.
49. OECD. OECD Science, Technology and Industry Outlook 2014. Available online: http://dx.doi.org.libproxy.lib.ilstu.edu/10.1787/sti_outlook-2014-en (accessed on 21 December 2015).
50. Gupta, P.; Trusko, B.E. *The Innovation Radar and enterprise Business System: Innovation in Five Nordic Countries and Beyond*; McGraw-Hill Professional: New York, NY, USA, 2014.
51. UNCTAD. UNCTAD at 50: A short History. 2014. Available online: http://unctad.org/en/PublicationsLibrary/osg2014d1_en.pdf (accessed on 23 December 2015).
52. Bank, W. *World Development Indicators 2010*; World Bank: Washington, DC, USA, 2010; p. xxiii.
53. Azubuike, V.M.U. Technological innovation capability and firm's performance in new product development. *Commun. IIMA* **2013**, *13*, 43–55.
54. Carcary, M.; Doherty, E.; Thornley, C. Business innovation and differentiation: Maturing the IT capability. *IT Prof.* **2015**, *17*, 46–53. [CrossRef]
55. Daqi, X.U. Research on improving the technological innovation capability of SMEs by university-industry collaboration. *J. Eng. Sci. Technol. Rev.* **2013**, *6*, 100–104.
56. Fagerberg, J.; Feldmany, M.P.; Srholec, M. Technological dynamics and social capability: US states and European Nations. *J. Econ. Geogr.* **2014**, *14*, 313–337. [CrossRef]
57. Hansen, U.E.; Ockwell, D. Learning and technological capability building in emerging economies: The case of the biomass power equipment industry in Malaysia. *Technovation* **2014**, *34*, 617–630. [CrossRef]
58. Tseng, C.-Y. Technological innovation capability, knowledge sourcing and collaborative innovation in Gulf Cooperation Council countries. *Innov. Manag. Policy Pract.* **2014**, *16*, 212–223.
59. Raymond, L.; St-Pierre, J.; Uwizeyemungu, S.; Dinh, T. Internationalization capabilities of SMEs: A comparative study of the manufacturing and industrial service sectors. *J. Int. Entrep.* **2014**, *12*, 230–253. [CrossRef]
60. Manseau, A.; Seaden, G. *Innovation in Construction: An International Review of Public Policies*; Spon Press: London, UK; New York, NY, USA, 2001.
61. Brooker, P.; Wilkinson, S. *Mediation in the Construction Industry: An International Review*; Routledge: London, UK, 2010.
62. Altenburger, R. Green product innovation: Values and networks in open innovation processes. In Proceedings of ISPIM Conferences, Dublin, Ireland, 8–11 June 2014.
63. Bindroo, V.; Mariadoss, B.J.; Pillai, R.G. Customer clusters as sources of innovation-based competitive advantage. *J. Int. Mark.* **2012**, *20*, 17–33. [CrossRef]
64. Chan, I.; Liu, A.; Fellows, R. Role of leadership in fostering an innovation climate in construction firms. *J. Manag. Eng.* **2014**. [CrossRef]
65. Elmualim, A.; Gilder, J. Bim: Innovation in design management, influence and challenges of implementation. *Archit. Eng. Design Manag.* **2014**, *10*, 183–199. [CrossRef]

66. Blindenbach-Driessen, F.; van den Ende, J. Innovation in project-based firms: The context dependency of success factors. *Res. Policy* **2006**, *35*, 545–561. [CrossRef]

67. Chen, L.; Marsden, J.R.; Zhang, Z. Theory and analysis of company-sponsored value co-creation. *J. Manag. Inf. Syst.* **2012**, *29*, 141–172. [CrossRef]

68. Gann, D.; Salter, A. Innovation in project-based, service-enhanced firms: The construction of complex products and systems. *Res. Policy* **2000**, *29*, 955–972. [CrossRef]

69. Iammarino, S.; Piva, M.; Vivarelli, M.; von Tunzelmann, N. Technological capabilities and patterns of innovative cooperation of firms in the UK regions. *Reg. Stud.* **2012**, *46*, 1283–1301. [CrossRef]

70. Leiringer, R.; Schweber, L. Managing multiple markets: Big firms and PFI. *Build. Res. Inf.* **2010**, *38*, 131–143. [CrossRef]

71. Sexton, M.; Barrett, P. Appropriate innovation in small construction firms. *Constr. Manag. Econ.* **2003**, *21*, 623–633. [CrossRef]

72. Kuo, Y. Technology readiness as moderator for construction company performance. *Ind. Manag. Data Syst.* **2013**, *113*, 558–572. [CrossRef]

73. Ruwanpura, J.; Mohamed, Y.; Lee, S. Construction research congress 2010: Innovation for reshaping construction practice. In Proceedings of the 2010 Construction Research Congress, Banff, AL, Canada, 8–10 May 2010.

74. Pellicer, E.; Correa, C.L.; Yepes, V.; Alarcón, L.F. Organizational improvement through standardization of the innovation process in construction firms. *Eng. Manag. J.* **2012**, *24*, 40–53. [CrossRef]

75. Pryke, S.; Ebooks Corporation. Construction supply chain management concepts and case studies. In *Innovation in the Built Environment*; Wiley-Blackwell: Chichester, UK; Malden, MA, USA, 2009.

76. Barrett, P.; Sexton, M.; Lee, A. *Innovation in small Construction Firms*; Taylor & Francis: London, UK; New York, NY, USA, 2008; p. 107.

77. Patanakul, P.; Pinto, J.K. Examining the roles of government policy on innovation. *High Technol. Manag. Res.* **2014**, *25*, 97–107. [CrossRef]

78. Chesbrough, H.W.; Appleyard, M.M. Open innovation and strategy. *Calif. Manag. Rev.* **2007**, *50*, 57–76. [CrossRef]

79. Wu, I.-L.; Chiu, M.-L. Organizational applications of it innovation and firm's competitive performance: A resource-based view and the innovation diffusion approach. *J. Eng. Technol. Manag.* **2015**, *35*, 25–44. [CrossRef]

80. Kamasak, R. Determinants of innovation performance: A resource-based study. *Procedia-Soc. Behav. Sci.* **2015**, *195*, 1330–1337. [CrossRef]

81. Han, J.-W.; Lim, H.-S. Strategic analysis and success factors of the enterprises through the convergence. *Int. J. Appl. Eng. Res.* **2014**, *9*, 15715–15726.

82. Lusch, R.F.; Nambisan, S. Service innovation: A service-dominant logic perspective. *MIS Q.* **2015**, *39*, 155–176.

83. Palm, K. Understanding innovation as an approach to increasing customer value in the context of the public sector. 2014. Available online: https://www.diva-portal.org/smash/get/diva2:773180/FULLTEXT01.pdf (accessed on 21 December 2015).

84. Wu, J. Cooperation with competitors and product innovation: Moderating effects of technological capability and alliances with universities. *Ind. Mark. Manag.* **2014**, *43*, 199–209. [CrossRef]

85. Aalbers, R.; Dolfsma, W. *Innovation Networks: Managing the Networked Organization/Rick Aalbers and Wilfred Dolfsma*; Routledge: London, UK, 2015.

86. Cabanelas, P.; Omil, J.C.; Vázquez, X.H. A methodology for the construction of dynamic capabilities in industrial networks: The role of border agents. *Ind. Mark. Manag.* **2013**, *42*, 992–1003. [CrossRef]

87. Macaulay, L.A.; Miles, I.; Wilby, J.; Tan, Y.L.; Zhao, L.; Theodoulidis, B. *Case Studies in Service Innovation*; Springer: Berlin, Germany, 2012.

88. Anumba, C.J.; Egbu, C.O.; Carrillo, P.M. *Knowledge Management in Construction*; Blackwell Pub.: Oxford UK; Malden, MA, USA, 2005; xiv; p. 226.

89. Connaughton, J.; Meikle, J. The changing nature of UK construction professional service firms. *Build. Res. Inf.* **2013**, *41*, 95–109. [CrossRef]

90. Gabbott, M.; Hogg, G. Consumer involvement in services: A replication and extension. *J. Bus. Res.* **1999**, *46*, 159–166. [CrossRef]

91. Halpin, D.W.; Senior, B.A. *Construction Management*, 4th ed.; Wiley: Hoboken, NJ, USA, 2011; p. 448.

92. Giang, D.T.H.; Pheng, L.S. Role of construction in economic development: Review of key concepts in the past 40 years. *Habitat Int.* **2011**, *35*, 118–125. [CrossRef]

93. Kazi, A.S. *Knowledge Management in the Construction Industry: A Socio-Technical Perspective*; Idea Group Pub.: Hershey, PA, USA, 2005; p. 384.

94. Korman, T.M.; Huey-King, L. Industry input for construction engineering and management courses: Development of a building systems coordination exercise for construction engineering and management students. *Pract. Period. Struct. Design Constr.* **2014**, *19*, 68–72. [CrossRef]

95. McCarthy, J.F. *Construction Project Management*; Pareto–Building Improvement: Westchester, IL, USA, 2010; p. 432.

96. Chinese Academy of Science and Technology for Development. China National Innovation Index Report 2013. Available online: http://www.most.gov.cn/kjtj/201511/P020151117383919061369.pdf (accessed on 21 December 2015).

97. Zhao, K.; Xuan, A. Set pair theory-a new theory method of non-define and its applications. *Syst. Eng.* **1996**, *14*, 14–26.

98. Xing, W.; Ye, X.; Kui, L. Measuring convergence of China's ICT industry: An input–output analysis. *Telecommun. Policy* **2011**, *35*, 301–313. [CrossRef]

99. Bereziński, P.; Jasiul, B.; Szpyrka, M. An entropy-based network anomaly detection method. *Entropy* **2015**, *17*, 2367–2408. [CrossRef]

100. Faed, A.; Chang, E.; Saberi, M.; Hussain, O.K.; Azadeh, A. Intelligent customer complaint handling utilising principal component and data envelopment analysis (PDA). *Appl. Soft Comput. J.* **2015**. [CrossRef]

101. Dong, X.; Guo, J.; Höök, M.; Pi, G. Sustainability assessment of the natural gas industry in China using principal component analysis. *Sustainability* **2015**, *7*, 6102–6118. [CrossRef]

102. Chen, J.; Yang, X.; Wang, Z.; Zhang, L. Vulnerability and influence mechanisms of rural tourism socio-ecological systems: A household survey in China's Qinling mountain area. *Tour. Trib.* **2015**, *30*, 64–75.

103. Likar, B.; Kopa, J.; Fatur, P. Innovation investment and economic performance in transition economies: Evidence from Slovenia. *Innov. Manag. Policy Pract.* **2014**, *16*, 53–66. [CrossRef]

104. Hemphill, T.A. Policy debate: The US advanced manufacturing initiative: Will it be implemented as an innovation—Or industrial—Policy? *Innov. Manag. Policy Pract.* **2014**, *16*, 67–70. [CrossRef]

105. Cabrilo, S.; Grubic-Nesic, L. Ic-Based Innovation Gap Assessment: A Support Tool for the Creation of Effective Innovation Strategies in the Knowledge Era. In Proceedings of the 4th European Conference on Intellectual Capital, Helsinki, Finland, 23–24 April 2012.

106. Martinez, M.G. Co-creation of value by open innovation: Unlocking new sources of competitive advantage. *Agribusiness* **2014**, *30*, 132–147. [CrossRef]

107. Hsieh, M.; Wu, C.; Ting, P.; Lin, T. A study on project partner's alignment process and value innovation. *Mark. Rev.* **2013**, *10*, 345–370.

108. Reitzig, M.; Puranam, P. Value appropriation as an organizational capability: The case of IP protection through patents. *Strat. Manag. J.* **2009**, *30*, 765–789. [CrossRef]

109. Giannopoulou, E.; YstrÖM, A.; Ollila, S. Turning open innovation into practice: Open innovation research through the lens of managers. *Int. J. Innov. Manag.* **2011**, *15*, 505–524. [CrossRef]

110. Roy, M.; Donaldson, C.; Baker, R.; Kerr, S. The potential of social enterprise to enhance health and well-being: A model and systematic review. *Soc. Sci. Med.* **2014**, *123*, 182–193. [CrossRef] [PubMed]

111. Bolanos, A.B. External Vulnerabilities and Economic Integration: Is the Union of South American Nations a Promising Project? *J. Econ. Dev.* **2014**, *39*, 97–131.

112. Culpepper, P.D.; Reinke, R. Structural power and bank bailouts in the United Kingdom and the United States. *Polit. Soc.* **2014**, *42*, 427–454. [CrossRef]

113. Murphy, E.; Scott, M. Household vulnerability in rural areas: Results of an index applied during a housing crash, economic crisis and under austerity conditions. *Geoforum* **2014**, *51*, 75–86. [CrossRef]

114. Ala, M.U. A firm-level analysis of the vulnerability of the Bangladeshi pharmaceutical industry to the trips agreement: Implications for R&D capability and technology transfer. *Proced. Econ. Finance* **2013**, *5*, 30–39.

115. Tomes, A. UK government science policy: The 'enterprise deficit' fallacy. *Technovation* **2003**, *23*, 785–792. [CrossRef]

116. Al-Sudairi, M.; Bakry, S.H. Knowledge issues in the global innovation index: Assessment of the State of Saudi Arabia versus countries with distinct development. *Innov. Manag. Policy Pract.* **2014**, *16*, 176–183. [CrossRef]

117. Kiskiene, A. Scientific knowledge and technology transfer policy in the EU. *Econ. Bus.* **2014**, *26*, 36–43. [CrossRef]

118. Ljungquist, U. Unbalanced dynamic capabilities as obstacles of organizational efficiency: Implementation issues in innovative technology adoption. *Innov. Manag. Policy Pract.* **2014**, *16*, 82–95. [CrossRef]

9

Diversification Models of Sales Activity for Steady Development of an Enterprise

Nestor Shpak [1], Tamara Kyrylych [1,*] and Jolita Greblikaitė [2,*]

[1]   Department of Management and International Business Undertakings,
      Economics and Management Education Research Institute, National University "Lviv Polytechnic",
      Metropolitan Andrey street 3, 79013 Lviv, Ukraine; dida_05@ukr.net

[2]   Faculty of Economics and Management, Business and Rural Development Management Institute,
      Aleksandras Stulginskis University, Studentu str. 11, Akademija, 53361 Kaunas, Lithuania

*   Correspondence: povstenkot@mail.ru (T.K.); jolita19@gmail.com (J.G.);

Academic Editor: Adam Jabłoński

Abstract: The paper substantiates the importance of the optimal directionality choice of sales activity as one of the main lines of enterprise activity, the functioning of which should be complete, synchronous and complementary. Diversification is one of the powerful instruments to ensure the steady development of the sales activity of an enterprise. Three models of sales activity diversification of an enterprise are developed. The first model is based on unveiling the potential of sales channels and allows us to show the peculiarities of their use. The second model of the optimal quantitative distribution of production between sales channels is based on profit maximization. This approach not only takes into account the evaluation of the prescribed parameters of sales channels, but also provides the high profitability of each assortment item and of the whole enterprise. The third model of the optimal distribution of production between sales channels accounts for the experience of collaboration between the enterprise and sales channels during the past period and ensures the minimal risk and appropriate profitability for each sales channel. The proposed models are tested and compared to actual data of the enterprise; the advantages and peculiarities of each model are discussed.

Keywords: sales activity; diversification; optimal production distribution; sales channels; profitability; business risk

---

1. Introduction

Market fluctuations are noticeably observed in modern conditions of uncertainty, disbalance and disproportions between the expected and actual state of the market. A reaction of enterprises on these processes is manifested by the adaptation to such conditions, an active search for new instruments and methods, which allow a company to ensure steady development, to confine the competitive positions and to reduce exogenous and endogenous risks appearing during the economic activity of market entities. One of such instruments providing the steady development of an enterprise consists of diversification, which is directed toward expanding the domain of company operation. Diversification of sales activity is a process of extended use of innovative tools, mechanisms, methods and models for achieving marketing goals and determining optimal sales channels and the optimal distribution of products in each sales channel. Diversification provides an instrument for varying the enterprise operation and constructive optimal decision-making to improve enterprise conditions.

Today, more and more companies choose multichannel distribution systems; the use of such systems has increased greatly in recent years [1]. It was emphasized in [2] that the increasing complexity of the competitive environment requires new approaches to stating company strategy and tactics. Enterprises diversify their sales activities to vary the use of distribution channels and to reduce a risk of profit deficiency caused by exploiting only a few sales channels or by cooperation with undisciplined intermediaries.

In this paper, we present three models of sales activity diversification of a company. Section 2 includes a review of existing approaches to the selection of sales channels, the conceptual discussion and presentation of models. The potential of sales channels and the peculiarities of their use are discussed in Section 3. The second approach to the optimal quantitative distribution of production between distribution channels based on profit maximization is considered in Section 4. The third model of the optimal distribution of production between distribution channels based on risk minimization is described in Section 5. The proposed models are tested and compared to actual data of the company; a comparison of predicted income is presented in Section 6. The advantages and peculiarities of each model are discussed in Section 7. Conclusions are reported in Section 8.

2. Theoretical Framework

The problem of the optimal selection of sales channels has attracted considerable interest of many researchers. Coughlan *et al.* [3] discussed the structure, function, framework, development, maintenance and management of distribution channels to attain significant competitive advantages. Developing relationships between sales channels and control mechanisms in such channels was reviewed in [4,5]. Nevin [5] emphasized that to be effective in designing channels, marketing managers need to understand the alternative mechanisms for controlling the individual channel members. Different kinds of consumers and their behavior on a market to provide the effective selling distribution were analyzed in [6,7]. Various aspects of sales channels choice by consumers have also been studied in [8–10]. Sutton and Klein [11] considered the optimization of marketing instruments to drive profitable sales channels of an enterprise. They underlined the need of optimizing the performance of each marketing channel (which channels perform better than others?) and of identifying risks and critical success factors to hit performance targets. Ingene and Parry [12] analyzed channel performance, channel strategy and mathematical models of sales channels. Evaluating channel choice, Magrath and Hardy [13] considered three groups of criteria: efficiency (cost, capacity), effectiveness (coverage, control, competence) and adaptability (flexibility, vitality). Criteria characterizing producers, markets, purchasing peculiarities, goods, intermediaries, customers, behavior of sales channels participants, *etc.*, were examined in [14–18]. Kotler [19] described economical, control and adaptive criteria of channels' evaluation. Criteria for selecting and evaluating intermediaries in indirect sales channels were discussed in [19–21]. Rolnicki [22] provides a comprehensive list of channel member selection criteria, including reputation, business and managerial stability, financial strength, type of market coverage, sales competency, *etc.* Various aspects of the sustainability of distribution channels were discussed by Dent [23]. Different profit-maximization models for distribution channels were proposed in [24]. Several examples of using the linear programming methods in management were presented by Anderson *et al.* [25]. A game-theoretical approach to modeling distribution channels was used in [26,27].

At the present time, the problem of selecting the best sales channels and arranging the movement of goods in them is still investigated incompletely, especially taking into account the specificity of Ukrainian economic relations. This determines the need of system research ensuring the steady development of sales activity of enterprises based on diversification principles. Choosing optimal sales channels, enterprises have to deal with a set of questions and problems. To solve these problems, the authors have proposed three approaches to the diversification of sales activity of a company. The presented complex of criteria has been formulated by the authors based on the large amount of literature on this topic, taking into account the practice of sales activity in Ukraine and previous authors' investigations. Three models considered in the paper present a new solution of a problem of sales channels' selection using the present-day mathematical technique. The mathematical tools are known in the literature, but the authors have implemented and adapted these models to existing conditions of enterprise functioning and development taking into account special features of proposed qualitative and quantitative characteristic criteria for comparing direct and indirect sales channels.

The choice of a model depends on the production type, the product life cycle stage, the goals of an enterprise (maximal profit or minimal risk) and other parameters. The model of determining the sales channel potential assumes comparing the sales channels based on qualitative and quantitative characteristic criteria, which reflect the peculiarities of cooperation between a company and intermediaries or take into account the sales results of individual direct sales channels. The second model of the optimal quantitative distribution of production between sales channels is based on profit maximization. This approach not only takes into account the evaluation of the prescribed parameters of sales channels, but also provides the high profitability of each assortment item and of the whole enterprise. The third model of the optimal distribution of production between sales channels accounts for the experience of collaboration between the enterprise and sales channels during the past period and ensures the minimal risk and appropriate profitability for each sales channel.

3. The Model of Determining the Sales Channel Potential

Based on the research mentioned above, the practice of economic entities and our own study [16], the qualitative-quantitative criteria were elaborated for evaluating and comparing the direct and indirect sales channels. The importance of elaborating such criteria was also emphasized by Magrath and Hardy [13]: "Products or services must be graded, assembled, bundled, converted, augmented, promoted, displayed, sold, warranted, repaired, transported, and so on. Any channel of distribution can be compared in terms of its inherent ability to fulfill such functions".

As an example, Svitovyr, LLC (Lviv, Ukraine), was considered. The characteristic criteria of comparing direct sales channels are presented in Table 1. We also give recommendations for their calculation. The obtained criteria will be used to compare the direct channels' potentials using the improved radar method (see Figure 1a).

Recommendations for the calculation of the qualitative and quantitative characteristic criteria for direct channels:

(1) The channel having the largest total production turnover gets 10 points; the points of other channels are calculated proportionally to the leading channel.

(2) The channel having the largest increase of sales volume gets 10 points; the points of other channels are calculated proportionally to the leading channel.

(3) $\frac{\text{The sum of strengths and opportunities positions}}{\text{The sum of weaknesses and threats positions}}$ .The direct channel having the maximum value of the ratio gets 10 points; the points of other channels are calculated proportionally to the leading channel.

(4) Independent experts interview top-management representatives of direct sales channels forming the expert opinion according to a 10-point grading scale.

(5) The direct channel having the lowest markup rate gets 10 points. Points for other channels are calculated subtracting 0.5 points for every additional 5% of markup rate.

(6) The direct channel having the shortest period of goods delivery from the producer to a consumer gets 10 points. Points for other channels are calculated subtracting 0.5 points for every additional day.

(7) A secret shopper evaluates sales personnel according to the 10-point grading scale.

(8) $\frac{\text{Total population of settlements, where production is presented}}{\text{Population of Ukraine}}$.

(9) The leading direct channel gets 10 points; the points of other channels are calculated proportionally to the leading channel.

(10) $\frac{\text{The number of months in use}}{\text{The number of months of company existence}}$.

Table 1. Characteristic criteria of comparing direct sales channels of Svitovyr.

No	Criterion Weight	Characteristic Criteria for the Selection of a Direct Sales Channel	Actual Value of a Characteristic of a Direct Channel		The Number of Points of Each Sales Channel (According to a 10-Point Scale)		The Number of Points for Each Sales Channel Corrected by the Weight	
			ES	IS	ES	IS	ES	IS
1	0.20	Year turnover of a sales channel	29,000 UAH	21,000 UAH	10	7.24	2	1.45
2	0.13	Increase of sales volume	5%	3%	10	6	1.3	0.78
3	0.11	Enterprise efficiency index according to SWOT analysis	1.4	1.1	10	7.86	1.1	0.86
4	0.11	Competence and professionalism of management personnel	-	-	7.8	9	0.86	0.99
5	0.10	Markup rate	19%	10%	9	10	0.9	1
6	0.09	Averaged velocity of commodities circulation from the producer to a consumer	At once	At once	10	10	0.9	0.9
7	0.08	A level of service and a level of production presentation by sales personnel	-	-	8.4	9.5	0.67	0.76
8	0.08	Territorial coverage	0.22	0.09	2.2	0.9	0.18	0.07
9	0.05	The number of visitors (the number of customers in a database)	19,000 visitors	16,000 visitors	10	8.42	0.5	0.42
10	0.05	Using period	1	0.2	10	3	0.5	0.15

Abbreviations: ES, Exhibition Sales; IS, Internet Sales.

The qualitative and quantitative characteristic criteria of comparing indirect sales channels of Svitovyr, LLC (Lviv, Ukraine), are presented in Table 2. We briefly characterize these criteria and give recommendations for their calculation. It should be emphasized that the number of qualitative and quantitative characteristic criteria for indirect distribution channels should be substantially larger than that for direct channels, as the manufacturer has less possibilities of control and influence on the intermediary behavior. The obtained criteria will be used to compare the indirect channels' potentials using the improved radar method (see Figure 1b).

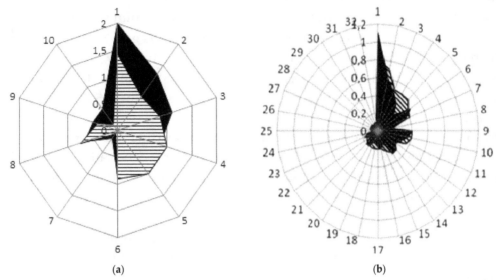

(a)   (b)

Figure 1. Graphical interpretation of the evaluation of direct (**a**) and indirect (**b**) sales channels for Svitovyr using the improved radar method (data from 2014). Nomenclature for Figure 1a: ■, internet sales; ≡, exhibition sales; nomenclature for Figure 1b: ◥, specialized hypermarket; ■, distribution network.

Recommendations for the calculation of qualitative and quantitative characteristic criteria for indirect channels:

(1) The intermediary having the largest year turnover of the producer production gets 10 points; the points of other indirect sales channels are calculated proportionally to the leading channel.

(2) Data from the last two years are compared. The intermediary having the largest sales increase gets 10 points; the points of other indirect sales channels are calculated proportionally to the leading channel.

(3) The intermediary having the least credit debt gets 10 points. For each additional 1000 UAH, 0.5 points are subtracted.

(4) The direct channel having the maximum value of the ratio gets 10 points; the points of other indirect sales channels are calculated proportionally to the leading channel.

(5) The intermediary having the largest increase in sales gets 10 points; the points of other sales channels are calculated proportionally to the leading channel.

(6) The intermediary having no debts during the last year gets 10 point. 0.5 points are subtracted for each debt month.

(7) Independent experts give the number of points according to a 10-point grading scale.

(8) $\dfrac{\text{Total population of settlements, where production is presented}}{\text{Population of Ukraine}}$.

(9) The indirect sales channel having the lowest markup rate gets 10 points. Points for other channels are calculated subtracting 0.5 points for every additional 5% of markup rate.

(10) The intermediary having the lowest discount gets 10 points; 0.5 point are subtracted for each additional percentage.

(11) Independent experts interview top-management representatives of an indirect sales channel forming the expert opinion according to a 10-point grading scale.

(12) Independent experts give the number of points according to a 10-point grading scale.

(13) The intermediary having the lowest freight charges gets 10 points; 0.5 point are subtracted for each additional 1000 UAH.

(14) The intermediary with the largest year turnover gets 10 points; the points of other indirect sales channels are calculated proportionally to the leading channel.

(15) A secret shopper evaluates sales personnel according to a 10-point grading scale.

(16) The intermediary having the largest frequency of promotions gets 10 points; the points of other sales channels are calculated proportionally to the leading channel.

(17) The intermediary having the least increase in sales of the analogical production of competitors gets 10 points. The points of other channels are calculated subtracting 0.5 points for each additional 5% increase.

(18) The duration of intermediary activity is compared; the leading indirect channel gets 10 points; the points of other indirect sales channels are calculated proportionally to the leading channel.

(19) The part of producer's costs in joint promotions is compared to that of the intermediary. The channel in which the part of producer's costs is the lowest gets 10 points; the points of other indirect sales channels are calculated proportionally to the leading channel.

(20) The intermediary having the shortest period of product delivery from the producer to a consumer gets 10 points. Points of other channels are calculated subtracting 0.5 points for each additional day.

(21) $\frac{\text{Turnover of producer production}}{\text{Total turnover of the intermediary}}$. The indirect channel having the largest ratio gets 10 points; the points of other indirect sales channels are calculated proportionally to the leading channel.

(22) The Marketing Department and Sales Department give the number of points according to a 10-point scale.

(23) Independent experts give the number of points according to a 10-point grading scale.

(24) Independent experts give the number of points according to a 10-point grading scale.

(25) $\frac{\text{The number of months in use}}{\text{The number of months of company existence}}$.

(26) The dates of the last investment in fixed assets are compared. The indirect channel with the last investment gets 10 points. The points of other channels are calculated by subtracting one point for each year earlier than the leading channel.

(27) The use of ecological modes of transport and the use of rendering plant facilities are estimated. The indirect channel having at least one of the abovementioned items gets 10 points.

(28) The indirect sales channel having no returns gets 10 points. The points for other channels are calculated subtracting one point for each return.

(29) Independent experts give the number of points according to a 10-point grading scale.

(30) $\frac{\text{The number of nonstandard situations solved positively}}{\text{The number of nonstandard situations}}$.

(31) The dates of the last purchase are compared. The indirect channel with the latest purchase gets 10 points. The points of other channels are calculated subtracting 0.5 points for each month earlier than the leading channel.

(32) Volumes of the last purchase are compared. The indirect channel with the largest purchase volume gets 10 points; the points of other indirect sales channels are calculated proportionally to the leading channel.

Table 2. Qualitative and quantitative characteristic criteria of comparing indirect sales channels of Svitovyr.

No	Criterion Weight	Characteristic Criteria for the Selection of an Indirect Sales Channel	Actual Value of a Characteristic of an Indirect Channel		Points (According to a 10-Point Scale)		The Number of Points Corrected by the Weight	
			SH	DN	SH	DN	SH	DN
1	0.11	Year turnover of a sales channel	16,200 UAH	19,100 UAH	7.5	10	0.825	1.1
2	0.07	Increase of sales volume of producer production	14%	12%	10	8.6	0.7	0.602
3	0.05	The quantity of credit debt	1000 UAH	2200 UAH	10	9.4	0.5	0.47
4	0.05	Enterprise efficiency index according to SWOT analysis	0.95	0.7	10	7.4	0.5	0.37
5	0.05	Increase of total sales volume	6%	3%	10	5	0.5	0.25
6	0.05	Exact time payment for shipped production	3 months	2 months	8.5	9	0.425	0.45
7	0.05	Consistency between a target consumer of the intermediary and the producer	-	-	8	7	0.4	0.35
8	0.05	Territorial coverage	0.22	0.32	2.2	3.2	0.11	0.16
9	0.04	Markup rate	29%	32%	10	9.8	0.4	0.392
10	0.04	Discount for production	6%	8%	10	9	0.4	0.36
11	0.04	Competence and professionalism of management personnel	-	-	9	7	0.36	0.28
12	0.04	Existence and quality of marketing strategy	-	-	5	6	0.2	0.24
13	0.03	Freight charges	7500 UAH	8000 UAH	10	9.8	0.3	0.294
14	0.03	Total year turnover of the indirect channel	144,000 UAH	153,000 UAH	9.4	10	0.282	0.3
15	0.03	A level of service and a level of production presentation by sales personnel	-	-	8	5	0.24	0.15
16	0.02	Frequency of joint promotions	2 times a year	2 times a year	10	10	0.2	0.2
17	0.02	Increase in sales of the analogical production of competitors	11%	17%	10	9.4	0.2	0.188
18	0.02	Duration of intermediary activity	1.9 year	1.4 year	10	7.4	0.2	0.148
19	0.02	Participation in joint promotions	26%	41%	10	6.3	0.2	0.126
20	0.02	Averaged velocity of goods circulation from the manufacturer to a consumer	3 days	2 days	9.5	10	0.19	0.2
21	0.02	A part of the turnover of producer production in the total turnover of the indirect channel	0.11	0.12	9.2	10	0.184	0.2
22	0.02	Elasticity in decision-making	-	-	8	6	0.16	0.12
23	0.02	Quality of promotions	-	-	7	9	0.14	0.18
24	0.02	Existence and quality of the review of branch markets for a channel	-	-	7	6	0.14	0.12
25	0.02	Using period	0.3	0.3	3	3	0.06	0.06
26	0.01	Date of the last investment in fixed assets	2010	2010	10	10	0.1	0.1
27	0.01	Ecological compatibility of commodity circulation	-	-	10	10	0.1	0.1
28	0.01	Merchandise returns	-	2007	10	9	0.1	0.09
29	0.01	Image, professionalism and reputation	-	-	10	8	0.1	0.08
30	0.01	Elasticity and accommodation of sales channel personnel to nonstandard situations	0.7	0.9	7	9	0.07	0.09
31	0.01	Date of the last purchase	8 July 2013	5 October 2013	7	10	0.07	0.1
32	0.01	The last purchase volume	100 items	110 items	9.1	10	0.091	0.1

Abbreviations: SH, Specialized Hypermarket; DN, Distribution Network.

On the basis of the described criteria, the direct and indirect channels' potentials will be compared. The existing radar method [28,29], which does not account for the criterion weights, involves building a circle with a radius equal to 10 conventional units. Next, a graphical cyclogram is constructed at the radial axis at which the criteria values are marked. These marks are connected creating a polygon (the number of axes is equal to the number of criteria). The proposed improved radar method [16] consists of building a circle with a radius equal to the maximum value of all of the criteria, sorting the criteria into groups according to the weight decrease and according to points adjusted by the weight coefficient. It should be mentioned that the recommended values of criteria weights reflect their significance and are set based on the experience of enterprise activity. At the radial axis of the graphical cyclogram, the criteria values corrected by their weights are marked. The area S_p^* of the obtained polygon is determined as follows:

$$S_p^* = \sin\left(\tfrac{2\pi}{n}\right)\ (a_1 \times \gamma_1 \times a_2 \times \gamma_2 + a_2 \times \gamma_2 \times a_3 \times \gamma_3 + a_3 \times \gamma_3 \times a_4 \times \gamma_4 + \ldots + \\ + a_{n-1} \times \gamma_{n-1} \times a_n \times \gamma_n + a_n \times \gamma_n \times a_1 \times \gamma_1) \times 0.5 \tag{1}$$

where n is the number of criteria, α_i is the value of the i-th characteristic criterion and γ_i denotes the weight coefficient of the i-th criterion.

Comparison of sales channels is carried out using the generalized characteristic index Y_k^* which is calculated as:

$$Y_k^* = \frac{S_p^*}{S_c^*} \tag{2}$$

In this equation, S_c^* is the area of a circle with a radius equal to the maximal value of all of the weighted criteria ($r = \max\ (a_i * \gamma_i)$). The greater is the value of Y_k^*, the more profitable is the sales channel (see Figure 1).

Based on graphical evaluation of the direct and indirect sales channels of Svitovyr, using the improved radar method, the correspondence between the actual and reference values of the characteristics of sales channels are presented in Table 3.

The analysis of the obtained results for Svitovyr allows us to conclude that exhibition sales has the largest potential among the direct sales channels, as its level of correspondence between the actual and reference values of the characteristics is equal to 0.125. According to this model, specialized hypermarket has the largest potential among the indirect sales channels, as its level of correspondence between the actual and reference values of the characteristics is equal to 0.067.

The recommended percentage of production distribution between the direct sales channels calculated on the basis of generalized characteristic indices is the following: 55% for exhibition sales and 45% for internet sales; whereas the recommended percentage of production distribution between the indirect sales channels is the following: 67% for specialized hypermarket and 33% for distribution network.

Actual values of income per unit and actual sales volumes of three-phase and single-phase transformers for direct and indirect distribution channels of Svitovyr, LLC (Lviv, Ukraine), are presented in Table 4.

The recommended sales volumes for the three-phase and single-phase transformers obtained on the basis of the considered model are shown in Table 5.

Table 3. The results of evaluation of direct and indirect sales channels for Svitovyr using the improved radar method (data from 2014).

The Names of Parameters	Types of Sales Channels		Parameter Values
Reference saturation of the characteristics of the sales channel, S_c^*	Direct channels	Exhibition Sales	6.602
		Internet Sales	12.56
Actual saturation of the characteristics of the sales channel, S_p^*		Exhibition Sales	0.821
		Internet Sales	1.266
A level of correspondence between the actual and reference values of the characteristics (the generalized characteristic index), Y^{*dir}_{kj}, $j = 1,2$		Exhibition Sales	0.125
		Internet Sales	0.101
Reference saturation of the characteristics of the sales channels, S_c^*	Indirect channels	Specialized Hypermarket	2.137
		Distribution Network	3.799
Actual saturation of the characteristics of the sales channel, S_p^*		Specialized Hypermarket	0.143
		Distribution Network	0.124
A level of correspondence between the actual and reference values of the characteristics (the generalized characteristic index), Y^{*indir}_{kj}, $j = 3,4$		Specialized Hypermarket	0.067
		Distribution Network	0.033

Table 4. The values of income per unit and actual sales volumes of direct and indirect sales channels of Svitovyr in 2014.

Production Items	Parameters / Sales Channels	Exhibition Sales	Internet Sales	Specialized Hypermarket	Distribution Network
Three-phase transformer	Income per unit	164.35	140.20	153.90	115.78
	Actual annual sales volume, $Q_{1j}, j = \overline{1;4}$	1890	2050	1820	3290
Single-phase transformer	Income per unit	161.13	152.46	166.71	101.42
	Actual annual sales volume, $Q_{2j}, j = \overline{1;4}$	1680	1658	1403	1779

Table 5. The recommended sales volumes of direct and indirect sales channels of Svitovyr in 2014 following from the model of determining the sales channels' potential.

Production Items	Sales Volumes Sales Channels	Exhibition Sales	Internet Sales	Specialized Hypermarket	Distribution Network
Three-phase transformer	Recommended annual sales volume, $Q_{1j}, j = \overline{1;4}$	2167	1773	3424	1686
Single-phase transformer	Recommended annual sales volume, $Q_{2j}, j = \overline{1;4}$	1836	1502	2132	1050

The actual annual income of Svitovyr from sales of two types of transformers is 2,196,843 UAH; after redistribution of production between sales channels, it will be 2,313,626 UAH, *i.e.*, it will be larger by 116,783 UAH or by 5.32%. The advantage of such a redistribution for the three-phase transformer will be also discussed in Section 6. It should be mentioned that the model of determining the sales channels' potential does not assume the redistribution of the product from direct channels to indirect and *vice versa*. The models discussed below allow such a redistribution.

4. The Model of the Optimal Distribution of Production between Sales Channels Based on Profit Maximization

The model of determining the sales channel potential described in the previous section can be used for further investigation of sales activity diversification of an enterprise. The results obtained for the generalized characteristic indices will be used to formulate the constraints in the linear optimization problem discussed in this section. The objective function of the optimal distribution of production between sales channels should guarantee the maximal profit:

$$\sum_{i=1}^{m}\sum_{j=1}^{n} G_{ij} = \sum_{i=1}^{m}\sum_{j=1}^{n} \left[P_{ij} \times \frac{(100 - \gamma_j)}{100} - (S_i + W_{ij} + U_{ij} + A_{ij} + C_{ij}) \right] \times Q_{ij} \rightarrow \max \qquad (3)$$

where:

G_{ij} is the profit for the i-th assortment item using the j-th sales channel;

P_{ij} is the price of the production unit for the i-th assortment item with the use of the j-th sales channel;

γ_i denotes the discount for the intermediary when the j-th sales channel is used, %;

S_i is the prime cost of the i-th assortment item;

W_{ij} are the costs of warranty repair and guarantee maintenance of the production unit guarantee for the i-th assortment item when the j-th sales channel is used;

U_{ij} stands for expected logistics costs per i-th output unit with the use of the j-th sales channel;

A_{ij} are the administrative costs for the i-th assortment item when the j-th sales channel is used;

C_{ij} denotes the stimulation costs of intermediary for the i-th assortment item in the j-th sales channel;

Q_{ij} is the production volume of the i-th assortment item when the j-th sales channel is used;

m is the number of assortment items;

n is the number of sales channels.

Now, we formulate a system of constraints of the linear optimization problem:

(1). In the proposed optimization model, the planned output volume of every assortment item is equal to or less than the initial output one W_i^{beg} as its increase leads to the corresponding cost increase. Hence:

$$\sum_{j=1}^{n} Q_{ij} \leqslant W_i^{beg}, \ i = \overline{1,m} \qquad (4)$$

(2). Expert interview of sales channels managers of Svitovyr has shown that the channels will continue the collaboration with this enterprise under conservation of at least 25% of actual sales volume. Such a constraint is written as:

$$Q_{ij} \geqslant 0,25 \times U_{ij}^{beg}, \ i = \overline{1,m}; \ j = \overline{1,n}$$ (5)

where U_{ij}^{beg} is the actual sales of the i-th assortment item in the j-th sales channel.

(3). To take into account the potential of each direct and indirect sales channel, we use the results of their evaluation obtained in Section 2 by the improved radar method, which allows us to calculate the profitability of each channel. Mathematically, this constraint has the following form:

$$\sum_{i=1}^{m} Q_{ij} = \lambda_j \sum_{i=1}^{m} \sum_{j=1}^{\alpha} Q_{ij}, \ j = \overline{1,\alpha}, \ \sum_{j=1}^{\alpha} \lambda_j = 1$$ (6)

$$\lambda_j = \frac{Y_{kj}^{*dir}}{\sum\limits_{j=1}^{\alpha} Y_{kj}^{*dir}}, \ j = \overline{1,\alpha}$$ (7)

where λ_j is the ratio of the generalized characteristic index Y_k^{*dir} of the direct sales channel (see Equations (2) and (7)); α is the number of direct channels.

Similarly, for indirect sales channels, we have:

$$\sum_{i=1}^{m} Q_{ij} = \mu_j \sum_{i=1}^{m} \sum_{j=\alpha+1}^{n} Q_{ij}, \ j = \overline{\alpha+1,n}, \ \sum_{j=\alpha+1}^{n} \mu_j = 1$$ (8)

$$\mu_j = \frac{Y_{kj}^{*indir}}{\sum\limits_{j=\alpha+1}^{n} Y_{kj}^{*indir}}, \ j = \overline{\alpha+1,n}$$ (9)

where μ_j is the ratio of the generalized characteristic index Y_k^{*indir}.

(4). The standard constraint of the optimization problems of such a type is the requirement of the non-negativity of sales volumes:

$$Q_{ij} > 0$$ (10)

Actual data necessary for formulating and solving the corresponding optimization problem for direct and indirect sales channels of Svitovyr can be found in Table 4. Based on these data, the objective function is stated as:

$$164.35 \times Q_{11} + 140.20 \times Q_{12} + 153.90 \times Q_{13} + 115.78 \times Q_{14} + 161.13 \times Q_{21}$$
$$+152.46 \times Q_{22} + 166.71 \times Q_{23} + 101.42 \times Q_{24} \rightarrow \max$$ (11)

The constraints are the following:

$$Q_{11} + Q_{12} + Q_{13} + Q_{14} \leqslant 9050,$$ (12a)

$$Q_{21} + Q_{22} + Q_{23} + Q_{24} \leqslant 6520,$$ (12b)

$$Q_{11} + Q_{21} = 0.45 \times (Q_{11} + Q_{12} + Q_{21} + Q_{22}),$$ (12c)

$$Q_{13} + Q_{23} = 0.33 \times (Q_{13} + Q_{14} + Q_{23} + Q_{24}),$$ (12d)

$$Q_{11} \geqslant 473,$$ (12e)

$$Q_{12} \geqslant 513,$$ (12f)

$$Q_{13} \geqslant 455, \tag{12g}$$

$$Q_{14} \geqslant 823, \tag{12h}$$

$$Q_{21} \geqslant 420, \tag{12i}$$

$$Q_{22} \geqslant 415, \tag{12j}$$

$$Q_{23} \geqslant 351, \tag{12k}$$

$$Q_{24} \geqslant 445. \tag{12l}$$

The solution of the optimization problem Equations (11) and (12) ensuring profit maximization was obtained using the simplex method realized by the computer program [30]. The solution results are presented in Table 6.

Table 6. The values of optimal sales volumes of direct and indirect sales channels of Svitovyr obtained in the profit maximization model.

Production Items	Parameters	Exhibition Sales	Internet Sales	Specialized Hypermarket	Distribution Network
Three-phase transformer	Optimal annual sales volume, $Q_{1j}^*, j = \overline{1;4}$	5487	1916	455	1192
Single-phase transformer	Optimal annual sales volume, $Q_{2j}^*, j = \overline{1;4}$	420	5304	351	445

The actual annual income of Svitovyr from two analyzed types of transformers is 2,196,843 UAH; after optimization, it will be 2,358,439 UAH. The proposed redistribution of production between the sales channels allows the enterprise to raise the annual income by 161,596 UAH, *i.e.*, by 7.35%.

5. The Model of the Optimal Distribution of Production between Sales Channels Based on Risk Minimization

The model considered in the previous section takes into account only the last annual income, but it is worthwhile to account for annual incomes for several previous years, as the experience of preceding years may be essential for decision-making. Every enterprise tends to maximize its income, but there appears the admissible risk that the company owner is ready to incur. According to [31,32], risk is incorporated into different types of decision models, and there are different types of risk management strategies: risk sharing, risk pooling and risk diversification. Some enterprises are of the opinion that it is better to restrict slightly their income to a certain level, but to minimize their risks ("safety first" objectives [31,32]).

In this section, we investigate the diversification of marketing activity from the viewpoint of minimal risk and formulate the new model of the optimal distribution of product between the sales channels based on risk minimization. Steady development of an enterprise is also possible under the use of such a strategy. The solution of the formulated problem can be obtained by adapting Markowitz's portfolio theory [33,34] to risk estimation under conditions of using the specified sales channels. This approach allows us not only to compare the sales channels from the viewpoint of their profitability, but also to investigate their risk level.

To illuminate the proposed approach, we present the information of Svitovyr about the profitability of three-phase transformer (Table 7) and single-phase transformer (Table 8) in direct (exhibition sales, internet sales) and indirect (specialized hypermarket, distribution network) sales channels during 2010–2014.

The use of Markowitz's portfolio theory for the investigation of the optimal integration of sales channels based on risk minimization is motivated by its origin approach to the mathematical formulation of the relation between profitability and risk.

Table 7. The values of profit per production unit (UAH) for the three-phase transformer in the sales channels of Svitovyr.

Sales Channels Years	Exhibition Sales	Internet Sales	Specialized Hypermarket	Distribution Network
2010	107.90	100.20	102.00	101.70
2011	134.02	102.70	130.90	114.81
2012	165.72	128.16	145.45	154.47
2013	172.13	135.50	147.98	145.80
2014	164.35	140.20	153.90	115.78
The mean profit value per production unit during 2010–2014	148.82	121.35	136.05	126.51

Table 8. The values of profit per production unit (UAH) for the single-phase transformer in the sales channels of Svitovyr.

Sales Channels Years	Exhibition Sales	Internet Sales	Specialized Hypermarket	Distribution Network
2010	117.50	126.20	127.75	109.00
2011	124.44	162.97	154.22	105.78
2012	132.15	170.16	178.40	129.65
2013	175.27	172.35	187.45	133.80
2014	161.13	152.46	166.71	101.42
The mean profit value per production unit during 2010–2014	142.10	156.83	162.91	115.93

The general stages of implementation of the optimal production distribution between sales channels based on risk minimization are the following:

(1) Gathering data about profitability $P_i^{(k)}$ of the selected assortment item in the i-th sales channel within the span of some period.
(2) Determining the mean value of profitability r_i of every sales channel.
(3) Calculating the covariance between profitability of sales channels:

$$\text{cov}(P_i, P_j) = \frac{1}{N-1} \sum_{k=1}^{N} (P_i^{(k)} - r_i)(P_j^{(k)} - r_j) \,,\ i = \overline{1,n}\,,\ j = \overline{1,n}\,, \tag{13}$$

where N is the number of periods (years).

(4) Arranging a symmetric covariance matrix of the profitability of sales channels:

$$\mathbf{A}(\text{cov}) = \begin{pmatrix} A_{11} & A_{12} & \dots & A_{1n} \\ A_{21} & A_{22} & \dots & A_{2n} \\ \dots & \dots & \dots & \dots \\ A_{n1} & A_{n2} & \dots & A_{nn} \end{pmatrix} \tag{14}$$

where $A_{ij} = \text{cov}(P_i, P_j)$.

(5) Finding the inverse matrix $\mathbf{A}(\text{cov})^{-1}$.
(6) Calculating the mean squared deviation based on the percentage relation between the sales channels. The essence of the considered model of the optimal production distribution between the sales channels consists of risk minimization. If x_i denotes the part of the production distributed

using the i-th sales channel, then the mean squared deviation, which reflects the risk level of the sales channel, is written as:

$$\sigma = \mathbf{X} \cdot \mathbf{A}(\text{cov})^{-1} \cdot \mathbf{X}^T, \tag{15}$$

where $\mathbf{X}$ is the vector with components x_i; $\mathbf{X}^T$ is the transpose of the vector $\mathbf{X}$; $\mathbf{A}(\text{cov})^{-1}$ denotes the matrix inverse to the covariance matrix.

The problem formulation, including the objective function and constraints according to the Markowitz model [35]:

$$\sigma = \mathbf{X} \cdot \mathbf{A}(\text{cov})^{-1} \cdot \mathbf{X}^T \rightarrow \min,$$
$$\sum_{i=1}^{n} x_i = 1, \tag{16}$$
$$x_i \geqslant 0, \; i = \overline{1, n}.$$

(7)   Solving the optimization problem (finding the optimal production distribution between sales channels that ensures minimal risk).

We will illustrate the described approach by the study of the profitability of sales channels for Svitovyr. The necessary input data for the formulation of the optimization problem are presented in Table 9 for the three-phase transformer.

Table 9. Covariance of profitability of sales channels for Svitovyr (sales of the three-phase transformer).

Sales Channels	Exhibition Sales	Internet Sales	Specialized Hypermarket	Distribution Network
			Covariance	
Exhibition Sales	740.9	469.8	545.9	486.0
Internet Sales	469.8	349.3	346.4	251.0
Distribution Network	545.9	346.4	433.8	301.6
Specialized Hypermarket	486.0	251.0	301.6	505.4

The covariance matrix takes the form:

$$\mathbf{A}(\text{cov}) = \begin{pmatrix} 740.9 & 469.8 & 545.9 & 486.0 \\ 469.8 & 349.3 & 346.4 & 251.0 \\ 545.9 & 346.4 & 433.8 & 301.6 \\ 486.0 & 251.0 & 301.6 & 505.4 \end{pmatrix} \tag{17}$$

The inverse matrix is calculated as:

$$\mathbf{A}(\text{cov})^{-1} = \frac{1}{10^8} \cdot \begin{pmatrix} 33.62 & -14.05 & -23.01 & -11.62 \\ -14.05 & 7.25 & 8.54 & 4.81 \\ -23.01 & 8.54 & 16.97 & 7.76 \\ -11.62 & 4.81 & 7.76 & 4.36 \end{pmatrix} \tag{18}$$

The objective function of the optimization problems is written as:

$$\sigma = (x_1, \; x_2, \; x_3, \; x_4) \cdot \begin{pmatrix} 33.62 & -14.05 & -23.01 & -11.62 \\ -14.05 & 7.25 & 8.54 & 4.81 \\ -23.01 & 8.54 & 16.97 & 7.76 \\ -11.62 & 4.81 & 7.76 & 4.36 \end{pmatrix} \cdot \begin{pmatrix} x_1 \\ x_2 \\ x_3 \\ x_4 \end{pmatrix} \rightarrow \min \tag{19}$$

or:

$$\sigma = 33.62x_1^2 - 28.10x_1x_2 - 46.02x_1x_3 - 23.24x_1x_4 + 7.25x_2^2 + \\ + 17.08x_2x_3 + 9.62x_2x_4 + 16.97x_3^2 + 15.52x_3x_4 + 4.36x_4^2 \rightarrow \min. \tag{20}$$

The constraints are the following:

$$x_1 + x_2 + x_3 + x_4 = 1 \tag{21}$$

$$x_1 \geqslant 0, \ x_2 \geqslant 0, \ x_3 \geqslant 0, \ x_4 \geqslant 0 \tag{22}$$

The convexity property of a quadratic form ensures that any local minimum must be a global minimum. A quadratic optimization problem is convex if and only if the inverse covariance matrix in the objective function is positively defined, *i.e.*, its eigenvalues are positive. In our case, the characteristic polynomial of the inverse covariance matrix:

$$\lambda^4 - 62.20\lambda^3 + 171.32\lambda^2 - 73.18\lambda + 3.63 = 0 \tag{23}$$

has the following roots:

$$\lambda_1 = 0.05707 > 0, \ \lambda_2 = 0.45535 > 0, \ \lambda_3 = 2.35422 > 0, \ \lambda_4 = 59.33336 > 0 . \tag{24}$$

Hence, the objective function is positively defined.

The problem is solved using the Lagrange multipliers: to find the minimum of the function:

$$\begin{aligned} L = 33.62x_1^2 - 28.10x_1x_2 - 46.02x_1x_3 - 23.24x_1x_4 + 7.25x_2^2 + 17.08x_2x_3+ \\ +9.62x_2x_4 + 16.97x_3^2 + 15.52x_3x_4 + 4.36x_4^2 - \lambda(x_1 + x_2 + x_3 + x_4 - 1) \to \text{min.} \end{aligned} \tag{25}$$

The conditions of existence of an extremum read:

$$\begin{aligned} \frac{\partial L}{\partial x_1} &= 67.24x_1 - 28.10x_2 - 46.02x_3 - 23.24x_4 - \lambda = 0 , \\ \frac{\partial L}{\partial x_2} &= -28.10x_1 + 14.50x_2 + 17.08x_3 + 9.62x_4 - \lambda = 0 , \\ \frac{\partial L}{\partial x_3} &= -46.02x_1 + 17.08x_2 + 33.94x_3 + 15.52x_4 - \lambda = 0 , \\ \frac{\partial L}{\partial x_4} &= -23.24x_1 + 9.62x_2 + 15.52x_3 + 8.72x_4 - \lambda = 0 . \end{aligned} \tag{26}$$

From system Equation (26), we obtain:

$$x_1 = 11.14\lambda, \ x_2 = 7.12\lambda, \ x_3 = 8.14\lambda, \ x_4 = 7.48\lambda \tag{27}$$

Inserting these values of x_i in the constraint Equation (21), we get that $\lambda = 0.0295$; hence, the optimal production distribution (for the three-phase transformer) between the sales channels of Svitovyr will be the following:

$$x_1 \approx 0.33, \ x_2 \approx 0.21, \ x_3 \approx 0.24, \ x_4 \approx 0.22, \tag{28}$$

i.e., 33% for Exhibition sales, 21% for internet sales, 24% for specialized hypermarket and 22% for distribution network. Based on data presented in Table 7, a similar optimization problem can be also solved for the single-phase transformer.

6. Comparison of Predicted Income

Analyzing three models of the diversification of sales activity shows that every model gives the possibility to optimize the product distribution between sales channels. The owner or top-managers, which have the right of decision-making, decide about the global strategy of enterprise development taking into account the peculiarities of the competitive position, the market environment situation, *etc.* Table 10 shows the prediction results for sales of the three-phase transformer on the bases of the three discussed models of distribution channels' diversification.

Table 10. Results of the diversification of sales channels for Svitovyr using different models (sales of the three-phase transformer).

Model	Recommended Sales Volume for Sales Channels								Total Income, UAH
	Exhibition Sales		Internet Sales		Specialized Hypermarket		Distribution Network		
	Pieces	%	Pieces	%	Pieces	%	Pieces	%	
Determining sales channel potential	2167	24	1773	20	3424	38	1686	18	1,326,880
Optimal production distribution between sales channels based on profit maximization	5487	61	1916	21	455	5	1192	13	1,378,446
Optimal production distribution between sales channels based on risk minimization	2986	33	1901	21	2172	24	1991	22	1,322,058
Actual sales volume (2014)	1890	21	2050	23	1820	20	3290	36	1,259,046
Actual profitability per production unit, UAH (2014)	164.35		140.20		153.90		115.78		

As can be seen from the presented calculations, all three models predict the excess of the total income in comparison with the actual income (by the example of the three-phase transformer); this testifies that every model can be used. The largest total income is predicted by the model based on profit maximization, whereas the model based on risk minimization predicts the least total income (though larger than the actual one). The model of determining sales channels potential predicts that the product redistribution between sales channels allows the firm to increase the annual income by 67,834 UAH or by 5.39%. According to the model based on profit maximization, the annual income will increase by 119,400 UAH or by 9.48%. The model of optimal production distribution between sales channels based on risk minimization forecasts the increase of annual income by 63,012 UAH or by 5%.

7. Verification and Comparison of Models

The model of determining the sales channel potential is a general-purpose tool for all kinds and types of enterprises (large, medium, small). This model is simple in use, reveals the sales channel potential, covers a wide spectrum of estimated parameters and takes into account the weight of each parameter. The use of the model lays down no special technical requirements. The processing of results is conducted by simple analytical methods using graphical tools (Excel environment or some analogue). The considered model includes qualitative and quantitative characteristic criteria. We have proposed the quantitative measurement of qualitative criteria using expert estimation. Such an estimation assumes that independent experts synthesize information by quantitative evaluation of a criterion that characterizes the compared sales channels. For example, a level of service and a level of production presentation by sales personnel is evaluated by a secret shopper according to the 10-point grading scale. Similarly, the competence and professionalism of management personnel is estimated on the basis of the interview of top-management representatives according to a 10-point grading scale. For Svitovyr, LLC (Lviv, Ukraine), such an estimation was carried out in 2014. The shortcoming of this model consists of the possibility of giving rise to inadequate or "warped" information; the more so as the data volume required for getting relevant data in each sales channel is sufficiently large. To ensure a well-grounded and balanced management decision, such studies should be conducted systematically, in the dynamics, immediately determining undesirable changes in sales channels.

The model of the optimal distribution of production between sales channels based on profit maximization ensures the maximal profit of an enterprise by choosing the most profitable sales channel. The advantages of this model are the following: the accuracy of the obtained results, a high level of their processing, the possibility of formulating additional constraints according to the needs and interests of a company, the possibility of comparing current and potential sales channels, the possibility of changing undisciplined intermediaries and redistributing production into more profitable direct and indirect sales channels. The shortcomings of the considered model are connected with the need to have specialists in linear programming, the risk of sales channel "overestimation" and the failure to take account of dynamic conditions.

The model of the optimal distribution of production between sales channels based on risk minimization is helpful for enterprises of those countries, the economy of which develops under indeterminate and chaotic conditions. This model can also be used when the product life cycle is at an initial stage and when an enterprise tries to enter into a new market where gathering information is complicated and there is high probability of product "aversion" by customers. The advantages of this model consist of the balance of risks and profits in the selection of the optimal sales channel and in elimination of the influence of subjective factors. The shortcomings of this model are connected with the threat of profit deficiency due to "underestimation" of the future sales channel potential and with the need of invoking experts-mathematicians to formulate a one-off optimization problem or the need for employing one's own specialists in this field.

8. Conclusions

Steady development of an enterprise is ensured by harmonious, synchronous and complementary realization of all of the directions of company activity. Our paper is devoted to one of such directions: sales activity. Mathematical modeling provides the tools for the optimal choice of sales channels based on diversification. Three models of such a choice have been proposed: the model of determining sales channels' potential, the model based on profit maximization and the model of the optimal production distribution between sales channels based on risk minimization. The first model allows us to throw light on the potential of sales channel, to show the peculiarities of its use and to introduce the qualitative and quantitative characteristic criteria for comparing direct and indirect sales channels.

To ensure steady development of a company, it is necessary not only to determine the key parameters of sales channels, but also to provide high profitability of every assortment item, as well as high profitability of the whole enterprise. The second model solves this problem as a problem of linear optimization. At the same time, the second model takes into account only current profitability and does not consider the comparison with the previous periods. This aspect is investigated by the third model based on accounting for the experience of the previous periods and risk minimization. The use of every model forecasts larger income than that brought by the current product distribution. The proposed models can be used by individual enterprises, as well as by consulting companies that offer facility for analysis and optimization of sales activity.

Author Contributions: All authors contributed equally to this work for drafting the paper, reviewing relevant studies, compiling and analyzing the data. All authors wrote, reviewed and commented on the manuscript. All authors have read and approved the final manuscript.

References

1.   Kotler, P.; Armstrong, G. *Principles of Marketing*, 12th ed.; Prentice Hall: Upper Saddle River, NJ, USA, 2008.
2.   Lambin, J.J.; Schuiling, I. *Market.-Driven Management: Strategic and Operational Marketing*, 3rd ed.; Palgrave Macmillan: London, UK, 2012.
3.   Coughlan, A.T.; Anderson, E.; Stern, L.W.; El-Ansary, A.I. *Marketing Channels*, 7th ed.; Prentice Hall: Upper Saddle River, NJ, USA, 2006.

4.   Weitz, B.A.; Jap, S.D. Relationship marketing and distribution channels. *J. Acad. Mark. Sci.* **1995**, *23*, 305–320. [CrossRef]

5.   Nevin, J.R. Relationship marketing and distribution channels: Exploring fundamental issues. *J. Acad. Mark. Sci.* **1995**, *23*, 327–334. [CrossRef]

6.   Jobber, D.; Lancaster, G. *Selling and Sales Management*, 8th ed.; Prentice Hall: London, UK, 2009.

7.   Trenz, M. *Multichannel Commerce: A Consumer Perspective on the Integration of Physical and Electronic Channels*; Springer: Heidelberg, Germany, 2015.

8.   Gupta, A.; Su, B.; Walter, Z. Risk profile and consumer shopping behavior in electronic and traditional channels. *Decis. Support. Syst.* **2004**, *38*, 347–367. [CrossRef]

9.   Konuş, U.; Verhoef, P.C.; Neslin, S.A. Multichannel shopper segments and their covariates. *J. Retail.* **2008**, *84*, 398–413. [CrossRef]

10. Verhagen, T.; van Dolen, W. Online purchase intentions: A multi-channel store image perspectives. *Inf. Manag.* **2009**, *46*, 77–82. [CrossRef]

11. Sutton, D.; Klein, T. *Enterprise Marketing Management: The New Science of Marketing*; John Wiley & Sons: Hoboken, NJ, USA, 2003.

12. Ingene, C.A.; Parry, M.E. *Mathematical Models of Distribution Channels*; Kluwer Academic Publishers: Boston, MA, USA, 2005.

13. Magrath, A.J.; Hardy, K.H. Selecting sales and distribution channels. *Ind. Mark. Manag.* **1987**, *16*, 273–278. [CrossRef]

14. Hertsyk, V.A. *Distribution Management of Enterprise Production*; Volodymyr Dahl East Ukrainian National University: Luhansk, Ukraine, 2011. (In Ukrainian)

15. Kovalchuk, S.V., Ed.; *Marketing Innovations in Economics and Business*; Poligrafist-2: Khmelnytskyi, Ukraine, 2013; pp. 1–321. (In Ukrainian)

16. Shpak, N.; Kyrylych, T. Sales channels selection for small industrial enterprises based on qualitative-quantitative characteristic criteria. *Int. Quart. J. Econ. Technol. New Technol. Model. Process.* **2013**, *2*, 79–88.

17. Shpak, N.O.; Kyrylych, T. The method of optimal planning of distribution activity for small industrial enterprises. *Econ. State* **2014**, *4*, 15–22. (In Ukraininan)

18. Emrich, C. *Multi-Channel Communications- und Marketing-Management*; Gabler Verlag: Wiesbaden, Germany, 2008.

19. Kotler, P. *Marketing Management: Millenium*, 10th ed.; Prentice Hall: Upper Saddle River, NJ, USA, 2000.

20. Capon, N.; Capon, R.; Hulbert, J.M. *Managing Marketing in the 21st Century: Developing & Implementing the Market. Strategy*; Wessex: Bronxville, NY, USA, 2009.

21. Kotler, P.; Armstrong, G.; Harris, L.C.; Piercy, N. *Principles of Marketing*, 6th European ed.; Pearson: Harlow, UK, 2013.

22. Rolnicki, K. *Managing Channels of Distribution: The Marketing Executive's Complete Guide*; AMACOM: New York, NY, USA, 1998.

23. Dent, J. *Distribution Channels: Understanding and Managing Channels to Market*; Kogan Page: London, UK, 2008.

24. Chen, J.M.; Chen, T.H. The profit-maximization models for a multi-item distribution channel. *Transp. Res. Part E Logist. Transp. Rev.* **2007**, *43*, 338–354. [CrossRef]

25. Anderson, D.R.; Sweeney, D.J.; Williams, T.A.; Camm, J.D.; Martin, K. *An. Introduction to Management Science: Quantitative Approaches to Decision Making*; South-Western Cengage Learning: Mason, OH, USA, 2011.

26. Park, S.Y.; Keh, H.T. Modelling hybrid distribution channels: A game-theoretical analysis. *J. Retail. Consum. Serv.* **2003**, *10*, 155–167. [CrossRef]

27. Dong, Y.; Shankar, V.; Dresner, M. Efficient replenishment in the distribution channel. *J. Retail.* **2007**, *83*, 253–278. [CrossRef]

28. Kuz'min, O.Y.; Chernobay, L.I.; Romanko, O.P. Methods of analysis of the enterprise competitiveness. *Sci. Bull. Ukr. Natl. Forest. Univ.* **2011**, *21*, 159–166. (In Ukrainian)

29. Kalashnik, O.V.; Omelchenko, N.V.; Tovt, V.M. The use of graphical models for evaluating the competitiveness of goods. *Commod. Res. Innov.* **2011**, *3*, 234–241. (In Ukrainian)

30. Library of Practical Software Open Access "Optimizing Resources with Linear Programming". Available online: http://www.phpsimplex.com/en/index.htm (accessed on 27 April 2011).

31. Robinson, L.J.; Barry, P.J. *The Competitive Firm's Response to Risk*; Macmillan: New York, NY, USA, 1987.

32. Tsay, A.A. Risk sensitivity in distribution channel partnerships: Implications for manufacturer return policies. *J. Retail.* **2002**, *78*, 147–160. [CrossRef]

33. Markowitz, H.M. *Portfolio Selection. Efficient Diversification of Investments*; John Wiley & Sons: New York, NY, USA, 1959.

34. Fabozzi, F.J.; Markowitz, H.M. *The Theory and Practice of Investment Management*, 2nd ed.; John Wiley & Sons: Hoboken, NJ, USA, 2011.

35. Zakharin, S.V. Economic diversification as an efficient mechanism of ensuring enterprise development. *Bull. Kyiv Nat. Univ. Technol. Design* **2012**, *1*, 139–145. (In Ukrainian)

10

Analytical Business Model for Sustainable Distributed Retail Enterprises in a Competitive Market

Courage Matobobo and Isaac O. Osunmakinde *

School of Computing, College of Science, Engineering and Technology, University of South Africa, P.O. Box 392, UNISA, Pretoria 0003, South Africa; 49116762@mylife.unisa.ac.za
* Correspondence: osunmio@unisa.ac.za.

Academic Editors: Adam Jabłoński and Giuseppe Ioppolo

Abstract: Retail enterprises are organizations that sell goods in small quantities to consumers for personal consumption. In distributed retail enterprises, data is administered per branch. It is important for retail enterprises to make use of data generated within the organization to determine consumer patterns and behaviors. Large organizations find it difficult to ascertain customer preferences by merely observing transactions. This has led to quantifiable losses, such as loss of market share to competitors and targeting the wrong market. Although some enterprises have implemented classical business models to address these challenging issues, they still lack analytics-based marketing programs to gain a competitive advantage to deal with likely catastrophic events. This research develops an analytical business (ARANN) model for distributed retail enterprises in a competitive market environment to address the current laxity through the best arrangement of shelf products per branch. The ARANN model is built on association rules, complemented by artificial neural networks to strengthen the results of both mutually. According to experimental analytics, the ARANN model outperforms the state of the art model, implying improved confidence in business information management within the dynamically changing world economy.

Keywords: sustainable business models; retail enterprises; analytical business model; analytics; distributed enterprises

---

1. Introduction

Business information (BI) analytics are groups of methodologies, organizational techniques and tools used collectively to gain information, analyze it and predict the outcomes of solutions to problems [1]. The field of BI analytics through the use of operational data generated from transactional systems has given business users better insight into the problems they face [2]. These insights can assist business users or managers to make better and informed decisions. BI analytics are commonly applied in sustainable retail enterprises. Retail enterprises purchase goods from manufacturers or wholesalers in large quantities. They break up the bulk and resell those goods in smaller quantities directly to consumers. Consumers can go around the shop, pick the items of their choice from the shop shelves, place them into their baskets and then the contents of each basket are captured into transactional systems. These transactional systems generate data that can be used for analysis purposes. There are two major types of retail enterprises: centralized and distributed retail enterprises. This paper concentrates on distributed retail enterprises as a way of alleviating analytics issues of enterprises in a competitive market environment.

A distributed retail enterprise issues decision rights to the branches or groups nearest to the data collection [3]. Each branch can make its own decisions, depending on the data generated. A distributed retail enterprise often maintains clustered databases for each branch for the storage of data. Data generated in a distributed retail enterprise branch usually reflects the true customer purchasing habits at that particular branch. Data analysis per branch might reveal better results than a centralized data management system. It is, therefore, important to analyze data generated in each branch to realize meaningful patterns. Analysts can apply BI analytics to branch data in order to generate meaningful patterns for each particular branch.

Retail enterprises strive for survival in view of the current challenging sales optimization models. These models affect product arrangements in retail enterprises, leading to a decline in sales levels [4], high research and marketing costs, a decline in market share, wrong product target markets and poor management decisions [5]. Figure 1 presents the quantitative impact of these challenging sales optimization models in retail enterprises. Figure 1a shows the sales decline in Hungarian retail enterprises in June 2013. The sales level of computer equipment and books declined drastically by 4.8%, while sales of non-food items had the lowest level of decline of 0.4%. Figure 1b shows the causes of the reduction in sales level. The highest scoring reason for the reduction in sales was expensiveness (48%), followed by 41% of products with features unavailable. The least common reason for a reduction in sales was lack of functionality (20%).

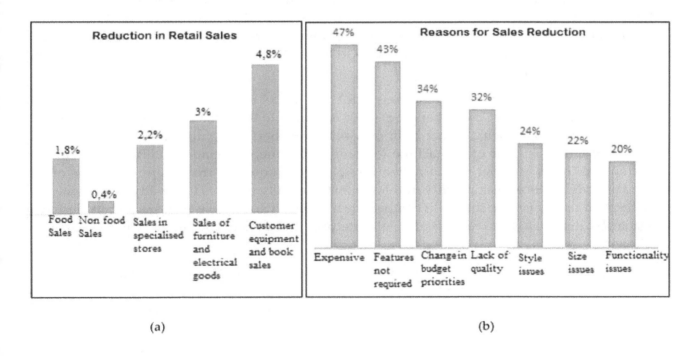

(a)   (b)

Figure 1. Impact of current sales optimization models on retail enterprises. (**a**) reduction in retail sales. Adapted from [6]; (**b**) reasons for reduction in sales. Adapted from [7].

Data quality problems also affect the quality of decisions made by managers on different levels of a retail enterprise [5]. Poor data has caused problems in both traditional and e-business companies, as shown in Figure 2. In both types of companies, extra cost to prepare reconciliations was seen as the main problem caused by inadequate data. This was seen to have an impact of 58% and 57% respectively. Inability to deliver orders or loss of sales was also a poor data quality challenge that had a higher impact in e-business (33%) than in traditional (24%) companies. The lowest-scoring problem caused by poor data was failure to meet a significant contractual requirement.

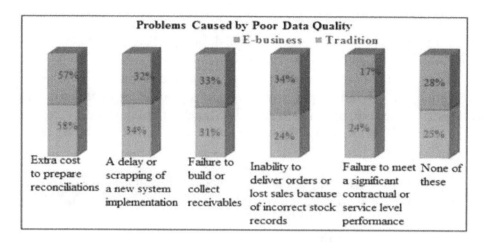

Figure 2. Problems caused by poor data quality. Adapted from [8].

An organization implemented an easy-to-use desktop and server analytics software program for the development of several business units and to improve the basis for decision-making [9]. The challenge was to test the most effective BI analytics for solving theoretical business problems. A data consolidation project was undertaken in South Africa by Altron to organize and deliver high-quality data successfully to its executives on their Apple iPads [10]. The smart phones' interfaces were too small for the style and amount of information they wanted to deliver. This approach posed the following challenges: lack of an analytics-based marketing program, failure to make BI a "matchmaker", lack of business-driven analytic strategies and failure to test the most effective BI analytics for solving theoretical business problems.

This paper develops an analytical business (ARANN) model that can be used in distributed retail enterprises within the dynamically changing world economy to implement the best arrangement of shelf products at each branch in order to improve the weaknesses highlighted in Figures 1 and 2. The ARANN model is built on a machine learning technique, association rules (AR) technique, complemented by an artificial neural network (ANN) technique to strengthen the results of the individual models. Since sustainability in this context generally requires the ability of a business to sustain itself in times of crisis, similar to competitive markets, ARANN has been specifically designed for sustainable distributed and centralized retail enterprises. The major contributions in this paper are the following:

- Development of a newly proposed analytical ARANN model that could intelligently assist distributed retail enterprise management within competitive markets to arrange products optimally on store shelves so that customers will purchase more products than planned in order to achieve an optimal profit level.

- Detailed experimental evaluations conducted on the sustainable ARANN model as measures of its performance using publicly available data and a volume of real-life retail data sets captured in ever-changing markets.

- Application of a robust business model in terms of (i) deployment scenarios, (ii) distributed and centralized analytics, (iii) time and memory scalability, and (iv) benchmark with classical methods for ease of implementation for managerial practices in IT.

To our knowledge, not enough research has presented user-friendly models and work examples to make technical information and BI available to professional managers. This paper is structured as follows: Section 2 previews work done in the area of AR and ANN, Section 3 proposes an intelligent model for distributed retail enterprises, Section 4 focuses on experimental evaluations and finally, Section 5 concludes the paper.

2. Background Studies

2.1. Related Work

Besides the analytics software programs and projects mentioned above, classical applications of AR and ANN are highlighted here. From the research conducted in [11], the authors applied AR to medical data containing combinations of categorical and numerical attributes to discover useful rules and from this experiment, useful and concise AR were discovered for prediction purposes. In [12], the authors implemented a system for the discovery of AR in web log usage data as an object-oriented application and discovered excellent associations within the data. They put forward "interestingness measures" as future work. In [13], the researchers applied an AR algorithm to a large database of customer transactions from a large retailing company to test the effectiveness of the algorithm and it exhibited excellent performance. In the study conducted in [14], it was observed that AR is effective in revealing associations though it does not take into account special interests. A comprehensive survey was conducted in [15] regarding AR on quantitative data in data mining. The authors examined it using different parameters and they concluded that the direct application of AR might produce a large number of redundant rules. This is also supported in the article in [16].

AR was applied in [4] to a sport company struggling with the arrangement of sports items in accordance with customer purchasing patterns. The retail company had no computerized mechanism for providing the best item arrangement. The study was performed to identify purchasing patterns that could be adopted by the retail enterprise. The authors analyzed historical data to identify the associated patterns from transactional data. From the study, they found relationships between sports items purchased and the best ways of arranging items, either side by side or in the same retail area, so that the items were frequently purchased together to yield high sales. In this study, AR was used for mining relationships between items purchased.

AR was applied in [11] to medical data containing combinations of categorical and numerical attributes to discover useful rules and from this experiment, useful and concise associations were discovered for prediction purposes. Ordonez [17] used AR to predict the level of contraction in four arteries and risk factors. The experiment predicted accurate profiles of patients with localized heart problems, specific risk factors and the level of disease in one artery.

ANN have been used in the past to search for patterns and predict future sales [18]. In research conducted in [19], the authors evaluated the predictive accuracy of ANNs and logistic regression (LR) in marketing campaigns of a Portuguese banking institution and their results showed that ANNs are more efficient and faster than LR. In [20], the researchers applied ANNs to a Pima Indians diabetes database and it generated rules with strong associations, thereby enhancing the decision-making process by doctors. In research conducted in [21], ANNs were applied for retail segmentation. The authors compared an ANN technique based on Hopfield networks against k-means and mixture model clustering algorithms. The results showed the usefulness of ANNs in retailing for segmenting markets. Many articles mentioned in [22] consider ANNs to be a promising machine learning technique.

In research conducted in [23], it was observed that the combination of data mining methods and a neural network model can greatly improve the efficiency of data mining methods. Craven and Shavlik [24] also supported ANN in data mining because of the ability to learn the target concept better than when using data mining methods. However, they presented two limitations that make ANNs poor data mining tools: excessive training times and incomprehensible learning. The proposed analytical model seeks to use AR complemented by ANNs to implement the best arrangement of shelf products, branch by branch, in order to use the cooperative result to make managerial decisions.

This research is undertaken to improve the following challenges of current sales optimization models: lack of analytics-based marketing programs, lack of business-driven analytic strategies and failure to leverage BI to become "matchmakers". To our knowledge, not enough research has presented working examples and considered non-expert users in proposing models that are user-friendly to professional managers. Sections 2.2 and 2.3 explain the building blocks of the analytic model where the processed data from different branches is entered.

2.2. Association Rules

AR mining is an unsupervised data mining method to find interesting associations in large sets of data items [25]. It was originally derived from point-of-sale data that describes which products are purchased simultaneously. AR discovers interesting associations that are often used by businesses such as retail enterprises for decision-making purposes; an example could be to find out which products are frequently purchased simultaneously by different customers [26]. It is one of the most common and widely used techniques in data mining, aimed at finding interesting relations [27,28] or correlations between large data items [29]. AR provides decision-makers at retail enterprises with marketing insights for cross-selling by providing information about product associations [30]. The most common AR algorithm used in market basket analysis is Apriori. However, the Apriori algorithm has an important drawback of generating numerous candidate item sets that must be repeatedly contrasted with the whole database [31]. We are going to use two measures to quantify the interestingness of a rule: support and confidence.

2.2.1. Support Value

Support determines how frequently a rule is contained in a given dataset. It is defined as the fraction of transactions that contains $A \cup B$ to the total number of transactions in the database [32] and this can be expressed as shown in Equation (1):

$$Support(A \Rightarrow B) = P(A \cup B) = \frac{n(A \cup B)}{N} \tag{1}$$

If support (A⇒B) is greater than or equal to the minimum support threshold (min_sup) then it is a frequent item set. An item set is frequent if support (A⇒B) ⩾ min_sup().

2.2.2. Confidence Value

Confidence is the ratio of the number of transactions containing A and B to the number of transactions containing A, and can be further expressed as shown in Equation (2):

$$Confidence(A \Rightarrow B) = P(B/A) = \frac{n(A \cup B)}{n(A)} \tag{2}$$

If confidence (A⇒B) is greater than or equal to the minimum confidence (min_con) then we are confident about the rule generated.

Furthermore, rules that satisfy both the minimum support threshold (min_sup) and the minimum confidence threshold (min_con) are called strong AR. A rule is strong if support (A⇒B) ⩾ min_sup ∧ confidence (A⇒B) ⩾ min_con. These two measures are used as inputs in the ANN technique.

2.3. Artificial Neural Networks

ANNs simulate the behavior of biological systems and are used to discover patterns and relationships. They are useful for studying complex relationships between input and output variables in a system [33]. The main advantage of an ANN is the ability to extract patterns and detect trends that are too complex to be noticed by other computer techniques or humans [34]. In [35], the research done shows that ANNs are now commonly used to solve data mining problems because of the following advantages: robustness, self-organizing adaptiveness, parallel processing, distributed storage and a high degree of fault tolerance. The ANN sums the inputs x_i against corresponding weights w_i and compares the ANN output to the threshold value, $\ominus$. The threshold is determined by the inputs used.

Let X be the net weighted input of the neuron, as shown in Equation (3). The decision of X is for discrete cases since it takes only certain values:

$$X = \sum_{i=1}^{n} xiwi \qquad (3)$$

where x_i is the input signal, w_i is the weight of input and n is the number of neurons.

If the net input is less than the threshold, the neuron output is -1; if the net input is greater than or equal to the threshold then the neuron is activated and the output attains a $+1$.

Let Y be the ANN output. The decision of Y is for continuous cases, since it can take any values in the range. The actual output of the neuron with the sigmoid activation function is expressed as shown in Equation (4):

$$Y = \frac{1}{1 + e^{-x}} \qquad (4)$$

3. Proposed Methodology for Sustainable Business Enterprises

3.1. Proposed System Model for Distributed Retail Enterprises

This section explores the proposed system model for BI analytics in distributed retail enterprises. The proposed model has three layers, namely data cleaning and formatting, intelligent model and distributed product shops, as shown in Figure 3. The data cleaning and formatting layer is found at the bottom of the proposed model. In this proposed model, data is collected from transactional systems branch per branch. The data is cleaned and formatted to the appropriate file type accepted by the proposed model. Processed data is input into the ARANN model branch per branch at the middle layer of the analytical model. The ARANN model cooperatively works between AR and ANN. Processed data from the bottom layer is passed into the AR model and it outputs confidence and support values. These values are passed into the ANN model as inputs in order to get the degree of belief (DoB). The DoB of sets generated is compared to the ARANN activations set. The accepted sets generated are applied on the top layer of the proposed model. This proposed model is deployed to each branch and patterns are generated independently. The choice is left for every retail enterprise branch to adopt the best results, depending on the market competitiveness and profit levels.

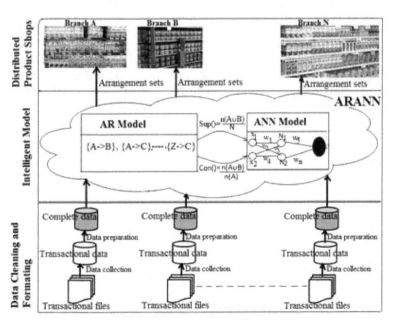

Figure 3. Proposed intelligent analytics-based framework.

The proposed intelligent analytics-based framework has the following benefits: reduction in risk of passing misleading results to all branches, no one point of failure, consumption of fewer resources, faster construction of distributed systems and no need for data integration.

This proposed analytics-based model can be implemented using the pseudo-code presented in Table 1. Table 1 shows how ARANN generates product arrangement sets that can be used by retail enterprise managers to arrange products on shop shelves so as to attract customers to purchase more products than planned. The pseudo-code is further presented mathematically, as shown in Equations (5)–(14).

Table 1. Pseudo-code for ARANN model.

		Pseudo-code
Steps	Input:	Transactional data in database (D) = {t$_1$, t$_2$, t$_3$, .., t$_n$} Support () Confidence () Weights (W) = {w$_1$, w$_2$, w$_3$, .., w$_n$}
	Output:	Products pattern

Step 1: D = {t$_1$, t$_2$, t$_3$, .., t$_n$} //Transactions in the database
Step 2: C$_k$ = Candidate item set of size k
Step 3: F$_k$ = frequent item set of size k
{
    for (k =1; F$_k$!= Ø; k++) // F$_k$ is not equal to empty set.
    {
        Scan the entire D to generate candidate sets C$_k$
        {
        Compare candidate support count from C$_k$ with the minimum support count to generate F$_k$
        }
    }
Step 4: Generate Support () & Confidence ()
    {
    Step 5: Input Support () & Confidence () into Neuron 1 (N$_1$) and Neuron 2 (N$_2$) as inputs
    Step 6: Generate N_1 by summing of the inputs with the corresponding weights and apply the output into sigmoid function
    Step 7: Generate N_2 by summing of the inputs with the corresponding weights and apply the output into sigmoid function
    Step 8: Generate the summation of N_1 & N_2 after the sigmoid function and apply the output into sigmoid function to obtain Degree of Belief (DoB)
    Step 9: Display products pattern where **DoB ⩾ ARANN activation**
    }
}

Mathematical description for the ARANN Model

$$Support\ (Sup) = \frac{n\,(AuB)}{N} \tag{5}$$

$$Confidence\ (Con) = \frac{n\,(AuB)}{n\,(A)} \tag{6}$$

The sup and con values feed the N$_1$ as the inputs and are multiplied with the corresponding weights.

$$N_1 = SupW_1 + ConW_3 \tag{7}$$

The output of N_1 after the sigmoid function

$$O_2 = \frac{1}{1 + e^{-N_2}} \tag{8}$$

The sup and con values feed the N_2 as the inputs and are multiplied with the corresponding weights:

$$N_2 = ConW_4 + SupW_2 \tag{9}$$

The output of N_2 after the sigmoid function

$$O_2 = \frac{1}{1 + e^{-N_2}} \tag{10}$$

$$F = W_5O_1 + W_6O_2 \tag{11}$$

$$= \frac{W_5}{1 + e^{-N_2}} + \frac{W_6}{1 + e^{-N_2}} \tag{12}$$

$$Degree\ of\ Belief\ (DoB) = \frac{1}{1 + e^{-F}} \tag{13}$$

$$Product\ Patterns = \begin{cases} Accepted, if & DoB \geqslant ARANN\quad activation \\ Rejected, if & otherwise \end{cases} \tag{14}$$

where N_1 and N_2 are Neuron 1 and 2 respectively; W_1, W_2, W_3, W_4, W_5 and W_6 are the corresponding weights; O_1 is Neuron 1 output after sigmoid function; O_2 is Neuron 2 output after sigmoid function, F is input to final Neuron and $ARANN\ activation$ is the threshold value set.

3.2. Evaluation Mechanism

The purpose of model evaluation is to assess the performance of the models so as to identify the best-performing model. To test the performance of the models, three sets were used. The confusion matrix shown in Table 2 was used to represent actual values and predictions.

Table 2. Confusion matrix. Adapted from [36].

		Predicted	
		True	False
Actual	True	a	b
	False	c	d

$$Error\ Rate = \frac{b + c}{a + b + c + d} \tag{15}$$

where a is the number of sets predicted true when they are true, b is the number of sets predicted false when they are true, c is the number of sets predicted true when they are false and d is the number of sets predicted false when they are false. Error rate is then defined as shown in Equation (15).

3.3. Scenario—Arrangement of Products on Shelves for Distributed Retail Branches

Figure 4 shows a scenario of how the analytical model displays placement results in distributed branches. Transactional data from each retail branch is loaded into the ARANN model to determine the arrangement sets.

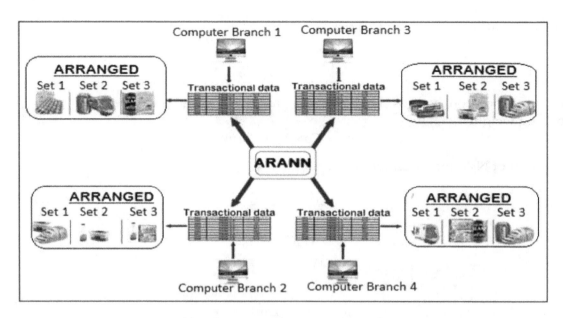

Figure 4. Intelligent Analytics-based Model for Four Branches.

Table 3. Market basket transactional data for branch 3 of a retail enterprise.

Market-basket Transaction Data—Branch 3	
TID	ITEMS
T300	Colgate, Vaseline, Geisha, Margarine, Bread
T301	Margarine, Bread, Coke, Colgate, Vaseline
T302	Coke, Colgate, Chocolate, Bread, Sweets, Margarine
T303	Geisha, Colgate, Chocolate, Towel, Vaseline, Sweets
T304	Colgate, Vaseline, Sweets, Chocolate, Bread, Margarine, Coke

Even weights were applied to each corresponding input to avoid bias on products. This was obtained by dividing the count of a_union_b over a number of records within the data set, where a, and b are different products. The following ARANN activation was used:

>= 0.75 strongly connected products (strongly accepted)

>= 0.65 moderately connected products (accepted)

< 0.65 weakly connected products (rejected)

Analysis of ARANN on   tab:sustainability-08-00140-t003

{Colgate, Vaseline} => {Bread}

$$\text{Support} = \frac{n(A \cup B)}{N} = \frac{3}{5} = 0.6 \qquad \text{Confidence} = \frac{n(A \cup B)}{n(A)} = \frac{3}{4} = 0.75$$

$N_1 = \text{Supw}_1 + \text{Conw}_3$ $\qquad\qquad$ N_2 $\qquad = \text{Conw}_4 + \text{Supw}_2$

$\qquad = (0.6 \times 0.6) + (0.75 \times 0.6)$ $\qquad\qquad\quad = (0.75 \times 0.6) + (0.6 \times 0.6)$

$\qquad = 0.81$ $\qquad\qquad\qquad\qquad\qquad\qquad\quad = 0.81$

$$O_1 = \frac{1}{1 + e^{-N1}} = \frac{1}{1 + e^{-0.81}} = 0.69 \quad O_2 \qquad = \frac{1}{1 + e^{-N2}} = \frac{1}{1 + e^{-0.81}} = 0.69$$

$F \quad = \text{w5}O_1 + \text{w6}O_2$

$\qquad = (0.6 \times 0.69) + (0.6 \times 0.69) = 0.83$

$$\text{DoB} = \frac{1}{1 + e^{-F}} = \frac{1}{1 + e^{-0.83}} = 0.70$$

Product pattern => 0.70 >= 0.65

Therefore it is moderately connected and is accepted.

{Coke} => {Bread}

Support $= \frac{3}{5} = 0.6$ Confidence $= \frac{3}{3} = 1.0$

N1 $= (0.6 \times 0.6) + (1.0 \times 0.6)$ N2 $= (1.0 \times 0.6) + (0.6 \times 0.6)$

   $= 0.96$ $= 0.96$

01 $= \frac{1}{1 + e^{-0.96}} = 0.72$ O2 $= \frac{1}{1 + e^{-0.4}} = 0.72$

F $= w5O_1 + w6O_2$

   $= (0.6 \times 0.72) + (0.6 \times 0.72) = 0.86$

DoB $= \frac{1}{1 + e^{-86}} = 0.70$

Product pattern => 0.70 >= 0.65

Therefore it is moderately connected and is accepted.

Table 4. Market basket transactional data for branch 4 of a retail enterprise.

Market-basket Transaction Data—Branch 4	
TID	ITEMS
T400	Maize meal, Beef, Fish, Cooking oil, Soups, Bread, Coke
T401	Cooking oil, Beans, Beef, Soups, Maize meal
T402	Rice, Fish, Soups, Cooking oil, Bread
T403	Fruits, Coke, Bread, Milk, Chocolate, Soups
T404	Bread, Beef, Fruit, Coke, Sweets, Maize meal

Analysis of ARANN on   tab:sustainability-08-00140-t004

{Maize meal} => {Beef}

Support $= \frac{3}{5} = 0.6$ Confidence $= \frac{3}{3} = 1.0$

N1 $= (0.6 \times 0.6) + (1.0 \times 0.6)$ N2 $= (1.0 \times 0.6) + (0.6 \times 0.6)$

   $= 0.96$ $= 0.96$

01 $= \frac{1}{1 + e^{-0.96}} = 0.72$ O2 $= \frac{1}{1 + e^{-0.4}} = 0.72$

F $= w5O_1 + w6O_2$

   $= (0.6 \times 0.72) + (0.6 \times 0.72) = 0.86$

DoB $= \frac{1}{1 + e^{-86}} = 0.70$

Product pattern => 0.70 >= 0.65

Therefore it is **moderately** connected and is **accepted.**

{Chocolate} => {Towel}

Support $= \frac{1}{5} = 0.20$ Confidence $= \frac{1}{3} = 0.33$

N_1 $= (0.20 \times 0.20) + (0.33 \times 0.20)$ N_2 $= (0.33 \times 0.20) + (0.20 \times 0.20)$

   $= 0.11$ $= 0.11$

O_1 $= \frac{1}{1 + e^{-0.11}} = 0.53$ O_2 $= \frac{1}{1 + e^{-0.11}} = 0.53$

F $= (0.2 \times 0.53) + (0.2 \times 0.53) = 0.212$

DoB $= \frac{1}{1 + e^{-0.212}} = 0.55$

Product pattern => 0.55 < 0.65

Therefore it is **weakly** connected and is **rejected.**

4. Experimental Evaluations: Results and Discussions

4.1. Experimental Setup

Real-life data was collected from a retail enterprise situated in South Africa with several branches nationwide. The data for the experiments was collected from only eight branches within different demographics of a developing country. The retail enterprise has database servers at each branch for the storage of data. Real-life datasets consisting of 66 records were taken from each branch, to be used for running experiments. In the experiment, the 11 most frequently purchased products were considered. This data was collected for research purposes. The data was then exported to notepad application for storage. Each row in Tables 5–7 represents a transaction performed by the customer. Tables 5 and 6 show samples of real-life data from different branches.

In the public dataset 1000 transactions were used. This data set was randomly broken up into five chunks representing branches and the records for each branch contained 200 transactions. The data was saved in .txt format. The public data set in Table 7 is found in [37]. The data contains the following products: bread, beer, tea, wine, orange juice, chocolate milk and canned soup.

Table 5. Sample of real-life data for branch 1.

Body lotion	Colgate	Rice	Maize meal		
Meat	Rice	Roll on	Cooking oil	Body lotion	
-	-	-	-	-	-
Drink	Roll on	Mince	Coke	Colgate	Perfume

Table 6. Sample of real-life data for branch 2.

Bread	Sugar	Rice	Meat	Salt	Cooking oil	Flour	Soup
-	-	-	-	-	-	-	-
Fruits	Sugar	Meat	Cooking oil	Salt	Soap	Bread	

Table 7. Sample of public data [37].

Fish	Orange juice	Tea	Wine	Peanuts	Canned soup	Bread	Beer
-	-	-	-	-	-	-	-
Cookies	Fish	Orange juice	Tea	Wine	Peanuts	Canned soup	Chocolate milk

Perl programming language was used to implement the ARANN model. Notepad was used as the text editor and results were displayed through the command prompt. Figures 5 and 6 show sample sets generated by the ARANN model using a real life dataset and public dataset respectively.

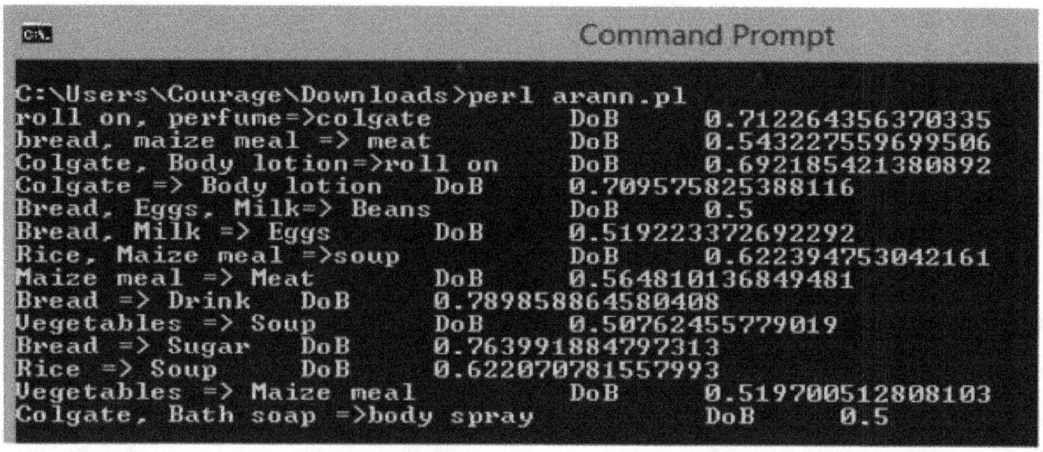

Figure 5. ARANN rules on real-life data.

Figure 6. ARANN rules on public dataset.

4.2. Experiment 1: Observations of ARANN with Varying Activation in Distributed Analytics

In this experiment, Equation (14) was used to determine the decisions to be applied to Tables 8–11 of the analytical model. This analytical model accepts product patterns defined in Equation (14) and uses the following ARANN activations: DoB < 60%, 60% >= DoB < 70% and DoB >= 70%. The analytical model rejects arrangement sets where the DoB is less than 60% and accepts arrangement sets between 60% and 69%, while those with a DoB greater or equal to 70% are strongly accepted. To make the decision, ARANN compares the DoB value generated with the ARANN activations and a decision is made. Managers use the decision to determine how products are to be arranged in each branch.

Table 8. Real-life ARANN results for branch 1.

Dataset Branch 1	Patterns Generated	DoB	ARANN Cooperative Decision with	
			60 >= DoB < 70	DoB >= 70
	Roll on, perfume => Colgate	0.71	N/A	Strongly accepted
	Colgate, Body lotion => roll-on	0.69	Accepted	N/A
	Colgate => Body lotion	0.71	N/A	Strongly accepted
	Bread, Milk => Eggs	0.70	N/A	Strongly accepted
	Rice, Maize meal => soup	0.62	Accepted	N/A
	Bread => Drink	0.79	N/A	Strongly accepted
	Bread => Sugar	0.76	N/A	Strongly accepted

Using ARANN activation of DoB >= 70, the following sets from Table 8 are strongly accepted: {Roll-on, Perfume => Colgate}, {Colgate => Body lotion}, {Bread => Drink} and {Bread => Sugar}; these are strongly connected products. Using ARANN activation of 60 >= DoB < 70, the following examples of sets from Table 8 are accepted: {Colgate, Body lotion => Roll on}, {Rice, Maize meal => Soup} and {Rice => Soup}; these are moderately connected products. The choice is left to every retail enterprise to adopt either moderately or strongly connected products, depending on the market competitiveness and profit levels. Note that the analytical model rejects the sets with DoB < 60 (*i.e.*, weakly connected products), which are not included. One can see in Table 8 of branch 1 that the "strongly accepted" products at higher activation implies that some specific toiletry products are strongly connected, while bakery products and refreshments are strongly connected at this branch.

Table 9. Real-life ARANN results for branch 2.

Dataset Branch 1	Patterns Generated	DoB	ARANN Cooperative Decision with	
			60 >= DoB < 70	DoB >= 70
	Meat, Salt => Cooking_oil	0.64	Accepted	N/A
	Meat => Salt	0.71	N/A	Strongly Accepted
	Bread, rice => Eggs	0.66	Accepted	N/A
	Bread => Lotion	0.65	Accepted	N/A
	Bread => Eggs	0.65	Accepted	N/A

Applying ARANN activation of DoB >= 70, the following "strongly accepted" set is generated; {Meat => Salt}; these are strongly connected products. When ARANN activation of 60 >= DoB < 70 is used, the following examples of sets are accepted in Table 9: {Meat, Salt => Cooking oil}, {Bread, Rice => Eggs} and {Bread => Eggs}; these are moderately connected products. It is up to the retail enterprise's decision-makers to adopt either moderately or strongly connected products, depending on the market competitiveness and profit levels. On the other side, the analytical model rejects the sets with DoB < 60 (*i.e.*, weakly connected products), which are not included. It can be seen in Table 9 of branch 2 that the "strongly accepted" products at higher activation implies that some specific meat products are strongly connected with salt products at this branch.

Table 10. Public DATA ARANN results for branch 3.

Dataset Branch 1	Patterns Generated	DoB	ARANN Cooperative Decision with	
			60 >= DoB < 70	DoB >= 70
	Fish, Canned soup => Wine	0.64	Accepted	N/A
	Fish => Canned soup	0.74	N/A	Strongly Accepted
	Tea, Cookies => Peanuts	0.61	Accepted	N/A
	Bread => Chocolate milk	0.73	N/A	Strongly accepted
	Bread, Chocolate milk => Tea	0.64	Accepted	N/A
	Beer => Tea	0.67	Accepted	N/A
	Beer => Chocolate milk	0.69	Accepted	N/A
	Wine => Beer	0.69	Accepted	N/A
	Canned soup => Bread	0.79	N/A	Strongly Accepted
	Orange juice => Bread	0.73	N/A	Strongly Accepted
	Peanuts, Bread => Canned soup	0.67	Accepted	N/A
	Tea, Bread => Orange juice	0.65	Accepted	N/A

When ARANN activation of DoB >= 70 is applied, the following "strongly accepted" sets from Table 10 are generated: {Fish => Canned soup}, {Bread => Chocolate milk} and {Canned soup => Bread}; these products are strongly connected. Using ARANN activation of 60 >= DoB < 70, the following are examples of "accepted" sets that are generated in Table 10: {Fish, Canned soup => Wine}, {Tea, Cookies => Peanuts} and {Wine => Beer}; these are moderately connected products. Every retail enterprise is left with the choice to adopt either moderately or strongly connected products, depending on the market competitiveness and profit levels. Note that the analytical model rejects the sets with DoB < 60 (*i.e.*, weakly connected products), which are not included. In Table 10 of branch 3, one can see that the "accepted" product sets at moderate activation implies that some specific beverages are moderately connected at this branch.

Table 11. Public data ARANN results for branch 4.

Dataset Branch 1	Patterns Generated	DoB	ARANN Cooperative Decision with	
			60 >= DoB < 70	DoB >= 70
	Fish, Canned soup => Wine	0.64	Accepted	N/A
	Fish => Canned soup	0.74	N/A	Strongly Accepted
	Tea, Cookies => Peanuts	0.61	Accepted	N/A
	Bread => Chocolate milk	0.72	N/A	Strongly Accepted
	Bread, Chocolate milk => Tea	0.66	Accepted	N/A
	Beer => Tea	0.67	Accepted	N/A
	Beer => Chocolate milk	0.67	Accepted	N/A
	Wine => Beer	0.70	N/A	Strongly accepted
	Canned soup => Bread	0.80	N/A	Strongly accepted
	Orange juice => Bread	0.73	N/A	Strongly accepted
	Peanuts, Bread => Canned soup	0.68	Accepted	N/A
	Tea, Bread => Orange juice	0.67	Accepted	N/A

In Table 11 the following "strongly accepted" sets were generated using ARANN activation of DoB >= 70: {Bread => Chocolate milk} and {Fish => Canned soup}, which are strongly connected products. Using ARANN activation of 60 >= DoB < 70, the following example of sets from Table 11 were accepted: {Fish, Canned soup => Wine}, {Orange juice => Bread} and {Tea, Bread => Orange juice}, which are moderately connected products. The decision-makers of every retail enterprise are left with the choice to adopt either moderately or strongly connected products, depending on the market competitiveness and profit levels. Note that the analytical model rejects the sets with DoB < 60 (*i.e.*, weakly connected products), which are not included. In Table 11 of branch 4 one can see that the "strongly accepted" product sets at higher activation implies that some specific bakery products are strongly connected with dairy products at this branch.

4.3. Experiment 2: Performance Evaluations of ARANN in Comparison with Classical Methods

Table 12 shows the error rate of the individual AR and ANN techniques against the analytical model. Equation (15) is used to determine the error rate of each technique. The column "No. of patterns" indicates the number of sets evaluated. The column "Correctly classified sets" is composed of sets the analytical model predicted as true when they were actually true (a) and sets predicted as false when they were actually false (d), as shown in Table 2. The column "Incorrectly classified sets" is composed of sets the analytical model predicted as false when they were actually true (b) and sets predicted as true when they were false (c). Randomly generated sets were used to evaluate the performance of the three models. For example, in Branch 1 (real life), 10 rules where used in AR: five rules were predicted as true when they were actually true (a); two were predicted as false when actually false (d); three were predicted as true when actually false (c) and 0 were predicted as false when actually true (b). From the results displayed in Table 12, it is clear that the analytical model (ARANN) has a lower error rate compared to the individual classical methods.

Table 12. Quantitative evaluations of the cooperative model in distributed branches.

Dataset	Algorithms	No. of Patterns	Correctly Classifies sets (a, d)	Incorrectly Classified sets (b, c)	Error Rate
Real life Branch 1 (66 Records)	AR	10	7	3	30%
	ANN	10	6	4	40%
	ARANN	6	5	1	17%
Branch 2 (66 Records)	AR	10	8	2	20%
	ANN	10	8	2	20%
	ARANN	7	6	1	14%
Public Branch 3 (200 Records)	AR	10	8	2	20%
	ANN	10	6	4	40%
	ARANN	6	5	1	17%
Branch 4 (200 Records)	AR	10	8	2	20%
	ANN	10	7	3	30%
	ARANN	8	6	2	25%

4.4. Experiment 3: Comparing Performance of Distributed and Centralized Retail Analytics

This research compares the performance of the analytical model in a distributed retail enterprise with a centralized retail enterprise. In the distributed retail enterprise, a computer was used to represent a branch and the time taken by the analytical model to generate arrangement patterns was observed. Figure 7a shows raw integration time. Figure 7b shows the time of response (ToR) taken by the analytical model to integrate a number of records from various workstations. Figure 7c shows the ToR taken by the analytical model to generate patterns in distributed and centralized retail enterprises.

Figure 7d shows the ToR taken by the analytical model to generate product arrangement patterns across different data sizes.

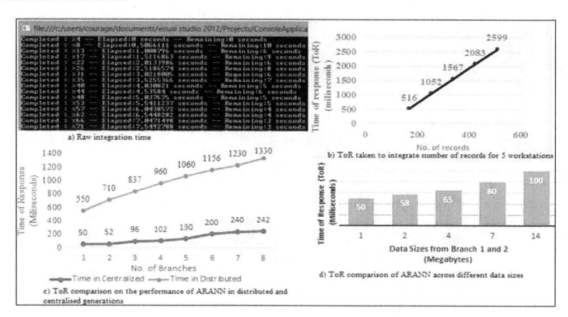

Figure 7. Comparison of the performance of ARANN in distributed and centralized retail enterprises.

From the experiment conducted, it was observed that the analytical model performs faster in distributed retail enterprises than in centralized retail enterprises, as shown in Figure 7c. The analytical model takes more time to generate patterns in a centralized retail enterprise than in a distributed retail enterprise. The ToR to integrate data depends on the number of records being integrated. The more records, the more time is needed to integrate those records. This was observed in Figure 7b. In addition, the performance time taken by the analytical model depends on the size of the data set being used. The analytical model's performance is affected by the size of the data set, as shown in Figure 7d.

5. Conclusions

In this paper, a sustainable model was proposed that can be used in distributed retail enterprises in an ever-changing economic environment to address the current laxity through the best arrangement of shelf products branch by branch. It can intelligently assist distributed retail enterprise management to arrange products optimally on shelves of shops so that customers will purchase more products than planned, in order to achieve an optimal profit level. The analytical model takes branch data and processes the data to determine the best ways of arranging items on the shelves of a retail enterprise branch by branch. It is built on AR, complemented by ANN.

The proposed analytical model for sustainable business in distributed retail enterprises was developed. A logical demonstration of working scenarios and experiments of the proposed analytical model for management practices in distributed retail enterprises was presented. This was done by inputting support and confidence values from the AR technique into the ANN technique in order to get DoB values of the analytical model. The analytical model accepts product patterns with a DoB greater than or equal to ARANN activation.

In the proposed analytical model performance evaluation experiment, ARANN proved to be better than the classical methods because of its lower error rate, implying improved confidence in the decision-making process in a competitive environment. To get the best results, the weights of the neurons need to be determined appropriately and the quality of data needs to be improved. The DoB values of the analytical model can sometimes be affected by the weights used.

It was observed that sets generated in a distributed retail enterprise portray the real purchasing habits of customers per branch better than in a centralized retail enterprise. In this research, real life datasets from eight branches of a retail enterprise and public datasets were used to conduct the experiments.

Observations of our distributed BI analytics model are: the proposed model retains complete control of product pattern generation, arrangement sets generated by the analytical model show a lower error rate (Table 12), they reveal the real buying habits of each branch, the model reduces the risk of passing misleading results to all branches (Tables 8–11) and the software runs a single process; there is no need for data integration (Figure 3). In addition, the ARANN incorporates the strengths of the AR and ANN models, improves generation of product arrangement sets, has the ability to discover complex nonlinear associations discreetly among different products, effects a reduction in poor data quality problems and losses, as well as an improvement in the effectiveness of current product sales optimization models. Since sustainability in this context generally requires the ability of a business to sustain itself in times of crisis, similar to competitive markets, ARANN has been specifically designed for sustainable distributed and centralized retail enterprises.

In future, we wish to; (i) improve on ARANN performance by considering nature-inspired algorithms; (ii) investigate a standard method of selecting the threshold; and (iii) integrate a sophisticated learning algorithm into ARANN. The strategy and observations in this research are therefore good for addressing challenges in an ever-changing economic environment.

Acknowledgments: Acknowledgments: The authors gratefully acknowledge the financial support and resources made available by the University of South Africa, South Africa.

Author Contributions: Author Contributions: All authors contributed equally to this article. They have read and approved the final manuscript.

References

1. Trkman, P.; McCormack, K.; de Oliveira, M.P.V.; Ladeira, M.B. The Impact of Business Analytics on Supply Chain Performance. *Decis. Support Syst.* **2010**, *49*, 318–327. [CrossRef]
2. Kohavi, R.; Rothleder, N.; Simoudis, E. Emerging Trends in Business Analytics. *Commun. ACM* **2002**, *45*, 45–48. [CrossRef]
3. Velu, C.; Madnick, S.; van Alstyne, M. Centralizing Data Management with Considerations of Uncertainty and Information-Based Flexibility. *J. Manag. Inf. Syst.* **2013**, *30*, 179–212. [CrossRef]
4. Abbas, W.; Ahmad, N.; Zaini, N. Discovering Purchasing Pattern of Sport Items Using Market Basket Analysis. In Proceedings of the 2013 International Conference on Advanced Computer Science Applications and Technologies (ACSAT), Kuching, Malaysia, 23–24 December 2013; pp. 120–125.
5. Haug, A.; Zachariassen, F.; van Liempd, D. The Costs of Poor Data Quality. *J. Ind. Eng. Manag.* **2011**, *4*, 168–193. [CrossRef]
6. Halford, Q.; Staff, S. Gap Cost Key Categories Billions. Furniture/Today, 3 September 2001, 14.
7. Hungary retail sales down in June. Regional Today, 26 August 2013, 1.
8. Data Quality. *Controller's Report*; EBSCOhost: Ipswich, MA, United States, 2001; Volume 7, p. 7.
9. Stoodley, N. Democratic Analytics: A Campaign to Bring Business Intelligence to the People. *Bus. Intell. J.* **2012**, *17*, 7–12.
10. Briggs, L. Case Study. *Bus. Intell. J.* **2011**, *16*, 39–41.
11. Aldosari, B.; Almodaifer, G.; Hafez, A.; Mathkour, H. Constrained Association Rules for Medical Data. *J. Appl. Sci.* **2012**, *12*, 1792–1800.
12. Dimitrijević, M.; Bošnjak, Z.; Cohen, E. Web Usage Association Rule Mining System. *Interdiscip. J. Inf. Knowl. Manag.* **2011**, *6*, 137–150.
13. Agrawal, R.; Imieliński, T.; Swami, A. Mining Association Rules between Sets of Items in Large Databases. In Proceedings of the 1993 ACM SIGMOD International Conference on Management of Data, Washington, DC, USA, 25–28 May 1993; pp. 207–216.
14. Klemettinen, M.; Mannila, H.; Ronkainen, P.; Toivonen, H.; Verkamo, A.I. Finding Interesting Rules from Large Sets of Discovered Association Rules. In Proceedings of the Third International Conference on Information and Knowledge Management, Gaithersburg, MD, USA, 29 November–2 December 1994; pp. 401–407.

15. Gosain, A.; Bhugra, M. A Comprehensive Survey of Association Rules on Quantitative Data in Data Mining. In Proceedings of the 2013 IEEE Conference on Information & Communication Technologies (ICT), JeJu Island, Korea, 11–12 April 2013; pp. 1003–1008.

16. Xu, Y.; Li, Y. Generating Concise Association Rules. In Proceedings the Sixteenth ACM Conference on Information and Knowledge Management, Lisbon, Portugal, 6–10 November 2007; pp. 781–790.

17. Ordonez, C. Association Rule Discovery with the Train and Test Approach for Heart Disease Prediction. *Inf. Technol. Biomed.* **2006**, *10*, 334–343. [CrossRef]

18. Vornberger, O.; Thiesing, F.; Middleberg, U. Short Term Prediction of Sales in Supermarkets. In Neural Networks, Proceedings of the IEEE International Conference, Perth, WA, USA, 27 November–1 December 1995; pp. 1028–1031.

19. Koç, A.; Yeniay, Ö. A Comparative Study of Artificial Neural Networks and Logistic Regression for Classification of Marketing Campaign Results. *Math. Comput. Appl.* **2013**, *18*, 392–398.

20. Anbananthen, S.; Sainarayanan, G.; Chekima, A.; Teo, J. Data Mining using Artificial Neural Network Tree. In proceedings of the 1st International Conference on Computers, Communications and Signal Processing with Special Track on Biomedical Engineering (CCSP), Kuala Lumpur, Malaysia, 14–16 November 2005; pp. 160–164.

21. Boone, D.; Roehm, M. Retail Segmentation using Artificial Neural Networks. *Int. J. Res. Mark.* **2002**, *19*, 287–301. [CrossRef]

22. Cerny, P. Data Mining and Neural Networks from a Commercial Perspective. In Proceedings of the ORSNZ Conference Twenty Naught One, University of Canterbury, Christchurch, New Zealand, 30 November–1 December 2001.

23. Arockiaraj, C. Applications of Neural Networks in Data Mining. *Int. J. Eng. Sci.* **2013**, *3*, 8–11.

24. Craven, M.W.; Shavlik, J.W. Using Neural Networks for Data Mining. *Future Gener. Comput. Syst.* **1997**, *13*, 211–229. [CrossRef]

25. Cios, K.; Pedrycz, W.; Swiniarski, R.; Kurgan, L. *Data Mining a Knowledge Discovery*; Springer: New York, NY, USA, 2007.

26. Berry, M.; Linoff, G. *Data Mining Techniques for Marketing, Sales, and Customer Relationship Management*; Wiley: Indianapolis, IN, USA, 2004.

27. Liu, H.; Su, B.; Zhang, B. The Application of Association Rules in Retail Marketing Mix. In Proceedings of the 2007 IEEE International Conference on Automation and Logistics, Jinan, China, 18–21 August 2007; pp. 2514–2517.

28. Chen, M.; Chiu, A.; Chang, H. Mining Changes in Customer Behavior in Retail Marketing. *Expert Syst. Appl.* **2005**, *28*, 773–781. [CrossRef]

29. Zhao, Y. *R and Data Mining: Examples and Case Studies*; Academic Press: New York, NY, USA, 2012.

30. Ahn, K. Effective Product Assignment Based on Association Rule Mining in Retail. *Expert Syst. Appl.* **2012**, *39*, 12551–12556. [CrossRef]

31. Dhanabhakyam, M.; Punithavalli, M. An Efficient Market Basket Analysis based on Adaptive Association Rule Mining with Faster Rule Generation Algorithm. *SIJ Trans. Comput. Sci. Eng. Its Appl.* **2013**, *1*, 105–110.

32. Kotsiantis, S.; Kanellopoulos, D. Association Rules Mining: A Recent Overview. *GESTS Int. Trans. Comput. Sci. Eng.* **2006**, *32*, 71–82.

33. Poh, H.; Jasic, T. Forecasting and Analysis of Marketing Data Using Neural Networks: A Case of Advertising and Promotion Impact. In Proceedings of the the 11th Conference on Artificial Intelligence for Applications, Los Angeles, CA, USA, 20–23 February 1995; pp. 224–230.

34. Mistry, J.; Nelwamondo, F.; Marwala, T. Estimating Missing Data and Determining the Confidence of the Estimate Data. In Proceedings of the Seventh International Conference on Machine Learning and Applications ICMLA '08, San Diego, CA, USA, 11–13 December 2008; pp. 752–755.

35. Nirkhi, S. Potential Use of Artificial Neural Network in Data Mining. In Proceedings of the the 2nd International Conference on Computer and Automation Engineering (ICCAE), Singapore, 26–28 February 2010; pp. 339–343.

36. Witten, I.; Frank, E.; Hall, M. *Data Mining: Practical Machine Learning Tools and Techniques*, 3rd ed.; Morgan Kaufmann: Amsterdam, The Netherlands, 2011; pp. 403–440.

37. Informatics. Available online: http://www.informatics.buu.ac.th/~ureerat/321641/Weka/Data%20Sets/supermarket/supermarket_basket_transactions_2005.arff (accessed on 21 January 2014).

11

Research on Consumers' use Willingness and Opinions of Electric Vehicle Sharing

Ning Wang * and Runlin Yan

School of Automotive Studies, Tongji University, Shanghai 201804, China; woaiwojia13147@163.com
*   Correspondence: wangning@tongji.edu.cn.

Academic Editor: Adam Jabłoński

Abstract: An empirical study in Shanghai was performed to explore consumers' use willingness and opinions on electric vehicle sharing (EVS) to help operators effectively operate and expand the new business model. Through the multinomial logistic regression developed for different groups, the results show that the factors of the main trip mode in daily use, monthly transportation expenditure, driving range of electric vehicles, gender, age, marital status and occupation have significant influences on consumers' use willingness. In short, the population characteristics of people choosing to use EVS are male, aged between 18 and 30 and usually taking the subway and bus as the daily transportation modes. Otherwise, the factors of the acceptable highest price of EVS, occupation and personal monthly income have significant impacts on the use willingness of people who keep a neutral stance. These people pay more attention to convenience and the economy of EVS. These results reveal that a reasonable price, accurate positioning of target groups, convenient site layout and usage are required for operators to successfully launch a new transportation mode of EVS.

Keywords: electric vehicle sharing; multinomial logistic regression; survey; use willingness

1. Introduction

Research indicates that electric vehicles are not only able to decrease vehicle emissions [1] and slow global warming [2], but also are able to enhance the sustainability of road traffic in the future [3]. With energy, environment and other issues becoming increasingly prominent, many countries began to realize the importance of environmentally-friendly electric vehicles. Most manufacturers also have started to develop and commercialize environmentally-friendly electric vehicles [4]. However, electric vehicles are currently limited by insufficient charging infrastructures and driving mileage (the longest driving range per battery charge). Considering that car sharing is more suitable for people's short-term travel demands, the combination of electric vehicles and car sharing is a good way to avoid these weaknesses and to provide a cleaner transport mode.

Certain cities in the world, such as Barcelona, Paris, Berlin, Hamburg, Rotterdam and Stockholm, are implementing electric vehicle sharing (EVS) [5]. In China, EVS is still in the initial development phase. China Car Club in Hangzhou and Eduoauto in Beijing are the pioneers for developing EVS. China Car Club was invested in by Intunecapital in early 2013, and it is based on the model of self-purchasing cars. Eduoauto is based on the model of light assets, and the operational vehicles are mainly provided by enterprises qualified for car rental, not bought by the company itself. eHi Car Services launched a pilot EVS program in Jading district of Shanghai in June 2013, but the progress is very slow. At present, there are several EVS services, such as EVCARD hosted by Shanghai International Automobile City, YiKaZuChe in Beijing, Weigongjiao in Hangzhou, *etc.*

In recent years, governments have begun to attach more importance to EVS, which contributed to the rapid development of EVS. In July 2014, the General Office of the State Council in China released the No. 35 document of "Instructions on accelerating the promotion and application of new energy vehicles" [6], which emphasized the needs of "exploring innovative business models, such as the time-sharing leasing, car sharing, vehicle leasing, mortgage purchase for new energy vehicles, *etc.*". The EVS program also has received support from the local governments. The Beijing Municipal Science and Technology Commission has listed EVS as a key supported project and set up many operational indicators. Other cities, such as Shanghai, Hangzhou, Shaoxing, Ningbo, Wuhan, Shenzhen, Yancheng, Chongqing, and so on, have launched or are actively ready to launch an EVS program.

From the analysis above, it can be known that the number of EVS enterprises operating is few, and most of them lack experience. With the support from the government, there will be more and more domestic companies involved in EVS in the next few foreseeable years. Nevertheless, how consumers think about EVS, whether they will use the service and their related preference are still unclear. Therefore, in order to promote all-round development of EVS and to help the enterprises achieve better operation, a questionnaire was designed to collect information about the acceptance of consumers and influencing factors for using EVS. Some suggestions are provided for EVS operators to promote its rapid development in China.

2. Literature Review

In the late 1980s, a preliminary model of car sharing appeared abroad. However, scholars started to research car sharing in the 1990s. At the beginning of the research, most studies were at the qualitative level, and scholars paid more attention to the feasibility of the car sharing model and consumer usage. Based on a large number of empirical studies, Meijkamp [7] in The Netherlands pointed out that car sharing as an alternative to private cars, because it had higher economic and ecological efficiency. Barth and Shaheen [8] had an opinion that car sharing could improve the traffic efficiency by reducing the number of private cars and improve the efficiency of energy and emissions. They also introduced a variety of car sharing systems and described the development prospect of car sharing in China. Prettenthaler and Steininger [9] researched how driving mileage influenced the car sharing users to make decisions. Results showed that using car sharing was better than using private cars when user's travel range was less than 18,000 km per year. However, if insurance and the vehicle depreciation rate are taken into account, the balanced driving distance of users decreased to 15,000 km. Seik [10] studied car sharing in Singapore and found that members still mainly used public transport for travelling to work after attaining membership, but turned more often to shared cars rather than public transport for marginal uses, such as leisure and social trips. Most of them chose car sharing for its marginal use and cost savings.

Entering the 21st century, foreign scholars gradually began to study the operation system of car sharing, the optimization of staff, site layout, vehicle allocation, *etc.*, from the quantitative perspective. Barth and Todd [11] used a computer to simulate the distribution of available vehicles and energy consumption in car sharing sites. Results showed that the influencing factors of the car sharing system were the proportion of demand, the charging strategy for the electric vehicles and the vehicle allocation algorithm. The main problems of the car sharing service that should be considered at the beginning of the establishment were service pricing, target customer selection, vehicle type selection, site location, *etc.* [12]. Xu and Lim [13] established a mathematical model for the vehicles sharing site layout in Singapore and used the improved neural network model to predict the car sharing net flows. Kek *et al.* [14] provided a three-stage decision optimization model for the car sharing operator. They analyzed the optimal distribution of staff and vehicles and used operational data from the Singapore sharing company to verify the model. Correia and Antunes [15] had studied the problem of car sharing site planning. Under the goal of maximizing the profit for the car sharing operating company, they established a mixed integer programming model to solve the unbalanced number of sharing cars between different sites.

At present, there are few research works on EVS abroad, and most of them focus on operating status analysis and consumer surveys. Quantitative studies on EVS are rare. Alessandro *et al.* [16] introduced the EVS project of Green Move and studied the shared service strategies and objectives. By investigating the feasibility of EVS as a private car for elderly, Shaheen *et al.* [17] found that 30% of respondents were interested in participating, but all participants would make a plan before they would use the car, indicating that EVS still has the range anxiety problem. This problem is caused by the limited driving range of electric vehicles. Using data from 533 members of the EVS program in Seoul, Kim *et al.* [18] found that the participants were rather reluctant to change their car ownership, but had intentions to continue participating in the program. Social and economic perspectives were the most important factors affecting the participants' attitudes. In addition, the attitudes varied depending on personal characteristics, such as gender, age and income.

Domestic research progress on the car sharing model is relatively late. In 2000, Huang and Yang [19] were the first to research car sharing and introduced its development history abroad. They summarized the benefits of this new public transport pattern, the impact on travel behavior and its possible target market (people who have no private cars or have a high cost of ownership). Market demand, quality of service and advanced public transportation are important factors for successful car sharing. Ye and Yang [20] summarized and introduced the concept, development status and influence of car sharing. They also explained its characteristics (low-cost, flexible) and target group (replacement selection for people who wanted to buy a second car). Gao [21] explained the concept of "shared car" in detail and presented the concept of "Auto Club". Its development prospect in China was also studied. Qiu [22] analyzed the key influencing factors for car sharing development in China. Results showed that educational level of respondents, number of owned private cars and convenience of EVS had impacts on consumers' use willingness. Xue *et al.* [23] combed the classification of car sharing and analyzed the impact of this service on car ownership, travel cost, usage cost, energy savings and emission reduction. Through an empirical study, they found that the target group of car sharing was people who are 25–40 years old and have an above average educational level. The model of Zipcar in the United States was studied by Wu [24]. He investigated the potential market of car sharing service in Guangzhou and demonstrated the significance of promoting car sharing. He pointed out that car sharing is very promising in China and will be an alternative to other means of transportation. By introducing the development of car sharing in Hanover, He [25] pointed out that a shared car could replace 6–10 private cars and radically reduce automobile usage. Xia *et al.* [26] had carried out empirical research on an informal car sharing service in Beijing from the perspective of economic and ecological efficiency. They suggested that the government should regulate such an industry and formulate relevant policies to support the development of shared services.

From the analysis above, it is obvious that domestic research on EVS is very small in quantity. More studies are focused on the operating model description, case analysis and the prospect forecast of traditional vehicle sharing. From the perspective of operators, a questionnaire was implemented in Shanghai to find factors affecting consumers' use willingness of electric vehicle sharing, including travel characteristics, expectation of EVS and socio-demographics and then proposed corresponding suggestions for station location, driving range choice and model selection for EVS. At the same time, the target group and potential market in Shanghai for using EVS were pointed out. This will help the operations of enterprises effectively.

3. Research Method

3.1. Questionnaire Design

The paper questionnaire was implemented and disseminated offline. Through this, we have learned comprehensive knowledge about EVS acceptance. Finally, the target population of EVS was pointed out by analysis.

The questionnaire was divided into three parts. The first part has three questions about travel characteristics, including main trip mode in daily use, factors considered when choosing the trip mode and monthly transportation expenditure. Based on a simple explanation of EVS, the second part was questions about the expectations of EVS, including the use willingness, the attractive point for the respondent, the suitable usage scenario, *etc.* The last part was personal information, including gender, age, occupation, educational level, marital status, personal monthly income, *etc.* The whole questionnaire was designed as shown in Table 1.

Table 1. The designed questionnaire for investigation. EVS, electric vehicle sharing.

	Variable	Description
Travel characteristics	Main trip mode in daily use	Subway, bus, private car, taxi, walking, bicycle, **motorcycle/scooter riders**
	Factors considered when choosing the trip mode	Time, expenditure, weather condition, degree of comfort, travel distance, travel purpose, body condition, others
	Monthly transportation expenditure	≤100 yuan, 101–200 yuan, 201–300 yuan, 301–400 yuan, **≥401 yuan**
Expectation of EVS	Whether to choose EVS	Will choose, keep neutral stance, **will not choose**
	Attractive points of using EVS	Convenient appointment, cost-effective, shorter distance, parking space saving, no overhead cost, others
	Suitable usage scenario of EVS	Work, school, shopping, entertainment, seeing a doctor, visiting relatives or friends, individual business, work business, others
	Suitable vehicle type for EVS	Mini car, small car, compact car, midsize car, medium and large size car, luxury car, SUV, MPV (multi-purpose vehicles), microvan
	Acceptable minimum driving range of EV	Not less than 50 km, not less than 80 km, not less than 120 km, not less than 150 km, not less than 200 km, not less than 250 km, not less than 300 km, **not less than 350 km**
	Acceptable maximum duration for going to stations	Time for walking is 5 min, time for walking is 10 min, **time for walking is 15 min**
	Acceptable maximum duration for waiting and handling procedure	5 min, 10 min, **15 min**
	Acceptable highest price of EVS	30 yuan/month + 60 yuan/h, 30 yuan/month + 40 yuan/h, **30 yuan/month + 20 yuan/h**
Socio-demographics	Gender	Male, female
	Age	Under 18, 18–25, 26–30, 31–40, 41–50, **above 50**
	Number of owned private cars	None, one, **not less than two**
	Marital status	Single, married, but have no child, **married and have kids**
	Educational level	Junior high school and the following: senior high school, junior college, Bachelor's, **Master's and above**
	Occupation	Party and government cadre/teacher/police, clerk, business owner/shareholder, *etc.*, technicist, worker/server, company management personnel, freelancer, **retired staff/student**
	Personal monthly income	Under 1000 yuan, 1000–3000 yuan, 3001–6000 yuan, 6001–10,000 yuan, 10,001–15,000 yuan, above 15,001 yuan, **no fixed income**

* The black bold items are reference categories used in the multinomial logistic regression model.

3.2. Data Collection

From May 2014–November 2014, 410 respondents participated in the survey. As is known to all, EVS is more convenient than bus, more predictable and accurate than taxi and more economical than private cars. For the above reasons, EVS will replace part of the public and private transportation in the future. Therefore, the investigation object should be universal to balance people with different characteristics. Choosing residents in Shanghai as the main investigation object, questionnaires were distributed randomly at railway stations, commercial shopping centers, bus stop waiting areas, public squares, university areas, and so on. According to the standard that the number of answers for one questionnaire should be not less than half, 394 effective questionnaires were received.

3.3. Model Formulation

In this paper, choice willingness for EVS ("will not choose" is coded as 1, "keeping neutral" as 2, "will choose" as 3) is the dependent variable, which is ordinal. Ordinal regression was used, and a test of the parallel lines was done to check whether the method was appropriate. According to the research of Zhang [27] and Li *et al.*, [28], when the value of P for the test of parallel lines is far less than 0.05, this indicates that the ordinal regression is not appropriate, and multinomial logistic regression should be used. As shown in Table 2, the value of significance (Sig.) is 0.001, which is far less than 0.05. Therefore, multinomial logistic regression is used in this paper, finally.

Table 2. Test of parallel lines.

Model	−2 Log Likelihood	Chi-Square	df	Sig.
Null Hypothesis	667.011			
General	579.259	87.751	51	0.001

The multinomial logistic regression model is often used to handle the case where the dependent variable has several classified categories (N > 2). During the process, the model will choose one category of dependent variable as the reference category to establish the general logits models. Furthermore, if the dependent variable Y is coded 0, 1 or 2 and using Y = 0 as the baseline, the probabilities of each dependent variable category [29] are:

$$P(Y = 0) = \frac{1}{1 + e^{g_1(x)} + e^{g_2(x)}} \tag{1}$$

$$P(Y = 1) = \frac{e^{g_1(x)}}{1 + e^{g_1(x)} + e^{g_2(x)}} \tag{2}$$

$$P(Y = 2) = \frac{e^{g_2(x)}}{1 + e^{g_1(x)} + e^{g_2(x)}} \tag{3}$$

where:

$$g_1(x) = \text{logit}\frac{P(Y = 1)}{P(Y = 0)} = \beta_{10} + \beta_{11}x_1 + \ldots + \beta_{1p}x_p \tag{4}$$

$$g_2(x) = \text{logit}\frac{P(Y = 2)}{P(Y = 0)} = \beta_{20} + \beta_{21}x_1 + \ldots + \beta_{2p}x_p \tag{5}$$

where $\beta_{10}, \beta_{11}, \beta_{1p}, \ldots, \beta_{2p}$ are coefficients for the logistic regression model, which can be obtained by using SPSS software.

4. Analysis Results

4.1. Descriptive Statistics

4.1.1. Demographic Variable

Table 3 illustrates the demographic characteristics of respondents. As shown in Table 3, most respondents are male (61.6%), which is higher than the proportion of women. The main age groups are 20s and 30s, which should be the major groups for using EVS. Forty one-point-seven percent of respondents are single, and the percentage of married having kids is 37.6%. Fifty eight-point-six percent of people have private cars, and 7.9% of them even have two or more cars. Most respondents (68.3%) had a Bachelor's degree or above. The monthly income is mainly concentrated in 3001–10,000 yuan (49.1%), and more than 15,000 yuan or below 1000 yuan are the least, which accords with the research. The distribution of the occupation is relatively balanced overall. Ordinary staff and technical staff account for 20.2%, respectively.

Table 3. Descriptive statistics for the demographic characteristics of respondents.

Variable	Description	Percentage
Gender	Male	61.6%
	Female	38.4%
Age	Under 18	1.5%
	18–25	28.1%
	26–30	30%
	31–40	24.6%
	41–50	8.4%
	Above 50	5.4%
Number of owned private cars	None	41.4%
	One	50.7%
	Not less than two	7.9%
Marital status	Single	41.7%
	Married, but have no child	20.7%
	Married and have kids	37.6%
Educational level	Junior high school and the following:	3.6%
	Senior high school	10.2%
	Junior college	17.9%
	Bachelor's	49.1%
	Master's and above	19.2%
Occupation	Party and government cadre/teacher/police	7.2%
	Clerk	20.2%
	Business owner/shareholder, *etc.*	4.3%
	Technicist	20.2%
	Worker/server	5.4%
	Company management personnel	7.9%
	Freelancer	5.4%
	Retired staff/student	29.4%
Personal monthly income	Under 1000 yuan	5.3%
	1000–3000 yuan	18.5%
	3001–6000 yuan	26.6%
	6001–10,000 yuan	24.0%
	10,001–15,000 yuan	10.6%
	Above 15,001 yuan	6.6%
	No fixed income	8.4%

4.1.2. Travel Characteristics

As shown in Figure 1, 83.5% of percipients have a monthly transportation expenditure within 300 yuan. The percentage spending more than 400 yuan monthly is only 10.4%. In the aspect of factors considered when choosing the trip mode, most respondents consider time primarily. The secondary is travel purpose, and cost is the least considerable factor (Figure 2). The above result conforms to the normal situation that residents in big cities consider travel time, cost, convenience, safety and comfort when they choose the trip mode [30].

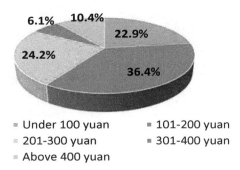

Figure 1. Distribution of monthly transportation expenditure.

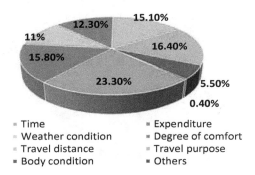

Figure 2. Factors considered when choosing the trip mode.

4.1.3. Expectations for EVS

With assistance from the investigators, respondents had preliminarily knowledge of EVS. The percentage of people who chose to use EVS is 42.4%. About 27% of people kept a neutral stance, which means quite a few people still maintain a wait-and-see attitude towards new things. This will be a customer resource to pursue during the development of EVS in the near future. The distribution of use willingness is shown as Figure 3.

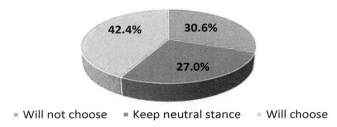

Figure 3. Whether to choose EVS.

When the respondents were asked about the attractiveness of EVS, their opinions were rather dispersed. More respondents selected the options of "the appointment and self-help picking cars are convenient and efficient", "it charges by hour and that is more cost-effective than renting for one day" and "it is more flexible than leasing and has no overhead costs" (as shown in Figure 4). It can be concluded that most consumers pay more attention to the convenience and economic benefits of the EVS service. Therefore, the service price should be as low as possible to offer consumers a chance to experience its economy and convenience, thus enlarging customer population.

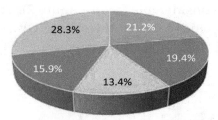

- The appointment and self-help picking cars are convenient and efficient
- Its meter charges by hour and is more cost-effective than renting for one day
- Shorter distance from starting/terminal point
- Saving parking space
- It is more flexible than leasing and has no overhead costs

Figure 4. Attractive points of using EVS.

When the respondents were asked about the suitable usage scenario of EVS, the two options that had the largest proportions are shopping and entertainment, with percentages of 22.1% and 23.8%, respectively (Figure 5). As a result, stations for EVS can be deployed around shopping malls, entertainment and leisure centers, so it can be convenient for users to rent and return vehicles.

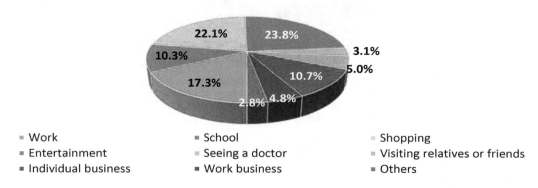

- Work
- Entertainment
- Individual business
- School
- Seeing a doctor
- Work business
- Shopping
- Visiting relatives or friends
- Others

Figure 5. Suitable usage scenario of EVS.

For the question of suitable vehicle type for EVS, respondents said that compact, small or mini cars would be more suitable. Cars of the A0 segment (small cars) accounted for the highest percentage of 27.2%. Respondents also preferred compact cars and mini cars (Figure 6). This also suggests that EVS is mainly used to meet people's needs for daily short-distance flexible transportation, and their demand for space is small.

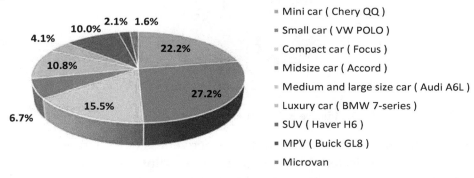

- Mini car (Chery QQ)
- Small car (VW POLO)
- Compact car (Focus)
- Midsize car (Accord)
- Medium and large size car (Audi A6L)
- Luxury car (BMW 7-series)
- SUV (Haver H6)
- MPV (Buick GL8)
- Microvan

Figure 6. Suitable vehicle types for EVS.

When asked about the acceptable minimum driving range of electric vehicles, 26.8% of respondents held the opinion that it should not be less than 150 km, as shown in Figure 7. The sum of percentages for "not less than 50 km", "not less than 80 km", "not less than 120 km" and "not less than 150 km" is 79.2%. A deep travel behavior investigation was done in 2014 with 67 residents in Shanghai. All travel behaviors were recorded for 14 days, including trip mode, time, distance, *etc.* The results show that the average travel distance for a single trip is 15.8 km, and the average daily travel range is 33.8 km, which is far lower than what the mainstream models on the market can offer. Another research work showed that when consumers were asked about the driving range for private electric vehicles, 35.8% of them responded that it should be between 120 km and 160 km [31]. Thus, it can be seen that most participants have higher tolerance towards the driving range of shared electric vehicles than private ones.

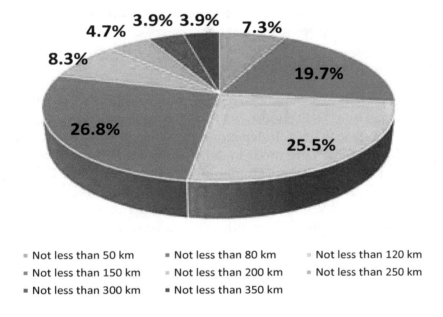

Figure 7. Acceptable minimum driving range of EV.

4.2. Statistics in Cross Tabulation Table

Figure 8 indicates that the number of owned private cars has an impact on the willingness to use EVS.

(1) With an increase in the number of owned private cars, the ratio of people who are willing to use the service shows a declining trend soon after rising. That is to say, the EVS acceptance of people in possession of only one private car is higher than that of people who do not have or have more than one private car. The reasons for this phenomenon may be that: (i) people in possession of private cars have more driving experience, and it is easier for them to accept a new transportation pattern; (ii) the EVS is a new type of transportation, and even the people who have a private car want to experience this new transportation system; (iii) because of severe traffic jams during rush hour, parking difficulty and high parking fees, a car owner is more willing to choose EVS as a method for short trips; (iv) the economic environment of people who have two or more private cars is better, and they tend not to consider whether the means of travel is economical. Compared to people who only have one car, reducing their usage willingness is also reasonable. At the same time, it also indicates that the target group of EVS is not only the people who have no private cars.

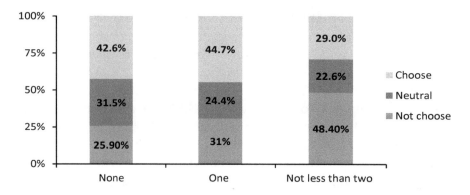

Figure 8. The relationship between willingness and the number of owned private cars.

(2) Along with the increase of owned private cars, people's attitude towards whether to adopt EVS becomes clearer. The ratio of keeping neutral decreases.

4.3. Multinomial Logistic Regression for the Target Group

In this paper, the dependent variable is the choice willingness for EVS ("will not choose" is coded as one, "keeping neutral" as two, "will choose" as three). In order to define the target group of EVS, multinomial logistic regression was used. Independent variables were selected from three aspects: (1) travel characteristics (including main trip mode in daily use and monthly transportation expenditure), (2) expectations for EVS (including acceptable minimum driving range of the EV, acceptable maximum duration for going to stations, acceptable maximum duration for the waiting and handling procedure and acceptable highest price of EVS) and (3) demographic characteristics (including gender, age, number of owned private cars, marital status, educational level, occupation and personal monthly income).

4.3.1. Model Fitting Test

SPSS20.0 was used to analyze the questionnaires, and Table 4 shows the likelihood ratio test for the final model and the intercept-only model. Here, the value of chi-squared is equal to the difference value between the −2 log likelihood in the intercept-only model and the final model. The significance level of the chi-squared test was 0.001, which is far less than 0.05. Therefore, the final model is superior to the intercept-only model, which means that the final model is established, and the fitting effect is significantly good. The indexes of Cox and Snell R-squares, Nagelkerke R-squared and McFadden R-squared were used to test the explainable degree of the equations on the variation of the explained variables. The bigger the R-squared is, the better the goodness of fit is. The value of these three indexes are 0.353, 0.400 and 0.204, and they indicate that independent variables can explain 35.3%, 40% and 20.4% of the variation of the explained variables. Although the three R-squared values are not very high, the result is acceptable.

Table 4. Model fitting information.

Model	Model Fitting Criteria	Likelihood Ratio Tests			R^2		
	−2 log likelihood	Chi-square	Sig.	Cox and Snell	Nagelkerke	McFadden
Intercept-only	762.673	-	-	-	-	-
Final	607.323	155.350	0.001	0.353	0.400	0.204

4.3.2. Coefficient Test of Variables

Table 5 shows the likelihood-ratio test in the final model for each independent variable. Through the statistical results, it can be seen that main trip mode in daily use, monthly transportation expenditure, acceptable minimum driving range of the EV, acceptable highest price of EVS, age and marital status have significant influences on the willingness to use EVS when the significance level is 0.1 [18]. People who usually take the subway or bus for daily transportation have a strong willingness to use EVS. People with a high monthly transportation expenditure are more likely to pursue the economical mode of EVS. Marital status often decides whether the respondents need to buy private cars, and this has a great impact on the decision to use the EVS service. The driving range of EV affects respondents' decisions of whether to choose the shared service instead of other modes of transportation. Respondents aged between 20 and 40 years old show a stronger receptivity to new things and the concept that they must have private cars is weaker. This makes them more willing to use the EVS service.

Table 5. Likelihood ratio test.

Effect	Model Fitting Criteria	Likelihood Ratio Tests	
	−2 log likelihood of reduced model	Chi-square	Sig.
Intercept	607.323 [a]	0.000	0.000
Main trip mode in daily use	632.206	24.883	0.015
Monthly transportation expenditure	631.696	24.373	0.002
Acceptable minimum driving range of EV	638.755	31.432	0.005
Acceptable maximum duration for going to stations	611.525	4.202	0.379
Acceptable maximum duration for waiting and handling procedure	612.404	5.081	0.279
Acceptable highest price of EVS	615.445	8.122	0.087
Gender	611.914	4.591	0.101
Age	633.589	26.266	0.003
Number of owned private cars	610.889	3.566	0.468
Marital status	624.302	16.979	0.002
Educational level	620.193	12.870	0.116
Occupation	624.859	17.536	0.229
Personal monthly income	621.654	14.331	0.280

[a] The ellipsis effect does not increase the degree of freedom. As a result, the simplified model is equal to the final model.

4.3.3. Parameter Estimation Results

Tables 5 and 6 show the parameter estimation results of different groups. The reference category for the dependent variable is choose not to use. The reference categories for the independent variables are in black bold, as shown in Table 1.

If the estimated coefficient of a factor (B) is significantly positive, then the probability of this factor belonging to the current category level is higher than the probability of it belonging to the reference category, with all of the other factors being fixed [32].

Estimated Model Results of the Choose to Use Group

As shown in Table 6, the factors of main trip mode in daily use, monthly transportation expenditure, driving range of electric vehicles, gender, age, marital status and occupation are statistically significant. The following is a detailed analysis of these results. (1) People who usually take the subway, bus or bike are more willing to use EVS. (2) With the increase of monthly transportation expenditure, its regression coefficient changes from negative to positive, which indicates that the higher the monthly transportation expenditure is, the more consumers prefer to choose EVS. (3) The driving range of electric vehicles has a significant influence on consumers' willingness to use EVS, with a negative coefficient. The absolute value of the coefficient increases as the driving range of electric vehicles increases, indicating that when the driving range of electric vehicles is higher, more consumers tend not to use EVS services. This result conflicts with previous expectations. The reasons may be that EVS is designed to provide a short commute for people, and the driving range of general electric vehicles has been able to meet that demand. The total cost of the operator increases as the driving range of electric vehicles increases, and then, the single use price for EVS may increase. For reasons of travel economy, consumers are more reluctant to use this business. It should be pointed out that the front reason is just guesswork; further research is required to give more information and to find out the cause. (4) Gender is significant to consumers' use willingness, with the probability ratio of male being 2.081-times higher than that of female. This means that males are more willing to use EVS than females. (5) Age has a significant influence on consumers' choices, and the coefficient is positive. The absolute value of the coefficient decreases as the age increases, which indicates that consumers' use willingness of EVS will be reduced as the age increases. People who are aged between 18 and 30 have the strongest use willingness. The reasons may be that this group is at the beginning of economic independence and usually pursue economic and effective ways to travel, and their receptivity to new modes of transportation is better. (6) Marital status is significant with a negative coefficient, indicating that the use willingness of unmarred people is lower than that of married people. This may controvert the former expectations. However, through the former analysis, the results can be obtained that people who own private cars have a stronger use willingness than people having no cars (that can be found in Figure 8). In this investigation, 73.2% of participants having private cars are married. Therefore, the use willingness of married people being higher than that of unmarried people is understandable. From the analysis above, the population characteristics of people choosing to use EVS are male, aged between 18 and 30, and usually taking the subway and bus as the daily transportation modes.

Table 6. Parameter estimation results: choose to use.

Independent Variables	B	Wald	Sig.	Exp(B)
Intercept	−2.283	1.437	0.231	
[Main trip mode in daily use = 1]: subway	1.705	2.870	0.090	5.499
[Main trip mode in daily use = 2]: bus	2.016	3.750	0.053	7.508
[Main trip mode in daily use = 6]: bicycle	3.226	7.190	0.007	25.173
[Monthly transportation expenditure = 1]: 0–100 yuan	−1.260	3.092	0.079	0.284
[Monthly transportation expenditure = 4]: 301–400 yuan	1.606	3.593	0.058	4.981
[Minimum driving range of EV = 4]: not less than 150 km	−1.882	3.523	0.061	0.152
[Minimum driving range of EV = 6]: not less than 250 km	−2.564	4.403	0.036	0.077
[Minimum driving range of EV = 7]: not less than 300 km	−4.939	12.600	0.000	0.007
[Gender = 1]: male	0.733	4.517	0.034	2.081
[Age = 2]: 18–25 years old	3.571	10.951	0.001	35.556
[Age = 3]: 26–30 years old	2.194	4.545	0.033	8.969
[Marital status = 1]: single	−2.289	11.271	0.001	0.101
[Occupation = 3]: business owner/shareholder, *etc.*	2.154	4.159	0.041	8.619

Estimated Model Results of the Choose to Remain Neutral Group

As shown in Table 7, the factors of acceptable highest price of EVS, occupation and personal monthly income have significant impacts on the use willingness of people who keep a neutral stance. The detailed analysis is as follows. (1) The acceptable highest price of EVS is significant to consumers' use willingness with a negative coefficient, indicating that the increasing service price could reduce consumers' willingness to use it. (2) Business owners/shareholders hold a neutral opinion about the EVS service. This may relate to their existing economic and social status, *etc.* These people have better living conditions, and they may not need this service to save money or improve travel conditions. (3) The probability of keeping neutral is higher than that of not choosing, which indicates that the exclusion effect of people with lower average monthly income for EVS is reduced. From the analysis above, people who keep a neutral stance have lower personal monthly income. If we want to encourage these people to change their existing attitude to use the EVS, a reasonable price should be offered to attract them to join in on the premise of guaranteeing profits.

Table 7. Parameter estimation results: choose to remain neutral.

Independent Variables	B	Wald	Sig.	Exp(B)
Intercept	−2.888	1.743	0.187	
[Acceptable highest price of EVS = 1]: 30 yuan/month + 60 yuan/h	−0.829	2.864	0.091	0.436
[Occupation = 3]: business owner/shareholder, *etc.*	1.887	2.924	0.087	6.598
[Personal monthly income = 1]: below 1000 yuan	2.348	4.402	0.036	10.463
[Personal monthly income = 2]: 1000–3000 yuan	1.767	4.051	0.044	5.854

Prediction for Use Proportion

As shown in Table 2, most respondents are male clerks aged 26–30 years old and have an average monthly income of 3001–6000 yuan. For a respondent having these features, the probability that he will choose, not choose and keep a neutral stance can be calculated by Equations (1)–(5) according to the multinomial logistic regression results.

$$g_1 = -2.283 + 0.733 + 2.194 + 1.169 = 1.758 \tag{6}$$

$$g_2 = -2.888 + 0.363 + 0.817 + 0.768 = 0.215 \tag{7}$$

$$P\,(Y = \text{will choose}) = \frac{e^{g_1}}{1 + e^{g_1} + e^{g_2}} = 0.721 \tag{8}$$

$$P\,(Y = \text{wil keep a neutral stance}) = \frac{e^{g_2}}{1 + e^{g_1} + e^{g_2}} = 0.154 \tag{9}$$

$$P\,(Y = \text{will not choose}) = \frac{1}{1 + e^{g_1} + e^{g_2}} = 0.125 \tag{10}$$

Therefore, the probability for a 26–30-year-old male clerk who has a personal monthly income of 3001–6000 yuan to use EVS is 72.1%.

According to the calculation method above, when other factors remain unchanged, the relationship between age and the use probability ratio of male clerks who have a 3001–6000 yuan monthly income can be obtained and is shown in Figure 9. It is possible to see that age has a great influence on personal decisions to use the EVS, which is consistent with the former analysis. People aged 18–30 are more likely to use EVS. When people's age is more than 30 years old, the probability of not choosing is bigger than that of choosing. Additionally, as the age increases, the probability of a neutral stance increases, and consumers are more reluctant to use EVS. Furthermore, the post-1990s generation in China is growing up, and their receptivity is better than other groups. They will be the major customers of EVS in the near future. Therefore, the market space for EVS business is huge. The suggestion is that the EVS service could aiim at young people aged between 18 and 30 as their customers.

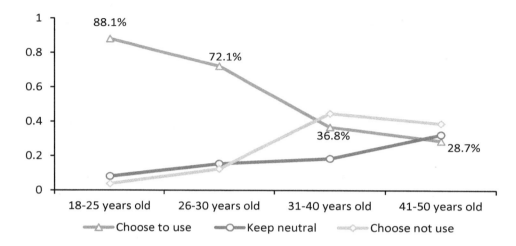

Figure 9. The relationship between age and the willingness to using EVS.

In a similar way, when other factors keep constant, the relationship between personal monthly income and the willingness to use EVS is shown as Figure 10. The following is the results. (1) Overall, with the increase of personal monthly income, the choice probability of individuals to use EVS decreases after rising first. When the personal monthly income is 3001–6000 yuan, the probability of choosing reaches the maximum of 72.1%. (2) When the personal monthly income is low, the probability of not choosing is high. The reason may be the relatively weak economic capacity of the low income group. When the monthly income is higher (more than 15,001 yuan), the probability of choosing is higher than that of not choosing. However, the value of the former is still below 50%, which indicates that the probability of not choosing for consumers with high monthly income (more than 15,001 yuan) is very big. This may be related to their social status, economic condition, *etc.* Therefore, EVS should be geared toward the needs of the main group at middle-income level.

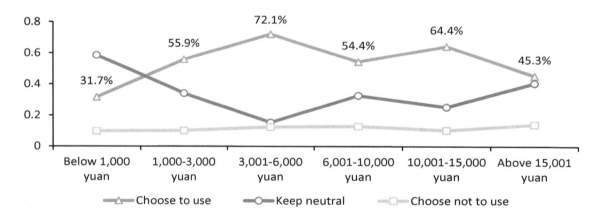

Figure 10. The relationship between monthly income and the willingness to use EVS.

5. Suggestions

In the operational aspect, the following suggestions are offered for the development of EVS.

(1) According to the regression analysis results (Tables 6 and 7), people who are male, aged between 18 and 30 and usually taking the subway and bus as the daily transportation mode are the target group for using EVS. Combined with the probability calculation (Figures 9 and 10), the suggestion is that operators should pay more attention to young people who are 18–30 years old and have a middle-level income.

(2) In the early development of EVS, the type of shared electric vehicles should give priority to compact, small or mini cars.

Car sharing is designed to satisfy people's short, temporary and flexible transportation demand. Most people will use it for shopping and entertainment (Figure 5), and they expect that the EVS would be economical (Figure 4). Most people who would like to use EVS are young, and their income is not very high (Figure 10). In order to decrease consumers' use-cost to show the economy of sharing and satisfy the need to carry certain items at the same time, the type of shared EV should focus on compact, small or mini cars. This can reduce the cost of operators and indirectly reduce the use-cost of shared cars. On the other hand, governments can offer certain subsidies to reduce the enterprises' pressure on operating funds in the early stage. This can promote the industrialization of electric vehicles and also improve the operational enterprises' enthusiasm.

(3) In the early developmental stage, the driving range of shared electric vehicles should reach 120 km.

More than half of the respondents (Figure 7) said the driving range of shared electric vehicles should reach 120 km at least, which indicates that most people hold tolerant attitudes towards the problem of driving range. However, there were more than a quarter of people who hoped that the driving range could reach 150 km. From regression the result in Table 6, it is indicated that the increasing driving range will decrease consumers' use willingness (the reason is stated in Section 4.3.3). Therefore, in the early stage of development, for reasons of cost, capital, *etc.*, it is recommended that the driving range of shared electric vehicles should reach 120 km.

(4) When laying out the sites, the walking time for consumers to stations should be controlled to be within 10 min.

Theoretically, the walking time for consumers to the stations should be as short as possible, which means more sites are needed. However, more sites mean large amounts of money for investment, and it is also likely to cause high operational and maintenance cost, a low utilization rate, *etc.* Therefore, a reasonable number and layout of sites are needed to improve vehicle utilization, reduce operating costs, and at the same time, meet consumers' need for the convenient usage of cars. According to Figures 11 and 12 92.5% of participants accept the walking time within 10 min. When the walking time increases from five to 10 min, the percentage of people who are willing to use EVS decreases by 4.7%, which is acceptable. Considering the cost and utilization rate, the suggestion is that the walking time for consumers to the station should be controlled to be within 10 min.

Figure 11. Acceptable maximum duration for going to stations (N = 385).

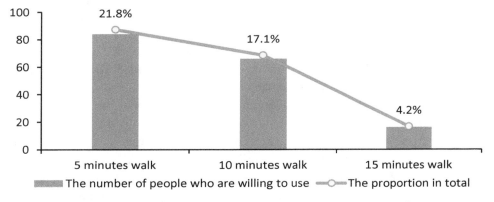

Figure 12. The relationship between time for going to stations and use willingness (N = 385).

(5) The waiting time for consumers to go through the formalities and pick up cars should be controlled within five minutes.

Convenient appointments and self-help picking up cars are some of the most attractive points that consumers think the EVS service should have. As shown in Figures 13 and 14 89.4% of participants can accept that the longest waiting time is within 10 min. However, when waiting time increases from five to 10 min, the percentage of people who are willing to use EVS decreases from 24% to 14%, which is a big decline. Therefore, services, such as picking up the cars or returning the cars, should be automatic and self-supported. The suggestion is that operators should open a variety of channels for customers to complete the procedures of booking, picking up cars, returning cars and paying the bill conveniently and effectively. These can help control the total waiting time to be within five minutes.

Figure 13. Acceptable maximum duration for the waiting and handling procedure (N = 385).

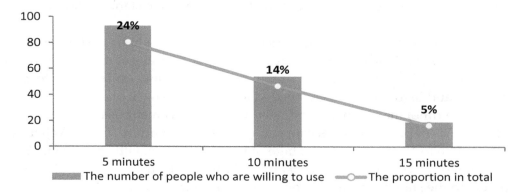

Figure 14. The relationship between waiting time and use willingness (N = 385).

6. Conclusions

In the early development of EVS, in order to achieve a good commercial operation, it is necessary to investigate with respect to the consumers the important influencing factors for the acceptance of EVS. Therefore, to solve these problems, a questionnaire was conducted in Shanghai. According to the results, relevant suggestions are offered to achieve a wide range promotion of EVS.

Through the multiple logistic regression analysis, the factors of the main trip mode in daily use, monthly transportation expenditure, acceptable minimum driving range of electric vehicles, gender, age, marital status and occupation have significant influences on the willingness to choose EVS. Males are more willing to use EVS than females. Younger people have a stronger receptivity to new things than the old. As age increases, the use willingness of consumers decreases. In short, the population characteristics of people choosing to use EVS are male, aged between 18 and 30 and usually taking the subway and bus as the daily transportation modes. Otherwise, the factors of acceptable highest price of EVS, occupation and personal monthly income have a significant impact on the use willingness of people who keep a neutral stance. The increase of service price will reduce the use willingness, and the exclusion effect of people with a low average monthly income is lower. As a result, if we want to encourage these people to change their existing attitude to use EVS, a reasonable price should be made to attract them to join on the premise of incurring no deficit. The probability for a 26–30 year-old male clerk who has a personal monthly income of 3001–6000 yuan in Shanghai to use EVS is as high as 72.1%, which indicates that the development prospect for EVS in Shanghai is good.

In the operational aspects, suggestions are provided for operators as follows. (1) The operators should pay more attention to people who are 18–30 years old and have a middle-level income. (2) In the early development of EVS, the electric vehicles used for sharing should be concentrated on compact, small or mini cars to achieve the aim of low-cost operation and good sharing economy. (3) The driving range of shared electric vehicles should not be less than 120 km to reduce consumers' range anxiety. (4) During the laying out of sites, a reasonable number of sites are necessary to guarantee that the walking time to stations is within 10 min for consumers. (5) Operators need to optimize the leasing system and implement automation and self-support as far as possible. This can help control the total waiting time to within five minutes.

Acknowledgments: Acknowledgments: The research has been funded under the China MOST project of Electric Car Sharing Technology Integration and Demonstration Operation (2015BAG11B00).

Author Contributions: Author Contributions: Ning Wang designed and performed this research. Runlin Yan analyzed the data and wrote this paper. All authors have read and approved the final manuscript.

References

1. Brady, J.; O'Mahony, M. Travel to work in Dublin. The potential impacts of electric vehicles on climate change and urban air quality. *Transp. Res. Part D* **2011**, *16*, 188–193. [CrossRef]
2. Hawkins, T.R.; Singh, B.; Majeau-Bettez, G.; Stromman, A.H. Comparative environmental life cycle assessment of conventional and electric vehicles. *J. Ind. Ecol.* **2013**, *17*, 53–64. [CrossRef]
3. Hanschke, C.B.; Uyterlinde, M.A.; Kroon, P.; Jeeninga, H.; Londo, H.M. Duurzame Innovatie in Het Wegverkeer. Available online: https://www.ecn.nl/docs/library/report/2008/e08076.pdf (accessed on 2 December 2015). (In Dutch)
4. Sierzchula, W.; Bakker, S.; Maat, K.; Van Wee, B. The competitive environment of electric vehicles: An analysis of prototype and production models. *Environ. Innov. Soc. Transit.* **2012**, *2*, 49–65. [CrossRef]
5. IEA (International Energy Agency). EV City Casebook. 2012. Available online: http://www.iea.org/publications/freepublications/publication/EVCityCasebook.pdf (accessed on 2 December 2015).
6. Instructions of the General Office of the State Council in China on Accelerating the Promotion and Application of New Energy Vehicles. Available online: http://www.gov.cn/zhengce/content/2014-07/21/content_8936.htm (accessed on 21 July 2014).
7. Meijkamp, R. Changing consumer behaviour through eco-efficient services: An empirical study of car sharing in the Netherlands. *Bus. Strateg. Environ.* **1998**, *7*, 234–244. [CrossRef]
8. Barth, M.; Shaheen, S.A. The Potential for Shared-Use Vehicle Systems in China. Available online: http://76.12.4.249/artman2/uploads/1/UCD-ITS-RR-03-11.pdf (accessed on 2 December 2015).
9. Prettenthaler, F.E.; Steininger, K.W. From ownership to service use lifestyle: The potential of car sharing. *Ecol. Econ.* **1999**, *28*, 443–453. [CrossRef]
10. Seik, T.F. Vehicle ownership restraints and car sharing in Singapore. *Habitat Int.* **2000**, *24*, 75–90. [CrossRef]
11. Barth, M.; Todd, M. Simulation model performance analysis of a multiple station shared vehicle system. *Transp. Res. Part C* **1999**, *7*, 237–259. [CrossRef]
12. Brook, D. Carsharing–Start Up Issues and New Operational Models. In Poceedings of the Transportation Research Board Annual Meeting, Chicago, IL, USA, 18–20 November 2004.
13. Xu, J.X.; Lim, J.S. A new evolutionary neural network for forecasting net flow of a car sharing system. In Proceedings of the Evolutionary Computation, Singapore, 25–28 September 2007.
14. Kek, A.G.; Cheu, R.L.; Meng, Q.; Fung, C.H. A decision support system for vehicle relocation operations in carsharing systems. *Transp. Res. Part E* **2009**, *45*, 149–158. [CrossRef]
15. Correia, G.H.; Antunes, A.P. Optimization approach to depot location and trip selection in one-way carsharing systems. *Transp. Res. Part E* **2012**, *48*, 233–247. [CrossRef]
16. Luè, A.; Colorni, A.; Nocerino, R.; Paruscio, V. Green move: An innovative electric vehicle-sharing system. *Procedia Soc. Behav. Sci.* **2012**, *48*, 2978–2987. [CrossRef]
17. Shaheen, S.; Cano, L.; Camel, M. Exploring Electric Vehicle Carsharing as a Mobility Option for Older Adults: A Case Study of a Senior Adult Community in the San Francisco Bay Area. *Int. J. Sustain. Transp.* **2015**. [CrossRef]

18. Kim, D.; Ko, J.; Park, Y. Factors affecting electric vehicle sharing program participants' attitudes about car ownership and program participation. *Transp. Res. Part D* **2015**, *36*, 96–106. [CrossRef]

19. Huang, Z.Y.; Yang, D.Y. The development of car sharing abroad. *Urban Plan. Forum* **2000**, *6*, 50–55.

20. Ye, L.; Yang, D.Y. The development and applied research on car sharing and mobile management in China. In Proceedings of the China's Sustainable Development Forum, Shandong, China, 2010; Available online: http://cpfd.cnki.com.cn/Article/CPFDTOTAL-ZKZC201010001051.htm (accessed on 2 December 2015).

21. Gao, Y.M. Car Sharing—A new model of automobile consumption. *Traffic Trans.* **2005**, *4*, 39–40.

22. Qiu, L. Market prospects and marketing research on car sharing service in China's. Master's Thesis, Fudan University, Shanghai, China, 2009.

23. Xue, Y.; Yang, T.Y.; Wen, S.B. Social Characteristics and Development Models of Car Sharing. *Techno-econ. Manag. Res.* **2008**, *1*, 54–58.

24. Wu, W.D. Research on car sharing pattern and analysis on its development in Chinese market. Master's Thesis, Zhongshan University, Guangzhou, China, 2010.

25. Jing, H. The green traffic of car sharing in Hanover. *Traffic Trans.* **2005**, *6*, 13.

26. Kaixuan, X.; Mingsheng, H.; Hua, Z. The economic and ecological efficiency of car sharing service and the feasibility to implement the service in Beijing. *China Soft Sc.* **2006**, *12*, 64–70.

27. Zhang, W.T. *Advanced Courses for SPSS Statistical Analysis*; Higher Education Press: Beijing, China, 2004; pp. 189–203. (In Chinese)

28. Li, K.; Guo, Z.; Hu, L.; Xu, Y. Analysis method for ordered categorical data of cumulative score model. *Chin. J. Health Stat.* **1993**, *4*, 35–38.

29. Hosmer, D.W.; Lemeshow, S. *Applied Logistic Regression, Second ed*; Wiley: New York, NY, USA, 2000.

30. Wen, X.X.; Tan, G.X.; Yao, S.S.; Huang, Z. Traffic flow characteristics and short-term prediction model of urban intersection. *J. Traffic Transp. Eng.* **2006**, *1*, 103–107.

31. Zhou, M.J. An empirical study of factors affecting electric car purchase decision. *Shanghai Auto* **2013**, *4*, 39–44.

32. Sun, Y.; Shang, J. Factors affecting the health of residents in China: a perspective based on the living environment. *Ecol. Indic.* **2015**, *51*, 228–236. [CrossRef]

12

Weak and Strong Compensation for the Prioritization of Public Investments: Multidimensional Analysis for Pools

Gianluigi De Mare [1,*], **Maria Fiorella Granata** [2,†] **and Antonio Nesticò** [1,†]

[1]   Department of Civil Engineering, University of Salerno, Via Giovanni Paolo II, 132, Fisciano (SA) 84084, Italy; anestico@unisa.it

[2]   Department of Architecture, University of Palermo, Viale delle Scienze, ed, 14, Palermo 90128, Italy; maria.granata@unipa.it

*   Correspondence: gdemare@unisa.it.

†   These authors contributed equally to this work.

Academic Editor: Adam Jabłoński

Abstract: Despite the economic crisis still heavily affecting most of Europe, a possible resumption can be found in the revitalization of public and private investments. These investments should be directed not only towards the strategic areas of infrastructures and production, but also to those which allow for a higher level of the quality of life (sports facilities, parks, *etc.*). In such cases, the need to balance the reasons of financial sustainability with environmental and social profiles is even more evident. Thus, multicriteria techniques, supporting complex assessments, should be implemented together with a monetary feasibility study (cost-benefit analysis). Multidimensional methods allow for the aggregation of different profiles into overall indicators. This study gives an account of how the application and comparison of multi-criteria approaches based on tools characterized by a higher or lower level of compensation between criteria can broaden the spectrum of analysis of the problems and lead to a more subtle logic of funding for public works and works of public utility, with a more current and mature sharing of profitability between private investors and users of community infrastructures.

Keywords: multicriteria evaluation; economic assessment; sports facilities; strong and weak sustainability; SMART; PROMETHEE II

1. Introduction

The formation of metropolitan cities, with geographic extensions much greater than the past, and the integration of original cultures from different countries raise the level of complexity of infrastructures in urban systems (transport, education, health, sports, *etc.*). At the same time, the recent economic crisis has placed the institutions that have historically been producers of the investment needed for such public works in front of the problem of having to find sufficient financial resources. In Europe, the financing channels have been primarily identified as the resources made available by the European Community, as well as the most advanced forms of public-private partnership. Private partners base the decision about their adhesion to projects of public interest on the fundamental criterion of the economic and financial convenience, which must be verified by using the appropriate financial evaluation techniques. Although the verification of the economic and financial feasibility is a necessary requirement for the realization of the project by private parties, the interest of the local community can be measured through a purely monetary analysis [1–4]. Therefore, the point of view of the public authority is broader. Based on the adopted strategic policies, it is interesting to know the level of satisfaction on social, cultural and environmental requests [5].

Public authorities should therefore be able to expertly mediate between the monetary feasibility of investments and its social and political coherence compared to the demands of growth and development from the population. In this perspective, it is important to be capable of "measuring" the suitability of either a public project or a project of public interest, in meeting the needs expressed by the local community. The measure of this capacity can be applied to a dual purpose: (1) identification of local priority projects to be considered within the definition of tools for territorial government; and (2) preparation of appropriate measures supporting the projects of public interest, which, although possibly characterized by a smaller economic attractiveness for private investors, can make a more significant contribution to the welfare of the community.

The assessment of the ability of a project of public interest in meeting the needs of the local community has a multidimensional nature and must be able to integrate the local political preferences delegated to land management.

To this end, the definition of composite indices, capable of integrating the quality of the urban projects from the point of view of the community into an overall assessment, is useful. These synthetic indexes can be used as evaluation instruments of the quality of urban projects from the perspective of the community and can pose parameters of judgment to identify reliefs, for example of a financial or tax nature, that can direct the membership of private partners to projects that are more favorable to the community. They can also be used to identify priority actions in the field of local strategic and financial planning.

The main functions of a composite index of sustainability related to a public work or a work of public interest can be identified in the ability to synthetically express the quality of the project in terms of the objectives of sustainability, to encourage communication with all of the involved parties and to legitimize choices derived from a rational and transparent analysis of the available alternatives [6].

The purpose of this paper is the construction of socio-environmental convenience indexes and integrated sustainability indexes for the provision of sports facilities. The index must summarize the main needs expressed by the stakeholders. Composite indicators of this type can also be defined for different types of projects.

This objective is pursued using different multi-criteria evaluation techniques, in view of the distinction between "weak sustainability" and "strong sustainability", opposing the idea of the almost complete against the idea of only the limited substitutability of natural capital with physical capital, respectively [7]. In particular, two different decision-making models, suitable for evaluating the contribution of public investments and private investments of public interest from the two-fold point of view of sustainability understood in a weak and strong sense, are proposed.

The model described in this paper is useful for the construction of a multi-dimensional index of "restricted social convenience" and "overall social convenience" or "overall sustainability" for investments targeted at the creation or adaptation of municipal swimming pools in the province of Salerno (Italy). The paper is organized in some introductory Section 2, Section 3, Section 4, Section 5, Section 6 and Section 7 on multicriteria tools for the construction of convenience indicators, in sections on the processing of models (8 and 9) and sections summarizing and discussing the results in Section 10 and Section 11.

2. The Formulation of a Social Convenience Index for Investments of a Public Nature

Synthetic indexes or composite indicators are evaluation tools widely used in decision-making on economy, environment, globalization, society, innovation and technology [8], public policies [9], sustainability about single civil engineering works [10] and at a local level [11], as well as in ranking countries [12].

Several aggregation procedures have been proposed to build a composite indicator integrating manifold issues [13,14]; however, from an operational point of view, they are the result of an aggregation rule applied to values representing the performance of a given alternative on a set of criteria.

The construction of a social synthetic index includes the following fundamental steps:

1. the carrying out of a detailed analysis of the basic needs of the local community as an instrument guiding the identification of the relevant points of view in the analysis of alternatives [15];
2. the choice of a suitable aggregation procedure, considering the use of the composite indicator in the sustainable management of the territory and the necessity of being easily understandable for local administrators, even if they do not have specific technical competences in decision analysis;
3. the weighting of considered indicators;
4. the implementation of the aggregative model for each alternative, in order to obtain the value of the indexes.

In general, either weights are directly attributed by experts or special techniques used in order to achieve more objective values. The assignment of weights to single indicators for their aggregation is considered a crucial step in social multicriteria evaluation, and a good solution could be the renunciation of their same assignment, considering, therefore, equal weights for all of the indicators. In this case, the number of the considered indicators will represent the importance of the criterion that they express [8].

The choice of aggregation procedure is also an important step for the essential implications of each procedure. Furthermore, it is known that the application of different decision models can lead to different results for the same decision problem [6,16].

The main aggregation approaches belong to Multiple Attribute Utility Theory (MAUT) [17,18], outranking methods, introduced by Bernard Roy [19], and other "non-classical" approaches [20].

Procedures belonging to classical approaches are all suitable for handling the aggregation of single one-dimensional indicators in a comprehensive index, since they can deal with both quantitative and qualitative information, as well as give as an outcome a measure of the performance of the considered alternatives.

The procedures belonging to the outranking approach, like the PROMETHEE (Preference Ranking Organization METHod for Enrichment Evaluations) [21] and ELECTRE (ELimination Et ChoixTraduisant la REalité) methods [19], which are based on a pair-wise comparison of the alternatives, use weights representing the coefficient of importance and are not, in general, totally compensatory methods [22]. This is the reason why they are able to support a strong sustainability concept in which a bad performance on an indicator is not fully compensated by a good performance on another one [8]. The outranking approach assumes the hypothesis of the preferential independence of any sub-family of indicators [22].

Approaches based on multi-attribute utility theory require the consideration of an n-dimensional utility function that assigns a value to each alternative, representing its preferability. In general, the n-dimensional utility function is constructed by aggregating one-dimensional utility functions on a single criterion, to which a weight may be associated [18]. Using this kind of procedure, the preferential independence of the family of indicators is also assumed, so that the marginal utilities can be assessed; the different indicators have to be expressed on the same scale; and the weights represent substitution rates [22].

The additive and multiplicative techniques are the most widely used form of aggregation function [23]. Other aggregation techniques, such as the class of Ordered Weighted Averaging (OWA) operators [24] and the Choquet integral [25,26], belong to the MAUT framework and are extensions of weighted means. OWA operators are able to express vague quantifications, and the Choquet integral can model interactions among criteria [27].

3. Social Convenience Indexes for Investments in Swimming Pools

In the present paper, a synthetic index of "restricted social convenience" related to projects for supplying sports facilities to a local community is defined. The proposed composite indicator comprehends both environmental aspects, as well as appropriate social aspects. Furthermore, a composite index of "overall social convenience", also called "overall sustainability", for the same projects is defined. It synthesizes the environmental, social and financial aspects.

Various reasons can explain the preference commonly given to the use of procedures based on additive value functions in the construction of synthetic indexes of sustainability:

- the modeling of preferences is rather intuitive and therefore easily understandable by non-experts;
- the value functions assign a comprehensive value to each alternative and not a measure of the degree of preference of an alternative over another;
- unlike the outranking methods, the comparability of alternatives is always possible [22];
- the outcomes are robust due to the independent evaluation of each alternative [28].

The above-mentioned reasons also justify the decision to use the MAUT approach, in the weighted linear form, for the formulation of an index of social convenience relating to investments for the creation or adaptation of sports facilities [29]. Furthermore, MAUT approaches allow for compensation among the different points of view integrated in the assessment procedure [22], with the result being agreeable to the assumption of a weak conception of sustainability [8], that is suitable for local contexts with several social needs to be satisfied.

With the aim of testing the results obtained with different aggregation techniques, in relation to the conception of sustainability in the strong or weak sense, in the present study, a comparison is made between the results achieved with the use of a compensatory aggregation procedure and of one that tends to partly compensate for the poor performance on some criteria with the favorable performance on other criteria. Therefore, the outcomes of the available alternatives' evaluation through the weighted linear sum aggregation model, in the simplified version SMART (simple multi-attribute rating technique), will be compared to those obtained by using a less compensatory aggregation technique. In particular, the PROMETHEE II procedure will be used. The choice of the two aggregation procedures is justified in the following section.

4. Reasons for the Choice of Aggregation Procedures

Using multi-criteria assessments for real decision-making problems in the public sector, the easiness of understanding the method and the minimum request for preference information from the decision-makers have been highlighted as key features of a suitable decision-making model [6]. Since in the evaluation process for the formulation of the aggregate index of the investments' social convenience, the role of the decision-maker is held by political institutions, in general not equipped with specific skills in the field of mathematical techniques for multi-criteria evaluation; the simplicity of the method is considered essential for the contribution of the decision-makers in eliciting their preferences, with it being more conscious and less prone to errors of interpretation.

As stated, the use of the MAUT approach is a widespread choice in the elaboration of sustainability indexes. In view of the difficulties detected in practice for defining the trade-off between the criteria [28] and due to the lack of information on the marginal utility functions, it was decided to resort to the simplified formulation of the linear model MAUT, known as SMART. In contrast to the SMART method, which like the other additive models is fully compensatory, an outranking method is used. Procedures belonging to this class may have more or less a degree of compensation between the criteria [22].

Endowed with a greater comprehensibility for the decision-makers than ELECTRE methods [30], the PROMETHEE II procedure is implemented here. It provides a single complete preorder, although the non-compensatory level is more limited compared to other ELECTRE methods, in particular in the absence of thresholds of preference, indifference and veto [31]. Applying the PROMETHEE II, we opt for the functional form of the "usual criterion", which avoids the definition of indifference and/or preference thresholds, which is typically a complex [28,31,32] and time-consuming [33] exercise for decision-makers. Neglecting the use of thresholds implies that any difference between two evaluations produces a strict preference for the alternative having a better, even if small, evaluation with respect the considered criterion.

SMART and PROMETHEE II are relatively simple multi-criteria evaluation procedures and therefore easily comprehensible by non-expert actors involved in the assessment. In particular, as previously mentioned, among the possible forms adoptable for the preference function of the outranking procedure, the "usual criterion" is chosen, since it does not require the definition of additional parameters and whose understanding is intuitive. The application domains of both procedures fit our decision problem [34], since they can treat discrete cardinal and ordinal information; they can also solve choice and ranking decision problems; they use the same type of inter-information between criteria, since weights reflect the relative importance between criteria [21,35]; they can be implemented using a simple spreadsheet. In addition, weights do not depend on the measurement scale of the criteria, both in the PROMETHEE II procedure [30] and in SMART, since in the latter, the measurement scales are normalized [35]. These circumstances make their task easier for decision-makers [33] and allow for the comparison of the results obtained by the two procedures.

5. Insertion of the Present Work in Literature Reviews

SMART and PROMETHEE methods are among the most used aggregation tools and have been applied to a wide variety of decision problems.

A literature review up to the year 2010 is given by Behzadian *et al.* [30], revealing an abundant production of the applications of PROMETHEE methods concerning logistic and transportation problems; energy, water, environment and business management; chemistry, manufacturing and social topics. In more recent years, there has been a great deal of interest in applying the various PROMETHEE methods, and a large number of applications about the management of natural resources is available; see Kuang *et al.* [36]. Only a recent interest has been shown for the specific field of assessment for the sustainability of cities and territories. The surveyed applications are on decisions at a building scale [37], urban scale [32,38] and on an overall assessment of global cities [39].

The main application of SMART is on environmental management decisions [40–42], but it is also proposed for a public assessment application for mitigation and adaptation policy [43], as well as transport [44]. On an urban scale, it is used in assessing the sustainability of built heritage [45], local energy systems [46] and urban ecosystems [47–50].

The main aspects central to the present work are the comparison between different aggregation procedures in multicriteria assessment and the issue of weak and strong sustainability. Previous works have made comparisons between different assessment methods, according to the technical characteristics of algorithms, as in [16,51], in order to make choices coherent with sustainability assessment problems [23] or to compare the results with aided decisions [52]. Compared to previous works, we aim to compare the outcomes from different assessment methods with regard to the compensatory effect, and confronting SMART and PROMETHEE II, we exclude the use of thresholds, as in [51], in order to investigate the differences between the considered methods under maximum similarity conditions. Regarding sustainability assessment, there is a very large amount of literature on every sector and, in particular, urban areas, as in [53], while the issue of weak and strong sustainability has been mainly addressed from a methodological point of view [8,13,54–56]. Although there have been some specific applicatory works on regions [57], countries [58,59], fisheries [60] and urban heritage [61], the need to address the issue of assessment application on weak and strong sustainability [62] has been recognized. In this work, the SMART and PROMETHEE II methods are used to assess the sustainability of single public projects in an urban context. In particular, they are applied to a swimming pool ranking problem.

6. Aggregation by the SMART Procedure

The weighted linear aggregation is the usual procedure used in the computation of composite indicators. Using SMART, a simplified form of MAUT [35,63] given a set of alternatives $\{A_1, A_2, \ldots A_m\}$, a set of indicators $\{c_1, c_2, \ldots c_n\}$ and their respective weights $\{w_1, w_2, \ldots w_n\}$, a synthetic index (V)

related to the alternative j is obtained by applying a weighted additive aggregation model, according to the following mathematical rule:

$$V(A_i) = \sum_i v_{ij} \cdot w_i \quad i = 1, 2, ..., n \tag{1}$$

with:

$$\sum_i w_i = 1 \text{ and } 0 \leqslant w_i \leqslant 1 \tag{2}$$

where $v_{i,j}$ is the normalized performance value on the indicator ci and w_i is the normalized weight [8].

The assessment $v_{i,j}$ is standardized to a 0–1 scale, where zero and one represent the worst and best performances, respectively [36]. The weights can be assigned by the direct rating method, according to which raw weights are assigned to criteria ranked according to their importance, attributing a score of 10 to the least important criterion, then assigning increasing scores to the other criteria in relation to the first score and, finally, normalizing the sum of the assigned weights to one [35].

While in MAUT models, weights reflect both scale and importance, in SMART, weights reflect only importance, since the scales are transformed to a common basis [64].

7. Aggregation by the PROMETHEE II Procedure

PROMETHEE procedures are based on the outranking relation, according to which an alternative outranks another alternative if, given the preferences of the decision-makers, there are sufficient arguments for recognizing that the first alternative is not less preferable than the second one [22]. The construction of the outranking relation in the PROMETHEE II method is characterized by the use of variables and parameters that are easily understandable by unexperienced decision-makers [22].

Introduced by Brans and Vincke [21], the PROMETHEE methods have been used in applications related to multiple fields [32], but their use is not widespread in the construction of composite indicators.

Given a set of alternatives $\{A_1, A_2, ... A_m\}$ and a system of indicators $\{c_1, c_2, ... c_n\}$ with their respective weights $\{w_1, w_2, ... w_n\}$ and knowing the performances of alternatives on single criteria, the outranking degree corresponding to an ordered couple of alternatives (A_r, A_s) is defined by the aggregated preference index, expressing the preference of A_r over A_s according to all of the criteria [65]:

$$\pi(A_r, A_s) = \sum_{i=1}^{n} P_i(A_r, A_s) w_i \text{ with } i = 1, 2, ..., n \tag{3}$$

in which $P_i(A_r, A_s)$ is a preference function related to the criteria i. Preference functions are defined by suitable functional forms and associated parameters, assigning to the differences between the performance of two alternatives on a criterion, $d_i(A_r, A_s) = c_i(A_r) - c_i(A_s)$, a preference degree ranging from 0–1. Among the available forms of the preference function [65], the one able to better express the preferences of the decision-makers will be chosen for each criterion. In the proposed assessment model, the usual criterion has been adopted for all of the considered criteria. In case of a criterion i to be maximized, comparing the alternatives A_r and A_s, the usual criterion expresses a strict preference of A_r in comparison with A_s only if the difference di (A_r, A_s) is positive. The choice is founded on the need to use a very simple assessment model that can be easily understood by decision-makers and on the advisability of not requiring the use of a threshold of indifference and/or of strict preference. Thus, the generalized usual criterion does not require additional information in comparison to the simple formulation of MAUT considered here. The preference function related to the usual criterion is expressed as follows [65]:

$$P_i(A_r, A_s) = \begin{cases} 0 \text{ if } d_i(A_r, A_s) \leqslant 0 \\ 1 \text{ if } d_i(A_r, A_s) > 0 \end{cases} \tag{4}$$

This form of the generalized criterion corresponds to the "true criterion" [66], expressing a strict preference for any difference between two evaluations [67].

Finally, the PROMETHEE II procedure leads to a unique complete preorder ranking the alternatives according to a decreasing order of values of the net outranking flow $\varphi(A_r)$ for each alternative that is given by:

$$\varphi(A_r) = \varphi^+(A_r) - \varphi^-(A_r) \tag{5}$$

where $\varphi^+(A_r)$ is the positive flow and $\varphi^-(A_r)$ is the negative flow, representing how the alternative A_r outranks the other ones and how A_r is outranked by the other alternatives. Positive and negative flows are expressed as follows [65]:

$$\varphi^+(A_r) = \frac{1}{m-1} \sum_{k \neq i} \pi(A_r, A_s) \text{ with } r = 1, 2, ..., m \tag{6}$$

$$\varphi^-(A_r) = \frac{1}{m-1} \sum_{k \neq i} \pi(A_s, A_r) \text{ with } r = 1, 2, ..., m \tag{7}$$

8. Three Projects for Municipal Pools in the Province of Salerno (Italy)

8.1. The swimming pool in Nocera Inferiore

The project involves the construction of an indoor swimming center to be built in the town of Nocera Inferiore (Salerno). The plant will be able to be approved by the Italian Swimming Federation, based on the safety standards of the Italian Olympic National Committee (CONI) and the Ministry of Interior, which set the size of the tanks according to the activities that must take place. The plant is designed to emit into the atmosphere the least possible amount of pollutants and adopts alternative methods of energy production, in the present case thermo-photovoltaic hybrid panels.

The project involves the construction of a semi-Olympic indoor pool with a size of 25 per 16.66 m and of two smaller swimming pools of 16.66 per 8 m, one dedicated to children and the other for rehabilitation activities and water aerobics. Some services dedicated to users are also planned. They include a bar, a solarium, a sauna and a gym. The structure is articulated on a single level consisting of a space for the swimming pools and a service block. The structure of external cladding of the service block will be made of panels with improved thermal performances, while the coverage of the swimming pool area will be in curved laminated wood.

8.2. The swimming pool in Sapri

This swimming pool will be realized in the city of Sapri, more precisely in the south, in Brizzi, close to the town center. Currently, the area is a sports ground, and with the realization of the structure, it will become a real sports center. This project involves the construction of a concrete structure cast *in situ* to be used as a reception and dressing room for athletes. The construction of the roof of the swimming pool is planned in precast prestressed concrete.

The pool for sports (swimming, water polo) has dimensions of 12.60 m for 25.00 m and a constant depth of 2.00 m, with an area of 315 m² and a volume of 630 m³. The flat roof around the pool will have a width of 2.50 m along the long side and of 4.00 m along the other side, according to the norms of the Italian Olympic National Committee (CONI).

The pool cover, entirely prefabricated, will consist of prestressed elements and pillars, with a total area of 747 m² (40.60 m for 18.40 m) and a practicable deck.

8.3. The swimming pool in Salerno

The plant is located in the center of Salerno. The project will cover the top of the adult pool, the reconstruction of the same pool, the construction of adjacent changing rooms, the renovation of the existing building and the installation of parking areas equipped with photovoltaic shelters. The projected plant includes an outdoor swimming pool of 28 m × 20 m × 1.60 m, an outdoor swimming pool for children of 11 m × 6 m × 0.50 m, a solarium around the swimming pools, two changing rooms with toilets and showers, a waiting room with reception, an infirmary, a bar room, an engine room, a boiler room, an outdoor parking area for about fifty cars and a green area adjacent to the swimming plant.

9. Calculation of the Composite Indicators for the Three Municipal Pools

Relevant indicators have been selected on the basis of an in-depth analysis of the local context conducted by the provincial public authority [68], as well as data taken from ISTAT (Istituto Nazionale di Statistica—National Institute of Statistics) on the local social, environmental and economic characteristics. According to ISTAT, young people are the main users of sports facilities; some student associations as the potential user basin of each swimming pool were involved in a discussion aimed at understanding their opinions about what features they expected a sustainable swimming pool should have. Table 1 presents the final value tree, including the goal, criteria and indicators, while Table 2 describes the single indicators, and Table 3 shows their direction and the measurement scales. The set of selected criteria represents all of the key sustainability aspects in relation to the specific context, avoiding redundancy [66].

While the environmental and social aspects define the "restricted social convenience" of the investments in question, the addition of the pre-taxation internal rate of return allows for the assessment of the "overall sustainability", which integrates the financial feasibility.

The aesthetic quality of the projects has not been included in the set of criteria, because the alternatives can be considered as having the same level of architectonic quality.

While indicators I1, I4, I6 and I7 are measured in their natural scales, indicators I2, I3 and I5 express qualitative judgments. Their levels of performance are measured according to the values shown in Table 4.

Table 1. Value tree.

Goal	Criteria	Codes-Indicators
Overall sustainability	Environmental issues	I1—Spared emissions from plants I2—Preservation of natural land I3—Accessibility
	Social issues	I4—Level of supply of swimming services I5—Synergistic effect I6—Employment effect
	Financial issue	I7—Pre-taxation internal rate of return

Table 2. Description of indicators.

Codes-Indicators	Description
I1—Spared emissions from plants	It measures the spared emission of CO_2 per user due to the reduction of energy consumption from traditional energy sources
I2—Preservation of natural land	It expresses the quality of a project regarding the shift of natural land to artificial areas
I3—Accessibility	It regards the presence of dedicated parking for users and the quality of a suitable public transport service
I4—Level of supply of swimming services	It concerns the level of the supply of swimming services against the local level of demand.
I5—Synergistic effect	It is achieved if the swimming plant is localized near other sports facilities, creating an integrated system of sports facilities useful also as a center for social gathering
I6—Employment effect	It expresses the contribution to the development of new employment
I7—Pre-taxation internal rate of return	It expresses the financial feasibility of the investment

Table 3. Information on indicators.

Codes-Indicators	Direction	Measurement Scale
I1—Spared emissions from plants	To be maximized	kg CO_2/year
I2—Preservation of natural land	To be maximized	Judgment measured on an ordinal scale
I3—Accessibility	To be maximized	Judgment measured on an ordinal scale
I4—Level of supply of swimming services	To be maximized	Supply of swimming services/relative demand
I5—Synergistic effect	To be maximized	Judgment measured on an ordinal scale
I6—Employment effect	To be maximized	Number of employees
I7—Pre-taxation internal rate of return	To be maximized	Value on 0–1 scale

Table 4. Levels of performance for indicators I2, I3 and I5.

I2		I3		I5	
Performance-Score		Performance-Score		Performance-Score	
Reuse of already built land	10	Presence of dedicated parking and of a suitable public transport service	10	Nearness to more than one sports facility	10
		Presence of dedicated parking and of an insufficient public transport service	5	Nearness to one sports facility	5
Shifting of natural land to artificial area	0	Absence of dedicated parking and of a suitable public transport service	0	Nearness to no sports facility	0

Table 5 summarizes the performance of the considered projects for swimming facilities on the set of indicators. The projects cover three geographical areas of the province of Salerno, which are the city of Salerno, the city of Nocera and the city of Sapri.

Table 5. Performance table.

Indicators		Projects		
		Salerno	Nocera	Sapri
Environmental issues	I1 (kg CO_2/year)	81,620	80,465	106,000
	I2 (ordinal judgment)	10	0	0
	I3 (ordinal judgment)	10	5	5
Social issues	I4 (supply/demand)	0.96	1	1
	I5 (ordinal judgment)	5	10	5
	I6 (number of employees)	25	40	15
Fin. issue	I7 (Pre-taxation internal rate of return)	0.129	0.117	0.140

For the purposes of the aggregation of the performances of the alternatives using the SMART method, we consider the standardized marginal utility functions assigning the value one to the best performance according to the considered indicator and the value zero to the worst one with the linear form of marginal utilities for indicators.

The aggregation of performances by the PROMETHEE II method does not require the transformation into a common scale, thanks to a pairwise comparison between the alternatives.

Initially, we calculated the synthetic index of the "restricted" social convenience relative to the alternatives under consideration. Regarding the weights, in the first assessment, we attached the same value to all of the indicators (0.166), by giving the same importance to the social and environmental criteria. This choice is justified by the consideration that the social and environmental issues are the main topics of sustainability in the considered local context.

Using the "distance from the best and worst performers" technique [6], the normalized performance table is obtained (Table 6).

Finally, according to Equations (1) and (5), the composite indicators of the restricted social convenience (RSC) related to the considered projects are calculated (Table 7). They express the environmental and social quality of each project.

The local administrations involved can choose the system of weights that best suit their policies. The composite indicators shown in Table 7 refer to a situation in which the same importance is attached to individual indicators and then to the two social and environmental criteria. However, if the social aspects are considered doubly more important than the environmental ones, the composite indicators will become the RSC' ones of Table 8.

Table 6. Normalized performance table.

Criteria	Projects		
	Salerno	Nocera	Sapri
I1	0.05	0	1
I2	1	0	0
I3	1	0	0
I4	0	1	1
I5	0	1	0
I6	0.40	1	0

Table 7. Composite indicators of social convenience obtained by assuming equal importance of the social and environmental aspects. RSC, restricted social convenience; SMART, simple multi-attribute rating technique.

Projects	Composite Indicators	
	RSC (SMART)	RSC (PROM.)
Salerno	0.41	0.083
Nocera	0.50	0.082
Sapri	0.33	−0.167

On the contrary, if the environmental issues are twice preferred in comparison to the social issues, the requested synthetic indexes are those in the columns RSC" of Table 8. The different preferences related to the relative importance among the indicators could still be considered to better represent the preferences of the decision-maker.

Table 8. Composite indicators of social convenience obtained taking a double preference for the social aspects with respect to the environmental ones (RSC') and *vice versa* (RSC").

Projects	RSC' (SMART)	RSC' (PROM.)	RSC" (SMART)	RSC" (PROM.)
Salerno	0.316	−0.111	0.499	0.278
Nocera	0.667	0.333	0.333	−0.167
Sapri	0.333	−0.222	0.333	−0.111

We then calculated the composite indicators of the overall sustainability (SC) obtained by integrating in the evaluation the contribution of the financial feasibility to the aspects of social convenience.

Table 9 shows the composite indexes of integrated sustainability obtained with the SMART and PROMETHEE II procedures assuming equal importance to the three categories (the social, environmental and financial one) of the indicators.

Table 9. Composite indicators of integrated sustainability obtained by assuming equal importance for the social, environmental and financial aspects.

Projects	Composite Indicators	
	SC (SMART)	SC (PROM.)
Salerno	0.449	0.055
Nocera	0.333	−0.278
Sapri	0.555	0.222

Finally, Table 10 presents the aggregate indices obtained by attributing to the social aspects a double importance compared to the environmental ones, while the environmental and financial aspects are considered of equal importance (SC′) and the aggregate indices obtained by giving to the environmental aspects a double importance in comparison to the social ones, while the financial and social aspects are considered of equal importance (SC″).

Table 10. Composite indicators of integrated sustainability obtained by assuming a double preference for the social aspects over the environmental and financial ones (SC′) and *vice versa* (SC″).

Projects	SC′ (SMART)	SC′ (PROM.)	SC″ (SMART)	SC″ (PROM.)
Salerno	0.371	−0.083	0.509	0.208
Nocera	0.501	0.000	0.250	−0.375
Sapri	0.500	0.083	0.500	0.167

10. Summary and Discussion of the Results

In this paper, the simplified linear aggregative model SMART and the PROMETHEE II model have been tested with the aim of verifying their utility in the elaboration of synthetic indexes for the choice or ranking of investments in urban development. Table 11 presents the rankings obtained through the use of the two procedures for the aggregation of the partial evaluation of the alternatives on the criteria.

As expected, the outcomes of the evaluation carried out by the considered methods lead to different scenarios. The comparison between the evaluation table (Table 3) and the ranking table (Table 11) induces the following considerations.

Assuming the same importance attributed to the classes of indicators, the exclusion of the financial parameter in the valuation of the synthetic index penalizes the investment in the territory of Sapri, which is the most disadvantaged for two out of three indicators for both the social category and the environmental aspects. Using SMART, the best performances of the alternative A2 (Nocera) on the social indicators offset the very bad performances on the environmental aspects. On the contrary, PROMETHEE II rewards the more balanced performances of the alternative A1 (Salerno).

If an equal importance is recognized for the various classes of indicators, the inclusion of the financial parameter in the evaluation of the synthetic index reverses the ranking of the investment in Sapri, which is the most disadvantaged for two out of three indicators for both the social and environmental categories. The drawback is re-balanced by the best financial performance.

Assuming a greater importance is attributed to the class of indicators on the social aspects compared to all of the remaining considered classes, the exclusion of the financial parameter in the evaluation of the synthetic index rewards, using both aggregation procedures, the investment in the territory of Nocera, which has the best performance on the social category. For the successive positions of the ranking, while PROMETHEE II awards the most balanced performances for the environmental aspects of the alternative A1-Salerno, SMART gives the highest-ranking to the alternative A3-Sapri, for which the best performance on the indicator I1 is able to balance the bad performances on the remaining environmental indicators. Analogous considerations can be made about the remaining rankings.

Nevertheless, the analysis of the results outlines some clearly legible trends.

Table 11. The obtained rankings.

RSC (SMART)	RSC (PROM.)
Nocera	Salerno
Salerno	Nocera
Sapri	Sapri
SC (SMART)	**SC (PROM.)**
Sapri	Sapri
Salerno	Salerno
Nocera	Nocera
RSC′ (SMART)	**RSC′ (PROM.)**
Nocera	Nocera
Sapri	Salerno
Salerno	Sapri
SC′ (SMART)	**SC′ (PROM.)**
Nocera	Sapri
Sapri	Nocera
Salerno	Salerno
RSC″ (SMART)	**RSC″ (PROM.)**
Salerno	Salerno
Nocera-Sapri	Sapri
Nocera-Sapri	Nocera
SC″ (SMART)	**SC″ (PROM.)**
Salerno	Salerno
Sapri	Sapri
Nocera	Nocera

In the aggregation carried out neglecting the financial criterion, both aggregative models indicate that the project in Sapri is the poorer. In fact, four times it is the last in the ranking, and two times it is penultimate. On the contrary, the projects in Nocera and Salerno share the leadership, with three first positions and two second places in the rankings.

Moreover, the compensatory effect of the procedure SMART seems to show itself. In fact, the procedure favors the project in Nocera (two first places and one second place in the rankings), whose profile of performances consists of three maximum values and three minimum values (see Table 4). Instead, the PROMETHEE method favors the project with a more balanced profile (Salerno; two times in the first position in the rankings and one time in the second position).

The outlined framework dismantles itself with the introduction of the financial criterion. First, the project in Sapri becomes by far the dominant one (three times it is in the first position of the rankings and three times first in the second one). It is followed by the project in Salerno (two times in the first position of the rankings and two times in the second one) and then by the project in Nocera (one time in the first position of the rankings and one time in the second one).

However, what is most striking is the substantial stabilization of the rankings obtained using the two methods. In developing the indices SC and SC″, the rankings obtained by the two methods do not change. Sapri-Salerno-Nocera is the ranking outlined applying both SMART and PROMETHEE in the calculus of the index SC. Salerno-Sapri-Nocera is the ranking obtained using both SMART and PROMETHEE for the index SC″. In the calculation of SC′, the project in Salerno always occupies the third position in the rankings, regardless of the used aggregation procedure, while the projects in Nocera and Sapri are reversed in the leadership.

This last evidence has strategic implications that deserve attention. The substantial stabilization of the results achieved using a more compensatory aggregation procedure (SMART) or a less compensatory one (PROMETHEE) leads to distrust of easy propaganda proclamations. In fact, it would be easy for decision-makers to convey the use of a non-compensatory aggregation procedure as a political choice of strong sustainability, when the same results are reached using a compensatory method. Therefore, in such cases, the prevalence of a project over another one does not arise from the application of stricter selective rules, but from the same nature of the projects that shows a very stable relative placement (obviously with respect to the introduced criteria).

11. Conclusions

As previously stated, the reconciliation of social, environmental and financial requirements places decision-makers in front of scenarios that are often complex, articulated or even conflicting. Multicriteria analysis techniques can support decision-makers in making aware and rational choices.

In comparison with the analysis carried out by the same authors in a previous work [29] where the rankings of the considered investments for supplying swimming pools in the south of Italy were completely opposite when a sustainable approach from an exclusively socio-environmental point of view or a merely financial approach were alternatively considered, the analysis presented in this paper characterizes the use of a multicriteria technique and a more articulated pattern of evaluation with regards to the considered set of weights.

Unlike the previously mentioned experiences, the new pattern of valuation combines the financial profile with the socio-environmental one in the versions SC' and SC", and this integration destabilizes the previously obtained rankings.

In fact, if the overall effects are considered, the investment in Sapri, which according to the first analysis conducted neglecting the financial criterion ranks four times out of six in the bottom position, rises to a top position three times out of six when the financial criterion is taken into consideration. The investment in Nocera, which was the best one three times out of six, ranks in the bottom position four times out of six.

However, the main difference is recorded for the investment in Salerno. If only the criteria belonging to the social and environmental class are considered when calculating the synthetic index [29], it ranks in an intermediate position, both attributing a greater importance to the socio-environmental aspects. In the new implementation, it has a better position in the rankings, whether the financial criterion is neglected or is taken into consideration.

Figure 1 shows the prevailing projects according to the considered assessment procedures. Using SMART, the project in Nocera prevails three times over the others, while using PROMETHEE, the more balanced project in Salerno is preferred three times. This result confirms the less compensative effect of the used outranking method.

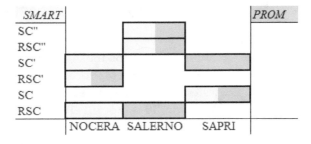

Figure 1. Prevailing projects according to the considered aggregation methods

The present analysis, which deserves further investigation from the point of view of the stability of outcomes on the basis of statistical techniques, highlights the huge responsibility of decision-makers when choices are also based on social and environmental principles and not merely on monetary criteria, even if a multidimensional assessment is carried out. This consideration is confirmed by the strictness imposed by the European Commission on the management of public funds, but also poses limits that must be revised when funds are of a private nature, considering the levels of profitability that can be shared with the community.

Another interesting development of this work could be a comparison of the outcomes of the assessment methods used with those coming from the use of specific aggregation procedures able to include interaction effects among the criteria, such as the Choquet integral or the ELECTRE III method with interactions between the criteria [69], in order to consider the different levels of strong and weak compensability.

Finally, it should be noted that the results of the implemented calculations seem to indicate that certain investment projects have performances on the criteria that make the rankings obtained robust through more or less compensatory aggregation procedures. This condition, where conveniently checked on a larger sample of study, leads to repudiation of the necessity of the adoption of a non-compensatory aggregation procedure in order to obtain a decision of strong sustainability. The adoption could instead simply hide manipulative intentions in the choices on the allocation of public resources.

Acknowledgments: The authors are grateful to the anonymous reviewers for the valuable comments that contributed to the improvement of the manuscript.

Author Contributions: The authors contributed equally to this work.

References

1.   Fusco Girard, L., Ed.; *Le Valutazioni per lo Sviluppo Sostenibile Della Città e del Territorio*; FrancoAngeli: Milano, Italy, 1997.

2.   Nijkamp, P., (Ed.) *Sustainability of Urban System*; Aldershot: Avebury, UK, 1990.

3.   Rizzo, F. *Il Capitale Sociale Della Città. Valutazione, Pianificazione e Gestione*; Franco Angeli: Milano, Italy, 2003.

4.   De Mare, G.; Nesticò, A.; Tajani, F. Building Investments for the Revitalization of the Territory: A Multisectoral Model of Economic Analysis. In Proceedings of the 3th International Conference, ICCSA 2013, Ho Chi Minh City, Vietnam, 24–27 June 2013; Murgante, B., Misra, S., Carlini, M., Torre, C., Nguyen, H.-Q., Taniar, D., Apduhan, B.O., Gervasi, O., Eds.; Springer Verlag: Berlin, Germany; Heidelberg, Germany, 2013; Volume 7973, pp. 493–508.

5.   European Ministers Responsible for Urban Development. *Leipzig Charter on Sustainable European Cities. Final Draft*; European Ministers Responsible for Urban Development: Leipzig, Germany, 2007.

6.   Lahdelma, R.; Salminen, P.; Hokkanen, J. Using Multicriteria Methods in Environmental Planning and Management. *Environ. Manag.* **2000**, *26*, 595–605. [CrossRef] [PubMed]

7.   Daly, H.E.; Cobb, J.B., Jr. *For the Common Good*; Beacon Press: Boston, MA, USA, 1989.

8.   Munda, G. Multiple Criteria Decision analysis and Sustainable Development. In *Multiple Criteria Decision Analysis: State of the Art Surveys*; Figueira, J., Greco, S., Ehrgott, M., Eds.; Springer: New York, NY, USA, 2005; pp. 953–986.

9.   Munda, G. *Social Multi-Criteria Evaluation*; Springer-Verlag: Heidelberg, Germany; New York, NY, USA, 2007.

10.   Bob, C.; Dencsak, T.; Bob, L. A Sustainability Model for the Assessment of Civil Engineer Works. In *Recent Advances in Energy, Environment, Biology and Ecology*, Proceedings of the 10th WSEAS International Conference on Energy, Environment, Ecosystems and Sustainable Development (EEESD '14), Tenerife, Spain, 10–12 January 2014; WSEAS Press: Sofia, Bulgaria, 2014; pp. 161–168.

11.   Lazăr, C.; Lazăr, M. Proposal of a sustainable development synthetic indicator at local level. In Proceedings of the 9th WSEAS International Conference on Mathematics & Computers in Business and Economics (MCBE '08), Bucharest, Romania, 24–26 June 2008; WSEAS Press: Sofia, Bulgaria, 2008; pp. 74–78.

12.   OECD. *JRC European Commission, Handbook on Constructing Composite Indicators. Methodology and User Guide*; OECD Publishing: Paris, France, 2008.

13. Munda, G. Choosing aggregation rules for composite indicators. *Soc. Indic. Res.* **2012**, *109*, 337–354. [CrossRef]
14. Granata, M.F. The city management: Methodological Considerations on the Multiple Criteria Techniques. In *The Right to the City. Human Rights and the City Crisis*; Beguinot, C., Ed.; Giannini Editore: Naples, Italy, 2012; pp. 295–319.
15. Sustainable Cities International—Canadian International Development Agency. *Indicators for Sustainability. How Cities Are Monitoring and Evaluating Their Success*; Sustainable Cities International—Canadian International Development Agency: Vancouver, BC, Canada, 2012.
16. Olson, D.L. Comparison of three multicriteria methods to predict known outcomes. *Eur. J. Oper. Res.* **2001**, *130*, 576–587. [CrossRef]
17. Von Neumann, J.; Morgenstern, O. *Theory of Games and Economic Behaviour*, 2nd ed.; Princeton University Press: Princeton, NJ, USA, 1947.
18. Keeney, R.L.; Raiffa, H. *Decisions with Multiple Objectives Preferences and Value Tradeoffs*; John Wiley&Sons: New York, NY, USA, 1976.
19. Roy, B. Classement et choix en presence de points de vue multiples (la méthode ELECTRE). *RAIRO* **1968**, *8*, 57–75.
20. Figueira, J.; Greco, S.; Ehrgott, M. Introduction. In *Multiple Criteria Decision Analysis: State of the Art Surveys*; Figueira, J., Greco, S., Ehrgott, M., Eds.; Springer: New York, NY, USA, 2005; pp. xxi–xxxvi.
21. Vincke, P.; Brans, J.P. A preference ranking organization method. The PROMETHEE method for MCDM. *Manag. Sci.* **1985**, *31*, 641–656.
22. Vincke, P. *Multicriteria Decision-Aid*; John Wiley & Sons: Chichester, UK, 1992.
23. De Montis, A.; de Toro, P.; Droste-Franke, B.; Omann, I.; Stagl, S. Assessing the quality of different MCDA methods. In *Alternatives for Environmental Valuation*; Getzner, M., Spash, C., Stagl, S., Eds.; Routledge: London, UK, 2005; pp. 99–133.
24. Yager, R.R. On ordered weighted averaging aggregation operators in multi-criteria decision making. *IEEE Trans. Syst. Man Cybernet. Part B* **1988**, *18*, 183–190. [CrossRef]
25. Choquet, G. Theory of capacities. *Ann. de l'Inst. Fourier* **1953**, *5*, 131–295. [CrossRef]
26. Sugeno, M. Theory of Fuzzy Integrals and Its Applications. Ph.D. Thesis, Tokyo Institute of Technology, Tokyo, Japan, 1974.
27. Grabisch, M. The application of fuzzy integrals in multicriteria decision making. *Eur. J. Oper. Res.* **1996**, *89*, 445–456. [CrossRef]
28. Munda, G. The issue of consistency: Basic discrete multi-criteria "Methods". In *Social Multi-Criteria Evaluation for a Sustainable Economy*; Munda, G., Ed.; Springer-Verlag: Berlin, Germany; Heidelberg, Germany, 2008; pp. 85–109.
29. De Mare, G.; Granata, M.F.; Nesticò, A. Complex efficiency of sports facilities. Multicriteria and financial analysis for swimming pools. In *Advances in Environmental and Geological Science and Engineering*, Proceedings of the 8th International Conference on Environmental and Geological Science and Engineering (EG '15), Salerno, Italy, 27–29 June 2015; WSEAS Press: Sofia, Bulgaria, 2015; pp. 96–103.
30. Behzadian, M.; Kazemzadeh, R.B.; Albadvi, A.; Aghdasi, M. PROMETHEE: A comprehensive literature review on methodologies and applications. *Eur. J. Oper. Res.* **2010**, *200*, 198–215. [CrossRef]
31. Polatidis, H.; Haralambopoulos, D.A.; Munda, G.; Vreeker, R. Selecting an appropriate multi-criteria decision analysis technique for renewable energy planning. *Energy Sources Part B* **2006**, *1*, 181–193. [CrossRef]
32. Cilona, T.; Granata, M.F. Multicriteria Prioritization for Multistage Implementation of Complex Urban Renewal Projects. In Proceedings of the 15th International Conference Computational Science and Its Applications—ICCSA 2015, Banff, BC, Canada, 22–25 June 2015; Gervasi, O., Murgante, B., Misra, S., Gavrilova, M.L., Rocha, A.M.A.C., Torre, C., Taniar, D., Apduhan, B.O., Eds.; Part III, LNCS 9157. Springer Verlag: Berlin, Germany; Heidelberg, Germany, 2015; pp. 3–19.
33. Cinelli, M.; Coles, S.R.; Kirwan, K. Analysis of the potentials of multi criteria decision analysis methods to conduct sustainability assessment. *Ecol. Indic.* **2014**, *46*, 138–148. [CrossRef]
34. Guitouni, A.; Martel, J.M. Tentative guidelines to help choosing an appropriate MCDA Method. *Eur. J. Oper. Res.* **1998**, *109*, 501–521. [CrossRef]
35. Von Winterfeldt, D.; Edwards, W. *Decision Analysis and Behavioral Research*; Cambridge University Press: Cambridge, UK, 1986.

36. Kuang, H.; Kilgour, D.M.; Hipel, K.W. Grey-based PROMETHEE II with application to evaluation of source water protection strategies. *Inf. Sci.* **2015**, *294*, 376–389. [CrossRef]

37. Le Téno, J.F.; Mareschal, B. An interval version of PROMETHEE for the comparison of building products' design with ill-defined data on environmental quality. *Eur. J. Oper. Res.* **1998**, *109*, 522–529. [CrossRef]

38. Juan, Y.-K.; Roper, K.O.; Castro-Lacouture, D.; Kim, J.H. Optimal decision making on urban renewal projects. *Manag. Decis.* **2010**, *48*, 207–224. [CrossRef]

39. Kourtit, K.; Macharis, C.; Nijkamp, P. A multi-actor multi-criteria analysis of the performance of global cities. *Appl. Geogr.* **2014**, *49*, 24–36. [CrossRef]

40. Ulvila, J.W.; Snider, W.D. Negotiation of international oil tanker standards: An application of multiattribute value theory. *Oper. Res.* **1980**, *28*, 81–96. [CrossRef]

41. Comer, J.L.; Kirkwood, C.W. Decision analysis applications in the operations research literature 1970–1989. *Oper. Res.* **1991**, *39*, 206–219.

42. Taylor, J.M., Jr.; Love, B.N. Simple multi-attribute rating technique for renewable energy deployment decisions (SMART REDD). *J. Def. Model. Simulat. Appl. Methodol. Technol.* **2014**, *11*, 227–232. [CrossRef]

43. Papadopoulos, A.M., Konidari, P., Eds.; *Overview and Selection of Multi-Criteria Evaluation Methods for Mitigation/Adaptation Policy Instruments*; PROMITHEAS—4: Athens, Greece, 2011.

44. Barfod, M.B., Leleur, M., Eds.; *Multi-Criteria Decision Analysis for Use in Transport Decision Making*, 2nd ed.; Technical University of Denmark: Copenhagen, Denmark, 2014.

45. Dutta, M.; Husain, Z. An application of Multicriteria Decision Making to Built Heritage. The case of Calcutta. *J. Cult. Herit.* **2009**, *10*, 237–243. [CrossRef]

46. Kılkış, S. Composite index for benchmarking local energy systems of Mediterranean port cities. *Energy* **2015**. [CrossRef]

47. Kılkış, S. Sustainable development of energy, water and environment systems index for Southeast European cities. *J. Clean. Product.* **2015**. [CrossRef]

48. Dizdaroglu, D.; Yigitcanlar, T. A parcel-scale assessment tool to measure sustainability through urban ecosystem components: The MUSIX model. *Ecol. Indic.* **2014**, *41*, 115–130. [CrossRef]

49. Dizdaroglu, D.; Yigitcanlar, T.; Dawes, L. A micro-level indexing model for assessing urban ecosystem sustainability. *Smart Sustain. Built Environ.* **2012**, *1*, 291–315. [CrossRef]

50. Yigitcanlar, T.; Dur, F.; Dizdaroglu, D. Towards prosperous sustainable cities: A multiscalar urban sustainability assessment approach. *Habitat Int.* **2015**, *45*, 36–46. [CrossRef]

51. Salminen, P.; Hokkanen, J.; Lahdelma, R. Comparing multicriteria methods in the context of environmental problems. *Eur. J. Oper. Res.* **1998**, *104*, 485–496. [CrossRef]

52. Hajkowicz, S. A comparison of multiple criteria analysis and unaided approaches to environmental decision making. *Environ. Sci. Policy* **2007**, *10*, 177–184. [CrossRef]

53. Kostevšek, A.; Klemeš, J.J.; Varbanov, P.S.; Čuček, L.; Petek, J. Sustainability assessment of the locally integrated energy sectors for a Slovenian municipality. *J. Clean. Product.* **2015**, *88*, 83–89. [CrossRef]

54. Roy, B. Decision aid and decision making. In *Readings in Multiple Criteria Decision Aid*; Bana e Costa, C.A., Ed.; Springer-Verlag: Berlin, Germany; Heidelberg, Germany, 1990; pp. 17–35.

55. Munda, G. Intensity of preference and related uncertainty in non-compensatory aggregation rules. *Theory Decis.* **2012**, *73*, 649–669. [CrossRef]

56. Pollesch, N.; Dale, V.H. Applications of aggregation theory to sustainability assessment. *Ecol. Econ.* **2015**, *114*, 117–127. [CrossRef]

57. Floridi, M.; Pagni, S.; Falorni, S.; Luzzati, T. An exercise in composite indicators construction: Assessing the sustainability of Italian regions. *Ecol. Econ.* **2011**, *70*, 1440–1447. [CrossRef]

58. Ostasiewicz, K. Ordering EU countries according to indicators of sustainable development. *Statistika* **2012**, *49*, 30–51.

59. Dietz, S.; Neumayer, E. Weak and strong sustainability in the SEEA: Concepts and measurement. *Ecol. Econ.* **2007**, *61*, 617–626. [CrossRef]

60. Garmendia, E.; Prellezo, R.; Murillas, A.; Escapa, M.; Gallastegui, M. Weak and strong sustainability assessment in fisheries. *Ecol. Econ.* **2010**, *70*, 96–106. [CrossRef]

61. Dalmas, L.; Geronimi, V.; Noël, J.-F.; Sang, J.T.K. Economic evaluation of urban heritage: An inclusive approach under a sustainability perspective. *J. Cult. Herit.* **2015**, *16*, 681–687. [CrossRef]

62. Janeiro, L.; Patel, M.K. Choosing sustainable technologies. Implications of the underlying sustainability paradigm in the decision-making process. *J. Clean. Product.* **2015**, *105*, 438–446. [CrossRef]

63. Edwards, W. How to use multiattribute utility measurement for social decision making. *IEEE Trans. Syst. Man Cybernet.* **1977**, *7*, 326–340. [CrossRef]

64. Edwards, W.; Barron, F.H. Smarts and Smarter: Improved Simple Methods for Multi Attribute Utility Measurement. *Organ. Behav. Hum. Decis. Process.* **1994**, *60*, 306–325. [CrossRef]

65. Brans, J.P.; Mareschal, B. Promethee methods. In *Multiple Criteria Decision Analysis: State of the Art Surveys*; Figueira, J., Greco, S., Ehrgott, M., Eds.; Springer: New York, NY, USA, 2005; pp. 163–195.

66. Roy, B. *Méthodologie Multicritère d'Aide à la Décison*; Economica: Paris, France, 1985.

67. Bouyssou, D. Building criteria: A prerequisite for MCDA. In *Readings in Multiple Criteria Decision Aid*; Bana e Costa, C.A., Ed.; Springer-Verlag: Berlin, Germany; Heidelberg, Germany, 1990; pp. 58–80.

68. Relazione Previsionale e Programmatica 2012–2014. Available online: http://googo.pw/url?sa=t&rct=j&q=&esrc=s&source=web&cd=1&ved=0ahUKEwiFwNDpxa3JAhXBF5QKHedtB08QFggcMAA&url=http%3A%2F%2Fwww.comune.rozzano.mi.it%2Findex.php%2Fmodulistica%2Fdoc_download%2F697-relazione-previsionale-e-programmatica-2012-2014.html&usg=AFQjCNHewDYQAw5x7gsCoUT-9znqiRisOQ&cad=rja (accessed on 18 November 2015).

69. Figueira, J.R.; Greco, S.; Roy, B. ELECTRE methods with interaction between criteria: An extension of the concordance index. *Eur. J. Oper. Res.* **2009**, *199*, 478–495. [CrossRef]

13

Effects of Employees' Work Values and Organizational Management on Corporate Performance for Chinese and Taiwanese Construction Enterprises

Jeng-Wen Lin [1,*], Pu Fun Shen [2] and Yin-Sung Hsu [3]

[1] Department of Civil Engineering, Feng Chia University, Taichung 407, Taiwan
[2] Ph.D. Program in Civil and Hydraulic Engineering, Feng Chia University, Taichung 407, Taiwan; p0043264@fcu.edu.tw
[3] Department of Water Resources Engineering and Conservation, Feng Chia University, Taichung 407, Taiwan; yshsu@fcu.edu.tw
* Correspondence: jwlin@fcu.edu.tw.

Academic Editors: Adam Jabłoński and Giuseppe Ioppolo

Abstract: Through questionnaire surveys, this study explored the discrepancies in work values and organizational management between employees and cadre members of construction enterprises on the two sides of the Taiwan Strait. Statistical methods including data reliability, regression analysis, and tests of significance were utilized for modelling a case study. The findings of this study included: (1) in terms of work values, employees from China focused on their lives "at present", while those from Taiwan focused on their lives "in the future", expecting to improve the quality of their lives later on through advanced studies and promotion; (2) according to the data obtained from the questionnaires, the answers regarding income and welfare in terms of work values and satisfaction were contradictory on the two sides of the Strait, which could be interpreted in terms of influence from society; and (3) there was a significant influence of organizational management on employees' intentions to resign. If enterprises could improve current organizational management systems, their employees' work attitudes would be improved and the tendency to resign would be reduced.

Keywords: corporate performance; organizational management; questionnaire survey; test of significance; work value

---

1. Introduction

Employees' work values change from generation to generation. Understanding employees' work values has become a key issue for organizations aiming to achieve higher performances. Choi and Kim recognized the individual human resource (HR) as a core asset of corporate value creation and devoted significant effort to developing and managing competency-based HR in order to strengthen corporate competitiveness [1]. Jia et al. addressed the concern that generational changes could be reflected in various management aspects such as organizational structure, HR, and enterprise culture [2]. Chau et al. indicated how to provide construction managers with information about and insight into the existing data, so they could make decisions more effectively [3]. Park showed that the effect of resource coverage on project performance was quantified and the policy implications were determined for dynamic resource management by simulating the model with heuristic and industry data [4]. Scholars in China have started to study work values of employees on either side of the Taiwan Strait. Chen pointed out that with increasingly frequent economic and trade exchanges across the Taiwan Strait, interdependency between Taiwan and mainland China was increasingly higher [5]. Through studies on cross-cultural exchange and on differences between the cultures of the two sides, it was revealed that, although there were some empirical research achievements made on the national culture and consumer culture of the two sides of the Taiwan Strait, reliable research about corporate culture is lacking and needs to be conducted [5]. For example, Phua examined three things regarding whether (1) national cultural differences influence individuals' preferences for types of remuneration and levels of job autonomy; (2) actual organizational human resource management (HRM) practices reflect such preferences; and (3) gaps between individuals' preferences and actual organizational HRM practices affect job satisfaction [6].

1.1. Organizational Management and Corporate Performance

Many factors may influence an organization's interests. Among them, two important ones are the organizational management and performance of HR. Kamath's empirical analysis found that HR was the one factor which had a major impact on the profitability and productivity of the firms studied [7]. Though there was growing importance and efficiency in the utilization of intellectual resources in the Indian pharmaceutical industry, its potential to impact the industry's financial performance was missing in the empirical analysis [7]. Kim et al. claimed that HRM had been identified as very important for site management compared with such management at other locations [8]. Cheng et al. applied business process reengineering and organization planning philosophy to HRM and focused on HR planning in construction management process reengineering (CMPR) to develop a team-based HR planning (THRP) method for deploying labor [9]. Druker et al. examined HRM practices in relation to the role of personnel departments, line management responsibility, performance management, and values and beliefs of personnel managers [10]. Fatimah claimed that HR improvement in an organization played an important role in determining the success of an organization [11].

Corporate organizational management is ultimately important to corporate performance. Rob et al. analyzed whether Japanese firms with many governance provisions had better corporate performance than firms with few governance provisions and discovered that well-governed firms significantly outperformed poorly governed firms by up to 15% per year [12]. Saito performed a comparative study according to two surveys conducted in Japan and the United States to understand how facility managers recognized and practiced universal design in their workplaces and to identify what factors were likely to facilitate or obstruct their practice [13]. Wong et al. claimed that workplace environment affected employees' well-being and comfort, which in turn influenced their productivity and morale [14]. Teizer et al. indicated that better safety and productivity could be achieved when construction resources, including people and equipment, could be monitored [15]. The work of Li et al. showed that the abilities of management and technology were two common factors that could transcend different institutions and systems [16].

On the other hand, an incentive system is also essential in an organization. Pattarin et al. proposed that employee perks were positively associated with current and future returns on assets, which supported the view that some types of perks might increase firm profitability and/or that perks were paid as a bonus to reward performance [17]. Findings from stratified samples suggested that perks might incentivize managers, even after controlling for firm size, growth opportunity, and leverage [17].

Pfeffer claimed that ignoring the influences of working environments on employees' performances might cause organizations to lose their competitiveness [18]. Hence, more emphases have been placed on studies of "person–organization fit" or "person–job fit", For example, Schein indicated that environment was an important factor for person–organization fit [19]. Schneider believed that person–organization fit might influence one's performance in an organization [20]. In short, HRM and its performance practice change due to the role of values and identity change and have also become the conceptual framework of this study.

1.2. Issues Regarding Work Values

In recent years, many scholars have studied issues related to work values. Ralston *et al.* assessed the impact of economic ideology and national culture on the individual work values of managers in the United States, Russia, Japan, and China [21]. Reichel *et al.* presented evidence that work values could be a good indicator for the selection and career development of personnel [22]. Lee and Yen explored the connection between work values and career orientation for employees in high-tech production [23].

All organizations are unique and, thus, practice different cultural values within the organization. In a university setting, it was discovered that leadership values have a significant impact on university-wide cultural values, employee values, and stakeholder values [24,25]. Cultural values considerably affect productivity values and employee values. Further, employee values have significant influence on productivity and stakeholder values [24,25]. Scholars believed there were many aspects of work values. For example, Wu and Chiang explored how Chinese values impacted employees' satisfaction (ES). Taiwanese employees viewed "career planning" as the most important, while Chinese employees thought "organizational management" was most important. For Taiwanese employees, "salary and benefits", "workload", and "organizational management" had effects on ES, while age and education were important to Chinese employees [26]. Leung *et al.* indicated that the construction industry had been recognized as a stressful industry, and a great deal of stress was placed on various construction professionals (CPs). However, due to the different "values" among CPs in Hong Kong, susceptibility to stressors varied a great range among workers. People who grew up and lived in different cultural environments had different values and this led to different perceptions of stressors [27]. Ochieng *et al.* examined challenges faced by senior construction managers in managing cross-cultural complexity and uncertainty [28]. Francis and Lingard claimed that societal attitudes and work values were changing and that these changes had been reflected in the employment practices of many construction companies [29]. Morrison and Thurnell addressed that, in order to attract and retain valuable employees, the New Zealand construction industry must provide useful work-life benefits, reasonable working hours, and supportive workplace cultures in line with such initiatives [30].

1.3. Prime Novelty Statements

Based on the arguments above regarding the effects of employees' work values and organizational management on corporate performance and based on the extension of the work by Lin *et al.* [31], Lin and Shen [32], Shen [33], we proposed three novelty statements.

(1) This paper is a "case study". It was conducted with a questionnaire survey to offer organizations some references, in which the reliability of the data was determined based on Cronbach's alpha values. According to the results of this study, all the Cronbach's alpha values from the reliability analyses were higher than 0.7, implying that all the organizational data were highly trustworthy.

(2) This study examined the results of questionnaires regarding issues of work values and organizational management, and compared the issues. The results clearly showed the needs and viewpoints of employees from the two sides of the Strait, and therefore the relevant organizational management skills that could be utilized as references.

(3) Three regression models were used to verify this study regarding the issues of work values and organizational management. Interpretations were provided of unpredictable outcomes, so that management could understand and compare the extent to which the employees from the two sides of the Strait devoted themselves to their jobs, whether the employees would like to stay or leave the enterprise, and what they thought about the welfare systems of the enterprise.

2. Analysis Methods for Questionnaires

The subjects of this study were Taiwanese and Chinese employees of branches of Taiwanese companies in China. The differences in work values and organizational management models were reviewed. The influences of the differences in work values and work satisfaction on organizations were also explored. The questionnaires were designed according to the job diagnostic survey by Hackman and Oldham [34], proposing to (1) diagnose existing jobs so to determine whether (and how) they might be redesigned to improve employee motivation and productivity and (2) assess the effects of job changes on employees. The tool is based on a theory of how job design affects work motivation and provides means of (a) individual psychological states because of these dimensions and (b) affective reactions of employees to the working environment. The survey questionnaire focused on the "work characteristics questionnaire", including questions for (1) work values and (2) organizational management. Participants used a five-point Likert Scale to answer the questionnaire.

This study analyzed the data using the software SPSS (Statistical Package for the Social Sciences). The statistical methods adopted in this study were listed below for quantitative measures.

(1) Reliability analysis for questionnaires: Reliability indicated stability and consistency. This study utilized Cronbach's alpha values, whose set of criteria were proposed by Guieford [35] to verify the reliability of the collected data. The standard value of Cronbach's alpha was 0.5. High alpha values (>0.7) represented high reliability and low alpha values (<0.35) meant low reliability.

(2) Descriptive statistics: They were used to describe the properties of the samples and the averages, standard deviations, and distributions of variables for the samples.

(3) Regression analysis: By adopting multiple regression analysis, the effects of the independent variables (work values and organizational management) on the dependent variables should be examined with moderating variables being controlled. In addition, work values and work satisfaction for employees from both sides of the Strait were modeled to determine their differences.

Using regression analysis, three models were established based on three most important indicators of managing an organization, as selected from the perspectives of business managers according to the interviews and to the works by Huang, Huang, and Tang [36–38]. The three indicators included (1) employees' devotion to their jobs; (2) their commitment to the organization and whether to resign; and (3) their salaries and welfare provided by enterprises. The capabilities of the independent variables to predict and explain the dependent variables were discussed. For employees' devotion to their jobs, the selected dependent variable Y was that "My boss thinks I am doing a great job at work". Huang believed that the more devoted employees are to their jobs, the more praises they are going to get from their bosses [36]. For whether employees will resign, the selected dependent variable Y was the "In order to stay employed by the company, I am willing to accept any assignment". Huang believed that only employees who can accept companies' arrangements are loyal to the companies [36]. For employees' salaries and welfare, the selected dependent variable Y was that "I am very satisfied with the welfare provided by the company I work for". On the other hand, the independent variables X for the three models were questions in the work values and organizational management questionnaires corresponding to the selected dependent variables.

(4) Test of significance: statistical significance is a kind of evaluation metric. For example: A and B are two sets of data with statistical significance at the 0.05 level, which indicates the possibility of the two data sets having significant difference of 5%, or 95% probability that the two sample sets have no difference. This 5% difference is caused by simple random sampling error. Typically, the statistical significance achieved at the .05 or .01 level can refer to significant differences between the data sets. If $P(X = x) < p = 0.05$ is significant, SPSS statistical analysis software uses * mark, while $P(X = x) < p = 0.01$ is considered extremely significant and is usually marked by **.

3. Results of Data Reliability, Data Validity, and Descriptive Statistics

A total amount of 250 questionnaires was handed out to Taiwanese and Chinese employees of different ranks in the company. After precluding 30 invalid questionnaires (non-response samples) and 69 unreturned ones, a total amount of 181 questionnaires were found to be valid. The response rate was 72.4% as illustrated in Table 1 (adapted from Lin et al. [31]). With the data obtained from the questionnaires, the reliability analysis was first conducted, followed by a series of statistical analyses.

Table 1. Information regarding returned questionnaires.

Sample	No. of Questionnaires Distributed	No. of Valid Questionnaires	Response Rate
All employees	250	181	72.4%
Taiwanese employees	90	58	64%
Chinese employees	90	73	81%
Taiwanese cadre members	50	36	72%
Chinese cadre members	20	14	70%

3.1. Reliability Analysis for Questionnaires

Reliability is the degree of consistency of results from repeated measurements of the same population or similar populations. It represents the correctness or precision of the tools used for measurement. In order to avoid the correctness of the collected and classified questionnaires being influenced by the low reliabilities for the measured categories, reliability analysis was applied for each of the categories as listed in Table 2. It shows that, in this study, all the reliabilities were greater than 0.7, implying that the collected samples were stable and satisfactorily consistent.

Table 2. Reliability analyses.

Cronbach's Alpha	Chinese	Taiwanese
Work values	0.736	0.703
Organizational management	0.716	0.743

3.2. Validity Analysis for Questionnaires

Validity means "exploratory factor analysis" [31], characteristics of main features being the following assessment, with the corresponding results listed in Table 3.

(1) Kaiser-Meyer-Olkin (KMO) measure of sampling adequacy assesses whether the partial correlations among variables are small (KMO > 0.6);

(2) Bartlett's Test of Sphericity assesses whether the correlation matrix is an identity matrix, indicating that the factor model is inappropriate (Sig < 0.05);

Table 3. Validity analyses.

Exploratory Factor	Chinese	Taiwanese
Work values	KMO = 0.817 Sig = 0.000	KMO = 0.809 Sig = 0.000
Organizational management	KMO = 0.738 Sig = 0.000	KMO = 0.743 Sig = 0.000

3.3. Descriptive Statistics

The research subjects of this study were employees of a company from Taiwan invested in China. After the questionnaires were retrieved, the number of samples was obtained and the frequencies and weighted averages of the questions were computed. From this information, how important work values were for the employees from both sides of the Strait and their differences could be determined. The ranking of work values for the employees from both sides of the Strait and the ranking of the organizational management of cadre members from both sides of the Strait were summarized in Tables 4 and 5 respectively (questionnaires adopted from [31–33]).

Table 4. Ranking of work values of employees from both sides of the Strait.

Chinese		Taiwanese	
The insurance system of the company is good.	4.79	The insurance system of the company is good.	4.93
When I am sick, the company takes good care of me.	4.44	When I am sick, the company takes good care of me.	4.89
The quality of my life can be improved through my work.	4.38	I never feel confused or scared while working.	4.69
My own dream can be realized at work.	4.28	There are chances for advanced studies at work.	4.67
My life becomes richer due to my work.	4.23	There are many chances of promotion.	4.59
There are chances for advanced studies at work.	4.05	I can arrange my own schedule properly because of the flexibility of my work.	4.37
I am proud of my work.	4.05	The quality of my life can be improved through my work.	3.82
I devote myself to my work.	3.95	My own dream can be realized at work.	3.67
I can arrange my own schedule properly because of the flexibility of my work.	3.92	My life becomes richer due to my work.	3.55
I want to be perfect when it comes to my work.	3.92	I want to be perfect when it comes to my work.	3.44
There are many chances of promotion.	3.69	I am proud of my work.	3.38
My income is higher than that of others with the same conditions as me.	3.49	I devote myself to my work.	3.31
Even if there is no extra pay for working overtime, I would still work overtime to finish my work at night.	3.47	I can get a raise or bonus of a proper amount.	3.07
I usually go to work earlier to prepare the tasks I have to handle.	3.33	The welfare system of the company is good.	3.07
I never feel confused or scared while working.	3.22	My income is higher than that of others with the same conditions as me.	3.07
I can get a raise or bonus of a proper amount.	3.22	I usually go to work earlier to prepare the tasks I have to handle.	2.93
The welfare system of the company is good.	3.22	Even if there is no extra pay for working overtime, I would still work overtime to finish my work at night.	2.66

Table 5. Ranking of the organizational management of cadre members from both sides of the Strait.

Chinese		Taiwanese	
I think the training provided by the company I work for can meet the demands of the employees.	4.21	Compared with other companies in the same field, I think the salary and welfare offered by the company I work for are better.	4.81
If there is a training opportunity, the management of the company I work for usually encourages the employees to participate.	4.14	I think the employees' salaries offered by the company are closely related to the employees' performances at work.	4.55
The company I work for would communicate with its employees regarding their achievements and offer them suggestions.	3.86	I think the training provided by the company I work for can meet the demands of the employees.	4.16
I think the employees' salaries offered by the company are closely related to the employees' performances at work.	3	If there is a training opportunity, the management of the company I work for usually encourages the employees to participate.	4.13
Compared with other companies in the same field, I think the salary and welfare offered by the company I work for are better.	2.93	The company I work for would communicate with its employees regarding their achievements and offer them suggestions.	3.83
I think the employees of the company I work for are highly involved in decision making at work.	2.5	I think the employees of the company I work for are highly involved in decision making at work.	3.36

According to the obtained statistical values, the Chinese cadre members believed that the most important thing was the demands of the employees, followed by the training opportunities and the communication between the company and its employees, and the least important ones were decision making at work, the salaries, and welfare offered by the company. On the other hand, the Taiwanese cadre members believed that the most important thing was the salaries and welfare offered by the company, followed by the employees' performances at work and the demands of the employees, and the least important ones were decision making at work and the communication between the company and its employees.

4. Correlation and Regression Analyses

4.1. Employees' Devotion to Their Jobs

The six variables from work values as listed in Table 6 (questions selected from [31–33]), including (1) "I devote myself to my work"; (2) "Even if there is no extra pay for working overtime, I would still work overtime to finish my work at night"; (3) "I usually go to work earlier to prepare the tasks I have to handle"; (4) "I am proud of my work"; (5) "I want to be perfect when it comes to my work"; and (6) "I never feel confused or scared while working", were selected as the independent variables X to explain the dependent variable Y: "My boss thinks I am doing a great job at work". The R value was 0.709 with the Taiwanese employees and 0.791 with the Chinese employees, indicating that there was a relationship between superintendents' praise for the employees and the employees' devotion to their jobs. One explanation is that the more devoted the employees were to their jobs, the more praise they could get from their superintendents. Hence, one of the six important indicators from work values for selecting employees was their devotion to their jobs.

Table 6. Employees' devotion to their jobs from both sides of the Strait.

Independent variables (X)	1. I devote myself to my work. 2. Even if there is no extra pay for working overtime, I would still work overtime to finish my work at night. 3. I usually go to work earlier to prepare the tasks I have to handle. 4. I am proud of my work. 5. I want to be perfect when it comes to my work. 6. I never feel confused or scared while working.
Dependent variable (Y)	My boss thinks I am doing a great job at work.
R value with the Taiwanese employees	0.709
R value with the Chinese employees	0.791

4.2. Influence of Organizational Management on Employees' Decisions to Resign

The five variables from organizational management as listed in Table 7 (questions selected from [31–33]), including (1) "I think the employees of the company I work for are highly involved in decision making at work"; (2) "If there is a training opportunity, the management of the company I work for usually encourages the employees to participate"; (3) "I think the training provided by the company I work for can meet the demands of the employees"; (4) "The company I work for would communicate with its employees regarding their achievements and offer them suggestions"; and (5) "Compared with other companies in the same field, I think the salary and welfare offered by the company I work for are better", were selected as the independent variables X to explain the dependent variable Y: "In order to stay employed by the company, I am willing to accept any assignment". The results show that the cadre members from both sides of the Strait believed that identification with the company and decisions to stay were highly related to the company's organizational management. Of course, the organizational management system could not fully interpret its employees' decisions to stay or whether they associated themselves with the company. However, it was a reasonable indicator as to why some employees decided to resign.

Table 7. Influence of the organizational management on employees' decision to resign from both sides of the Strait.

Independent variables (X)	1. I think the employees of the company I work for are highly involved in decision making at work. 2. If there is a training opportunity, the management of the company I work for usually encourages the employees to participate. 3. I think the training provided by the company I work for can meet the demands of the employees. 4. The company I work for would communicate with its employees regarding their achievements and offer them suggestions. 5. Compared with other companies in the same field, I think the salary and welfare offered by the company I work for are better.
Dependent variable (Y)	In order to stay employed by the company, I am willing to accept any assignment.
R value with the Taiwanese employees	0.759
R value with the Chinese employees	0.736

4.3. Employees' Salaries and Welfare

The five variables among work values as listed in Table 8 (questions selected from [31–33]), including (1) "When I am sick, the company takes good care of me"; (2) "The insurance system of the company is good"; (3) The welfare system of the company is good"; (4) My income is higher than that of others with the same conditions as me"; and (5) "I can get a raise or bonus of a proper amount", were selected as the independent variables X to explain the dependent variable Y: "I am very satisfied with the welfare provided by the company I work for". The R values with both the Taiwanese and Chinese employees were relatively low, implying that it was not adequate to explain the employees' satisfaction with the company's welfare using their work values. Such results of both sides of the Strait are similar to the work of Huang [36]. This means that the employees were not satisfied when their superintendents used one of their work values as standards to offer welfare, due to the fact that the welfare satisfaction may be relevant to "the influence of social desirability" [36]. Excluded variables in Table 8 further show that the factor "I can get a raise or bonus of a proper amount" showed a very significant difference (p-value = 0.00) than other factors. Thus, the factor was removed and the regression analysis was rerun once again. The consequent R values were drastically increased for the Taiwanese and Chinese employees from 0.435–0.764 and from 0.308–0.687, respectively, as listed in Table 9 (questions selected from [31–33]). This verifies the assumption that the welfare satisfaction may be relevant to "the influence of social desirability".

Table 8. Employees' salaries and welfare on both sides of the Strait.

Independent variables (X)	1. When I am sick, the company takes good care of me. 2. The insurance system of the company is good. 3. The welfare system of the company is good. 4. My income is higher than that of others with the same conditions as me. 5. I can get a raise or bonus of a proper amount.					
Dependent variable (Y)	I am very satisfied with the welfare provided by the company I work for.					
R value with the Taiwanese employees	0.435					
R value with the Chinese employees	0.308					
Excluded Variables						
Model	Beta	t	Sig.	Partial Correlation	Collinearity Statistics Tolerance	p-value
I can get a raise or bonus of a proper amount.	.	.	.	.	0.000	0.000

Table 9. Employees' salaries and welfare on both sides of the Strait with a variable excluded.

Independent variables (X)	1. When I am sick, the company takes good care of me. 2. The insurance system of the company is good. 3. The welfare system of the company is good. 4. My income is higher than that of others with the same conditions as me.
Dependent variable (Y)	I am very satisfied with the welfare provided by the company I work for.
R value with the Taiwanese employees	0.764
R value with the Chinese employees	0.687

5. Evaluation by Test of Significance

Analyses via the statistical significance assists in comprehending the differences in work values and organizational management of the employees and cadres between the two sides of the Strait, as listed in Tables 10 and 11 (questionnaires adopted from [31–33]). Table 10, regarding the work values of employees of both sides of the Strait, shows significant differences for the three questions: (1) "There are many chances of promotion"; (2) "Even if there is no extra pay for working overtime, I would still work overtime to finish my work at night"; and (3) "I never feel confused or scared while working". Table 11, regarding the organizational management of cadre members of both sides of the Strait, shows significant differences for the three questions: (1) "I think the employees' salaries offered by the company are closely related to the employees' performances at work"; (2) "Compared with other companies in the same field, I think the salary and welfare offered by the company I work for are better"; and (3) "I think the employees of the company I work for are highly involved in decision making at work".

Table 10. Test of significance of work values of employees of both sides of the Strait.

Work Values	Chinese	Taiwanese	p-Value
The insurance system of the company is good.	4.79	4.93	0.082
When I am sick, the company takes good care of me.	4.44	4.89	0.057
The quality of my life can be improved through my work.	4.38	3.82	0.044 *
My own dream can be realized at work.	4.28	3.67	0.037 *
My life becomes richer due to my work.	4.23	3.55	0.034 *
There are chances for advanced studies at work.	4.05	4.67	0.039 *
I am proud of my work.	4.05	3.38	0.032 *
I devote myself to my work.	3.95	3.31	0.036 *
I can arrange my own schedule properly because of the flexibility of my work.	3.92	4.37	0.056
I want to be perfect when it comes to my work.	3.92	3.44	0.054
There are many chances of promotion.	3.69	4.59	0.005 **
My income is higher than that of others with the same conditions as me.	3.49	3.07	0.058
Even if there is no extra pay for working overtime, I would still work overtime to finish my work at night.	3.47	2.66	0.009**
I usually go to work earlier to prepare the tasks I have to handle.	3.33	2.93	0.061
I never feel confused or scared while working.	3.22	4.69	0.000 **
I can get a raise or bonus of a proper amount.	3.22	3.07	0.081
The welfare system of the company is good.	3.22	3.07	0.082

Table 11. Test of significance of the organizational management of cadre members of both sides of the Strait.

Organizational Management	Chinese	Taiwanese	p-value
I think the training provided by the company I work for can meet the demands of the employees.	4.21	4.16	0.093
If there is a training opportunity, the management of the company I work for usually encourages the employees to participate.	4.14	4.13	0.098

Table 11. *Cont.*

Organizational Management	Chinese	Taiwanese	p-value
The company I work for would communicate with its employees regarding their achievements and offer them suggestions.	3.86	3.83	0.096
I think the employees' salaries offered by the company are closely related to the employees' performances at work.	3	4.55	0.000 **
Compared with other companies in the same field, I think the salary and welfare offered by the company I work for are better.	2.93	4.81	0.000 **
I think the employees of the company I work for are highly involved in decision making at work.	2.5	3.36	0.007 **

Statistical significance is a kind of evaluation metric; significant is indicated by an * and extremely significant is usually marked by **. Thus, it is clear to see the differences in work values and organizational management of the employees and cadres between the two sides of the Strait from Tables 10 and 11.

6. Conclusions

The conclusions of the analyses in this study are summarized, anticipating that they will offer domestic enterprises some references when developing and implementing organizational management strategies on both sides of the Strait.

(1) Comparative results of Chinese and Taiwanese employees:

(a) Work values: The Chinese employees valued "The quality of my life can be improved through my work", "My own dream can be realized at work", and "My life becomes richer due to my work", which all focused on their lives "at present". On the other hand, the Taiwanese employees valued "I never feel confused or scared while working", "There are chances for advanced studies at work", and "There are many chances of promotion", which all focused on "the future". From this perspective, the Chinese employees focus on their current situation and how it can improve the quality of their lives, while the Taiwanese employees tend toward a stable job that reflects the opportunity for promotion.

(b) Organizational management: The Chinese cadre members were satisfied with the employee training provided by the company, while the Taiwanese cadre members thought that the salaries and welfare offered by the company were better than other companies. In general, the Taiwanese cadre members thought more highly of their organization's management than their Chinese counterparts did. It appeared that the management model used in China was similar to the one used in Taiwan, showing that the Chinese cadre members were unable to integrate in the company completely. The Taiwanese cadre members thought better welfare could improve employees' performances, while the Chinese cadre members focused on encouragement and communication.

(2) An organization should know how devoted its employees are to their jobs:

Another important indicator influencing the company's performance was the employees' devotion to their jobs. When recruiting new staff, applicants' devotion and enthusiasm for their jobs should be tested so that the organization's performance could be improved.

(3) An organization should pay attention to defects in its organizational management and reduce employees' tendency to resign:

In this study, we discovered that the influences of organizational management on employees' tendency to resign were significant. If an enterprise could improve its current organizational management, its employees' work attitudes could be improved as well, and their tendency to resign should be reduced. The interviews revealed that many enterprises in Taiwan that were invested in China did not have well-established systems for employees' repatriation. Those assigned to work in

China felt uncertain about their future, and this was reflected in their performance. Besides increasing employees' salaries, a repatriation system should be established: this ought to entail not only allowing staff to return to their jobs in Taiwan, but also proper in-service training for Taiwanese employees in China so that they may remain in China for long-term development. Otherwise, it is very likely that further salary raises would be futile in increasing employees' commitment to an organization.

Acknowledgments: Acknowledgments: The work described in this paper comprises part of the research project sponsored by Ministry of Science and Technology, Taiwan (Contract No. MOST 102-2221-E-035-049), whose support is greatly appreciated.

Author Contributions: Author Contributions: Jeng-Wen Lin designed the research and wrote the paper; Pu Fun Shen performed research and analyzed the data; and Yin-Sung Hsu revised the paper.

References

1. Choi, J.H.; Kim, Y.S. An analysis of core competency of construction field engineer for cost management. *J. Constr. Eng. Manag.* **2013**, *14*, 26–34. [CrossRef]
2. Jia, G.; Ni, X.; Chen, Z.; Hong, B.; Chen, Y.; Yang, F.; Lin, C. Measuring the maturity of risk management in large-scale construction projects. *Autom. Constr.* **2013**, *34*, 56–66. [CrossRef]
3. Chau, K.W.; Cao, Y.; Anson, M.; Zhang, J. Application of data warehouse and decision support system in construction management. *Autom. Constr.* **2003**, *12*, 213–224. [CrossRef]
4. Park, M. Model-based dynamic resource management for construction projects. *Autom. Constr.* **2005**, *14*, 585–598. [CrossRef]
5. Chen, C.-C. Comments on relevant study on corporate culture across the Taiwan Straits. *Asian Soc. Sci.* **2011**, *7*, 59–63. [CrossRef]
6. Phua, F.T. Do national cultural differences affect the nature and characteristics of HRM practices? Evidence from Australian and Hong Kong construction firms on remuneration and job autonomy. *Constr. Manag. Econ.* **2012**, *30*, 545–556. [CrossRef]
7. Kamath, G.B. Intellectual capital and corporate performance in Indian pharmaceutical industry. *J. Intellect. Cap.* **2008**, *9*, 684–704. [CrossRef]
8. Kim, J.H.; Cho, H.H.; Lee, U.K.; Kang, K.I. Development of a hybrid device based on infrared and ultrasonic sensors for human resource management. In Proceedings of the 24th International Symposium on Automation & Robotics in Construction, Kochi, India, 19–21 September 2007; pp. 111–115.
9. Cheng, M.Y.; Tsai, M.H.; Xiao, Z.W. Construction management process reengineering: Organizational human resource planning for multiple projects. *Autom. Constr.* **2006**, *15*, 785–799. [CrossRef]
10. Druker, J.; White, G.; Hegewisch, A.; Mayne, L. Between hard and soft HRM: human resource management in the construction industry. *J. Constr. Eng. Manag.* **1996**, *14*, 405–416. [CrossRef]
11. Fatimah, P.R. The development of FFMD pyramid: Fuzzy Family Marriage Deployment as decision support method to improve human resources performance. *Qual. Quant.* **2014**, *48*, 659–672. [CrossRef]
12. Rob, B.; Bart, F.; Rogér, O.; Alireza, T.-R. The impact of corporate governance on corporate performance: Evidence from Japan. *Pac. Basin Financ. J.* **2008**, *16*, 236–251.
13. Saito, Y. Awareness of universal design among facility managers in Japan and the United States. *Autom. Constr.* **2006**, *15*, 462–478. [CrossRef]
14. Wong, J.K.W.; Li, H.; Wang, S.W. Intelligent building research: A review. *Autom. Constr.* **2005**, *14*, 143–159. [CrossRef]
15. Teizer, J.; Cheng, T.; Fang, Y. Location tracking and data visualization technology to advance construction ironworkers' education and training in safety and productivity. *Autom. Constr.* **2013**, *35*, 53–68. [CrossRef]
16. Li, J.; Chiang, Y.H.; Choi, T.N.; Man, K.F. Determinants of Efficiency of Contractors in Hong Kong and China: Panel Data Model Analysis. *J. Constr. Eng. Manag.* **2013**, *9*, 1211–1223. [CrossRef]
17. Pattarin, A.; Ilan, A.; Tianyu, Z. Executive perks: Compensation and corporate performance in China. *Asia Pac. J. Manag.* **2009**, *28*, 401–425.
18. Pfeffer, J. Fighting the War for Talent is Hazardous to Your Organization's Health. *Organ. Dyn.* **2001**, *29*, 248–259. [CrossRef]

19. Schein, E. *Organization Culture and Leadership*; Jossey-Bass: San Francisco, CA, USA, 1985.

20. Schneider, B. The People Make The Place. *Pers. Psychol.* **1987**, *40*, 437–453. [CrossRef]

21. Ralston, D.A.; Holt, D.H.; Terpstra, R.H.; Yu, K.-C. The impact of national culture and economic ideology on managerial work values: A study of the United States, Russia, Japan, and China. *J. Int. Bus. Stud.* **1997**, *28*, 177–207. [CrossRef]

22. Reichel, A.; Neumann, Y.; Pizam, A. The Work Values and Motivational Profiles of Vocational, Collegiate, Nonconformist, and Academic Students. *Res. High. Educ.* **1981**, *14*, 187–199. [CrossRef]

23. Lee, H.W.; Yen, K.W. A study of the relationship between work values and career orientation of employed in the high technology industry. *Qual. Quant.* **2013**, *47*, 803–810. [CrossRef]

24. Ab Hamid, M.R.; Mustafa, Z.; Idris, F.; Abdullah, M.; Suradi, N.M.; Ismail, W.R. Multi-factor of cultural values: a confirmatory factor analytic approach. *Qual. Quant.* **2013**, *47*, 499–513. [CrossRef]

25. Ab Hamid, M.R.B. Value-based performance excellence model for higher education institutions. *Qual. Quant.* **2015**, *49*, 1919–1944. [CrossRef]

26. Wu, C.-C.; Chiang, Y.-C. The impact on the cultural diversity to employees' job satisfaction between mainland China and Taiwan: A comparison of Taiwanese invested companies. *Int. J. Hum. Resour. Manag.* **2007**, *18*, 623–641. [CrossRef]

27. Leung, M.Y.; Chan, Y.S.; Chong, A.M.L. Chinese values and stressors of construction professionals in Hong Kong. *J. Constr. Eng. Manag.* **2010**, *136*, 1289–1298. [CrossRef]

28. Ochieng, E.G.; Price, A.D.F.; Ruan, X.; Egbu, C.O.; Moore, D. The effect of cross-cultural uncertainty and complexity within multicultural construction teams. *Eng. Constr. Archit. Manag.* **2013**, *20*, 307–324. [CrossRef]

29. Francis, V.; Lingard, H. The case for family-friendly work practices in the Australian construction industry. *Aust. J. Constr. Econ. Build.* **2012**, *2*, 28–36. [CrossRef]

30. Morrison, E.; Thurnell, D. Employee preferences for work-life benefits in a large New Zealand construction company. *Aust. J. Constr. Econ. Build.* **2012**, *12*, 12–25. [CrossRef]

31. Lin, J.-W.; Shen, P.F.; Lee, B.-J. Repetitive model refinement for questionnaire design improvement in the evaluation of working characteristics in construction enterprises. *Sustainability* **2015**, *7*, 15179–15193. [CrossRef]

32. Lin, J.-W.; Shen, P.F. Factor-analysis based questionnaire categorization method for reliability improvement of evaluation of working conditions in construction enterprises. *Struct. Eng. Mech.* **2014**, *51*, 973–988. [CrossRef]

33. Shen, P.F. Impact of Employees' Work Values at Two Sides of Taiwan Straits on Corporate Performance. Master's Thesis, Feng Chia University, Taichung, Taiwan, July 2011.

34. Hackman, J.R.; Oldham, G.R. Development of the Job Diagnostic Survey. *J. Appl. Psychol.* **1975**, *60*, 159–170. [CrossRef]

35. Guieford, J.P. *Fundamental Statistics in Psychology and Education*, 4th ed.; McGraw Hill: New York, NY, USA, 1965.

36. Huang, G.-L. The Differences in Work Values between Enterprise Employees on both Sides of the Strait. Paper Collection for the Differences in Work Values between Enterprise Employees on both Sides of the Strait Seminar, Taiwan, 1994. Available online: http://readopac2.ncl.edu.tw/nclserialFront/search/ref_book.jsp?la=ch&id=A00039972 (accessed on 18 December 2015).

37. Huang, T.C. *Human Resource Management of Taiwanese Businessmen in Mainland China*; Fongheh Publishing Co.: Taipei, Taiwan, 1995.

38. Tang, S.C. Discussions of corporate culture between different business strategies—A case study of Taiwan's home appliance industry. Master's Thesis, National Chung Hsing University, Taichung, Taiwan, July 1995.

Permissions

The contributors of this book come from diverse backgrounds, making this book a truly international effort. This book will bring forth new frontiers with its revolutionizing research information and detailed analysis of the nascent developments around the world.

We would like to thank all the contributing authors for lending their expertise to make the book truly unique. They have played a crucial role in the development of this book. Without their invaluable contributions this book wouldn't have been possible. They have made vital efforts to compile up to date information on the varied aspects of this subject to make this book a valuable addition to the collection of many professionals and students.

This book was conceptualized with the vision of imparting up-to-date information and advanced data in this field. To ensure the same, a matchless editorial board was set up. Every individual on the board went through rigorous rounds of assessment to prove their worth. After which they invested a large part of their time researching and compiling the most relevant data for our readers.

The editorial board has been involved in producing this book since its inception. They have spent rigorous hours researching and exploring the diverse topics which have resulted in the successful publishing of this book. They have passed on their knowledge of decades through this book. To expedite this challenging task, the publisher supported the team at every step. A small team of assistant editors was also appointed to further simplify the editing procedure and attain best results for the readers.

Apart from the editorial board, the designing team has also invested a significant amount of their time in understanding the subject and creating the most relevant covers. They scrutinized every image to scout for the most suitable representation of the subject and create an appropriate cover for the book.

The publishing team has been an ardent support to the editorial, designing and production team. Their endless efforts to recruit the best for this project, has resulted in the accomplishment of this book. They are a veteran in the field of academics and their pool of knowledge is as vast as their experience in printing. Their expertise and guidance has proved useful at every step. Their uncompromising quality standards have made this book an exceptional effort. Their encouragement from time to time has been an inspiration for everyone.

The publisher and the editorial board hope that this book will prove to be a valuable piece of knowledge for researchers, students, practitioners and scholars across the globe.

List of Contributors

Caterina Cavicchi and Emidia Vagnoni
Department of Economics and Management, University of Ferrara, 44121 Ferrara, Italy

Chloé Phan Van PhI, Maye Walraven, Marine Bézagu, Maxime Lefranc and Clément Ray
InnovaFeed, Route de Chaulnes, Lieudit Les Trente, 80190 Nesle, France

Barbara Kożuch
Institute of Public Affairs, Jagiellonian University, Łojasiewicza 4 Str., Kraków 30-348, Poland

Katarzyna Sienkiewicz-Małyjurek
Faculty of Organisation and Management, Silesian University of Technology, Roosevelta 26 Str., Zabrze 41-800, Poland

Jinhuan Tang
School of Economics and Management, Shenyang Aerospace University, Shenyang 110136, China

Shoufeng Ji and Liwen Jiang
School of Business Administration, Northeast University, Shenyang 110169, China

M. Isabel Sánchez-Hernández
Business Administration and Sociology Department, School of Economics, University of Extremadura, Ave. Elvas s/n, Badajoz 06006, Spain

Dolores Gallardo-Vázquez
Financial Economics and Accountancy Department, School of Economics, University of Extremadura, Ave. Elvas s/n, Badajoz 06006, Spain

Agnieszka Barcik
Department of Management and Transport, University of Bielsko-Biała, Willowa 2, Bielsko-Biala 43-309, Poland

Piotr Dziwiński
Department of Law and Administration, The University of Da̧browa Górnicza, Cieplaka 1c, Dąbrowa Górnicza 43-300, Poland

Tuananh Tran and Joon Young Park
Department of Industrial and Systems Engineering, Dongguk University, Pil-dong, Jung-gu, Seoul 100715, Korea

Seungkyum Kim and Yongtae Park
Department of Industrial Engineering, Seoul National University, 1 Gwanak-ro, Gwanak-gu, Seoul 151-742, Korea

Changho Son
Department of Weapon System Engineering, Korea Army Academy at Yeong-Cheon, 135-1 Changhari, Young-Cheon, Gyeongbuk 770-849, Korea

Byungun Yoon
Department of Industrial & Systems Engineering, Dongguk University, Seoul 04620, Korea

Jingxiao Zhang and Hui Li
Institution of Construction Economics, Chang'an University; NO.161, Chang'an Road, Xi'an 710061, China

Haiyan Xie and Klaus Schmidt
Department of Technology, Illinois State University; Normal, IL 61790, USA

Nestor Shpak and Tamara Kyrylych
Department of Management and International Business Undertakings, Economics and Management Education Research Institute, National University "Lviv Polytechnic", Metropolitan Andrey street 3, 79013 Lviv, Ukraine

Jolita Greblikaitė
Faculty of Economics and Management, Business and Rural Development Management Institute, Aleksandras Stulginskis University, Studentu str. 11, Akademija, 53361 Kaunas, Lithuania

Courage Matobobo and Isaac O. Osunmakinde
School of Computing, College of Science, Engineering and Technology, University of South Africa, UNISA, Pretoria 0003, South Africa

Ning Wang and Runlin Yan
School of Automotive Studies, Tongji University, Shanghai 201804, China

Gianluigi De Mare and Antonio Nesticò
Department of Civil Engineering, University of Salerno, Via Giovanni Paolo II, 132, Fisciano (SA) 84084, Italy

Maria Fiorella Granata
Department of Architecture, University of Palermo, Viale delle Scienze, ed, 14, Palermo 90128, Italy

Jeng-Wen Lin
Department of Civil Engineering, Feng Chia University, Taichung 407, Taiwan

Pu Fun Shen
Ph.D. Program in Civil and Hydraulic Engineering, Feng Chia University, Taichung 407, Taiwan

Yin-Sung Hsu
Department of Water Resources Engineering and Conservation, Feng Chia University, Taichung 407, Taiwan

Index

Printed in the USA
CPSIA information can be obtained
at www.ICGtesting.com
JSHW061729301023
51110JS00006B/45

9 781647 254599